M000163659

# DRIVEN TO DEATH

# DRIVEN TO DEATH

## Psychological and Social Aspects of Suicide Terrorism

### ARIEL MERARI

OXFORD
UNIVERSITY PRESS
2010

# OXFORD
UNIVERSITY PRESS

Oxford University Press, Inc., publishes works that further
Oxford University's objective of excellence
in research, scholarship, and education.

Oxford    New York
Auckland    Cape Town    Dar es Salaam    Hong Kong    Karachi
Kuala Lumpur    Madrid    Melbourne    Mexico City    Nairobi
New Delhi    Shanghai    Taipei    Toronto

With offices in
Argentina    Austria    Brazil    Chile    Czech Republic    France    Greece
Guatemala    Hungary    Italy    Japan    Poland    Portugal    Singapore
South Korea    Switzerland    Thailand    Turkey    Ukraine    Vietnam

Copyright © 2010 by Oxford University Press, Inc.

Published by Oxford University Press, Inc.
198 Madison Avenue, New York, New York 10016

www.oup.com

Oxford is a registered trademark of Oxford University Press, Inc.

All rights reserved. No part of this publication may be reproduced,
stored in a retrieval system, or transmitted, in any form or by any means,
electronic, mechanical, photocopying, recording, or otherwise,
without the prior permission of Oxford University Press

Library of Congress Cataloging-in-Publication Data
Merari, Ariel.
Driven to death : psychological and social aspects of suicide terrorism / by Ariel Merari.
p. cm.
Includes bibliographical references.
ISBN 978-0-19-518102-9
1. Suicide bombers—Psychology. 2. Terrorism—Psychological aspects. I. Title.
HV6431.M448 2010
363.325—dc22    2009038261

3 5 7 9 8 6 4 2

Printed in the United States of America
on acid-free paper

# ACKNOWLEDGMENTS

I started writing this book more than a decade ago, about three years before 9/11/2001. Over the years, I have been occasionally asked by friends and colleagues how was the book coming. Having received vague answers, I suppose that many of them stopped believing that the project would ever be completed. Presumably, every writer would like to see his book finished sooner rather than later. But in hindsight, I do not regret that it took so long. Had I published a book on suicide terrorism a decade ago, it would not have included important insights that I gained over the years.

Many people helped me in various ways along this road. During the 1990s, my assistants at the Political Violence Research Unit in the Department of Psychology of Tel Aviv University, Zvi Adar and Avigail Jacobson, compiled basic data on suicide attacks around the globe. The work with Nasra Hassan provided unprecedented information on Palestinian suicide bombers through the eyes of their parents and siblings. Ms. Hassan's ability to gain the frank cooperation of the suicides' family members was truly amazing and I am grateful for the opportunity I had to work with her.

Many people were involved in the studies in which would-be suicide bombers and organizers of suicide attacks were interviewed and tested. The open-minded approach of Maj. General (res.) Uzi Dayan, then Head of Israel's National Security Council, enabled the launching of the project. Throughout the years of conducting these studies I have worked closely with Brig. General (res.) Elkana Harnof of the Counter-Terrorism Bureau at Israel's National Security Council (formerly Deputy Director of Military Intelligence). In the many hours of discussions we have had, Gen. Harnof's immense experience in and vast knowledge on Palestinian affairs, and his acquaintance with the mysterious ways in which government bureaucracy functions, were of crucial importance in conducting these empirical studies. Without him the studies would have never been done. The research team that I headed included many people to whom I am indebted. Baruch Zadik, Ilan Baruch and Haim Aharoni carried out the clinical interviews and administered the tests with superb professional skill and great sensitivity. Special thanks are due to Ilan Diamant, Arie Bibi (who also conducted some of the interviews), Yoav Broshi, and Giora Zakin, who performed the comprehensive psychological assessment of the would-be suicide bombers, control group participants, and organizers of suicide attacks, and to Eran Shadach, who helped in this task. I am also indebted to the group of specialists on Palestinian affairs who interviewed the prisoners: Jonathan Fighel, Ephraim Lavie, Yohanan Tzoreff, and Arie Livne. Col. (res.) Fighel also contributed to the planning and management of the study and helped in the designing of the questionnaires which dealt with the preparation of suicide attacks. Boaz Ganor, Director of the International Institute for Counter Terrorism was also part and parcel of the planning and execution of these studies. Technical assistance was competently provided by Liron Levy, Yaniv Ofek, and David Peled.

I started working on the book at the time when I was a Senior Fellow at the International Security Program of the Belfer Center at Harvard University's Kennedy School of Government. I am deeply grateful to Dr. Steven Miller, Director of the International Security Program, who provided me with ideal conditions for research work as well as a highly stimulating intellectual environment. Later on, I enjoyed the warm hospitality of my brother-in-law Coby Dayan and his wife Riki, in whose home in California I spent several months in intensive work on the book.

Professor Bruce Bongar of the Pacific Graduate School of Psychology, one of the great suicidologists in the world, provided very helpful comments and has been an enormous source of knowledge on suicide. His encouragement and belief in the importance of this endeavor have been an important driving force along the way. I also benefited from the comments and encouragement of another great suicidologist, Professor David Lester from the Center for the Study of Suicide at Blackwood, New Jersey. I am much indebted to a dear friend, Professor Philip Heymann of the Harvard Law School, who invited me more than two decades ago to teach with him a course on terrorism. In our many discussions over the years we have covered just about every aspect of terrorism, including suicide attacks.

I would like to thank Beatrice Smedley for her good editing work of a large part of the book. Thanks are also due to Aaron van Dorn of Oxford University Press for his thorough editorial work. I am particularly indebted to Joan Bossert of OUP for her relentless trust in this project, her warm support, good spirit and sound advice. For me, Joan symbolizes the ideal publisher one can dream of.

Finally, my deepest gratitude goes to my beloved wife (Professor) Dalia Merari, who has been a true companion to this project. Her firm support and encouragement, as well as her wise advice, critique, and insight have had a great influence on my thinking. Without her heart and brain this book would have never been published. And, to my daughters, Amit and Yael, my son-in-law Benny and my grandchildren Tom, Noa, and Jonathan I am grateful for their patience and encouragement throughout the years in which I was partially relieved of my duties as a father and grandfather so as to enable me to work on the book.

# CONTENTS

# CONTENTS

# DRIVEN TO DEATH

# 1

# Introduction

A T ABOUT 6:20 AM on October 23, 1983, a yellow Mercedes truck, carrying three to six tons of hexogen, a high power explosive, drove toward the U.S. Marines' barracks in Beirut Airport. The driver sped through the barbed wire fence surrounding the building, broke through a gate, and exploded as the truck crashed into the four-story building housing the Marines, turning it into a huge pile of rubble. The death toll included 241 U.S. servicemen. Sixty were wounded. One of the Marine sentries who saw the truck racing towards the building noted later, in disbelief, that the suicide driver was smiling as he passed by him.

Two minutes after the attack on the barracks, another truck driven by a suicide hit the French Paratroopers' headquarters nearby, killing 58 French soldiers and wounding 15. The American and French forces belonged to a multinational peacekeeping force that had been sent to Lebanon to help the Lebanese government in its effort to stabilize the country after the 1982 war. The force withdrew from Lebanon four months after the attacks.

The attack on the Marines' barracks was the second suicide attack in Lebanon since Hizballah had started using this tactic systematically in 1983.[1] Since that time, suicide attacks have proliferated, first in Lebanon and later in many other countries on four continents. I chose to start this book with a description of the attack on the Marines' barracks because of its impact on public opinion and the far-reaching strategic consequences that followed—and especially because of the feeling of bewilderment, disbelief and awe generated by the description of the smiling suicide bomber just seconds before his terrible death and mass-murder. In several ways this assault epitomized the enigma of terrorist suicide attacks.

For many people, suicide attacks are the symbol of terrorism. More than any other terrorist tactic these attacks demonstrate terrorists' determination and devotion—to the extent of killing themselves for their

3

cause—alongside their ruthless willingness to kill others indiscriminately. The vigor of this resolve is frightening and, as it is probably intended to do, instills the impression that people who are willing to sacrifice themselves cannot be stopped, and their cause is bound to win. Suicide attacks have also been more lethal than other forms of terrorism. The attacks of September 11, 2001 in the United States caused about nine times more fatalities than any previous terrorist attack in history. In Israel, suicide attacks during 7 years of the second Palestinian intifada, which started on September 29, 2000, have constituted about one half of one percent of the total number of terrorist attacks but resulted in 49 per cent of the Israeli fatalities.[2] The U.S. National Counterterrorism Center's report for 2007 found that whereas suicide attacks constituted only 3.3% of the total number of terrorist attacks around the globe, they resulted in 25.3% of the fatalities.[3] The lethality of suicide attacks may explain the increasing attractiveness of this method for terrorist groups. Robert Pape (2003), for example, has attributed the proliferation of suicide attacks to their apparent effectiveness, arguing that campaigns of suicide terrorism have often succeeded in gaining at least partial concessions from the targeted governments. A survey of 117 foreign policy and terrorism experts conducted in 2006 by Foreign Policy magazine and the Center for American Progress, a Washington think tank, found that two-thirds of the respondents thought that a major suicide bomb attack was the most likely terrorist event to happen in the United States in the coming five-year period.[4] The experts surveyed included academics, retired military officers, think-tank analysts, and former administration, foreign service and intelligence officers. With this in mind, it is no wonder that suicide terrorism has attracted considerable media and academic attention.

Several books and many articles on suicide terrorism have been published in recent years. Those that tried to provide a comprehensive theory of suicide terrorism have related to three main elements in the production of suicide bombers: The community from which the suicide bombers emerge, the group that decides to use suicide attacks as a tactic, and the individuals who are willing to sacrifice themselves in the attacks. Indeed, these are the most important factors necessary for understanding the roots of the phenomenon. However, whereas data on the community sentiments, its cultural and social values, and its attitudes to the conflict are relatively easy to obtain, the other two basic factors are much less accessible. Although groups' decisions can be usually inferred from both their actual behavior and public declarations of their leaders, the considerations, decisions and practices that go into recruiting suicide bombers and preparing them for the mission, are much less known. Factual knowledge about the individual characteristics and motivations of suicide bombers is even more difficult to obtain.

Presumably, this is a major reason why most of the studies of suicide terrorism have dealt very little with group processes and with personality characteristics of suicide bombers, or have ignored these aspects altogether. Actually, the prevailing view is that suicide terrorists are normal, and have no distinctive personality traits. By and large, this view is influenced by the considerable diversity in suicide bombers' demographic characteristics. Empirical evidence shows that most suicide bombers are young, but some are old; most are men, but some are women; some are university educated but others have not even finished elementary school. Moreover, meager as it may be, the available evidence suggests that the great majority of suicide bombers had no record of mental illness. Given these facts, and in the absence of convincing evidence to the contrary, the conclusion that suicide bombers are just ordinary, normal people seems tentatively reasonable. The relatively few works that attribute to suicide terrorists a variety of personality characteristics have not relied on direct psychological examination of suicide bombers, and have therefore been regarded as speculative. Thus, while it is theoretically possible that suicide bombers have some personality characteristics that make them more susceptible to undertake suicide missions, no empirically based evidence has been presented so far. A valid assessment of suicide bombers' personalities and motivations must rely on psychological interviews and tests. The studies reported in this book were designed to fill this gap, at least partially.

Terrorism is not a phenomenon that renders itself easily to psychological study. Obviously, terrorists cannot be simply summoned to participate in psychological interviews and tests. For this reason, opinions on the psychological characteristics of terrorists have mainly relied on secondhand descriptions in the media of terrorists' personal backgrounds, or on short interviews that terrorists have occasionally granted to television reporters. Recognizing the importance of direct interviews with terrorists, however, over the years some researchers have made an effort to interview leaders or rank-and-file members of terrorist groups. In the early 1970s, when modern terrorism research was making its first steps, David Hubbard, an American psychiatrist, interviewed hijackers in jail (not all of them political terrorists). Hubbard summarized his interviews in a book titled, *The Skyjacker: His Flights of Fantasy* (1971). In Germany, a group of psychologists and sociologists interviewed suspected members of terrorist groups in jail in the early 1980s, as did Franco Ferracuti, a forensic psychiatrist in Italy.

My interest in suicide terrorism started in 1983, when this tactic emerged in Lebanon in a rather dramatic way, first with the attack on the U.S. Embassy on April 18, and then with the abovementioned attacks on the U.S. Marines and the French paratroopers in October. The temporal proximity of these three major incidents suggested that suicide attacks were turning out to be a threatening new form of terrorism. In my role as the Director of the Terrorism and Low Intensity Project at the Jaffee Center for Strategic Studies of Tel Aviv University, I started a systematic collection of information on suicide attacks, as a subset of the database on terrorism maintained by the Project. From the start, it was clear that the data provided by media reports enabled an educated analysis of the political context in which suicide attacks were carried out, as well as their consequences, but that information was woefully insufficient for a comprehensive understanding of the organizational and individual components of the phenomenon. In the Lebanese situation, the identity of the organizations that devised the suicide attacks and their objectives were clear enough; yet there was no information on the decision-making processes or how suicides were recruited and prepared, nor on the personality characteristics and motives of the suicides themselves. In Sri Lanka, where systematic suicide attacks began in 1990,[5] information on these aspects was even more meager: even the basic demographic details of the suicides remained unknown.

The onset of a campaign of suicide attacks in Israel opened new possibilities for research. The Palestinian groups espoused a policy of publicizing the identity of the suicide bombers and providing some details on their backgrounds. The relative openness of Israeli authorities has also been helpful, in allowing Israeli and international television and newspaper reporters to interview captured would-be suicides in jail. Some details on the process of recruitment of suicide bombers surfaced in trials of captured would-be suicides and of organizers of suicide attacks. Yet, more systematic and direct research is needed for gaining valid conclusions concerning the making of suicide bombers.

In 1997 I had an opportunity to conduct a comprehensive study of the families of Palestinian suicide bombers, in cooperation with Nasra Hassan. That study, in which the families of almost all of the Palestinian suicide bombers prior to the second intifada were interviewed, yielded important information on the background of the suicides, which made it possible to assess the influence (or lack thereof) on the decision to become a suicide bomber of factors such as religiosity, poverty, and personal revenge. However, the interviews with family members could not provide more than a superficial glimpse at the personality characteristics of the suicide bombers, their motivations, and their mental states throughout the preparation for the suicide attack, nor could they provide information on the perpetrating groups' decision-making processes concerning the use of this tactic. This information could only be obtained in interviews with the suicide candidates themselves, as well as with operatives involved in organizing suicide attacks. For that, I had to wait a few more years.

In recent years I headed a large group of psychologists and specialists on Palestinian affairs in a series of studies designed to obtain a direct and comprehensive picture of the making of suicide bombers. In the first study in the series, incarcerated Palestinian would-be suicide bombers–some of whom had been caught carrying an explosive charge on the way to the target, and some who actually reached their target and tried to detonate the charge but it failed to explode for technical reasons–were subjected to clinical psychological interviews and tests by a team of clinical psychologists, as well as interviews by specialists on Palestinian affairs. This has been the first direct psychological study of suicide bombers reported so far. The psychological and background characteristics of the would-be suicide bombers were compared with those of a control group of non-suicide terrorists, matched for age, marital status and organizational affiliation, so as to detect differences between suicide and other terrorists. In yet another unprecedented study, organizers of suicide attacks (typically local commanders of the Palestinian groups that used suicide attacks) were interviewed and tested by the research team in order to learn about their personality characteristics, their considerations in recruiting suicide candidates and preparing them for the mission, and factors that influenced their operational decisions. This information complemented the data obtained in the would-be suicides' study, to provide a full picture of the process by which suicide bombers are made. Additional data derived from the organizers' indictments and court records, in conjunction with the interview material, made it possible to reach some conclusions concerning the differences between those suicides who persisted in their mission and those who decided to abort it, and the factors involved in the decision to abandon the mission.

In the absence of comparable studies on suicide bombers in other countries, the generalizability of the psychological findings on Palestinian suicides to others remains questionable. When I launched the series of studies I hoped that similar studies in other countries would make it possible to identify similarities and differences in the psychological characteristics, motivation, and preparation processes across several countries. This would give us some idea what elements appear to be universal, and what elements are related to specific cultural, political, or organizational factors. Unfortunately, no such studies have been carried out in other countries.

The empirical subject matter of this book is dictated by the definition of suicide terrorism. Whereas to most people suicide terrorism means an act in which the perpetrator literally *kills himself* to kill others, some writers have also regarded as suicide terrorism acts in which the perpetrator carried out the attack knowing that he was highly likely to be killed, but did not actually kill himself (Atran, 2003) Gambetta (2005, p. vii) actually includes high-risk missions, which he calls "no escape missions," a term used earlier by Margalit (2003). Such "no escape" missions are described by Gambetta as events in which "the perpetrator's death is certain but not self-inflicted." As an illustration, Gambetta mentions cases where "the agents attack a target with some weapon—daggers, hand grenades, or firearms—knowing that the enemy will respond by killing them." This inclusion is problematic for several reasons. First, although many of these attackers have indeed been killed, some of them survived after being caught or even managed to escape despite the odds. Second, it is practically impossible to determine the precise subjective or objective likelihood of being killed in a given action. Soldiers in World War I who climbed out of the trenches to charge against machine gun and artillery fire knew that they had a very high chance of getting killed. The likelihood of death for a British or French soldier in the battle of the Somme was probably no less than that of a Palestinian terrorist who fires an automatic weapon at Israeli inhabitants of a West Bank settlement. Most, but certainly not all, of the assailants who perpetrated this kind of attack have indeed been killed, but certainly not all of them. Even if we agree that there is no meaningful difference between a perceived sure death and a subjective, 90 percent chance of being killed, there is no way of determining the actual or subjective likelihood of dying in action. And, most important, presumably there is a fundamental psychological difference between the act of self-destruction and the situation of being killed by others. The difference is not only in the perceived certainty of dying in the case of suicide and the chance, however meager, of surviving enemy fire, but in the mental state that allows a person to destroy himself by his own hand.

It is therefore necessary to define this form of behavior at the outset of this book. A suicide terrorist attack is a situation in which a person intentionally kills himself (or herself) for the purpose of killing others, in the service of a political or ideological goal. This definition excludes situations in which the person does not know that his/her action would result in certain death—as has occasionally happened when a person was carrying an explosive charge that was detonated from a distance by remote control operated by another person, so as to make it look like a suicide attack, although the courier of the device was unaware of this plan (Merari, 1990). A definition such as that offered by Ganor (2000), which reads: "operational method in which the very act of the attack is dependent upon the death of the perpetrator," as well as Gambetta's (2005, p. vi) definition phrased as "a violent attack designed in such a way as to make the death of the perpetrators strictly essential for its success" do not exclude these false suicide cases.[6] In my view, the *conscious self-destruction* is a crucial element in the definition of suicide terrorism. Furthermore, the assertion that the attacker's death is essential for the success of the operation is not always true, and certainly unnecessary for the definition of suicide attack. A bomb on board a bus or in a marketplace, detonated by a timer or remote control, would cause the same damage as a bomb operated by a suicide bomber. Bombs of this kind, as well as car bombs, have been used by terrorist groups around the world, sometimes causing a large number of casualties. It is true that suicide bombers have a greater chance of success because they can select a target while moving and explode at will if they are suspected, but in most cases the same physical effect could be obtained by non-suicide bombing.

The purpose of this book is to portray and explain suicide terrorism as a global phenomenon. However, the book relies heavily on the case of Palestinian suicide bombers, especially with regard to empirical evidence. This focus is mainly a result of the fact that much more data are available on Palestinian suicide attacks, their perpetrators, and on Palestinian public attitudes toward them, than on suicide attacks anywhere else around the world. In addition, of course, as an Israeli I am closer to and more familiar with the Palestinian case than with other arenas that have bred suicide terrorism. Still, with the exception of the chapters that report the empirical studies of Palestinian suicides, their families, and organizers of suicide attacks, the bulk of the book seeks to analyze suicide terrorism across countries and campaigns.

Chapter 2 describes the geographical and temporal scope of suicide terrorism and presents some of the main campaigns of suicide attacks in their strategic and political context. Chapter 3 reviews the demographic features of suicide terrorists around the world, as gleaned from various sources, including my own database. Chapter 4 presents the results of the study of families of Palestinian suicides, focusing on background factors that could, hypothetically, be perceived as motives for undertaking the suicide attack. The chapter also depicts the families' responses to their sons' suicides. Chapter 5 describes the study of Palestinian would-be suicides and suggests that, contrary to the prevailing opinion, most suicide terrorists do have distinctive personality characteristics. The chapter also looks at the would-be suicides' reports of their motives for undertaking their missions, and their experiences and behaviors throughout the period of preparation and on the way to the target. Palestinian organizers of suicide attacks are the subject of Chapter 6. This chapter delineates the organizers' personal characteristics, but most of it deals with the organizers' descriptions of the operational aspects of preparing a suicide attack and the factors that influence their decisions. Chapter 7 discusses the importance of public opinion in the terrorist suicides' community, focusing on the Palestinian population as a case in point. Chapter 8 considers suicide terrorism in the light of sociological and psychological theories of suicide. The chapter reaches the conclusion that existing theories cannot readily explain suicide terrorism, mainly because this phenomenon is first and foremost a group phenomenon, and because the individual risk factors for becoming a suicide bomber are by and large different from the risk factors for ordinary suicide. Chapter 9 offers a critical discussion of the literature on suicide terrorism. In the concluding chapter, I present an integrated view of the suicide terrorism phenomenon and a brief discussion of coping with this phenomenon.

*Endnotes*

1. The systematic campaign of suicide attacks in Lebanon began with the suicide car bombing of the American embassy in Beirut on April 18, 1983. However, two isolated suicide attacks were carried out in Lebanon before 1983. The first recorded suicide attack took place on December 15, 1981, apparently against the backdrop of the Iran–Iraq war. In that attack, a man exploded a car laden with explosives at the Iraqi embassy in Beirut. The other event took place November 11, 1982. A massive explosion destroyed the Israeli headquarters building in Tyre. An Israeli investigation concluded that the blast resulted from the ignition of a gas leak at the building's basement, but three years later Hizballah claimed that the attack had been carried out by a suicide car bomber by the name of Ahmed Qassir.

2. According to the Israeli Security Agency's statistics, in seven years of the second intifada, 1.065 Israelis were killed in 30,595 terrorist attacks of all kinds. Of these, 525 were killed in 155 suicide attacks. See: Israeli Security Agency's report, *Palestinian Terrorism in 2007 - Statistics and Trends*. Available at: http://www.shabak.gov.il/SiteCollectionImages/english/TerrorInfo/Terrorism2007report-ENGLISH.pdf, accessed on January 12, 2010.

3. See: National Counterterrorism Center, 2007 Report on Terrorism, 30 April 2008, Chart 3 (p. 24) and Chart 10 (p. 31).
4. New York Times, June 13, 2006. "Suicide Bombs Biggest Threat to US: Experts".
5. The first suicide attack in Sri Lanka took place on July 5, 1987 by an LTTE (Liberation Tigers of Tamil Eelam) officer who apparently acted on his own initiative. However, this event remained an isolated case for three years before the LTTE adopted suicide attacks as a systematic tactic in 1990.
6. This definition was adopted by some other writers, e.g., Weinberg, Pedhazur, & Canetti-Nisim (2003) and Moghadam (2008).

# 2

# The Spectrum of Suicide for an Ideological Cause

THE BIBLICAL STORY OF the death of Samson is often mentioned as the earliest recorded case of what we now call a suicide attack. Samson's self-inflicted death is described in Chapter 16 of the Book of Judges:

> Then Samson prayed to the Lord, "O Sovereign Lord, remember me. O God, please strengthen me just once more, and let me with one blow get revenge on the Philistines for my two eyes." Then Samson reached toward the two central pillars on which the temple stood. Bracing himself against them, his right hand on the one and his left hand on the other, Samson said, "Let me die with the Philistines!" Then he pushed with all his might, and down came the temple on the rulers and all the people in it. Thus he killed many more when he died than while he lived.

Samson's suicide, however, differed from terrorist suicide attacks, as we know them today, in several respects: First, it was a totally individual act, whereas practically all suicide attacks now are organized by a group in the course of a systematic strategy of struggle. Second, Samson committed suicide because he was irreversibly blinded and had no hope of regaining his previous powerful, carefree, independent life. For him, death was a better alternative than continuation of life. In this sense, his suicide was similar to that of ailing persons who suffer much and have no hope of recovery. This kind of personal reason for committing suicide cannot be found in the case of most suicide bombers nowadays, although some of them do show suicidal symptoms (see Chapter 5). Moreover, Samson's actions would not fit our definition of a suicide attack because his suicide was not politically or ideologically motivated.

Numerous authors (e.g., Taylor, 1988, p.109; Schweitzer, 2001a, p. 75; Silke, 2003, p. 93; Atran, 2003a; Reuter, C., 2004, pp. 23–27; Bloom, 2005, pp. 4–5; Pape, 2005, pp. 12–13) have attributed the use of suicide attacks as a systematic tactic to some ancient groups, notably the Jewish Sicarii of the 1st century CE, the Hindu Thugs of the 7th–19th centuries, and the Muslim Hashshashin (Assassins) of the 11th–13th centuries. The mention of these groups is meant to serve the claim that suicide terrorism is an old phenomenon, and to link it to religious fanaticism. These ancient examples, however, cannot be taken as genuine suicide, because in all cases the assailants did not kill themselves.[1]

The Sicarii were a violent, radical Jewish sect of the Zealots, who, in the 1st century CE, fought against the Roman rule of Judea. They used to assassinate their opponents—especially Jews who, in their view, collaborated with the Romans—using daggers (*sicae*, in Latin), which they concealed under their clothes. Contrary to the prevailing erroneous notion, however, their attacks were not suicidal. In fact, as noted by Flavius Josephus, the main source on the Sicarii, they did their best to escape unharmed after their attacks by posing as bystanders and expressing dismay at the crime. In Flavius' words:

> The murderers became a part of those that had indignation against them; by which means they appeared persons of such reputation, that they could by no means be discovered.[2]

The attribution of suicide attacks to the Hashshashin is also not quite accurate. The Hashshashin were members of the Nizari sect of the Ismaili branch of Shi'ite Islam. From the late 11th century until 1256, when the Mongols crushed them, they conducted a violent struggle against the Abbasid caliphate. Because they were no match for their opponents militarily, the founder and first leader of the sect, Hassan-i Sabbah, adopted as their main form of struggle the method of assassination for which they became known and feared. From their primary stronghold, the fortress of Alamut in the Elburz Mountains in Northern Persia, the sect's leaders sent their men to assassinate select personalities. The assassins would approach their targets in disguise and, at the first opportunity, kill them with a dagger. Because the prominent men whom they attacked were surrounded by guards, the assassins had no hope to escape and presumably knew that their action would result in their own death (Lewis, 1967; C. Reuter, 2004, pp. 23–26; Esposito, 2002, p. 43). However, they never killed themselves. In this respect they were quite similar to numerous modern terrorists who are not regarded as suicides. The anarchists of the 19th and early 20th centuries, for example, or the Russian members of the 19th-century

Narodnaya Volya and the 20th-century Social Revolutionary Party, who assassinated heads of state and high-ranking officials, were comparable to the Hashshashin in their methods, yet no one offers them as examples of suicide terrorists. Similarly, in numerous cases of modern terrorism, the assailants had a slim chance of escape, or no chance whatsoever.

Another sect considered by some writers to be an early example of terrorist suicide was the Thugee. The Thugee operated in India in the course of several centuries, until they were extinguished in 1828 (some authors trace their roots as far back as 2500 years ago).[3] Members of the sect, known as Thugs, used to murder travelers by strangulation and rob them. Not only did they not commit suicide after the murder, they did everything to conceal the crime and escape with the booty. The Thugs worshiped Kali, the Hindu goddess of killing and destruction (but also a motherly protector of her followers) and, according to some reports, their murders had a religious element—ritualistic sacrifice for Kali—in addition to the material goal of ordinary robbery. Their motivation notwithstanding, like the Sicarii and the Assassins, the Thugs do not qualify as suicide terrorists for the simple reason that they did not kill themselves.

The attribution of suicide to the Sicarii, the Hashshashin, and the Thugs, but not to the anarchists, Russian revolutionaries, and other members of secular terrorist groups who carried out similar high-risk attacks but did not kill themselves, probably reflects the writers' hidden assumption that members of religious sects wanted to die in order to reach paradise, or because they revered martyrdom, whereas members of secular groups did not seek death.[4] This presumed difference is questionable, because the assumption—that religious motivation, and the belief that dying in a "holy war" guarantees a place in paradise, are stronger motives to sacrifice one's life than, say, patriotism—is groundless.

The current myth that the willingness to die in a "holy war" is a distinctive attribute of Muslim fighters originated in the Iranian propaganda during the Iran–Iraq War (1980–1988). In an attempt to fuel fighting spirit among their people and to frighten the enemy, the Iranian authorities publicized with great fanfare stories about the Basij: young recruits (many of them teenagers) who, in some cases, were tasked to walk over mine fields, so as to clear them for the main forces that followed (Taheri, 1987, p. 92). Reputedly, the Basij were wearing symbolic keys to Paradise around their necks, as a token of their readiness to die. It is unclear whether this propaganda succeeded in hampering the Iraqi soldiers' morale, but it certainly impressed Western reporters, who expressed great astonishment at this show of devotion and willingness to sacrifice, driven by religious belief. An examination of the statistical facts, however, shows a less dramatic picture. At the time of the Iran–Iraq war, Iran's population was about 50 million.[5] An estimated 300,000 Iranian soldiers were killed in the course of the eight years of the war.[6] In comparison, during World War I the French population was about 55 million, and in the course of the four years of the war about 1.35 million French soldiers were killed.[7] The Western Front in World War I was characterized by the use of mass attacks of soldiers charging across mine fields against entrenched enemy troops, under heavy machine gun and artillery fire.[8] Considerably higher casualty rates per population were recorded in World War II. Germany, with a population of about 70 million, lost an estimated number of 2,850,000 soldiers in battle; the Soviet Union, with a population of about 170 million, lost 7.5 million soldiers.[9] These Western soldiers were not motivated by religious fervor or by the wish to reach paradise as soon as possible. Yet, they were willing to sacrifice their lives in far greater numbers than the Iranian youngsters who were ostensibly enthusiastic to die.

## Group Suicides

Mass suicide by cult members is not terrorist suicide as defined in Chapter 1, because the suicide is not committed in order to kill an enemy. Yet, as the suicide is ostensibly motivated by religious belief rather than by individual distress, these cases might add some information that helps us understand the phenomenon of suicide terrorism. This information pertains especially to two aspects: group influence and religious belief as a motive for suicide. Three of the better-documented cult suicides are described below.

### Masada

An early recorded case of mass suicide took place in Masada. During the uprising of the Jews against the Romans (66–73 CE), members of the Sicarii sect and their families found refuge in Masada, a desert fortress overlooking the Dead Sea. After the fall of Jerusalem, the rebellion was all but crushed, with Masada remaining as the last bastion of rebels. The Roman army committed a whole legion (at least 6000 men) to defeat this last Jewish stronghold. After a siege, which lasted a few months, the Romans succeeded in breaching Masada's outer wall. The defenders, meanwhile, had managed to build an inner wall made of wood, but the Romans set it on fire and were about to break in the next day. At this moment, when it was clear that the Romans would storm the fortress shortly, the Sicarii's leader, Elazar Ben Yair, decided to persuade his followers to carry out collective suicide. According to Flavius (the only source on the event), Elazar spoke to his congregation, but initially they wavered and hesitated. He then delivered another speech, and this time managed to convince them to carry out the communal suicide. Each man then killed his wife and children. Following that, the men drew lots and selected ten men, who killed the others. Then the remaining ten drew lots again to select one, who killed the nine and then finally fell on his sword. By Flavius' account, the number of dead—men, women and children—was 960. The only survivors were two women and five children, who hid in a cave to save their lives. Flavius' dramatic description is worth providing here in his own words:

> Now as Eleazar was proceeding on in this exhortation, they all cut him off short, and made haste to do the work, as full of an unconquerable ardor of mind, and moved with a demoniacal fury. So they went their ways, as one still endeavoring to be before another, and as thinking that this eagerness would be a demonstration of their courage and good conduct, if they could avoid appearing in the last class; so great was the zeal they were in to slay their wives and children, and themselves also! Nor indeed, when they came to the work itself, did their courage fail them, as one might imagine it would have done, but they then held fast the same resolution, without wavering, which they had upon the hearing of Eleazar's speech, while yet every one of them still retained the natural passion of love to themselves and their families, because the reasoning they went upon appeared to them to be very just, even with regard to those that were dearest to them; for the husbands tenderly embraced their wives, and took their children into their arms, and gave the longest parting kisses to them, with tears in their eyes. Yet at the same time did they complete what they had resolved on, as if they had been executed by the hands of strangers; and they had nothing else for their comfort but the necessity they were in of doing this execution, to avoid that prospect they had of the miseries they were to suffer from their enemies. Nor was there at length any one of these men found that scrupled to act their part in this terrible execution, but every one of them despatched his dearest relations. Miserable men indeed were they! whose distress forced them to slay their own wives and children with their own hands, as the lightest of those evils that were before them. So they being not able to bear the grief they were under for what they had done any longer, and esteeming it an injury to those they had slain, to live even the shortest space of time after them, they presently laid

all they had upon a heap, and set fire to it. They then chose ten men by lot out of them to slay all the rest; every one of whom laid himself down by his wife and children on the ground, and threw his arms about them, and they offered their necks to the stroke of those who by lot executed that melancholy office; and when these ten had, without fear, slain them all, they made the same rule for casting lots for themselves, that he whose lot it was should first kill the other nine, and after all should kill himself. Accordingly, all these had courage sufficient to be no way behind one another in doing or suffering; so, for a conclusion, the nine offered their necks to the executioner, and he who was the last of all took a view of all the other bodies, lest perchance some or other among so many that were slain should want his assistance to be quite despatched, and when he perceived that they were all slain, he set fire to the palace, and with the great force of his hand ran his sword entirely through himself, and fell down dead near to his own relations. So these people died with this intention, that they would not leave so much as one soul among them all alive to be subject to the Romans. Yet was there an ancient woman, and another who was of kin to Eleazar, and superior to most women in prudence and learning, with five children, who had concealed themselves in caverns under ground, and had carried water thither for their drink, and were hidden there when the rest were intent upon the slaughter of one another. Those others were nine hundred and sixty in number, the women and children being withal included in that computation.[10]

This event, as described by Flavius, warrants several comments. First, although Elazar's followers agreed to be killed, all but one were slain by others rather than killing themselves. Technically, this was a case of 959 murders and one suicide. This is not a mere pedantic observation. Psychologically, killing oneself is more demanding than letting oneself be killed by another's hands. Presumably, Eleazar preferred the method employed because he feared that some of the men would not have the fortitude to actually kill themselves (as we shall see, this was the case also in other instances of mass suicide).

Furthermore, as noted above, many of the congregation hesitated, at least initially. Flavius described it as follows:

This was Eleazar's speech to them. Yet did not the opinions of all the auditors acquiesce therein; but although some of them were very zealous to put his advice in practice, and were in a manner filled with pleasure at it, and thought death to be a good thing, yet had those that were most effeminate a commiseration for their wives and families; and when these men were especially moved by the prospect of their own certain death, they looked wistfully at one another, and by the tears that were in their eyes declared their dissent from his opinion. When Eleazar saw these people in such fear, and that their souls were dejected at so prodigious a proposal, he was afraid lest perhaps these effeminate persons should, by their lamentations and tears, enfeeble those that heard what he had said courageously; so he did not leave off exhorting them, but stirred up himself, and recollecting proper arguments for raising their courage, he undertook to speak more briskly and fully to them, and that concerning the immortality of the soul.

What made the hesitators change their mind? It is implausible that Eleazar's speech made all that difference, impassioned as it was. Presumably, it was a combination of the authority of the leader and group pressure that forced the reluctant members of the community to obey.

Elazar's speeches were, presumably, reconstructed if not fabricated by Flavius.[11] Nevertheless, it is interesting that only in the second speech, which succeeded in convincing the congregation to carry out the collective suicide, did Elazar refer to the survival of the soul after death. In his exhortation, he did not promise paradise as a prize for martyrdom, but stressed that death is the end of the existence of the body, while the soul survives. There is no way of knowing the importance of this argument in convincing his flock to die, but apparently Flavius thought that it was significant.

## Jonestown

A modern case of mass murder/suicide was carried out in 1978 by the Peoples Temple cult in the communal settlement of Jonestown in Guyana, named after the cult's leader, Jim Jones. The cult was founded in Indiana in the 1950s and moved to California in the 1960s. In 1977, Jones and his followers moved to a secluded place in Guyana, which he had purchased several years before. Before long, reports of abuse of children and adult members of Jones' community reached the media in the U.S. These reports included allegations of harsh beatings and torture—administered on Jones' orders to cult members as a means of discipline—as well as allegations that cult members were held in Jonestown against their will. In the wake of these reports, Congressman Leo Ryan decided to investigate the situation. He flew to Guyana and visited Jonestown, accompanied by media reporters, representatives of the Guyana government and the U.S. embassy, and concerned relatives of the cult members. Congressman Ryan and his companions reached Jonestown and interviewed members of Jones' community, some of whom asked to leave the place with him. Jim Jones presumably felt that Ryan's visit signified the end of his cult.

As they left Jonestown's compound, Ryan and his company arrived at an airstrip from where they were supposed to fly back. At the airstrip, Ryan's company was attacked by Jones' men. Ryan and four reporters were killed and several others were wounded. At the compound, Jones ordered the killing of all members of his community. This eventuality had been rehearsed several times in the past. All members of the community were made to drink a cyanide-laced soft drink. The lethal liquid was injected into children's mouths by syringes, and given to adults in paper cups. Apparently, at least some of the people thought that this was another drill designed to test their loyalty, as had happened several times before. This time, however, it was real. Nine hundred and thirteen members of the community died in this mass-murder-suicide event.

## Waco, Texas

The Branch Davidians was a cult led by David Koresh (whose name at birth was Vernon Howell), where members lived in a commune called Mount Carmel, on the outskirts of Waco, Texas. Like the communes in Masada and Jonestown, the Branch Davidians community included families as well as single people. At the onset of the chain of events, which led to the mass suicide/murder, they numbered 117 men, women and children. The cult espoused an apocalyptic belief, which maintained that Armageddon was imminent. For this reason, they stashed weapons and fortified their compound. The cult's confrontation with law enforcement agencies started when the Bureau of Alcohol, Tobacco and Firearms (ATF) decided to investigate allegations that the Branch Davidians were stockpiling illegal weapons.[12] On February 28, 1993, the ATF tried to enter the compound by force in order to search for weapons. The raid was meant to be a surprise, but the Branch Davidians had received warnings and were ready for the assault. They opened fire on the ATF agents, and in the exchange of fire that ensued, four ATF agents and five members of the Branch Davidian sect were killed. Following the failed raid, the FBI took over and placed a siege on the compound. For 51 days, FBI negotiators tried to persuade David Koresh to surrender, to no avail. At several points during the negotiations, however, Koresh agreed to let some members of the cult leave the compound. On April 19, 1993, the FBI tried to force the Branch Davidians out of the compound by pumping large amounts of tear gas into the buildings. Cult members responded by firing at the government forces. Several hours later, a small group of Koresh assistants poured gasoline throughout the compound and set it on fire, without informing the majority of the cult members of their intention. They also shot cult members who tried to escape. Autopsies revealed that at least 20 cult members, including infants and young children, were shot to death (all gunshot wounds were in the head or thorax, some of them from behind). One victim, a 3-year-old child, was stabbed.[13] Altogether 79 people, including 21 children, died as a result of the fire and shooting by Koresh henchmen.

## Common Factors in Communal Suicide

Collective suicide cases seem to have several characteristics in common. Perhaps the most salient feature is that in all cases, the ostensibly common suicide event was primarily a matter of mass murder rather than mass suicide, because the majority of the victims did not kill themselves but were killed by other cult members. It may be argued that the victims were willing to die, and their killing should therefore be regarded as assisted suicide rather than murder. However, the validity of this argument is questionable. The "free will" claim is certainly not applicable to the many children who were killed under these circumstances. Furthermore, adult victims in Jonestown and Waco who were shot from behind were apparently people who tried to escape, not people who asked to be killed.

In a more general sense, from a psychological rather than a legal perspective, free will is questionable even in the case of seemingly consenting adult cult members. In all three events, the decision to die was not taken in a group discussion and vote—it was imposed on the community by the leader (and in Jonestown and Waco, enforced and executed by his lieutenants). Typically, cult members submit totally to the leader and obey his orders. In Jonestown, as well as in Waco, cult members gave their property to the leader, and often accepted that their wives and daughters became his concubines (Maris et al., 2000, pp. 473–4).[14] This mental condition of submissiveness is presumably the result of an interaction of certain personality characteristics that make some persons more amenable to influence than others, and living under extreme pressure by the leader and the group. In this sense, the factors that play a crucial role in cult members' willingness to comply with the leader's order to commit suicide are similar to the critical factors in terrorist suicide, as explained in Chapter 5.

Often, albeit not always, cult suicide occurs against a backdrop in which the cult members (and especially the leader) perceive a critical impending threat to the continuation of the cult's existence, its belief system, and especially the leader's status. In Masada, the suicide was carried out when the Romans were about to break into the fortress; this was the only case of the three where the alternative to suicide was indeed death or miserable slavery and humiliation. In Jonestown and Waco, the genuine threat was loss of power and prosecution—which the cult leader and his assistants faced, but not the majority of the community members. The perceived threat is often interwoven with an apocalyptic belief of impending Armageddon, as was the case in both Jonestown and Waco. The apocalyptic belief provides the context for justifying the confrontation with agents of the government as war against the forces of evil, and entails the promise of eventual victory and resurrection.

In contrast to cult suicide, in which the whole group perishes, terrorist suicide is a calculated tactic consisting of sacrificing individual members in the service of the group.

## Kamikazes

The Japanese kamikaze pilots of World War II are another interesting example of suicide attacks that do not quite fit the definition of suicide terrorism, but can provide pertinent insights. Although, unlike cult suicides, the kamikazes did kill themselves to kill others, their attacks were conducted in the framework of a conventional war as part of an organized, large-scale military activity, and within their unit formations rather than as individuals.[15]

Systematic kamikaze attacks started in October 1944, during the American advance to the Philippines—but the idea of suicide attacks by Japanese pilots crashing into American ships with their bomb-carrying airplanes had been proposed six months earlier to the Japanese Imperial Headquarters by Vice Admiral Takijiro Onishi, commander of the Japanese naval air force in the Philippines.[16] In view of the mounting American superiority in naval power, Onishi was certain that Japan was doomed to defeat unless the Japanese could find a way to severely damage the American fleet. In April 1944, however, the Japanese supreme command was not yet ready to take such a radical step, and Onishi's idea was rejected on the grounds that it would be a waste of good pilots. In October, however, the situation seemed so grim that the Imperial Headquarters authorized Onishi to take whatever steps he deemed necessary in order to prevent the American takeover of the Philippines. Onishi immediately acted upon this permission. Captain Inoguchi was Onishi's personal representative for operations, and Commander Nakajima was second in command of the 201st Air Group, which was charged with the formation of the first kamikaze unit. After the war, they brought forward an eyewitness account of the initiation of the kamikaze program. According to them, Onishi, having received Imperial Headquarters' permission to use suicide crash-dive attacks, went to the 201st Air Group base in Mabalacat, near Manila, where he presented the idea to the top Air Group officers. The Air Group's commanding officer immediately set out to organize the suicide unit. According to Inoguchi and Nakajima (1958, p. 10), the first batch of suicides was recruited as follows:

> Commander Tamai, after consulting with his squadron leaders, ordered an immediate assembly of all non-commissioned pilots of the air group. He reviewed the critical war situation when all 23 of the men were assembled and then explained Admiral Ohnishi's proposal. In a frenzy of emotion and joy, the arms of every pilot in the assembly went up in a gesture of complete accord.

A second batch of kamikaze pilots was recruited a day later at another air base. This time, the recruiter was Nakajima. According to his account, he explained the necessity to the assembled pilots, and then asked them to write their names on a piece of paper and put it in an envelope as an indication of their willingness to join the suicide unit, or submit a blank piece of paper if they did not want to participate. Only two of 20 envelopes contained blank pieces of paper, and these were submitted by pilots who were sick at the time.

In assessing these descriptions of overwhelming joy and enthusiasm expressed by all of the pilots at the prospect of dying for their country and Emperor, one should remember that the writers were among those who sent the kamikazes to their death. Thus, they had an understandable need to depict the kamikazes as enthusiastic to die, rather than as cannon fodder sent by heartless commanders who knew better. It is noteworthy that Inoguchi and Nakajima themselves did not go on a suicide mission, and survived the war to write their story. Onishi, however, committed a ritual seppuku (hara-kiri) and another high-ranking commander of the kamikaze operations, Admiral Matome Ugaki, personally carried out a kamikaze attack and died, immediately after hearing the Emperor's announcement of Japan's surrender.[17]

Suicide attacks in a conventional war setting have not been a uniquely Japanese phenomenon. Suicide attacks by individuals or small groups of soldiers of many nations have been carried out before and after World War II. Yet the kamikaze phenomenon is unmatched in its scope and duration. As Inoguchi and Nakajima (1958, p. xv) point out:

> Kamikaze attacks shocked the world primarily because of their certain death aspect. History provides many cases of individual soldiers who fought under certain-death circumstances, but never before was such a program carried out so systematically and over such a long period of time. In the case of a do-or-die action, however great the risk involved, there is always a chance of survival. But the kamikaze attack could be carried out *only* by killing oneself. The attack and death were one and the same thing.

Indeed, the number of Japanese kamikaze pilots who died in action is astounding. Ohnuki-Tierney (2002, pp. 161, 167) makes several estimates, ranging from 2,392 to 3,843.[18] Thus, the number of kamikaze suicides in the course of 10 months (October 21, 1944 to August 15, 1945) was about as large, or even larger, than the total number of terrorist suicide attacks committed by dozens of groups around the globe in the period of 1981-2008, which stands at 2,622.

Similarly to Japanese nationalist writers who glorified the kamikazes, some Western scholars have also described the suicide pilots as unwavering volunteers who went enthusiastically to die for their country. A well-known scholar of Japanese culture, Pinguet (1993, p. 228), for example, wrote in an admiring, almost poetic, tone:

> We have a few photographs from just before the take-off, the pilots smiling and waving from their cabins, their foreheads bound with a cotton strip bearing a red sun. Lambs to the slaughter? No: it would insult them to deny their perfect concord with their own destiny. No need to force or cajole or even indoctrinate them. They were entirely free, their decision springing from their country's agony. However well-organized this death, they had chosen it and willed it unceasingly, from day to day, proud of it, and finding it in all their reasons for *living*.

The real picture, however, was much more complex. Presumably, many of the kamikazes were, indeed, keen to go on the mission; but many others were reluctant, and joined the Special Attack Force under social pressure and sometimes under direct coercion. Ohnuki-Tierney (2002) found evidence showing that many pilots, including the officer who was chosen to lead the first kamikaze attack, were assigned to kamikaze units against their will.[19] The practice of forcing recruits to enroll in kamikaze units was particularly prevalent towards the end of the war, as Japan's military situation became increasingly hopeless and conventional military methods could not halt the American offensive.

Like the group suicides in Masada, Jonestown and Waco, the Japanese Imperial Headquarters decision to resort to suicide attacks was reached out of desperation. Although, as noted above, several pilots crashed on American ships or rammed American airplanes on their own initiative before October 1944, the use of suicide attacks as an organized tactic was only adopted when the Japanese military leadership realized that the American advance toward the Japanese home islands could not be stopped by conventional tactics. The battle of Leyte Gulf was regarded by the Japanese military leadership as crucial for the future of the war. In their view, losing the Philippines meant losing the war. Since they had no hope of repelling the superior American forces by conventional means, they were willing to employ this extreme measure.

The kamikaze pilots demonstrate that the promise of paradise is not a necessary factor in the willingness to carry out suicide attacks. Japan's main religions, Shinto and Buddhism, do not espouse a concept of paradise as Judaism, Christianity and Islam do, although they do support the concept of survival of the soul through reincarnation (Buddhism) or in the form of a *kami*, or ancestral spirit (Shinto). In neither religion, however, does heroic death carry the prize of a better existence.

Above all, the kamikaze phenomenon is a demonstration of the power of the military organization as a source of extreme social pressure. Social pressure has also been a major factor in cult suicides—but armies, which are huge organizations that specialize in death en masse, can produce a much larger number of suicides, once they decide to do so. For soldiers in war, in contrast to cult members, the possibility of death is part of the terms of service.

## Terrorist Suicide

Genuine suicide attacks as defined in this book (i.e., killing oneself for the purpose of killing others), carried out by sub-state groups or individuals (that is, actors other than government agencies) are a relatively novel phenomenon, which began in the early 1980s. In the course of nearly three decades, suicide attacks have taken place in 37 countries.

Suicide terrorism is proliferating. The systematic use of suicide attacks by terrorist groups started in the early 1980s, but more than 88 percent of the attacks have taken place over the last six years (2003-2008). The growth is not only in the frequency of attacks, but also in their geographical spread and the number of groups involved. In the 20-year period from 1981 to 2000, suicide attacks took place in 19 countries, whereas in the 8-year period from 2001 to 2008, suicide attacks have occurred in 33 countries.[20] The problem has, therefore, been growing rapidly.

As shown in Figure 2.1, in a global perspective the rate of suicide attacks was fairly stable in the period of 1981–1999, ranging between one attack and 18 attacks per year. Since 2000, however, the rate of attacks has risen dramatically, reaching a peak of 608 attacks in 2007. This recent trend has been perceived as an alarming indication that this form of terrorism is spreading exponentially and may reach disastrous proportions. However, suicide terrorism, unlike a new technology (e.g., the use of the internet or cell phones), does not proliferate in ever growing circles. A closer look at the countries where suicide attacks have taken place reveals that the bulk of them have been the sites of acute conflicts at the time of the attacks. Table 2.1 shows the distribution of suicide attacks by country. Ninety percent of the world total of suicide attacks took place in five countries—Iraq, Afghanistan, Israel, Sri Lanka, and Pakistan. Three countries—Iraq, Afghanistan and Israel—account for 80.5% of the world total, and Iraq alone accounts for 58.2%. Why these places and not others? And why are most of the perpetrators of suicide attacks Muslims? These questions will be dealt with in the concluding chapter of this book.

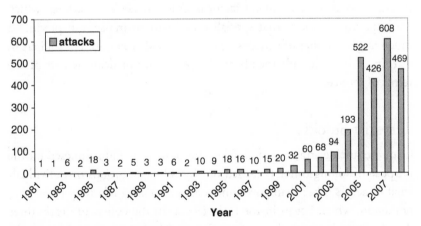

**Figure 2.1** Number of worldwide suicide attacks by year, 1981–2008.

**Table 2.1** Number of Suicide Attacks and Attackers, and Percentage of the World Total per Country, 1981–2008[*][#]

| Country | Number of attacks (and % of world total) | Number of attackers (and % of world total) |
|---|---|---|
| Iraq | 1,526 (58.2%) | 1,643 (55.9%) |
| Afghanistan | 399 (15.2%) | 415 (14.1%) |
| Israel (incl. Occupied Territories) | 187 (7.1%) | 216 (7.4%) |
| Pakistan | 155 (5.9%) | 169 (5.8%) |
| Sri Lanka | 101 (3.9%) | 167 (5.7%) |
| Lebanon | 41 (1.9%) | 41 (1.4%) |
| Russia (incl. Chechnya) | 38 (1.4%) | 50 (1.7%) |
| Turkey | 30 (1.1%) | 31 (1.1%) |
| Algeria | 20 (0.8%) | 20 (0.7%) |
| India | 14 (0.5%) | 14 (0.5%) |
| Somalia | 13 (0.5%) | 13 (0.4%) |
| Morocco | 9 (0.3%) | 20 (0.7%) |
| Saudi Arabia | 9 (0.3%) | 17 (0.6%) |
| United Kingdom | 9 (0.3%) | 10 (0.3%) |
| Egypt | 8 (0.3%) | 11 (0.4%) |
| Yemen | 8 (0.3%) | 12 (0.4%) |
| Bangladesh | 7 (0.3%) | 10 (0.3%) |
| Indonesia | 7 (0.3%) | 8 (0.3%) |
| Uzbekistan | 6 (0.2%) | 6 (0.2%) |
| China | 6 (0.2%) | 8 (0.3%) |
| USA | 5 (0.2%) | 20 (0.7%) |
| Jordan | 4 (0.2%) | 4 (0.1%) |
| Kenya | 2 (0.1%) | 4 (0.1%) |
| Argentina | 2 (0.1%) | 2 (0.1%) |
| Kuwait | 2 (0.1%) | 2 (0.1%) |
| Syria | 2 (0.1%) | 2 (0.1%) |
| Spain | 1 (0.0%) | 7 (0.2%) |
| Portugal | 1 (0.0%) | 5 (0.2%) |
| Bolivia | 1 (0.0%) | 1 (0.0%) |
| Croatia | 1 (0.0%) | 1 (0.0%) |
| Kosovo | 1 (0.0%) | 1 (0.0%) |
| Moldova | 1 (0.0%) | 1 (0.0%) |
| Philippines | 1 (0.0%) | 1 (0.0%) |
| Qatar | 1 (0.0%) | 1 (0.0%) |
| Sudan | 1 (0.0%) | 1 (0.0%) |
| Tanzania | 1 (0.0%) | 1 (0.0%) |
| Tunisia | 1 (0.0%) | 1 (0.0%) |
| Uganda | 1 (0.0%) | 1 (0.0%) |
| **World Total** | **2,622 (100%)** | **2,937 (100%)** |

[*]Two or more suicide attackers at the same place and time were counted as one attack.
[#]A suicide attack was defined as an event in which the bomber tried to detonate an explosive device that he/she was carrying, even when the bomber survived because the device failed to explode due to a technical reason. However, in a great majority of the cases (98.7%), the bomber was actually killed in the attack.

The countries and contexts in which suicide terrorism appeared are quite varied, and each case study would no doubt provide important lessons. However, a comprehensive description of all suicide campaigns would require a voluminous book in itself. For this reason, I shall only discuss in this section some of the major suicide campaigns—namely, those that have special significance in the development of suicide attacks or in understanding the phenomenon. The cases to be surveyed include Lebanon, where it all began; Israel, where a large number of suicide attacks took place and where information on the suicide bombers and the perpetrating organizations is much better than in any other country; Iraq, where the largest number of suicide attacks have taken place, signifying a concerted effort of militant Islamic groups around the globe; and Afghanistan, second in the world's frequency of suicide attacks, and where the number of these attacks has risen sharply in recent years.

### Lebanon

The first systematic use of suicide attacks as a terrorist tactic took place in Lebanon. This tactic was adopted against the backdrop of the Israeli invasion of June 1982, which led to the expulsion of the Palestine Liberation Organization (PLO) and Syrian forces from Beirut and South Lebanon in the last week of August 1982. As a part of the ceasefire agreement, a multinational force (MNF), composed of American, French, Italian and British soldiers, came to Lebanon with the mission of supervising the evacuation of the Palestinian and Syrian forces and, later, also to help stabilize the country.[21] The presence of the MNF was perceived by Syria as a threat to its dominant status in Lebanon. Iran, a vowed anti-American and anti-Israeli actor, who detested Western influence in the region, also viewed the MNF as an arrogant Western intervention in a Muslim country. In addition, the MNF was involved in several incidents that led Lebanese Muslim and Druze groups to believe that the MNF sided with the Christian forces (Wright, 1985; Jaber, 1997). Thus, through their protégé Lebanese groups, both Syria and Iran acted to oust the MNF and the Israeli forces from Lebanon by using guerrilla and terrorist attacks against them and their allies. These efforts intensified following the signing of a peace agreement between Israel and Lebanon on May 17, 1983.

Hala Jaber (1997), along with other observers, has surmised that the idea of suicide attacks was inspired in Lebanon by the model of Iran's practice of clearing minefields by sending children to walk over them.[22]

The Iranian regime exalted the bravery and devotion of the teenage Baseeji and made them national heroes. Given the immense Iranian influence on the leadership of the Lebanese Hizballah, it is quite possible that the latter decided to use suicide attacks under the influence of the Iranian example.

The first terrorist suicide attack in the country took place on December 15, 1981. A suicide bomber crashed a car containing about 100 kg of explosives into the Iraqi embassy building in Beirut. The explosion killed 61 persons and wounded about 100 others. The attack was presumably carried out against the backdrop of the Iran–Iraq war (1980–1988), and was attributed to pro-Iranian agents in Lebanon. At that time, however, this was an isolated event. The systematic use of suicide attacks only started about a year later, when Shiite factions, who later formed Hizballah, carried out a series of suicide attacks against American and Israeli targets. The first in the series was a suicide truck bomb attack on the Israeli military head-quarters building in the city of Tyre in South Lebanon, on November 11, 1982, which resulted in 89 fatalities.[23] On April 18, 1983, Hizballah carried out a suicide car bomb attack against the American Embassy in Beirut, which resulted in 63 fatalities.[24] Six months later, on October 23, two concurrent suicide truck bomb attacks were carried out against the multi-national force in Beirut: one targeted the U.S. Marines barracks, killing 273 people (including 241 American servicemen) and the other destroyed the French paratroopers' headquarters, killing 58 people. On September 20, 1984, a suicide bomber targeted the U.S. embassy again, this time killing 23 people.

The first suicide attacks in Lebanon were directed against American targets. But once the multinational force left Lebanon, Israeli forces and soldiers of the South Lebanese Army—Israel's ally—became the chosen targets. On November 4, 1983, a suicide bomber drove a car laden with explosives into the Israeli government compound in Tyre. The driver was shot by soldiers standing guard at the compound's entrance, but the car continued a few meters before exploding and killing 61 people, 28 of them Israeli soldiers, and 33 Palestinian and Lebanese detainees. All in all, by the end of 1999, 24 suicide attacks were carried out against Israeli forces and nine against the South Lebanese Army. A few attacks were directed against other targets: One attack that targeted a Syrian checkpoint was carried out in September 1988, at the time that Syrian forces in Beirut were perceived by Hizballah as a threat to its independence. Another attack, on November 11, 1985, was carried out against the Christian Lebanese Front's headquarters in East Beirut. In one case, on November 20, 1986, a suicide car bomber exploded at a checkpoint of the United Nations Interim Force in Lebanon (UNIFIL).[25] Apparently, the suicide bomber was not sent to attack the Fijian soldiers who manned the checkpoint; the intended target was, presumably, a South Lebanese Army position nearby. However, the UN soldiers stopped the suicide's car for a routine search, and he may have lost his nerve.

Initially, suicide attacks in Lebanon were carried out by Hizballah (usually claimed under the name Islamic Jihad). However, in June 1984, Amal, another Shiite organization, joined in, sending a 17-year-old Lebanese boy by the name of Bilal Fahs to carry out a suicide car bombing attack against an Israeli military convoy in South Lebanon. Amal, founded in 1975, preceded Hizballah as the advocate of the cause of the under-privileged Shiite community in Lebanon. In the wake of Hizballah's rising popularity as the leader of the struggle against the Israeli occupation, Amal's leaders presumably felt that to maintain the organization's leadership status in the Shiite community, they needed to sponsor spectacular terrorist attacks as well. Although Amal cannot be properly described as a secular organization, its agenda has focused on promoting the Shiite community's social, economic and political interests in Lebanon, and it has never been a religiously militant group (Esposito, 1998, pp. 275–279).[26]

In 1985, several secular groups—all of them under Syrian influence—adopted the suicide tactics in Lebanon. They included the Syrian Social Nationalist Party (SSNP), the Lebanese Ba'ath party, the Lebanese Communist Party, and two Palestinian groups—the Popular Front for the Liberation of Palestine (PFLP) and the Popular Front for the Liberation of Palestine-General Command (PFLP-GC). Altogether, they carried out more attacks than the religiously motivated Hizballah. Table 2.2 details the distribution of suicide attacks in Lebanon by perpetrating organizations.

**Table 2.2**  Suicide Attacks in Lebanon by Perpetrating Group

| Group | Group's ideology | Number of attacks |
|-------|------------------|-------------------|
| Hizballah | Militant religious, sectarian Shiite | 14 |
| Amal | Sectarian Shiite | 3 |
| SSNP | Syrian nationalist | 10 |
| Ba'ath Party | Syrian nationalist, socialist (Lebanese branch of Syria's ruling party) | 7 |
| Communist Party | Pro-Syrian, communist | 1 |
| PFLP-GC | Nationalist Palestinian | 1 |
| PFLP | Nationalist Palestinian/Marxist | 2 |
| Unknown | | 3 |
| **Total** | | **41** |

As can be seen in Table 2.3, suicide attacks in Lebanon peaked in 1985 (17 attacks) and subsided afterward. One may presume that the reason for the drastic decline in the number of suicide attacks was the diminution of the insurgents' motivation following the withdrawal of Israeli forces from most of the occupied area, which was completed in June 1985. However, Israeli forces still remained in a "security zone" in South Lebanon until May 2000, and attacks on Israeli and South Lebanese Army forces continued throughout that period. Moreover, a significantly larger number of suicide attacks took place after the 1985 withdrawal than before this event—11 attacks before the 1985 partial withdrawal, compared to 29 after. Apparently, the reason for the decline in the frequency of suicide attacks was their diminishing effectiveness. As can be seen in Table 2.3, the average number of fatalities declined sharply after 1983. Thus, in 1985, effective Israeli countermeasures were able to reduce the number of fatalities of suicide attacks to an average of 2.7 per attack. Under these circumstances, the perpetrating groups viewed the tactic as operationally unwarranted. Toward the end of 1985, Hizballah's spiritual mentor, Sayyid Muhammad Husayn Fadlallah, who had initially endorsed suicide attacks, stated that martyrdom (suicide) attacks were no longer justified (Kramer, 1990).

**Table 2.3**  Number of Suicide Attacks and Fatalities in Lebanon by Year, 1983–1990

| Year | No. of attacks | No. of fatalities | Mean no. of fatalities per attack |
| --- | --- | --- | --- |
| 1983 | 4 | 455 | 114.7 |
| 1984 | 2 | 23 | 11.5 |
| 1985 | 17 | 46 | 2.7 |
| 1986 | 3 | 5 | 1.7 |
| 1987 | 1 | 0 | 0 |
| 1988 | 4 | 11 | 2.7 |
| 1989 | 3 | 0 | 0 |
| 1990 | 0 | | |
| 1991 | 0 | | |
| 1992 | 0 | | |
| 1993 | 0 | | |
| 1994 | 0 | | |
| 1995 | 2 | 12 | 6.0 |
| 1996 | 1 | 1 | 1.0 |
| 1997 | 0 | | |
| 1998 | 0 | | |
| 1999 | 1 | 1 | 1.0 |

## Israel

As a systematic, preplanned tactic, suicide attacks began in Israel in 1993. However, two cases of unplanned suicide attacks occurred as early as 1974. Because they can offer an insight into the circumstances that create terrorist suicide behavior, these incidents will be described here in some detail.

On the morning of April 11, 1974, a team of three members of Ahmad Jibril's PFLP-GC were sent to take hostages in Israel, so as to exchange them for Palestinian convicts that had been sentenced for terrorism offenses. The team crossed the Lebanese frontier into Israel and reached the border town of Kiryat Shmona. Originally, their plan was to take hostage a large number of elementary school students. When they reached the school, however, the three members of the team discovered that the school was closed, due to the Passover vacation. On the spur of the moment, they crossed the street and entered a four-story apartment house. Instead of taking hostages as instructed, however, they went from the first floor to the fourth, breaking into each and every apartment and killing every resident they could find—altogether 16 persons, including 9 children. At the top floor, they barricaded themselves, shooting at police and military forces that arrived on the scene. Using megaphones, security forces spokesmen tried to start negotiations, but the three terrorists never answered. Instead, they kept shooting at the security forces, who returned fire. After a while, an explosion was heard from the apartment in which the terrorists had barricaded themselves. Soldiers then entered the building, only to discover that all the residents were dead. On the fourth floor they found the bodies of the three terrorists, who apparently killed themselves by activating explosive belts that they carried on their bodies. At that time, it was not quite clear whether the terrorists committed suicide by intentionally activating the explosive belts, or whether the explosion was caused by an Israeli bullet. Another event, which occurred a couple of months later, strengthened the suicide hypothesis.

On June 13, 1974, a team of four PFLP-GC members again was sent on a hostage-taking mission. Again, they crossed the Israeli-Lebanese border and entered nearby Kibbutz Shamir. Kibbutz members encountered them as they entered. In the exchange of fire, two of the terrorists were wounded and after a few minutes were killed by their own hand grenade. As in the Kiryat Shmona event, it was unclear whether they killed themselves intentionally. The remaining two members of the team burst into a house where they found three women, two of them Kibbutz members and the third a visitor from abroad. Army units had not arrived yet, so armed kibbutz members gathered around the building. They tried to communicate with the terrorists through the closed doors but were never answered. After a while, shots were heard from inside the building, followed shortly by an explosion. As they entered the building, the kibbutz members found out that the terrorists had shot their hostages and then activated the explosive belts they were wearing. No shots had been fired at them from the outside. Autopsy findings suggested that the two hostage-takers exploded themselves while hugging each other.

These two incidents perpetrated by Ahmad Jibril's PFLP-GC were quite unusual in that although the perpetrating organization instructed the teams to take hostages and negotiate to exchange them for Palestinian prisoners—the teams were provided with leaflets intended to be conveyed to the Israelis, detailing the group's demands in return for the release of the hostages—the teams' members shot all Israelis they encountered and committed suicide. Palestinian groups never repeated this behavior, in more than two dozen hostage incidents perpetrated in the following years.[27] Why then, did the PFLP-GC teams in Kiryat Shmona and Shamir behave in this peculiar way?

In 1975, I established Israel's Hostage Negotiations Unit. In this capacity, I had to develop the unit's operational doctrine. For that purpose, among other things, I read all the data I could find on previous Palestinian hostage incidents. In my search, I found a plausible explanation of the odd behavior displayed by the PFLP-GC teams. Presumably, the key was in how the team members were prepared for their mission. In addition to technical instructions, weapons and navigation training, the men were asked to write farewell letters to their families and friends, in case they were killed in the mission. Also, posters were prepared in which they were displayed standing with their rifles against the backdrop of flames, and the legend presented them as fallen heroes. Probably, when the team members left for their mission, they had already resigned from life and felt themselves to be dead heroes.

Although two Palestinian groups—PFLP and PFLP-GC—carried out three suicide attacks in Lebanon in the 1980s[28] at a time when Lebanese groups used this method frequently, Palestinian groups inside the occupied territories started using suicide attacks only in 1993. The political context for the radical Palestinian groups' decision to resort to this method, which signified an escalation of the struggle, was the Israeli-Palestinian peace process, which gained momentum in 1993. For Hamas, the peace process meant bad news for both ideological and practical reasons. Ideologically, Hamas has always maintained that the state of Israel must be destroyed because it was founded on Palestinian land. The group therefore opposed any agreement that included a territorial compromise. Practically, Hamas leadership was worried that once a peace agreement was achieved and the PLO took control of the Territories, it would suppress Hamas, its main political rival. Thus, escalation of the struggle was meant to derail the peace process.

The radical Palestinian groups' decision to use suicide attacks was, presumably, influenced by Hizballah's experience in Lebanon. On December 17, 1992, Israel deported to Lebanon 415 leaders and operatives of Hamas and the Palestinian Islamic Jihad (PIJ). The deportees stayed in Lebanon about a year before they were permitted to return to the occupied territories. During that time, they were hosted by Hizballah, which provided them with all kinds of aid. Hizballah's operatives also shared with the Palestinians the experience they had accumulated over the years of fighting in Lebanon and, no doubt, discussed suicide attacks—their trademark tactic—as well. The deportees maintained constant contact with the remaining infrastructure in the Territories. It is noteworthy that by the time these men were allowed to return to their homes, half a dozen suicide attacks had already been carried out in the Territories by Hamas and PIJ.

On April 16, 1993, a 23-year-old Hamas member by the name of Sahir Hamdallah Tammam Nabulsi set off an explosives-laden van that he was driving between two Israeli buses in the parking lot of a restaurant near Mekholah, in the Jordan Valley. The buses carried Israeli soldiers, but at the time of the explosion almost all of them were inside the restaurant, so that only one person was killed and eight were wounded. Five months passed before the next Hamas-perpetrated suicide attack took place, this time near Sheikh Ajlin in the Gaza strip. On September 12, 1993, the suicide bomber, 20-year-old Ayman Salah Atallah, rammed a rigged car he was driving at an Israeli bus. Hamas announced that the operation was carried out in protest of the coming peace agreement between Israel and the PLO, which was formally signed in Washington, DC on September 13. Indeed, another three suicide attacks were carried out in the next three days, two of them in the Gaza Strip by Hamas, and one by PIJ, on a bus near Ashdod, inside Israel.[29]

Until April 1994, Palestinian suicide attacks were carried out mainly (albeit not exclusively) in the occupied territories, where the targets were Israeli soldiers and civilian settlers. Thereafter, most of the attacks were carried out against civilian targets inside Israel. Of the 190 suicide attacks carried out by Palestinian groups until the end of 2008, 118 took place within Israel, whereas 40 were in the Gaza Strip and 29 in the West Bank. Three attacks were carried out at sea, off the shores of Lebanon.

Some authors (e.g., Sprinzak, 2000; Hudson, 1999, p. 126; Hafez, 2006, p. 18; Hroub, 2006, p. 52)[30] have erroneously claimed that Palestinian groups resorted to suicide attacks inside Israel only after the February 25, 1994 massacre of Palestinian worshippers in the Tomb of the Patriarchs in Hebron. In that terrorist attack, a Jewish fanatic, a medical doctor by the name of Baruch Goldstein, entered the Muslim mosque at the Tomb during the Friday prayer, shot to death 29 worshippers and wounded 150 others before he was killed by the remaining men. Following that event, Hamas announced that they would carry out five attacks against Israelis in retaliation.[31] However, Hamas carried out several suicide attacks well before the Hebron attack, including attacks against civilians inside Israel (and, of course, many more in the following years). For example, on September 15, 1993, six months before Goldstein's attack in Hebron, Hamas sent 22-year-old Marwan Abu-Rumeillah to carry out a suicide attack on a bus in Jerusalem. Abu-Rumeillah boarded bus no. 23 near the city's open market and tried to detonate an explosive charge he was carrying on his body, but due to mechanical failure the charge did not explode.[32] Furthermore, in the preceding years, Hamas had claimed numerous non-suicide attacks against civilians inside Israel.[33] Clearly, it was not the Hebron massacre that prompted the group to carry out indiscriminate attacks against civilians.[34]

From 1993 until the breakout of the second intifada in September 2000, the only Palestinian groups that carried out suicide attacks were Hamas and PIJ. Hamas carried out about two-thirds of the suicide attacks in this period—24 out of 37—and PIJ carried out about one-third (13 attacks). For both groups, the political objective of the suicide attacks in that time period was to derail the peace process. Indeed, the suicide attacks—especially those in Israeli cities, which caused a large number of casualties—succeeded in impeding the peace process. Time and again, the Israeli government suspended negotiations with the PLO in response to suicide attacks carried out in public places in Israeli cities. The rationale was that the Palestinian Authority had not done enough to prevent terrorist attacks against Israel and had not punished the perpetrators, even when their identity was known. In addition to slowing down the progress of the Oslo Agreement, Israel also put into practice various measures, such as roadblocks and severe restrictions on Palestinian laborers' entrance into Israel. These measures were ostensibly intended to make it harder for terrorists to enter the country, but presumably also designed to make the Palestinian public turn against the terrorists. The result, however, was increased animosity among many Palestinians toward Israel. Thus, the vicious circle of terrorist attacks—especially suicide bombings in Israeli cities—and Israeli countermeasures created mutual distrust and effectively hampered the peace process.

A clear example of the deleterious political effect of suicide attacks is the chain of events in the first months of 1996. On January 5, 1996, the Israeli General Security Service located the whereabouts of Yahya Ayyash, nicknamed "the Engineer," who masterminded and prepared several suicide attacks in which many Israelis lost their lives. He was staying in an apartment in Gaza. A Palestinian, who was an Israeli agent, gave Ayyash a booby-trapped cellular telephone, which exploded and killed Ayyash when he tried to make a telephone call. Across the Palestinian community, Ayyash was regarded as a national hero. Although he was a Hamas operative, many Fatah supporters admired him as a great patriot who had taught the arrogant Israelis a lesson they deserved. For several months before his death, Hamas temporarily suspended suicide attacks for fear of alienating the Palestinian public, which was fairly satisfied with the progress of the peace process.[35] But in the wake of the killing of Ayyash, Hamas leadership felt that the Palestinian public expected retaliation. The group therefore carried out a series of four suicide attacks in Jerusalem, Tel Aviv, and Ashkelon, which caused the death of 59 Israelis and wounding of another 216. These attacks infuriated the Israeli public and resulted in a considerable weakening of support for the Oslo Accord. This shift in public opinion had a far-reaching effect on the results of the general elections, which were held in May 1996. Before the wave of suicide attacks, acting Prime Minister Shimon Peres, the originator of the Oslo Accord, was leading in public opinion polls by a margin of about 20%. After the wave of suicide attacks, Peres lost the elections by a small margin to Likud leader Benjamin Netanyahu. Although Netanyahu, who opposed the Oslo Accord, promised to honor agreements made by the previous government, his government effectively stalled the process. Thus, suicide attacks were a major factor in the eventual collapse of the Oslo Accord and the breakout of the second intifada.

As can be seen in Figure 2.2, the frequency of suicide attacks increased dramatically during the second intifada, which erupted on September 29, 2000. The Palestinians regarded the intifada as an all-out war. Whereas the highest rate of Palestinian public support for suicide attacks against civilian targets inside Israel in the period of 1993–2000 was 35.5%,[36] after the onset of the second intifada the level of support reached 74.5%.[37] Before the intifada, the Palestinian Authority tried, albeit half-heartedly, to prevent terrorist attacks against Israel. From the beginning of the September 2000 hostilities, this policy was discarded altogether. Hamas and PIJ operatives were released from Palestinian Authority prisons, either because Arafat felt that keeping them in prison would have been extremely unpopular, or because the intensification of the struggle fit his plans. Under these circumstances, the rate of suicide attacks grew rapidly. The number of suicide attacks leaped to 37 in 2001 and reached a peak of 55 in 2002: (see figure 2.2). Part of the increase was because, beginning in October 2001, the PFLP joined Hamas and PIJ in carrying out suicide attacks and, more significantly, in the following month Fatah's al-Aqsa Martyrs Brigades joined as well. Fatah's decision to resort to suicide attacks is often attributed to the killing by Israeli forces of Tanzim (Fatah's irregular militia) operatives,[38] especially Raed Karmi, the head of Fatah's forces in the town of Tul Karem, on January 14, 2002. Observers have speculated that the organization felt the need to avenge these deaths, and to deter Israel from further targeted killings of its operatives (e.g., Bergman, 2002, pp. 252–3; Hafez, 2006, p. 30). In fact, Fatah operatives had been involved in three suicide attacks (two of them against civilians inside Israel) before the killing of Karmi, but these attacks were carried out jointly with PIJ and were possibly the product of local initiatives rather than a central decision of Fatah leadership.[39] Hafez (2006, p. 29) is probably right in his evaluation that "secular groups [i.e., Fatah and the PFLP] adopted suicide terrorism, at least in part, to compete with their Islamic rivals in the factional struggle over public support." Mia Bloom (2005, pp. 95–6) has also stressed the importance of inter-organization competition as a factor in the decision to escalate violence in general, and suicide attacks in particular.[40]

As shown in Table 2.4, the group that carried out the largest number of suicide attacks by far over the years has been Hamas, followed by the PIJ and Fatah. The PFLP and the Popular Resistance Committees, on the other hand, perpetrated a relatively small number of attacks. The PFLP-GC was responsible for the two attacks in 1974 mentioned above, which were originally intended to be barricade-hostage events. One of the suicide attacks was carried out by a man who prepared the attack on his own, and was not sent by a group.

The incidence of intergroup cooperation in preparing suicide attacks increased in the later years of the second intifada. Whereas joint operations

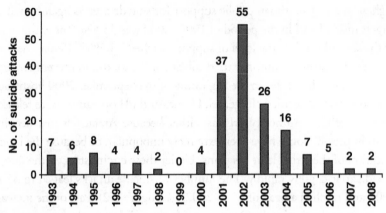

**Figure 2.2** Number of Palestinian suicide attacks per year, 1993–2008.

were very rare before the intifada, comprising less than 3% of the total number of attacks, their rate grew to 3.6% in 2002, 11.5% in 2003, and 37.5% in 2004. The growing intergroup cooperation has presumably been the result of intensified Israeli pressure, which made the preparation of a suicide operation increasingly difficult. For example, if a PIJ bombmaker in a town such as Jenin or Tul Karem were arrested or killed, the local PIJ group leader who wanted to prepare a suicide attack would have to try to

**Table 2.4** Distribution of Palestinian suicide attacks by perpetrating group and period*

| Group | Total no. of attacks | Before the 2nd intifada | After the onset of the intifada |
| --- | --- | --- | --- |
| Hamas | 79 | 20 | 59 |
| PIJ | 47 | 10 | 37 |
| Fatah | 33 | 0 | 33 |
| PFLP | 9 | 2 | 7 |
| PFLP-GC | 3 | 3 | 0 |
| Popular Resistance Committees | 1 | 0 | 1 |
| Independent | 1 | 0 | 1 |
| Unknown | 1 | 0 | 1 |
| Two or more groups | 16 | 1 | 15 |
| **Total** | **190** | **36** | **154** |

*With the exception of three attacks off the shore of Lebanon in 1988–1989, all attacks took place in Israel and the occupied territories.

obtain an explosive device from local Fatah or Hamas cells. In other words, ordinarily a group would prefer to be self-reliant, but circumstances can make intergroup cooperation a prerequisite for continuing this kind of terrorist activity.

THE DECLINE OF PALESTINIAN SUICIDE ATTACKS  The growing frequency and mounting casualties of Palestinian suicide attacks in 2001 and early 2002 caused great consternation in the Israeli public, and put growing pressure on the government to take a drastic approach to curb Palestinian violence. In the month of March 2002 alone, Palestinian groups managed to carry out 15 suicide attacks, an average of an attack every other day. These attacks occurred across Israel, in Jerusalem (five attacks), Tel Aviv, Haifa, Netanya, Afula, and other places. The suicide bombers exploded on board public buses and at bus stations, in hotels and coffee shops, in restaurants and on crowded streets, randomly hitting civilians. Eighty-two men, women, and children were killed and 519 others were wounded in the month of March alone.

For the Israeli public, the most shocking attack was the suicide bombing at the Park Hotel in the town of Netanya. On the evening of March 27, 2002, when Jews all over the country were celebrating Passover, a suicide bomber named Abd al-Basset Oudeh was sent by Hamas to carry out a suicide attack inside Israel. Odeh—a 25-year-old member of Hamas' military arm, Izz al-Din al-Qassam—lived in Tul Karem, less than 20 miles from Netanya, across the border. Dressed as a woman, to remove suspicion and to conceal the explosive belt he was carrying, he originally intended to carry out his attack in Tel Aviv.[41] He and his driver (a cell member who carried a counterfeit Israeli ID card), drove through the streets of Tel Aviv but found no suitable place for the attack. At that point, Oudeh told the driver to go to Netanya, a town that he had known because he used to steal cars there. In Netanya, Oudeh directed the driver to the Park Hotel. After bidding the driver farewell, he entered the large dining room where hundreds of people had gathered for the traditional Seder meal. The bomber's explosion killed 30 people and wounded 140 others. This event immediately triggered Operation Defensive Shield, which was launched on March 29, 2002. This operation had far-reaching consequences, not only with regard to the level of violence, but also for the status of the Palestinian Authority.

Operation Defensive Shield was intended to curtail terrorist activity by destroying the Palestinian groups' infrastructure and arresting or killing terrorists. In this operation, Israeli forces reoccupied the Palestinian autonomous

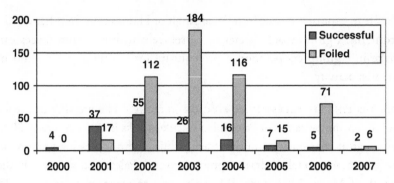

**Figure 2.3**  Successful vs. foiled suicide attacks, 2000–2007.

territories in the West Bank, which they had evacuated before the intifada. The Gaza Strip was the only area still controlled by the Palestinian Authority. This operation was largely responsible for reducing Palestinian terrorist attacks in general, and suicide attacks in particular. The presence of Israeli forces in the Palestinian Territories facilitated the collection of intelligence on planned attacks before their execution, and enabled Israeli forces to reach the perpetrators in real time. As can be seen in Figure 2.3, the number of successful suicide attacks, which reached a peak in 2002, declined steadily thereafter.

The remarkable effect of the Defensive Shield operation can be seen even more clearly if we look at the number of suicide attacks in 2002, month by month, as shown in Figure 2.4. Whereas in the first three months of the year the number of *successful* suicide attacks grew rapidly—from 3 in January to 15 in March—their frequency declined to 5 in the first month of the operation and reached a low level of 1 to 3 toward the end of the year. It is noteworthy that the combined number of successful and foiled suicide attacks did not decline throughout the year, indicating that the operation affected the Palestinian groups' *ability* to carry out suicide attacks, not their *motivation*. The groups continued to try to carry out suicide attacks at a high pace, but most of their attempts failed due to the presence of IDF forces in the West Bank.

Another factor that hampered Palestinian groups' ability to carry out suicide attacks inside Israel was the construction of the security fence between Israel and the West Bank. Although, as of this writing, the fence has not been completed, the parts that have been constructed, especially in the northern part of the border between Israel and the West Bank, have already been a significant impediment to the ability of the Palestinian

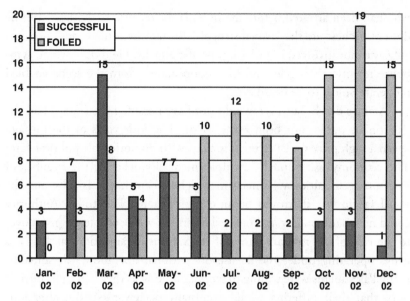

**Figure 2.4** Successful vs. foiled suicide attacks in Israel *by month*, 2002.

groups to send suicide bombers into Israel.[42] Most of the suicide bombers have been organized by cells in the northern area of the West Bank; to enter Israel they have to travel south, to the area of Jerusalem where the fence has not yet been completed. This long detour has exposed the suicide bombers' operations to detection by Israeli intelligence agencies.

Whereas Israeli countermeasures—especially the Defensive Shield operation and the security fence—did not reduce Palestinian groups' motivation to carry out suicide attacks, the death of Yassir Arafat in November 2004, and the change of PLO leadership that followed his departure, did have a moderating effect on Palestinian public opinion. The change in public attitude was reflected in the level of terrorist activity, including suicide attacks. Thus, the death of Arafat was immediately followed by a significant decline in Palestinian public support for suicide attacks, and a simultaneous reduction in the number of actual and attempted attacks (for an analysis of the relationship between public opinion and the frequency of suicide attacks, see Chapter 7). The temporal relationship between Arafat's demise and the decline in Palestinian militancy should not be interpreted as an indication that Arafat was the main conductor of Palestinian violence during the second intifada. Arafat certainly encouraged the use of violence,[43] authorized the financing of terrorist activities by members of al-Aqsa Martyrs Brigades, and ordered the release of members of Hamas and PIJ who had been arrested before the intifada for terrorist activities— but he did not orchestrate the "armed struggle" during the intifada and, presumably, was not involved in ordering specific attacks. He did, however, symbolize relentless struggle, and his disappearance from the scene enabled moderate voices to be heard.

Arafat's death, however, would not have heralded the change had the Palestinian public not been ready for it. The four years of the intifada levied a high price on Palestinian society, with no noticeable political gain. The economy was ruined, unemployment skyrocketed, the number of Palestinian casualties was three times higher than that of Israelis, and the social fabric was destroyed because the shattered Palestinian Authority could not maintain law and order. The streets were completely given over to the rule of the military wings of the various organizations and lawless gangs operating under the license of "national liberation." Presumably, many Palestinians were willing to sacrifice as long as they had a glimmer of hope that their suffering would eventually be rewarded. But after four years of intifada, there was no sign that Israel was about to cave in. On the contrary, in the course of the second intifada, Israeli public opinion turned right, and opponents of the Oslo Agreement gained considerable political strength. Having lost faith in the ability to achieve a negotiated settlement, most Israelis supported unilateral actions in dealing with the Palestinians and advocated harsh antiterrorist measures. Thus, in a poll conducted by Tel Aviv University's Steinmetz Center for Peace Research in February 2004, 84% of the respondents supported the construction of the security fence, and 70% were in favor of "targeted killing" of Palestinian terrorists, even if innocent civilians might be hurt in the process. The level of support for the Oslo peace process, and the belief that it would lead to peace, stood at less than 30%.[44]

Under these conditions, many Palestinians lost hope in the utility of the armed struggle and were ready to abandon it.

*Iraq*

Only a few suicide attacks were carried out in Iraq before the American invasion in March 2003. The first one, on June 1, 1988, was a car bomb attack on an oil installation in Baghdad, which was claimed by the "Islamic Amal" organization. This name was used in claiming responsibility for suicide attacks against American targets in Lebanon in 1983–84, and was generally believed to be a cover name for Hizballah. The attack was undoubtedly carried out by pro-Iranian agents in the context of the Iran–Iraq war. Three attacks were attempted in 2002 and 2003—before the American invasion—by the militant Muslim group, Ansar al-Islam. The intended targets of these attacks were not clear, because the suicides exploded themselves when they were stopped at checkpoints on the way.

The frequency of suicide attacks rose sharply in the wake of the American invasion, which started on March 18, 2003. Initially, there were only a few sporadic suicide attacks. One of these attacks, on March 23, 2003, targeted a roadblock manned by Kurdish soldiers in Northern Iraq, and was apparently perpetrated by Ansar al-Islam. Three attacks in March and April targeted American forces and were presumably carried out by Saddam Hussein's followers. Only in August, more than four months after the invasion, did suicide attacks start on a large scale. In less than five months, from August 7, 2003 through the end of the year, 29 suicide attacks were carried out, about half of them in Baghdad. Most of the others took place in the Sunni-populated areas, but some were carried out in predominantly Kurdish cities in northern Iraq. The latter were claimed by the militant Islamic groups, Ansar al-Islam and Ansar al-Sunna.[45] The time lag between the invasion and the onset of the large wave of suicide attacks was perhaps due to the fact that most of the suicides were foreign volunteers who came from a variety of Middle Eastern and North African countries. It took some time to organize the machinery of recruitment, travel arrangements, and incorporation in Iraq, and put it to work. Once in place, however, this organization produced a growing stream of suicide bombers. In 2004, there were already 137 suicide attacks, carried out by 157 suicide bombers, and they peaked in 2005 with 462 attacks involving 507 suicide bombers (see figure 2.5).

The frequency of suicide attacks declined somewhat in 2006 and 2007 (270 and 393 attacks, respectively), although it remained quite high, comprising 63% of the world's total in these two years. The frequency of suicide attacks continued to decline in 2008 (226 attacks). The decline was probably the result of several factors, including the increased participation of Iraqi forces in the struggle against the insurgency, reduced support for the insurgents among the Sunnis, and stabilization of the number of foreign volunteers for the fight against the Americans (although in 2007 the number of volunteers still remained quite high). Records seized by the American forces at an al-Qaeda-affiliated office near the Syrian border showed that about 600 foreign volunteers entered Iraq at that particular location in one year, between August 2006 and August 2007 (Felter & Fishman, 2007, 2008).

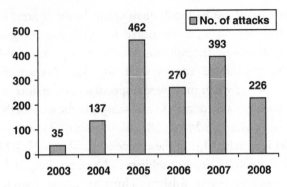

**Figure 2.5** Number of suicide attacks in Iraq per year, 2003–2008.

Data on the identity and background of the suicide bombers in Iraq is lacking. However, official Iraqi and American sources, as well as media reporters, suggest that most of them have been foreign volunteers rather than indigenous Iraqis.[46] Three studies, based on different types of data, have provided some details of these volunteers. The first study was authored by Reuven Paz, an Israeli scholar, who gleaned information on the volunteers from obituaries that appeared in Islamic websites (Paz, 2005). Of 154 fallen *"shahids"* (martyrs) mentioned in the obituaries, 61% were Saudis. Thirty-three of the *shahids* were identified as suicide bombers, and a clear majority of them (70%) were Saudi nationals. The other suicide bombers came from Syria (15%), Kuwait (6%), Libya, and Morocco (3% each). Only 3% were Iraqis.

Similarly to Paz, Mohammed Hafez (2007a) also collected information on the background of suicide bombers in Iraq from Islamic websites and chat rooms, which enabled him to identify the country of origin of 124 suicide bombers. Of these, 53 (42.7%) were Saudi nationals. Other countries of origin included Syria (6.5%), Italy (6.5%), Kuwait (5.6%), Jordan (3.2%), Belgium, France, and Spain (1.6% each). Others came from a variety of Middle Eastern and African countries. Only 18 suicides (14.5%) were Iraqi nationals.

Felter and Fishman (2007, 2008), who analyzed the abovementioned al-Qaeda records of foreign volunteers seized by the coalition forces in Iraq, reported that 41% of the volunteers whose country of origin was known were Saudi nationals. Other countries included Libya (19.2%), Syria (8.1%), Yemen (8.0%), Algeria (7.1%), Morocco (6.1%), and Jordan (1.9%). In many cases, the al-Qaeda records listed the role that the volunteer was designated to assume in Iraq. This designation was probably based on the volunteer's expressed wish.[47] Among the 376 volunteers whose intended role was mentioned in the records, 212 (56.4%) were designated to be suicide bombers. Saudi Arabians constituted 33% of the foreign volunteers for suicide missions, Libyans 24.1%, Moroccans 10.4%, Syrians 9%, Yemenis 8%, Tunisians 4.7%, and Algerians 2.4%.

The percentage of suicide bombers among the volunteers varied across countries, ranging from 10.7% (Algeria) to 91.6% (Morocco). Among Saudi volunteers, the rate of suicide bombers was 47.6%, and among Libyans it was 85.0%. Still, because the absolute number of volunteers from Saudi Arabia by far exceeded that of other countries, the number of designated suicide bombers from that country was considerably greater than that of other countries.[48]

The differences between the findings of these studies may be explained by the different periods that they covered—presumably, the number of volunteers from any given country fluctuated over time. Differences could also be the result of the different sources of the data—websites presumably published obituaries of *shahids* who had been connected with the website's editors in some way. Altogether, however, the studies show that the majority of the suicide bombers in Iraq have, indeed, been foreigners. At the same time, it is clear that the foreigners could not operate in Iraq without substantial support from the local Sunni population. Furthermore, the numerous and widespread non-suicide acts of violence in Iraq, which by far outnumber suicide attacks, suggest that most of them have been carried out by indigenous Iraqis. Thus, it appears that whereas most of the insurgents have been local Iraqis, suicide attacks have by and large been the specialty of foreign volunteers. This fact, combined with the statistics showing that Iraq has by far exceeded any other country in which suicide attacks have taken place since 2003, shows that the effort of Islamic militants worldwide has focused on Iraq. The struggle against the coalition forces there has become the main battlefield of the global Jihad against the enemy. Interestingly, the number of suicide attacks that have been carried out by Islamic militants in their own countries is small compared to the number of attacks that volunteers from those countries have carried out in Iraq. For example, Saudi nationals have apparently carried out hundreds of suicide attacks in Iraq, but only nine attacks (which involved 17 suicides) in their home country. No suicide attacks have been recorded in Libya, and only two incidental suicide episodes took place in Syria. But Felter and Fishman's study (2008) found that 51 and 19 volunteers came to Iraq for suicide bombing attacks from these two countries (respectively) in the course of one year.[49] Islamic militants in Morocco and Algeria have carried out several suicide attacks in their home countries (10 attacks involving 21 suicides in Morocco and nine attacks and suicides in Algeria), but a still higher number of suicide attacks in Iraq.

The large number of countries from which volunteers came to Iraq underscores the global nature of the war. Almost all Muslim countries are represented, although the bulk of volunteers came from the Middle East and North Africa. The fact that very few came from large Muslim countries such as Indonesia and Pakistan suggests that the volunteers have been motivated by a strong nationalist (pan-Arabic) sentiment, in addition to the Islamic religious motivation. The militant Islamic groups in Pakistan particularly have been rather active in their own country in the period of 2002–2008, carrying out 154 suicide attacks involving 167 suicides (most of these in 2007–2008). Nevertheless, Pakistanis were all but absent from the Iraqi scene.[50] This disparity between Arab and non-Arab Islamists may also be partly due to the greater ease of recruiting Arabic-speaking volunteers (e.g., greater exposure to Islamic websites; many of them are written in Arabic) as well as to the greater willingness of people to volunteer for fighting in a country whose language they speak. It is true, however, that Arab volunteers also constituted a large part of foreigners who came to fight the Soviet invaders in Afghanistan in the period of 1979–1989, although no exact numbers are available (Brown, 2008).

Initially, suicide bombing attacks mainly targeted coalition forces. Soon, however, attacks were conducted against every entity that was perceived as jeopardizing the Islamists' plan to seize power. Thus, targets for attacks included recruits for the newly established Iraqi police, foreign embassies, and the U.N, as well as Sunni militias that initially supported the insurgency but later turned against al-Qaeda.

As early as 2003, suicide attacks were frequently conducted also against Shiite targets. On August 29, 2003, a suicide car bomb at the Imam Ali mosque, in the Shiite holy city of Najaf, killed 83 people, including the pro-Iranian Ayatollah Mohammed Baqer al-Hakim, a high-ranking Shiite cleric. Later on, the number of attacks increased dramatically. By the end of 2008, at least 162 attacks were carried out against Shiite mosques, pilgrims, funeral processions, weddings, markets, and the random public in Shiite neighborhoods. Peter Bergen and Paul Cruickshank argue that these attacks have been al-Qaeda's biggest success in Iraq, because they provoked a sectarian war between the Shiite and the Sunni communities.[51]

Most of these attacks were carried out by al-Qaeda in Iraq—initially led by Abu Mus'ab al-Zarqawi under the name *Tawhid wal-Jihad* (monotheism and holy war) and then by the name *Tanzim Qa'idat al-Jihad fi Bilad al-Rafidayn* (al-Qaeda in Iraq) when Zarqawi formally pledged allegiance to al-Qaeda and Bin Laden in October 2004. In early 2006, al-Qaeda in Iraq established the Mujahedin Shura Council, which claimed to be a coalition of several groups but was actually a continuation of the original jihadi group. Since October 2006, the group has used the name Islamic State of Iraq (Felter & Fishman, 2008).

In 2008, suicide attacks in Iraq declined to the lowest level since 2004. The decline reflects the weakening in al-Qaeda's power in Iraq, which apparently resulted from several developments in that arena. The most important factor has been the turning of large segments of the Sunni population against al-Qaeda. Since 2005, the U.S. command has been able to increasingly convince Sunni tribal leaders, who had previously been an important part of the insurgency and collaborated with al-Qaeda, to join forces in fighting against al-Qaeda.[52] These tribal leaders established regional militias, known as Awakening Councils, which were armed and paid by the U.S. military. Their growing effectiveness has bothered al-Qaeda enough to direct a large number of suicide attacks against these councils' leaders. In an interview with the Qatari newspaper *Al Arab* in February 2008, a senior al-Qaeda commander said: "It is true that we have lost several cities and have been forced to withdraw from others, after a large number of [Sunni] tribal leaders betrayed Islam and when their tribe members joined forces against us."[53] This commander also attributed the decline of al-Qaeda's popularity among the Iraqi Sunnis to the indiscriminate killing of civilians by al-Qaeda militants. Another testimony showing that al-Qaeda perceived the Awakening Councils as the main reason for their decline was found in a captured diary of a senior commander in the organization.[54]

Another reason for the reduction in al-Qaeda activity has been the dwindling flow of foreign volunteers. In June 2008, American government and intelligence sources reported "a sharp drop in the number of foreigners entering Iraq to become al-Qaeda suicide bombers."[55] The decline was attributed to disenchantment with al-Qaeda among Muslims in Arab countries, coupled with al-Qaeda's growing difficulty in transporting volunteers across the Syrian border and absorbing them in Iraq.

In addition to the factors mentioned above, it is possible that the decline in the number of foreign volunteers also reflects a situation in which the immediate reservoir of potential recruits in Arab countries has been draining in the course of the five years since the invasion. Presumably, while the initial wave of ready zealots has been exhausted, the setbacks of al-Qaeda in Iraq and the growing criticism of the organization's conduct, coupled with more effective preventive measures by several Arab countries (especially Saudi Arabia), have reduced al-Qaeda's appeal to the new generation of potential recruits.

## Afghanistan

Guerrilla and terrorism war against the NATO occupying forces and their Afghani allies began immediately after the downfall of the Taliban regime in 2001. For several years, the intensity of the struggle was relatively low. Starting in 2005, however, there has been a significant increase in Taliban attacks, and in particular suicide bombing attacks, as shown in Figure 2.6.

The sharp increase in suicide attacks in Afghanistan has undoubtedly been a result of a decision by the Taliban leadership. Before the invasion of the NATO forces in October 2001, there was only one suicide attack in Afghanistan. It was perpetrated by the Taliban's protégé group, al-Qaeda, and was carried out in order to assassinate Ahmad Shah Masoud, leader of the Northern Alliance—the Taliban's main political and military opponent.[56] This attack preceded the attacks of 9/11/2001 by two days, and was presumably part of the general plot. Possibly, Bin Laden wanted to lock in the Taliban leadership's commitment to protect him, by eliminating their foremost rival.

During the first three years after the invasion, the Taliban carried out only a few, sporadic suicide attacks. Even though, in claiming responsibility for a suicide attack in Kabul on January 30, 2004, Taliban spokesmen

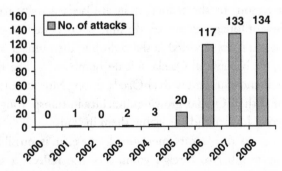

**Figure 2.6** Annual number of suicide attacks in Afghanistan, 2000–2008.

promised that similar attacks would follow, a systematic campaign of suicide attacks only started in May 2005. In the following three years, the annual number of suicide attacks was well over 100.[57] The rise in suicide attacks corresponded to the intensification of the Taliban's general military effort, but presumably also reflects the Taliban leadership's appreciation of the impact of suicide attacks in Iraq, where the number of suicide attacks reached 137 in 2004 and peaked at 462 in 2005 (see Figure 2.5).

Williams (2007) pointed out an interesting feature of the suicide attacks in Afghanistan: many of these attacks caused no fatalities, except for the suicide bomber himself. The percentage of suicide attacks with fatalities increased gradually from 2005 to 2008: 50.0% in 2005, 51.3% in 2006, 61.7% in 2007, and 67.2% in 2008. The average number of deaths per suicide attack in Afghanistan increased in parallel: 2.5 in 2005 and 2006, 4.1 in 2007, and 4.4 in 2008. Still, these figures are considerably lower than the average casualty rates in Iraq: 12.7 fatalities per suicide attack in 2004, 7.6 in 2005, 9.4 in 2006, 12.2 in 2007, and 6.8 in 2008. The disparity in the average death toll in these two arenas of militant Islamic operations may be explained by the different targeting policy. Whereas in Iraq, many of the attacks by Sunni militants have been directed against random civilians (especially Shiites and, more recently, Sunni tribesmen opposing al-Qaeda) and were intended to cause a large number of casualties, in Afghanistan the great majority of the attacks targeted international and local security forces. Usually, the targets were military patrols traveling in armored vehicles, or guards at the gates of government buildings or military camps. The targeted security forces were not only better protected, but were also ready for an attack and followed procedures designed to prevent a suspected suicide bomber from approaching. Thus, target preferences may well explain the lower average number of casualties in Afghanistan compared to Iraq.

Still, there may be another factor—namely, the quality of the suicide bombers. Several reports have suggested that some of the suicide bombers in Afghanistan were naïve, uneducated teenagers, who had been recruited in madrasas in Pakistan. Thus, Afghani authorities presented to the media a 13-year-old boy by the name of Rohullah, who told reporters that he ran away from his home in Gardez city in southwestern Afghanistan because he quarreled with his parents. He crossed the border to Miranshah in neighboring Pakistan, where an Afghani acquaintance he met incidentally directed him to a madrasa run by Afghanis. There he was offered free school and board alongside radical Islamic preaching. Together with the other youngsters in the madrasa, he was exposed to incendiary sermons and films describing Western atrocities against Muslims, and urging Muslims to wage a holy war against the infidels. After about a week, the boy was informed that he had been selected for a suicide mission in Afghanistan. He was promised that because of his martyrdom operation he would reach paradise and would be remembered as a hero. He was then taken back to Afghanistan, but was caught before he could carry out his suicide mission.[58] Moreover, some captured would-be suicide bombers said that they had been coerced to undertake the suicide mission.[59] Presumably, both the motivation and capability of these recruits are questionable.

As mentioned above, most of the suicide attacks in Afghanistan have been directed against the International Security Assistance Force (ISAF) and Afghani government forces and officials. However, according to a U.N. report, 80% of the victims were civilians,[60] probably because the attackers showed no regard whatsoever for casual victims who happened to be at the site of attack. Furthermore, some of the attacks were clearly intended to harm civilians perceived as cooperating with the regime. These attacks usually caused a large number of casualties because the bombs exploded in the midst of unprotected crowds rather than in the vicinity of armored vehicles, as was the typical case in attacks against military patrols.

In contrast to the struggle against the Soviet forces in Afghanistan in the period of 1979–1989, and to the insurgency against the coalition forces in Iraq following the 2003 occupation, Muslim volunteers have not flocked to Afghanistan in large numbers following the foreign intervention which began in October 2001 (with the notable exception of Pakistanis). Although the identity of the great majority of the suicide bombers in Afghanistan is unknown, and their nationality is therefore uncertain, the absence of eulogies specifying their background in international Jihadi websites suggests that most of them have been Afghanis. In his excellent analysis of suicide attacks in Afghanistan, Koenigs (2007) reports that Afghani and foreign intelligence officers believe that most suicide bombers have come from Pakistan, although many of them have been Afghanis living in Pakistan's tribal region.[61] There have been some Muslim volunteers from other countries, but these have, apparently, been rare.[62]

Until the end of 2007, radicalized Muslim youth in Arab countries tended to choose Iraq for implementing their desire to fight against what they perceived as the enemies of Islam. However, with the declining success of al-Qaeda in Iraq, and the growing share of the Muslim community engaged in the struggle against al-Qaeda, it is likely that Muslim volunteers will turn to Afghanistan instead. This shift may also fit al-Qaeda's policy, as recent successes of Islamic militants in Afghanistan and Pakistan may make this region more attractive for the organization. Thus, it is likely that al-Qaeda's propaganda machine and organizational efforts will be harnessed to funneling global jihadis to that region at the expense of their endeavor in Iraq.

*Endnotes*

1. Dale (1988) described "suicide attacks" carried out by Muslims fighters against Western colonialist forces in South-Western India, Sumatra, and the Philippines in past centuries. However, like in the cases of the Sicarii, the Hashshashin and the Thugs, these Muslim warriors were ostensibly eager to fight to death but did not kill themselves.
2. Flavius Josephus, *The Wars of the Jews or The History of the Destruction of Jerusalem*, Book II, Ch. 13. William Whiston, translator. Available at: http://www.earlychristianwritings.com/text/josephus/josephus.htm, accessed July 17, 2007.
3. See: Rapoport, 1984; Bloom, 2005, p. 5; Richardson, 2006, pp. 27–28.
4. Based on tales that circulated in his time in Persia, Marco Polo reported that the assassins were prepared for their missions by sophisticated manipulation. According to this story, the candidates for the assassination missions were drugged with hashish, and when they were in stupor were taken unconscious to a beautiful garden in the fortress. There they woke up surrounded by handsome trees and lawns, and served fine foods and wine in the company of beautiful women. They were also given more hashish, which eventually, stunned them again. Then they were carried back to their quarters, where they woke up. Wondering what happened to them, they were told that they were allowed to taste Paradise, and that they would be able to return there forever if they would die as shahids (C. Reuter, 2004, pp. 23–26). The Hashshashin were accused by their contemporaneous enemies of using hashish as a means instilling fearlessness in the assailants (a view maintained also by some modern writers, e.g., Taheri, 1987). This allegation probably generated the popular name of the sect, "Hashshashin" (hashish users), from which the term "assassins" was derived in Western languages.
5. In 1989 the Iranian population was estimated at 51,250,000 (see: Gazit, 1989, p. 163). A somewhat lower estimate of 45.2 million was mentioned by Segal (1988, p. 946).
6. Estimates of the number of Iranian casualties in the Iran–Iraq war vary widely. According to the official Iranian estimate, about 300,000 soldiers and civilians were killed in the war. See: http://www.globalsecurity.org/military/world/war/iran-iraq.htm (accessed May 15, 2008).
7. Dupuy, R. E. & Dupuy, T. (1986). *The Encyclopedia of Military History* (p. 990) London: Jane's Publishing Co.

8. In his book *On the Psychology of Military Incompetence*, Dixon notes: "On the first day of the Somme offensive the British Army suffered 57,000 casualties—the biggest loss ever suffered by any army in a single day." (Dixon, 1976, p. 82).

9. Dupuy & Dupuy, p. 1198.

10. Flavius Josephus, *Wars of the Jews or The History of the Destruction of Jerusalem*, Book VII, Ch. 9. William Whiston, translator. Available at: http://www.earlychristian writings.com/text/josephus/josephus.htm (accessed July 17, 2007).

11. Elazar Ben Yair's speeches as they are reported by Flavius are imagined approximations at best. Flavius, of course, was not on Masada at the time of the event. The only source of information was the two women and the five children who hid in a cavern at the time of the slaughter. It is doubtful that they heard Eleazar's speeches and even if they did, they could not provide a verbatim text. Thus, the text provided by Flavius is probably his creation.

12. For details of the ATF part of the story, see: *Report of the Department of the Treasury on the Bureau of Alcohol, Tobacco, and Firearms Investigation of Vernon Wayne Howell, also known as David Koresh*. Washington, DC: U.S. Government Printing Office, September 1993.

13. Details of the investigation of the Waco events can be found in the extensive and thorough reports issued by the U.S. Department of Justice. An early report, titled *Report to the Deputy Attorney General on the Events at Waco, Texas, February 28 to April 19, 1993*, was written by Department of Justice and FBI officials, and was submitted on October 8, 1993. Another report was submitted seven years later by Special Counsel (and former U.S. Senator) John Danforth: *Final Report to the Deputy Attorney General Concerning the 1993 Confrontation at the Mount Carmel Complex, Waco, Texas* (submitted on November 8, 2000). This report is available online at: http://www.apologeticsindex.org/pdf/finalreport.pdf (accessed on July 28, 2007).

14. See also the U.S. Department of Justice *Report to the Deputy attorney General* 1993, p. 16.

15. The Japanese official term for the kamikaze units was *Tokkotai* (Special Attack Force). See Ohnuki-Tierney (2002, p. 2).

16. Long before the adoption of suicide attacks as a systematic tactic, there were numerous occasions when Japanese pilots intentionally crashed their airplanes into enemy targets by ramming American airplanes or crash-diving into American ships. In some of these cases the pilots decided to carry out a suicide attack because their airplanes were damaged or out of fuel, and they had no hope of returning to base. However, in other cases there was no technical reason for these suicide attacks. Interestingly, suicide crashing on enemy ships was not an exclusive Japanese behavior. On at least a couple of occasions in 1942, American pilots exhibited the same behavior (Hill, 2005, pp. 1–3).

17. Admiral Ugaki radioed his last message from his plane, on his way to his suicide attack: "I alone am to blame for our failure to defend the homeland and destroy the arrogant enemy. The valiant efforts of all officers and men of my command during the past six months have been greatly appreciated. I am going to make an attack at Okinawa where my men have fallen like cherry blossoms. There I will crash into and

destroy the conceited enemy in the true spirit of Bushido, with firm conviction and faith in the eternity of Imperial Japan. I trust that the members of all units under my command will understand my motives, will overcome all hardships of the future, and will strive for the reconstruction of our great homeland that it may survive forever." (Hoyt, 1983, p. 299).

18. The lowest estimate of the number of pilots who died in Kamikaze missions— 2,392—was calculated from the figures provided by Ohnuki-Tierney (2002, p. 161). Quoting Hattori (1993, p. 23), Ohnuki-Tierney reports that 27.5% of the 3,300 kamikaze pilots returned to base, whereas 72.5% (2,392 pilots) are presumed dead.

19. See also Hill (2005, p. 21–23).

20. In the period of 1981–2000, suicide attacks took place in the following countries: Argentina, China, Croatia, Egypt, India, Iraq, Israel, Kenya, Kuwait, Lebanon, Morocco, Pakistan, Portugal, Russia, Sri Lanka, Tanzania, Turkey, Uganda, and Yemen. In the period of 2001–2008, suicide attacks were carried out in the following countries: Afghanistan, Algeria, Bangladesh, Bolivia, China, Egypt, India, Indonesia, Iran, Iraq, Israel, Jordan, Kenya, Kosovo, Lebanon, Moldova, Morocco, Pakistan, Philippines, Qatar, Russia, Saudi Arabia, Somalia, Spain, Sri Lanka, Sudan, Syria, Tunisia, Turkey, UK, USA, Uzbekistan, and Yemen. It should be noted, however, that in both periods under consideration, the great majority of suicide attacks took place in a small number of countries. In the 1981–1999 period, only 4 of 17 countries had more than 10 suicide attacks, and in the 2001–2008 period, only nine countries had more than 10 suicide attacks.

21. The multinational force (MNF) was sent to Lebanon twice. Initially, the force arrived in Lebanon in August 1982, at the final phase of the Israeli siege of Beirut, as part of the ceasefire agreement brokered by the American diplomat Philip Habib. At that stage, the MNF mission was to guarantee the peaceful evacuation of the PLO forces from Beirut, and to safeguard the civilian Palestinian population that remained behind. The MNF forces left Lebanon shortly after the evacuation of the PLO forces. However, they returned to Lebanon less than a month later, after the assassination of Lebanese President Bashir Jumayyil by a pro-Syrian group, and the massacre of hundreds of Palestinians at Beirut's Sabra and Shatila refugee camps by the Christian Phalangists.

22. During the Iran–Iraq war, Iran established the Basij, an organization of volunteers, which included 9- to16-year-old children. These were called "Children of the Imam" and were sent to the front after a brief training (Wright, 1985; Taheri, 1987; Jaber, 1997).

23. An Israeli commission of investigation determined that the cause of the explosion was a butane gas leak in the basement of the building. Hizballah claimed responsibility for the attack in May 1985, more than two years after the event, announcing that the attack was carried out by Ahmad Qassir, whose age was 15 or 17 years, depending on the source.

24. The suicide car bombing of the American embassy on April 18, 1993, was carried out when a meeting was taking place of CIA Middle Eastern experts with the Agency's operatives stationed in Beirut. Jaber (1977, pp. 81–3) asserts that the timing of the bombing was not incidental. According to her report, Russian

intelligence found out about the meeting and conveyed the information to Syria, who shared this information with Iran. The operation was planned jointly by Iranian and Syrian agents in meetings at the Iranian embassy in Beirut. Syria and Iran also oversaw the preparations for the October 1993 attacks on the MNF and provided logistical support.

25. The United Nations Interim Force in Lebanon (UNIFIL) was established in 1978 in accordance with the U.N. Security Council Resolutions 425 and 426. Initially, UNIFIL's objectives were to confirm Israeli withdrawal from South Lebanon, restore international peace and security, and assist the Lebanese government in restoring its effective authority in the area. In practice, UNIFIL has functioned as an observer force in South Lebanon, reporting to the U.N. breaches of the ceasefire agreements. See the United Nations Interim Force in Lebanon web page at: http://www.un.org/Depts/dpko/missions/unifil.

26. Nevertheless, Shaul Shay, quoting interviews in Lebanese newspapers, reported that both Bilal Fahs as well as Hassan Qasir—another suicide bomber sent by Amal, who carried out an attack on an Israeli military convoy on February 5, 1985—had consulted with Shiite clergymen before the attack, concerning the religious legitimacy of their intended suicide operations. See: Shay (2000, pp. 48–49).

27. In several incidents, Palestinian hostage-takers killed hostages after a rescue assault by security forces started. This was the case, for example, in an incident where an 8-man Fatah team took over a small hotel in Tel Aviv on March 5, 1975. In that event, the hostage-takers negotiated with Israeli negotiators for several hours. They then activated explosive charges that they had placed beforehand, thus killing several of their own men alongside the hostages. In another incident, on May 15, 1974, a team from the Democratic Front for the Liberation of Palestine (DFLP) took hostage about 100 Israeli high school students and negotiated for 12 hours. They started shooting, killing 20 hostages, when an Israeli antiterrorist unit stormed the place. In this incident, as in almost all others, the hostage-takers were killed by the security forces and did not commit suicide.

28. All three attacks consisted of attempts to crash explosive-laden speedboats at Israeli naval patrol boats off the shores of Lebanon.

29. In the bus attack, the suicide bomber, Ala'a Dhiyab Ismail al-Kahalut, tried to activate the explosive device but it failed to explode. He then tried to attack passengers with a knife but was shot dead by a soldier who happened to be traveling on that bus.

30. Hroub (2006, p. 52) actually claimed that Hamas had not used suicide attacks before Goldstein's attack at all, either in the occupied territories or inside Israel. As noted above, however, at the time of Goldstein's massacre, Hamas had already carried out five suicide attacks.

31. Ann Marie Oliver and Paul Steinberg (2005, p. 79) quote a communiqué issued by Hamas' military arm, Izz ad-Din al-Qassam, claiming responsibility for a suicide attack in Afula, a town inside Israel. The bomber, 19-year-old Ra'id Abdallah Zakarneh, detonated an explosive-laden car next to a civilian bus, killing eight people and wounding 42 (April 6, 1994). The communiqué said: ". . . Immediately after the disgusting slaughter that Doctor Baruch Goldstein carried out, which

changed the Eid al-Fitr lives of our people, the operations room of the Battalions of al-Qassam swore to reply to this attack with five violent attacks. We chose the passing of the forty-day anniversary of the Hebron slaughter and the beginning of the Israeli leadership's celebration of their false independence holiday to carry out the first attack so as to transform their holiday into a hell of tears and screaming and death . . ."

32. Hamas did not claim the operation, because it failed and the perpetrator was not caught on the spot. However, Abu Rumeillah was later arrested on another charge and described the failed bus attack in his interrogation, as well as in court.

33. Judith Barsky, Director of the American Jewish Committee's Division on Middle East and International Terrorism, compiled a list of Hamas operations, as reported by the group in Hamas websites. This list can be found on the internet at http://www.ajc.org/atf/cf/%7B42D75369-D582-4380-8395-D25925B85EAF%7D/HAMAS2006.PDF.

In Barsky's words: "Hamas communiqués claiming responsibility for suicide bombings and other attacks are catalogued on the official Internet site of the movement, the Palestine Information Center, in Arabic in a document entitled *Sijil Al-Majid*—'The Record of Glory.' The terrorists who carry out the attacks are referred to as '*shuhada*' or 'martyrs,' and the movement publishes a memorial page for each of them on its Web site in a section entitled *Shuhada' wa mu`ataqalun*— 'Martyrs and Prisoners.'

"The communiqués in English dating from January of 1999 through January 2004 were located at an earlier version of the Palestine Information Center Web site: 'Hamas –The Islamic Resistance Movement' under 'Communiqués,' http://Web.archive.org/Web/20010925193245/ http://www.palestineinfo.com/hamas/index.htm. The Arabic communiqués are located at '*Sijil Al-Majd – Amaliyat Hamas*,' 'The Record of Glory – Hamas Operations,' http://www.palestineinfo.info/arabic/hamas/glory/glory.htm, February 2006."

The following are examples of attacks on civilian targets which appear in this Hamas "Glory Record":

'**Keryat Youval Operation**: The militant Mohammed Mustafa Abu Jalala stabbed four Israelis and injured another at a bus station in Keryat Youval in Jerusalem before he was arrested by the Israeli forces.

**Eid Al-maskhara Operation**: The militant Ra'ed Al:reefy attacked an Israeli crowd in Jaffa on March 17, 1992. He was able to kill 2 and injure 21 Israelis who gathered to celebrate Eid Al:maskhara, also known as Al:boureem.

**Carlo Factory Operation**: Four militants belonging to Al Qassam Brigades broke into a citrus packing factory (Carlo) near Nahal Oaz at 2:30 p.m. on 25 June 1992. Three militants stabbed two Israelis while the other was guarding. The Hamas members wrote some slogans and considered this operation as a gift for Yitzhak Rabin on the occasion of winning the Israeli elections.

**Al Haram Al-Ibrahimy Operation**: Two militants belonging to Al Qassam Brigades attacked an Israeli group near Al Haram (the Shrine) in Hebron. One of the militants attacked the group while the other was on guard. The Israeli forces admitted that only one Israeli was killed and another was injured although the Israeli authorities were shocked by this audacious and well-planned operation. Thereafter, they arrested many members of Hamas.

**The Revenge Operation**: As soon as the Israeli forces announced the execution of the six heroes, Al Qassam Brigade militants put explosives in a 15-story shopping center in Tel Aviv on May 16, 1993. The building was completely destroyed and several Israelis were killed and others injured. The Israeli forces admitted that one Israeli had been killed and 40 were injured as a result of a gas bottle explosion in order to cover up the operation.'

34. Hafez (2006, p.18) recognizes that Hamas' decision to use suicide attacks was made before Goldstein's Hebron attack and was influenced by the group's leadership association with Hizballah during their deportation in South Lebanon. He maintains, however, that this decision was not implemented for a while, for fear of the PLO-controlled Palestinian Authority. He suggested that Goldstein's heinous attack provided Hamas with the circumstances that made suicide attacks acceptable. The fact, however, is that Hamas carried out suicide bombings before Goldstein's attack. Nevertheless, the observation that the attack made suicide attacks more justifiable for the Palestinian public is correct.

35. The last suicide attack perpetrated by Hamas before the wave of February–March 1996 took place on August 21, 1995.

36. CPRS Public Opinion Poll No. 29, September 18–20, 1997. Available at: http://www.pcpsr.org/survey/cprspolls/97/poll29a.html (accessed June 10, 2008).

37. PSR Public Opinion Poll No. 9, October 7–14, 2003. Available at: http://www.pcpsr.org/survey/polls/2003/p9a.html (accessed: June 10, 2008).

38. The Tanzim ("organization" in Arabic) was established by Yasser Arafat in 1995 to serve as Fatah's armed militia. It was meant to attract militant youth to counterbalance the influence of Hamas and the PIJ. Tanzim members have been loosely organized on a local basis and received arms and financing from the Fatah movement, which was the ruling party of the Palestinian Authority. The al-Aqsa Martyrs Brigades have been spawned by the Tanzim.

39. The suicide attacks in which Fatah operatives were involved, before the killing of Ra'ed Karmi, included a suicide explosion on board a bus near Karkur on November 29, 2001; a suicide attack at a bus station between Haifa and Akko on December 9, 2001; and a suicide attack near a roadblock outside Tul Karem on December 15, 2001. The leading perpetrating organization in all three attacks was PIJ, but Fatah operatives assisted in the preparation.

40. Competition between groups is an important factor on the strategic level (for example, in influencing a group's decision to escalate violence). In the field, however, inter-group cooperation between local operatives is quite common. Fourteen (9.2%) of the 152 suicide attacks in the period between the outbreak of the second intifada and the end of 2007 were carried out jointly by two or three groups.

41. According to the initial plan, the attack was intended to be carried out by two suicide bombers. However, the other would-be bomber, Nidal Qalaq, dropped out on the day before the operation on the pretext that he was sick.

42. Leaders of the main Palestinian groups that have carried out suicide attacks have attributed the decline in the frequency of such attacks to the security fence. Ramadan Shalah, the top leader of PIJ, said in an interview: ". . . they built a separation fence in the West Bank. We do not deny that it limits the ability of the resistance to arrive deep within [Israeli territory] to carry out suicide bombing attacks . . ." (Interview to *al-Sharq*, a Qatari newspaper, on March 23, 2008. Quoted by the Intelligence and Terrorism Information Center at the Israel Intelligence Heritage & Communication Center (IICC), March 26, 2008. Available at: http://www.terrorism-info.org.il/malam_multimedia/English/eng_n/pdf/ct_250308e.pdf. Mousa Abu Marzouq, Deputy Chairman of Hamas' Political Bureau, has made a similar statement (ibid.).

43. As Hafez (2006, p. 8) notes: ". . . the Palestinian Authority, headed by Yasser Arafat, failed to unequivocally denounce the bombings and indeed promoted a culture of martyrdom through its media."

44. *Haaretz* (Israeli daily), March 11, 2004.

45. Ansar al-Islam was a radical Islamist group operating in northern Iraq since 2001, allegedly with Iranian assistance. In September 2003, the group joined other militant elements to form Ansar al-Sunna (Rubin, 2004).

46. For example, U.S. military spokesman in Iraq, Brig. Gen. Kevin Bergner, said in July 2007 that up to 90% of the suicide attacks in Iraq were carried out by "foreign born al-Qaeda terrorists." He also said that 60 to 80 foreign fighters enter Iraq in any given month, 70% of them through Syria (*USA Today*, July 11, 2007. Available at: http://www.usatoday.com/news/world/iraq/2007-07-11-iraq-wednesday_N.htm, accessed July 13, 2007). Similarly, a Reuters report quoted Iraqi National Security Adviser Mowaffak Rubaie as saying: "We do not have the least doubt that 9 out of 10 of the suicide bombers who carry out suicide bombing operations among Iraqi citizens . . . are Arabs who have crossed the border with Syria" (Available at: http://www.outsidethebeltway.com/archives/12666, accessed November 19, 2005). Hafez (2007a, p. 1) presents estimates showing that although foreigners have constituted a small percentage of the total number of insurgents (4–10%), they carried out most of the suicide attacks in Iraq. Felter and Fishman (2008) estimate that about 75% of the suicide bombers in Iraq in the period of August 2006–August 2007 were foreigners listed in the Sinjar records. Assuming that some foreign volunteers entered Iraq through other points of entry, this estimate is quite close to the abovementioned high estimates in the 90% range.

47. Felter and Fishman (2008, p. 59) note that at least some of the volunteers designated as suicide bombers signed contracts pledging to carry out suicide attacks, suggesting that some of the volunteers changed their minds after initially expressing a wish to become suicide bombers. These authors note that some of the contracts stated that if the volunteer did not carry out the suicide mission, he had to divorce his wife immediately and renounce Islam.

48. A different composition of the insurgents was provided by Cordesman and Obaid (2005) of the Washington-based Center for Strategic and International Studies. Based primarily on Saudi Arabian intelligence sources, these authors asserted that

foreign volunteers comprised only 10% of the insurgents in Iraq, and that only 12% of the foreigners were Saudi nationals. These data should be regarded with caution, because the authors did not specify the precise manner by which their estimates had been obtained, except for identifying the source as "reports of Saudi and other intelligence services." On the other hand, the 12% estimate is not that far from the rate quoted by Felter and Fishman (2008). These authors reported that in April 2008 there were only 251 foreigners among about 24,000 insurgents detained in Camp Bucca, the largest detention facility in Iraq. Saudi Arabians comprised 16.7% of the foreign detainees. Hewitt and Kelley-Moore (2009) collected data from various sources on around 1000 foreign volunteers who had been killed or captured in Iraq through 2005. They found that Saudis comprised 27% of the foreign fighters who were killed or captured in Iraq. In any event, it should be noted that these data do not refer to suicide bombers but to insurgents in general.

49. One of the two incidents in Syria was counted as a suicide attack, although it was not planned as such. On November 28, 2006, Amer Abdallah, leader of the Syrian Tawhid wal Jihad group blew himself up when he was stopped for questioning at a Syrian border control as he tried to cross the border into Lebanon.

50. Felter and Fishman (2008) list only one Pakistani among 251 foreign volunteers detained in Camp Bucca in Iraq in April 2008. The only other non-Arabs in the camp at that time were 11 Iranians (10 of them Shiites and one Christian), three Turks, two U.S. nationals whose ethnic origin was not mentioned, one Kyrgyz and one Hindu from Sri Lanka. Altogether, these non-Arab nationals comprised a mere 7% of the total number of foreign volunteers at the camp. The only non-Arab volunteers counted by Hewitt and Kelley-Moore (2009) were Iranians, Turks, and Indonesians.

51. Bergen, P. & Cruickshank, P. (2007). *Al-Qaeda in Iraq: Self-Fulfilling Prophecy.* Available at: http://www.peterbergen.com/bergen/articles/details.aspx?id=315 (accessed: February 19, 2008). Reuven Paz (2005) quoted an al-Qaeda document stating that Zarqawi's attacks on Shiite targets were designed to hamper the power of Shiite militias, so that they would not stand in the way of establishing an Islamic Sunni rule once the American forces were defeated.

52. The Iraqi government later collaborated with the U.S. forces in managing the Awakening Councils, and since October 2008 has taken over the payment of Awakening Councils members' salaries. Despite their contribution to the struggle against al-Qaeda, however, the Councils are a reason for concern within the Iraqi government, because they constitute armed Sunni militias that are only partially under government control.

53. MEMRI Special Dispatch No. 1866, March 11, 2008. Al Qaeda Commander in Northern Iraq: We Are in Dire Straits. Available at: http://www.memri.org/bin/latestnews.cgi?ID=SD186608.

54. United States Central Command brief, February 10, 2008. Al Qaida leader's diary reveals organization's decline. Available at: http://www.centcom.mil/en/news/al-qaida-leaders-diary-reveals-organizations-decline.html.

55. Washington Times, June 11, 2008. Suicide Recruits Dropping in Iraq. Available at: http://www.washingtontimes.com/news/2008/jun/11/suicide-recruits-dropping-in-iraq.

56. Massoud was the leader of the United Islamic Front for the Salvation of Afghanistan, which was commonly referred to as the Northern Alliance. He was assassinated by two Tunisian members of al-Qaeda, who posed as journalists wanting to interview him.

57. The U.N. Assistance Mission to Afghanistan report offers somewhat different numbers from those presented in Figure 2.6: 17 suicide attacks in 2005, and 123 attacks in 2006. See: Koenigs, T. *Suicide Attacks in Afghanistan (2001–2007). A report of the United Nations Assistance Mission to Afghanistan, September 1, 2007.* Available at: http://www.unama-afg.org/docs/_UN-Docs/UNAMA%20-%20 SUICIDE%20ATTACKS%20STUDY%20-%20SEPT%209th%202007.pdf (accessed February 19, 2008).

58. IRIN News, October 20, 2008, available at: http://www.irinnews.org/HOVReport. aspx?ReportId=80996.

59. See, for example: Koenigs (2007) and Williams (2007).
Also: *Gulf Times*, March 28, 2008. Pakistan 'suicide bomber' confessed, reiterates Kabul. Available at http://www.gulf-times.com/site/topics/printArticle.asp?cu_ no=2&item_no=209753&version=1&template_id=41&parent_id=23; *Washington Post*, March 2008. The face of terror: Confessions of a failed suicide bomber. Available at: http://newsweek.washingtonpost.com/postglobal/ islamsadvance/2008/03/suicide_bomber_interview_afghanistan.html.

60. Koenigs, T. Suicide Attacks in Afghanistan (2001–2007). A report of the United Nations Assistance Mission to Afghanistan, September 1, 2007. Available at: http:// www.unama-afg.org/docs/_UN-Docs/UNAMA%20-%20SUICIDE%20AT- TACKS%20STUDY%20-%20SEPT%209th%202007.pdf. (accessed February 19, 2008).

61. Interviews in an Afghani prison with persons incarcerated for involvement in suicide attacks (conducted by workers from the U.N. Assistance Mission in Afghanistan) showed that 21 were Afghani nationals and the remaining two were Pakistanis. However, 14 of the Afghanis had been refugees in Pakistan and were probably recruited there for the mission. Another two had been refugees in Iran. See: Koenigs (2007), p. 68.

62. Cueneyt Ciftci, a 28-year-old resident of Germany born to Turkish immigrants, carried out a suicide attack in Zambar, Afghanistan, on March 3, 2008. Ciftci used to pray at a radical mosque in Germany and associated with a group of militant Muslims, some of them converts, linked to the Uzbek Islamic Jihad Union (Times Online, March 18, 2008. "Bavarian Cueneyt Ciftci is Germany's first suicide Bomber." available at: http://www.timesonline.co.uk/tol/news/world/europe/ article3571785.ece. Also: *Deutsche Presse-Agentur*, March 15, 2008. "German Turk behind suicide attack on US Afghan base" (summary).

# 3

# Demographic Characteristics
# of Suicide Bombers: A Global View

M ANY CURRENT SCHOLARS OF terrorism maintain that suicide bombers
have no common demographic profile: they include teenagers and
middle-aged people, men and women, poor and rich, the university educated and elementary school dropouts. What follows is that everyone can
become a suicide bomber. This assertion has far-reaching implications for
several aspects of coping with suicide terrorism, such as using profiles to
screen passengers, identifying population sectors at risk and monitoring their
militancy, and allocating social, educational and other resources as part of a
policy aimed at prevention. If suicide bombers have no identification marks
whatsoever, there is no point in directing preventive efforts toward specific
sectors. This chapter surveys the data on demographic characteristics of
suicide bombers, showing that most suicide bombers do fit a rough profile.

A broad range of sources underpins my analysis of the demographic
characteristics of terrorist suicides. Of these, the primary source is a database on suicide terrorism that I have compiled since 1983. This database
details all suicide terrorist attacks and attackers that I have been able to
document, though it surely misses some. Comprehensive media coverage
depends on the availability of sources, and varies greatly across countries.
In Israel and Lebanon the data are quite detailed, not only because of
extensive media coverage of the Israeli-Palestinian conflict, but also because
Israeli government agencies regularly release the perpetrators' basic demographic details (name, age, gender, and place of residence). More specific
information was obtained in a series of studies on suicides' families, organizers of suicide attacks, and surviving would-be suicides.

The amount of detail in reports on suicide attacks in other countries
varies with the prominence of the incident, its political context, and the
media's access to information. Government intelligence agencies are the

primary source of information in most cases, so the quality and detail of the information available to the authorities is a key factor in the quality of knowledge that gets to the public and to academic researchers. Yet, even in the best case, little important background information is readily accessible. Basic details such as name, age, and marital status of Palestinian suicides are easily available, but reliable information on the socioeconomic status of the suicide's family, religiosity, and life history in general, are much more difficult to obtain. Very little of this information is published in the media, and even then, only about a few individuals, who may not be representative of the entire suicide's population.[1] Gathering this kind of data requires systematic interviews of the suicide's family members and friends. Such large-scale research, which would offer a reliable and truly representative picture of the suicides' characteristics, is an arduous project. I have conducted this kind of study only on Palestinian suicides, and am unaware of any similar research in other populations. Thus, personal information on the suicides in most campaigns remains rather limited.

This chapter summarizes the available information on the demographic characteristics of suicide terrorists in the main campaigns that have used this tactic.

## Gender

The overall tally of suicide bombers worldwide clearly indicates that suicide attacks are mostly a man's job. In my database, of the 2,896 suicides during 1974–2008 whose gender is known, 2,750 (95.0%) were males and only 146 (5.0%) were females. There are, however, marked differences among the various groups.

### Lebanon

In Lebanon, 7 out of a total of 41 suicide bombers were women (17%), all sent by secular groups. However, Hizballah, the only militant Islamic group that used suicide attacks in Lebanon, recruited only men for these missions. Thus, in attacks perpetrated by secular groups the proportion of women was fairly high: 25.9%.

### Palestinians

In the Palestinian arena, during 1993–2000 and prior to the second intifada, all suicide attacks were carried out by males, and by two Islamic groups, Hamas and the PIJ. After the outbreak of the second intifada, which started in September 2000, there were 11 women among the 175 suicide bombers (6.3%). During this period the secular groups of Fatah and the PFLP also reverted to this tactic. Interestingly, however, PIJ also sent three women at that time (one of them in a joint operation with Fatah), and Hamas sent two female suicides. It does not seem surprising that Fatah, a secular organization, sent most of the female suicides. Yet, occasional use of females by the orthodox PIJ and Hamas strongly suggests that preference for males is determined by culture and social attitudes rather than formal religious prohibitions. This issue will be discussed further, following Table 3.1.

## Russia

While the Chechen rebels struggle to gain national independence and are motivated primarily by a nationalist ideology, they also observe fundamentalist Islamic tenets. It is interesting, therefore, that a large number of women have figured among Chechen suicide attackers. Out of a total of 47 suicide bombers whose gender is known, 23 (48.9%) have been women. John Reuter (2004) reported a larger proportion of women (nearly 70%), but his data is not reliably comprehensive, since his tally includes only 17 Chechen suicide bombers in the period of 2001–2004. Pape (2005, p. 208) found that out of 23 suicide attackers, 60% were women. A thorough study of Chechen suicide attackers was conducted by Akhmedova and Speckhard (2006), who acquired first-hand information by interviewing family members and acquaintances of Chechen suicide bombers. By their count, women made up 43% of the Chechen suicide bombers.[2]

## Tamil Tigers

There is a consensus that a significant proportion of the suicide bombers among Tamil Tigers have been women, although their exact number is still unknown. The Black Tigers, LTTE's (Liberation Tigers of Tamil Eelam) special operations unit, trained and launched suicide terrorists in Sri Lanka and had a special female subunit called "Birds of Freedom" (Joshi, 2000; Ramasubramanian, 2004). As Hindus, the Tamils believe in reincarnation of the soul, but the LTTE's nationalist ideology was initially expressed in Marxist-Leninist terms, as phrased in the organization's 1983 Theoretical Guide written by the LTTE Political Committee (Balasingham, 1983).

In later years the LTTE de-emphasized Marxist terminology in favor of a nationalist theme as the core of its ideology.

My database specifies the gender of only 137 of 168 LTTE suicide attackers, and 29 were women (21.0%). Pape found 20% women among 115 suicides (2004, p. 208) and Gunawardena (2004) reported 27% females among 242 LTTE bombers who exploded themselves. Relying on statistics of Black Tigers' combat deaths publicized in *eelamweb* by the LTTE, Hopgood (2005) estimated the rate of female deaths among them to be between 12.5% and 25% (the LTTE's own statistics for 1982–1996 reported 16 Black Tiger women and 78 men, i.e., 20.5%). Ramasubramanian (2004) reported a total number of 312 men and 92 women (22.8%) involved in Black Tiger operations. It should be noted, however, that although the Black Tigers have carried out suicide attacks, not all Black Tiger operations involved suicide in the strict sense used here, i.e., killing oneself to kill the enemy. As Hopgood notes, "Black Tigers do sometimes return from their missions" (p. 53). Overall, tallies based on a careful data search offer reasonably close estimates of women's proportion among LTTE suicide attackers. Ranging between 20% and 25%, these estimates are lower than the 30% to 40% figures loosely reported in the media and in some academic papers (e.g., Joshi, 2000; Schweitzer, 2001, p. 82; Zedalis, 2004, p. 2; Merari, 2005).

## Turkey

The only group where women comprised a clear majority of suicide bombers has been the PKK (Partiya Karkere Kurdistan—Kurdistan Workers Party). The gender of all 22 suicide attackers sent by this group is known, and of these, 13 (61.9%) were women. The PKK is a nationalist-separatist group fighting for Kurdish independence. While most Kurds are Sunni Muslims, the PKK's social ideology is Marxist (Ergil, 2001). In comparison, all six al-Qaeda affiliated suicide bombers in Turkey were males.

## Al-Qaeda

In stark contrast to the Marxist PKK, groups affiliated with al-Qaeda feature the lowest female proportion of suicide bombers. Excluding Iraq, Afghanistan and Pakistan after 2003 (where al-Qaeda's precise share of suicide attacks is hard to determine), 140 suicide attackers have been associated with al-Qaeda and its affiliated groups, and all but two were men.[3] In Iraq, the database records 1,643 suicide attackers through the end of 2008, of whom only 49 were women (less than 3%). As explained in Chapter 2, al-Qaeda affiliated groups sent the great majority of the suicide bombers in Iraq. In Afghanistan and Pakistan, where local militant Islamic groups have carried out the bulk of the suicide attacks, it is impossible to say how many have been perpetrated by local Taliban-affiliated tribesmen and how many by foreigners who organizationally belonged to al-Qaeda. In any case, female suicide attacks have been extremely rare in these countries. By the end of 2008 there have been only two women out of a total of 169 suicide bombers in Pakistan, and in Afghanistan all 415 suicide bombers have been men.

The rate of women suicides across groups clearly shows that groups motivated primarily by Islamic religious ideology have used males for suicide missions almost exclusively, whereas groups motivated mostly by nationalist/ethnic sentiments have often used females. Almost all terrorist suicides around the world were sent by one of three types of groups: (a) pure Islamic groups, i.e., whose agenda stresses mainly religious Islamic themes, (b) pure nationalist/ethnic groups, and (c) groups espousing a religious-nationalist ideology. Those in the first category are al-Qaeda and its affiliates. The second category includes such groups as the secular Lebanese organizations, the Tamil Tigers, the Palestinian Fatah, and the Kurdish PKK. Typical groups in the third category are the Lebanese Hizballah, the Palestinian Hamas and Islamic Jihad, and the Chechen rebels.[4] Table 3.1, which counts only the suicides whose gender and group affiliation could be ascertained, shows the distribution of male and female suicides in each of the three categories. The 1,045 cases whose group affiliation could not be ascertained are not included in the table. Most cases with uncertain group affiliation were suicide bombers in Iraq—1,022 out of the 1,045—and all but ten of these were males. An American military

**Table 3.1** Gender Distribution of Suicides by Group Ideology

| Group type | Males | Females | Total |
|---|---|---|---|
| Islamic | 96.4% (N=1,317) | 3.6% (N=49) | 100% (N=1,366) |
| Nationalist-Islamic | 86.4% (N=197) | 13.4% (N=31) | 100% (N=228) |
| Nationalist | 78.8% (N=204) | 21.2% (N=55) | 100% (N=259) |
| Total | 92.7% (N=1,718) | 7.3% (N=135) | 100% (N=1,853) |

spokesman in Iraq, Maj. Gen. Mark Lynch, stated in December 2005 that at least 96 percent of the suicide bombers had come from outside Iraq, implying that they were militant Muslims affiliated with the "al-Qaeda in Mesopotamia" group led at the time by Abu Musab al-Zarqawi.[5] Their addition would have further underscored the rarity of female suicides in Islamic groups.

As the table shows, religion is a strong factor in a group's willingness to use women for suicide missions (and, presumably, for combat missions in general)—though probably more as a result of tradition and gut sentiment than religious rulings. Yet, in recent years, several high-ranking Islamic figures have spoken in favor of women's participation in combat in general, and suicide missions in particular. Following the January 27, 2002 suicide attack of Wafa Idris, the first Palestinian woman suicide bomber, Hamas ideological leader Ahmad Yassin commented that "the Palestinian woman has an important role in society and in supporting the fighters . . . but the woman has uniqueness. Islam sets some restrictions for her, and if she goes out to wage Jihad and fight, she must be accompanied by a male chaperon."[6] Yassin's statement drew immediate rebuttals from both Islamic authorities and lay political leaders. Opinions permitting women to carry out suicide attacks have been voiced not only by radical Islamic clerics, but also by the establishment's religious authorities. Dr. Mohammed Sayyed Tantawi, Sheikh al-Azhar, arguably the most senior living religious authority for Sunni Muslims, said in an interview that suicide attacks carried out by members of the Palestinian resistance are acts of sacrifice intended for the sanctification of Allah, whether performed by men or by women. For the successful performance of a combat mission, a woman is even exempt from wearing traditional garb (e.g., a veil).[7] Dr. Abd al-Moati Bayoumi, Dean of the Faculty of Foundations of Religion at Cairo's al-Azhar University, also opposed Yassin's opinion, and even went as far as to question Yassin's religious authority.[8] A similar opinion was expressed by Sheikh Ali Abu Al-Hassan, chairman of the Religious Ruling Committee at al-Azhar University.[9] On the Shiite side, Ayatollah Muhammad Hussein Fadlallah, the Hizballah's spiritual leader in the 1980s, also stated that women are permitted to take part in fighting and to carry out suicide attacks if necessary (Zedalis, 2004; Kramer, 2004). These rulings, however, may reflect a recent shift by Islamic religious authorities in response to pressures of public opinion and social change. Notwithstanding Fadlallah's recent endorsement of female suicide attacks, when Hizballah carried out suicide attacks (1982–1999), the group never used women.

Martin Kramer (1991) cites a Hizballah-affiliated Shiite cleric in Lebanon, Shaykh Abd al-Karim Ubayd, from a 1986 interview:

> One of the nationalist women asked me, does Islam permit a woman to join in military operations of the resistance to the occupation, and would she go to paradise if she were martyred? The jihad in Islam is forbidden to women except in self-defense and in the absence of men. In the presence of men, the jihad is not permissible for women. My answer to this woman was that her jihad was impermissible regardless of motive or reason. She could not be considered a martyr were she killed, because the view of the law is clear. There can be no martyrdom except in the path of God. That means that every martyr will rise to paradise. I do not deny the value of the nationalist struggle (*nidal*) against Israel, but the jihad of women is impermissible in the presence of men. I do not deny women of the right to confront the enemy, but we must ask whether all of the nationalist men are gone so that only the women are left, or whether their men have become women and their women have become men.[10]

Given the increasing social and religious acceptance of female suicide attacks in traditional Muslim societies, we may well witness a growing number of female suicide attackers in militant Islamic groups, such as al-Qaeda. In fact, until September 2005 Zarqawi's "al-Qaeda in Mesopotamia" refrained from using women in suicide attacks, but late in the year it sent three women on such missions (two in Iraq and one in Jordan). In 2007, al-Qaeda in Iraq had already used 7 females in suicide attacks, and in 2008 the number reached 38. The rapid increase in the use of women for suicide missions probably resulted from operational needs, against the backdrop of the growing difficulties that al-Qaeda faced in Iraq.

Still, religion cannot account for the whole picture of women's participation in suicide attacks. Very few suicide terrorists have been coerced into carrying out this mission.[11] Women's participation in suicide attacks is, therefore, a function of their willingness to be drafted for these missions. Because of personality traits or cultural influences, women are arguably less inclined than men to engage in front-line combat activity in general and to carry out suicide missions in particular. Ordinary (nonterrorist) suicide rates of women are generally much lower than those of men (Bongar, 2002, p. 24; World Health Organization [WHO], 2001) not only in Western countries but also in the Third World. By the U.N.'s World Health Organization statistics, in 1991 the suicide rate of men in Sri Lanka was 44.6 per 100,000 population as opposed to women's, at 16.8. Thus, the ratio of female to male suicides was about 1:4 (WHO, 2003). *This is also (approximately) the rate of female to male terrorist suicides in nationalist groups.* Another striking finding concerns the rate of suicide in the Kurdish-inhabited regions of southeastern Turkey. To quote an Associated Press report:

> The suicide rate in the southeast, the most traditional area of Turkey, is skyrocketing, rising more than 50 percent since 1993. Although most suicides in Western countries are by men, 80 percent of suicides in the southeast of Turkey are by women and 75 percent of those women are between the ages of 13 and 25, according to government figures.[12]

As in the case of Sri Lanka, the gender distribution of "ordinary" suicides in the Kurdish population of Turkey roughly corresponds to the gender distribution of PKK terrorist suicides (61.9% women and 38.1% men).

Somewhat lower, but still quite high, ratios of female-to-male suicides were found in two other studies of suicide in the Kurdish areas of Turkey—the Batman Province (Altindag et al., 2005) and the Diyarbakir Province (Goren et al., 2004). The latter study showed that in the period of 1996–2001 (the time when PKK suicide attacks took place), 58% of the ordinary (nonterrorist) suicides in that Kurdish region were females and 42% males. Furthermore, the authors found that 56.3% of the female suicides were under 20 years of age. The authors rightly concluded that "the higher rate of suicide in females than in males, and the absolute female predominance in suicides in Diyarbakir, Turkey, are in contrast to most of the medical literature and statistical information about suicide rates by country, in which suicide rates are usually higher among males." The same is true for Kurdish *terrorist* suicides.

Unfortunately, I could not find reliable data for the distribution of ordinary suicide rates by gender in the Palestinian Authority and in Chechnya. Yet the findings on Sri Lanka and the Kurdish provinces in Turkey cautiously suggest that at least in communities where the selection of suicide terrorists is not influenced by religious constraints, the rate of female suicide bombers closely approximates the rate of "ordinary" suicides—thus, presumably reflecting the differential willingness to commit suicide among males and females.

Having acknowledged the factor of individual will, we must emphasize, as I have done over the recent decade, that the very choice of suicide attacks as a tactic and the selection of candidates for such missions, are not individual, but group decisions. While a woman may volunteer for a suicide mission, the group's leadership decides whether to recruit her or not. Hence, women's willingness to volunteer (or be solicited) for a suicide mission determines the potential upper limit of the female percentage of suicide terrorists, but the actual number is set by the organization's policy.

## Age

Suicide terrorists are generally young. In this they do not differ from other armed struggle combatants. There are, however, noteworthy age differences among suicides in various terrorist campaigns.

### Lebanon

In Lebanon, the mean suicide bombers' age was 21.6, with a range of 15–37. The mean age of females (all sent by secular groups) was 23.4, with a range of 17–37. The mean age of male suicides was 20.9, with a range of 15–30.[13] Kramer (1991) attributed the age of Hizballah's suicides to the organization's wish to avoid conflict with the suicides' families. Adolescents are obliged to obey their parents, who ordinarily would not concur with their son's willingness to commit suicide, and married men are obliged to their wives and children. As Shiites in Lebanon tend to marry young, the age "window of opportunity" for recruits is quite narrow.

### Palestinians

My database[14]—probably the most comprehensive on Palestinian suicide bombers—specifies the age of 200 out of 213 suicides (93.9%). The mean age, both before and during the second intifada, was quite similar—22.6 and 22.1, respectively, but during the intifada the range was broader than before (16–57 and 18–38, respectively). There have been slight differences between the three main Palestinian groups that have used suicide attacks: the mean age of Hamas suicides has been 23.6 (range: 18–57), of PIJ suicides 21.3 (range: 16–46), and of Fatah suicides 21.0 (range: 16–34). Hamas seems more selective, in that none of its suicides was under 18, as opposed to the other two groups (Fatah has sent two 16-year-olds and five 17-year-olds, and PIJ sent one 16-year-old and three 17-year-olds). The mean age of Palestinian female suicides has been 25.1, with a range of 18–57.[15]

Yom and Saleh (2004) found the mean age of 87 Palestinian suicides during the intifada to be also 22. Pape (2005, p. 208) found a mean age of 22.5 years for the period ending in 2003, but does not specify the number of cases included in his calculation. Weinberg, Pedahzur, and Canetti-Nisim (2003) reported that the mean age of 80 Palestinian suicide terrorists on whom they collected data was 24.5 years. This finding, along with other demographic characteristics they reported, is incongruent with findings of other researchers and with data made public by Israeli intelligence agencies.[16]

### Tamil Tigers

Only scanty data have been published on the age of Tamil suicides, and assessment of their age varies greatly among writers. As Hopgood (2005, p. 67) pointed out, the LTTE has provided little information on Black Tiger deaths. Joshi (2000), a journalist who conducted interviews in Sri Lanka, reported that LTTE suicides were generally very young, most of them 14–16 years old. Yet this assessment is probably impressionistic rather than the result of systematic data collection and calculation. A study of the New Delhi-based Institute of Peace and Conflict Studies reports that in 1990 about 75% of the second-generation LTTE members were below 30 years of age, with about 50% between the ages of 15 and 21 and about 25% between the ages of 25 and 29. However, according to the study, in 1998 Sri Lanka's Directorate of Military Intelligence estimated that 60% of LTTE fighters were below the age of 18 (Ramasubramanian, 2004). Robert Pape (2005), who created a database of suicide attacks around the world, reported that the average age of Tamil Tigers suicide attackers in the period of 1987–2002 was 21.9 years. Pape is the only researcher who based his assessment on a systematic tally of individual Tamil suicides as reported by the media. However, media reports of LTTE suicide attacks usually do not contain information on the attackers, and Pape does not disclose how many cases he used in calculating an average age. My own database lists the ages of only 10 of 167 suicides, yielding a mean of 23.7 and a range of 14–32. Obviously, the small number of cases makes these figures rather tentative.

### Turkey

By the end of 2008, there had been a total of 30 suicide attacks in Turkey, carried out by 31 suicide bombers. Of these, 21 were perpetrated by the PKK. My database lists the ages of 19 suicide bombers of all groups, with a mean age of 25.8 (range: 17-47). The average age of males was 26.9 (range: 20-47) and of females 24.6 (range: 17-35). The mean age of PKK suicide bombers was 24.7 (range: 17-35). Pape (2005) calculated the overall average age to be 23.6 years. Ergil (2001), a Turkish scholar who has extensively studied the PKK, reported an age range of members of that group as 17-27 for 11 females, and 18-40 for four males. Zedalis (2004) claimed (without specifying sources) that the average age of female suicide bombers in Turkey was 21.5.

The PKK has not been the only group to carry out suicide attacks in Turkey. In recent years, three other groups have used this tactic: the radical left-wing Revolutionary People's Liberation Party Front (known as DHKP-C, its Turkish acronym), another Marxist group by the name of TIKKO, and a militant Islamic group affiliated with al-Qaeda. The mean ages of seven of the 10 suicides who belonged to these groups was 27.7, with a range from 21 to 47.

## Russia

Suicide attacks in Russia have been carried out by Chechen rebels since June 2000. Data on the perpetrators' ages are lacking, and researchers have relied on a small proportion of the cases for studies. My database lists the ages of only 17 out of 50 suicides (including 3 would-be suicides caught on site). Their mean age was 23.9, but the range was quite broad: 15-46. Although the bulk fell in the 20-27 age bracket (47%), six (35%) were under 20, two (12%) under 17, and three (18%) 42 or older. Pape reports an average age of 29.8, though without specifying the number of cases included in his calculation.

## Al-Qaeda

Al-Qaeda differs in several respects from other groups that have carried out suicide attacks. First, its membership has included nationals of several countries, whereas other groups have been nationally uniform. Second, it has operated over a vast geographical range rather than in a single country. Third, unlike other groups, since the fall of the Taliban regime in Afghanistan in late 2001, al-Qaeda has been a cluster of like-minded groups rather than a single, monolithic organizational structure. Until September 11, 2001, terrorist attacks around the world were indeed planned and directly commanded by the original organizational apparatus of al-Qaeda, headquartered in Afghanistan. However, after the defeat of the Taliban regime in Afghanistan, terrorist attacks attributed to al-Qaeda were executed in various countries by local groups ideologically affiliated with al-Qaeda and logistically connected with its core group to varying degrees.

By far, the largest number of suicide attacks by groups affiliated with al-Qaeda has taken place in Iraq. Evidently, most of the suicides there have come from a variety of foreign countries (see Chapter 2). Outside Iraq, my database lists 145 al-Qaeda-associated suicide bombers, who carried out attacks in Afghanistan (before 9/11/2001),[17] the United States, Kenya, Tanzania, Yemen, Morocco, Tunisia, Algeria, Somalia, Turkey, Pakistan, Egypt, Saudi Arabia, Qatar, and Spain. The database provides the ages of 70 of them. The mean age was 26.6, and the range 15-63, with some differences among countries. The mean age of the 9/11 suicides in the U.S. was 25.0 (range: 20–33); in Morocco it was 26.0 (range: 22–31); in Spain 31.4 (range: 28–35); in the U.K. 25.0 (range: 19–30).

Pape (2005) found the average age for al-Qaeda to be 26.7 years, but did not report how many cases, nor what al-Qaeda-associated groups were used for calculating this average. Interestingly, Sageman (2004, p. 92), who analyzed data on 172 al-Qaeda members (only some of them committed suicide attacks), found that they were, on average, 25.69 years old when they "joined the jihad" (presumably: joined their groups). Paz (2005), who analyzed "al-Qaeda in Mesopotamia" obituaries of Arab Jihadi volunteers in Iraq, also notes that many of the Saudi suicides (who comprised the majority of Zarqawi's volunteers) were 25-30 years old. The most comprehensive data set on Al-Qaeda foreign volunteers in Iraq so far was reported by Felter and Fishman (2007; 2008). These authors, researchers at West Point's Combating Terrorism Center, analyzed al-Qaeda documents captured by the U.S. army in Iraq, which listed the registration details of 590 volunteers who arrived in Iraq across the Syrian border during the period from August 18, 2006 through August 22, 2007. Their findings indicate that the mean age of the volunteers was between 24 and 25 and the range was 15-54.[18] Fifty-six percent of these volunteers intended to be suicide bombers.

Overall, age differences between the groups are relatively minor. Mean ages of the suicides across groups that carried out more than 10 attacks ranged from 21.0 (Fatah) to 26.6 (al-Qaeda). The young age of suicide terrorists is not surprising. Young people are more easily attracted to radical action, have fewer family obligations, and are more willing to take risks.

An interesting question is whether the older suicide bombers, men and women in their thirties and forties differ psychologically from their younger counterparts. Unfortunately, reliable psychological data has so far only been collected on Palestinian suicide bombers, all of them less than 30 years old.

## Marital Status

Although many researchers have stated that the great majority of suicide terrorists have been single, the available data refer only to a small number of people, and a few groups. My database lists the marital status of only 266 out of 2,937 suicides (8.5%). Palestinian suicides have provided the most comprehensive data; in their case, the marital status of 186 out of 213 suicides could be ascertained (87.3%). Of these, 168 suicides were single (90.3%), 16 were married (8.6%), one was divorced, and one was a widow. Fourteen suicides had children (7.5%).

The distribution of suicides' marital status in Lebanon has been similar to the Palestinians'. Pape (2005, p. 204) found that 97% of 37 suicides were single. Data for other countries are much scantier, but nevertheless suggest that, like gender distribution, marital status also reflects the group's social and perhaps political idiosyncrasies. I was able to find the marital status of only 12 out of 50 (24%) Chechen suicides. Of these, none was married: only four were single, five were divorced, and three widowed. Two suicides had children. This distribution is probably a skewed representation of the total picture of Chechen suicides' marital status because 10 out of the 12 suicides whose marital status is known were females, and media reporting of the suicides' backgrounds has tended to ignore "ordinary" males and feature the image of Chechen suicides as "Black Widows," thus focusing on women with shattered family backgrounds.

A relatively high rate of married people, though still a minority, has been found also among al-Qaeda-affiliated suicides. Paz (2005) found that many of the Saudi suicides in Iraq (who comprised the majority of the foreign volunteers in his study) were married, but he did not provide exact figures.

The single status of almost all suicides may suggest that single persons are more willing to volunteer for suicide missions. However, in the Palestinian case, it has also usually been the policy of the organizations to refrain from recruiting married persons for such missions (see Chapter 6).

**Table 3.2** Education Distribution of 141 Suicide Terrorists

| Education level | Partial elementary and illiterate | Elementary | Partial high school | Complete high school | Partial university | Full university |
|---|---|---|---|---|---|---|
| **Percent** | 5.0 | 5.7 | 12.8 | 19.1 | 36.2 | 21.3 |

## Education

As in the case of other demographic characteristics, data are scanty on the educational level of suicide bombers except for the Palestinians. Of the 2,937 terrorist suicides in the database, educational data were found for only 147 (5.0%). Of these, 95 were Palestinians. Most of the other suicides whose educational level was known belonged to various militant al-Qaeda-affiliated Islamic groups, including the 9/11 hijackers, the London suicide bombers of July 7, 2005, al-Qaeda suicides in Iraq, the Uzbekistan Islam Movement, the Moroccan *Salafiya Jihadiya*, and the Indonesian *Darul Islam*. The rest belonged to the Lebanese groups Amal and Hizballah, and to the Chechen rebels. Overall, suicide terrorists are not uneducated. Table 3.2 shows their education distribution.

In the Palestinian case, where the number of suicide bombers with known educational levels is large enough to allow a meaningful comparison with the general population, the suicides' educational levels were shown to be higher than that of the general Palestinian society (the Palestinian National Authority's Central Bureau of Statistics, 2002). The comparative distribution is shown in Table 3.3.

The findings in Table 3.3 clearly show that Palestinian suicide bombers were, on average, much better educated than the population from which they emerged. Yom and Saleh (2004) analyzed data on 87 Palestinian suicide bombers. They found that 38% were university students or graduates (a figure somewhat smaller than my findings), and that 28% failed to finish high school (a figure somewhat higher than mine). Berrebi (2003) reached similar conclusions following his analysis of biographies of 44 Hamas and PIJ suicide bombers (his sample did not include Fatah members). By his tally, 36% had a high school education and 55% "academic institute" education (presumably including both undergraduates and graduates). A similar picture emerges from Pape's analysis (2005, pp. 213-4), where he presented data on the educational level of 67 Arab suicide bombers, including Palestinians, Lebanese, and al-Qaeda members. Pape found that the average educational level of his combined sample was higher than among Palestinian

**Table 3.3** Educational Levels of Palestinian Suicides and of the General Palestinian Population (percent)

| Education | No schooling | Partial elementary | Elementary | Partial high school | High school | Partial university | University |
|---|---|---|---|---|---|---|---|
| **Suicides** | 1.1 | 1.1 | 5.6 | 16.7 | 22.2 | 46.7 | 6.7 |
| **General population** | 11.6 | 16.9 | 26.1 | 22.8 | 17.6 | | 4.9 |

males or the general Shia population in Lebanon. Fifty-four percent of the suicides in his sample had some "post-secondary" education, compared to less than 20% of Palestinian males and less than 10% of the general Shia population. Although Pape's comparison is methodologically problematic because it weighs a mixture of Arab suicides from various countries against two specific national and subnational populations, it does underscore the large proportion of suicide bombers who had received higher education. Hassan (2001), who interviewed the families of 34 Palestinian suicide bombers, and a few would-be suicide bombers in a Palestinian Authority jail in Gaza, has even overstated the case: "None of them were uneducated, desperately poor, simple-minded or depressed" (p. 38). In fact, one suicide who completed his mission had only partial elementary school education (2.9% of the total in her report) and four others (11.8%) had merely elementary school education (for the details of this study see Chapter 4).

Contrary to the overwhelming evidence cited above, Weinberg, Pedahzur and Canetti-Nisim (2003) stated that Palestinian suicide bombers tended to have "limited education" (p. 144). These authors, however, do not provide a breakdown of the suicides' educational level.

It should be noted yet again that as in the case of most demographic characteristics, information on suicide terrorists' educational level is by and large limited to the Palestinians, some Lebanese, the U.K., and the 9/11 hijackers. As the educational background of suicides in other places, such as Afghanistan, Pakistan, Sri Lanka, Chechnya and Turkey, may be quite different, it would be irresponsible to use such scarce information to make sweeping generalizations on educational levels of suicide terrorists worldwide.[19]

## Economic Status

The economic status of terrorist suicides is hard to assess. Most cases offer no data whatsoever. In the few cases with rather scanty information, there are no data on indicators commonly used in socioeconomic studies, such as per capita income and family size per dwelling size. As Pape (2005, p. 213) correctly observed, "reliable data on education and income level are difficult to find even in native-language sources." Berrebi (2003, p.24), who invested tremendous effort in trying to glean socioeconomic data from Palestinian Hamas and PIJ terrorists' biographies, expressed similar frustration: "Inferring poverty status presented more of a challenge. Although some biographies clearly implied an individual's poverty status in statements such as 'he lived in poverty' or 'he was a wealthy man,' this was not the case for all observations." Researchers have therefore used bits and pieces of evidence to infer the socioeconomic status of suicide bombers. Pape, for example, resorted to the suicide bomber's or his family's occupation as an indicator of economic level, dividing the suicides into three categories: low class, which included those identified as poor, unemployed, or without a clear source of income; working/middle class, i.e., those employed in non-white-collar jobs, "such as technician, electrician, security guard, waiter, primary or secondary school teacher, etc.," and professional/ high class, which included lawyers, doctors, and members of families identified as wealthy. Pape found that out of 77 Arab suicide bombers (of various countries) 76% fell in the middle-class category. Only 17% were classified as poor. Berrebi (2003, p. 51) found fairly similar results for Palestinian suicide bombers. In trying to assess their economic level, he used clues in their biographies, such as car or computer ownership, from which he inferred the suicide's relative economic condition. His analysis covered 48 suicides, whom he classified into four economic strata: poor (13% of the suicides), average (54%), well off (25%), and very well off (8%).

In my database, I feel sufficiently confident about the suicides' economic status in only 72 cases, 49 of whom are Palestinians. For these I had two direct sources of evaluation: house visits (by Nasra Hassan) at the homes of 34 suicide bombers who died in the period of 1993-1997, before the beginning of the second intifada, and self-evaluation of 15 would-be suicide bombers captured after September 2000 (during the second intifada), who were interviewed in jail. Of the 49, 14 (28.6%) were classified as poor, 30 (61.2%) as middle-class, and five (10.2%) as well off. Table 3.4 summarizes the findings of these three studies.

Given the difficulties involved in trying to assess the economic status of suicide bombers, the differences among the evaluation methods and criteria, and the impressionistic rather than accurate estimates, the figures in Table 3.4 are reasonably close—even if we bear in mind that Pape's figures refer to "Arab," not just Palestinian, suicide bombers. In the absence

**Table 3.4**   Distribution of Palestinian and Arab Suicides by Economic Level According to Three Studies (percent)[20]

| Source | N | Low | Middle | High/very high |
|---|---|---|---|---|
| Berrebi | 48 Palestinian | 13% | 54% | 33% |
| Pape | 77 Arabs | 17% | 76% | 7% |
| Merari | 49 Palestinian | 29% | 61% | 10% |
| PNA general population ages 16–50 | | 32% | 48% | 20% |

of information on the suicides' income or other quantitative indicators of economic status, the validity of a comparison with the Palestinian general population data (which are based on such quantitative measures) is questionable. Yet the picture that emerges from these estimates is clear enough: at least in the Palestinian case, suicide terrorists come from all economic strata, with the majority of them from the middle class. The similarity between my results and the Palestinian National Authority census suggests that in terms of economic background, suicide bombers approximate a cross section of the general Palestinian population.

Nevertheless, while these figures may closely represent the Palestinian suicide population, they do not reliably represent other suicide bombers, not even those who are Arabs. For example, in a press report on the background of the Moroccan suicide bombers who concurrently attacked several sites in Casablanca on May 16, 2003, Liam Pleven (2005) wrote:

> There were no veterans of Osama bin Laden's training camps among them; they didn't even have passports. One was an unemployed shoemaker, another sometimes sold eggs. Many lived in a poor neighborhood of cinder-block homes with tin roofs held down by rocks.

The suicides of the 9/11/2001 attacks in the United States, on the other hand, the majority of them Saudis, came mostly from middle-class families (Holmes, 2005, pp. 143–4). In assessing the socioeconomic status of the families of 102 members of al-Qaeda-affiliated groups (most of them not suicide bombers), Sageman (2004) found marked differences between "core Arabs," Southeast Asians, and Maghreb Arabs. Whereas the latter were almost equally divided between lower class and middle-class, 80% of "core Arab" terrorists came from middle-class or upper class families.

Information on the socioeconomic background of suicides outside the Arab world, such as in Sri Lanka and Russia, does not permit any solid evaluation. There is no reason to assume, however, that a middle-class background is as prevalent among them as among Palestinians. Yet, as a rule of thumb, in cases where the struggle is supported by the majority of the population, it seems reasonable to assume that suicide bombers, as well as terrorists in general, come from all echelons of society. Broad popular support is usually a characteristic of nationalist/ethnic struggles, as in the Palestinian case.

## Religious Affiliation

A salient feature of suicide attacks in the past quarter of a century is that a great majority of them have been carried out by groups that follow a militant Islamic ideology, have emerged in Muslim countries, or both. Thus, most suicide bombers held a radical Islamic belief or were raised in a Muslim society. Although this conclusion is inferred from the characteristics of the perpetrating group and is not based on direct investigation of the religiosity of the suicides, it seems sufficiently sound.

With the exception of the Tamil Tigers, which account for 5.7% of the world's total number of suicide bombers, practically all suicide attacks around the globe have been carried out by militant Islamic groups, nationalist-Islamic groups, or groups that pursue a nationalist or social agenda established in Muslim societies.[21] The number of exceptions in addition to the Tamil Tigers is extremely small. It includes four members of the Armenian Revolutionary Army (ARA), who carried out a barricade-hostage event in Lisbon, Portugal, in 1983, which eventually ended in the perpetrators' suicide,[22] as well as five cases of suicide attacks for private reasons. Ninety-one percent of all suicide bombers whose group affiliation is known have been members of Muslim societies (whether or not they were practicing Muslims). Of these, 79.4% belonged to Islamic groups, 13.6% to Islamic-Nationalist groups, and 7.0% to nationalist or Marxist groups in Muslim countries.

## Demographic Profile of Suicide Bombers

The appearance of occasional diversity among suicide bombers, such as older people and females in certain cases, has led some scholars to claim that no profile of suicide bombers can be drawn. Bruce Hoffman, one of the foremost researchers of terrorism, for example, wrote:

> Today, though, suicide bombers are middle-aged and young, married and unmarried, and some of them have children. Some of them, too, are women, and word has it that even children are being trained for martyrdom.

"There is no clear profile anymore—not for terrorists and especially not for suicide bombers," an exasperated senior officer in the Israel Defense Forces told me last year. (Hoffman, 2003).

Hafez (2007a, p. 8) expressed the same frustration in his excellent book on suicide attacks in Iraq.

Still, in light of the data presented in this chapter, it is possible to point out several features shared by most suicide bombers. These features have to do with gender, age, marital status and religious affiliation. As has been pointed out above, 95% of the suicide bombers around the world on whom I have these data have been males; 89% of them have been under 30 years of age, and 69% under 25 years; 82% of them have been single; and 91% have been Muslims.

Using as the basis of calculation the 261 suicide bombers on whom we have data for all these four criteria—namely, gender, age, marital status and religious affiliation—we find that 67% have been single Muslim males, aged less than 25 years. Setting the age limit at 29 or younger would cover 77% of the suicide bombers, well over three quarters. These rates are as high as those used in consumer profiling, assessing risk factors for a variety of diseases, and tendency for involvement in criminal activity.

*Endnotes*

1. Marc Sageman, a forensic psychiatrist with on-site experience with the Mujahedin movement, used media sources and court records to collect data on members of militant Islamic groups (most of them not suicide bombers). Despite his extensive efforts, he was able to find "some fragments of childhood data" on only 61 out of hundreds of activists. See: Sageman, M., *Understanding Terror Networks*. (p. 81). Philadelphia: University of Pennsylvania Press, 2004.

2. The Akhmedova and Speckhard tally is not readily comparable to other authors' counts, because they also included in their data the 40 Chechen assailants of the Moscow theater barricade-hostage event (October 23, 2002), and the 32 assailants of the Beslan school event. In both cases the assailants do not qualify for a strict definition of suicide because although they threatened to commit suicide, they were actually killed by government forces.

3. One of the two incidents involving females was the June 14, 2002 car-bomb attack on the U.S. consulate in Karachi, Pakistan. A 17-year-old girl was driving the booby-trapped car that exploded as it passed the consulate entrance. The car belonged to a driving school, and investigators later suspected that the bomb had been secreted in the car and was detonated by remote control rather than by any of the car's passengers. The other incident was the November 9, 2005 suicide attack at the Radisson Hotel in Amman, carried out by a married couple. The wife, Sajida al-Rishawi, admitted that she had tried to activate the explosive device she was carrying but it failed to detonate.

4. In only five cases did the suicides not readily fall under one of the three categories.

5. New York Times, December 1, 2005. "General: Iraq Bombings Fell in November." In the following years, American spokesmen and Iraqi leaders have issued similar statements about the high proportion of foreign volunteers among suicide bombers in Iraq. Thus, in July 2007, U.S. military spokesman in Iraq, Brig. Gen. Kevin Bergner, said that up to 90% of the suicide attacks in Iraq had been carried out by "foreign-born al-Qaeda terrorists." (USA Today, July 11, 2007, available at: http://www.usatoday.com/news/world/iraq/2007-07-11-iraq-wednesday_N.htm Accessed: July 13, 2007).

6. MEMRI, Inquiry and Analysis Series No. 83, February 12, 2002, quoting Sheikh Ahmad Yassin interview in *Al-Sharq Al-Awsat* (London), January 31, 2002. Available at: http://memri.org/bin/articles.cgi?Page=subjects&Area=jihad&ID=IA8302 (accessed on November10, 2005).

7. Interview given to al-Quds Press agency, December 27, 2002, as quoted by the Intelligence and Terrorism Information Center at the Center for Special Studies, available at: http://www.intelligence.org.il/eng/bu/egypt/attacha.htm (accessed on September 25, 2005). This statement marked a basic change in Tantawi's opinion. In an earlier statement he opposed suicide attacks against civilians altogether.

8. Barel, Z. March 9, 2002. Hitabdut ha'isha, eimat hagever [Suicide of the woman, fear of the man.] *Haaretz*,. Available at: http://www.haaretz.co.il, [Hebrew].

9. MEMRI, op. cit.

10. Kramer's English translation of an interview with Shaykh Abd al-Karim Ubayd, *Al-Safir* (Beirut), 28 July, 1986.

11. The occurrence of some cases in Iraq in which people had been forced to carry out suicide attacks was reported by CNN on July 26, 2004 (available at: http://edition.cnn.com/2004/WORLD/meast/07/26/iraq.bombers.force). In Israel, on July 12, 2005 a Palestinian suspected of collaborating with Israel was sent by PIJ activists to explode with a booby-trapped car in the Israeli settlement of Shavei Shomron. The man was tied with rope to the driver's seat, and a heavy stone was placed on the accelerator pedal. Ergil (2001, p. 123) reported a case in which the PKK coerced a woman, Leyla Kaplan, to carry out a suicide bombing attack. According to his account, Kaplan agreed to undertake the suicide mission only after a friend of hers refused the task and had been therefore executed in Kaplan's presence. A case of forced suicide attack in Afghanistan was described by Koenigs (2007, p. 76). In that case, a 16-year-old boy was told by the Taliban operatives that they would behead him if he refused to carry out the attack. However, these sporadic reports apparently represent a tiny minority of the suicide bombing attacks.

12. Fraser, S. (2000). Turkey battles rash of suicides among young women. Available at: http://www.polygamyinfo.com/intnalmedia%20plyg%2075ap.htm

13. Similarly, Hurwitz (1999, p. 31–32) found that the average age of a Hizballah fighter's death was 22. The great majority of them (75%) were 19–24 years old; 15% were in the 25–38 age range, and 10% 15–18. Half of the persons in the higher age group (25–38) held command positions. Seventy-five percent of them were

married, and 75% of these had children. Hurwitz's study was based on biographical information of 130 fallen members of Hizballa's military echelon ("The Islamic Resistance"). Most were killed during operations against Israel, but only a few died as suicide bombers. A minority were killed in skirmishes with other Lebanese groups or in accidents (pp. 40–41).

14. I originally established the database in 1978 at Tel Aviv University's Jaffee Center for Strategic Studies, as a systematic dataset on terrorism in general. Since 1983, the database has included a specific subset on suicide attacks. After 1989 I moved the database to the University's Political Violence Research Unit.

15. The women's mean age is strongly affected by one exceptional suicide–a 57-year-old woman, a mother of nine children and grandmother of 41 grandchildren.
 The woman, Fatma Najar, lived in a refugee camp in the Gaza Strip. Reportedly, her husband died about a year before her suicide attack. One of her grandsons was killed and another crippled in clashes with the IDF, and five of her seven sons served time in Israeli jails. Hamas claimed responsibility for her attack, releasing her videotaped will. The next oldest Palestinian female suicide bomber was 31 years old.

16. For a list of Palestinian suicide attacks in Israel and demographic details of suicide bombers since 2000, see: *Netunei Mekhablim Mitabdim Hakhel Mishnat 2000 [Data on Suicide Bombers Since 2000]*. Retrieved from the Israeli Prime Minister's Office website www.pmo.gov.il, on July 13, 2005 [Hebrew].

17. Most of the suicide attacks in Afghanistan after the 2001 war have been carried out by the Taliban. Presumably, some of the attacks have been carried out by al-Qaeda, but their number is unknown (see Chapter 2).

18. The analysis of age distribution was based on 413 volunteers who reported a birth date.

19. For example, Ergil (2001, p. 123) described the background of female PKK suicide bombers as follows: "None of them possessed professional skills, and some were high-school dropouts. Most of them came from poor, crowded families." He characterized male PKK suicide bombers as "uneducated." Furthermore, the scanty evidence concerning suicide bombers in Afghanistan suggests that the prevalence of youngsters with just of few years of madrasa education among them may be high.

20. Data for the Palestinian general population were taken from Berrebi (2003).

21. Only four suicide bombers belonged to organizations whose agenda was classified as social. These were members of the Turkish groups, Revolutionary People's Liberation Party-Front (commonly known by Turkish acronym DHKP-C) and Tikko. These groups pursue a radical left-wing ideology, but they too emerged in a Muslim country (Turkey).

22. On July 27, 1983, five young Armenians attacked the Turkish Embassy in Lisbon, Portugal. One of them was killed at the outset by embassy guards and the remaining four barricaded themselves at the embassy residence and held hostage the wife and son of the Turkish chargé d'affaires. Communicating with the Portuguese authorities, the terrorists posed no demands but stated that they wanted to "sacrifice themselves on the altar of freedom." Shortly afterwards, they detonated explosive charges they had brought with them, killing themselves, the chargé's wife, and a Portuguese policeman (See: Cordes, B., Hoffman, B., Jenkins, B, Kellen, K.,

Moran, S., & Sater, W. (1984). *Trends in International Terrorism 1982 and 1983*. Santa Monica, CA: Rand Corporation Publication No. R-3183-SL). The attack was claimed by the Armenian Revolutionary Army (ARA), which was probably a cover name or an offshoot of the Justice Commandos for the Armenian Genocide (JCAG). This incident is of particular interest not only because it was carried out by Christians, but because it took place very shortly after Shiite groups in Lebanon started using suicide attacks—long before this method was established as a popular terrorist tactic and a trademark of Islamic (Shiite or Sunni) groups.

# 4

# Palestinian Suicide Bombers in the Eyes of Their Families

IN AN EARLY PAPER on suicide terrorism (Merari, 1990), I suggested that personality characteristics must play a crucial role in this phenomenon, as most terrorists have neither tried nor committed suicide. At the time, however, when the number of suicide bombers around the globe was less than 50 (the great majority of them in Lebanon) I was rather skeptical about the possibility of obtaining the data necessary for a valid assessment of their personalities. Hizballah, the dispatcher of a significant number of these suicides, usually did not disclose the perpetrators' identities. Thus, even basic demographic data were very scanty or nonexistent, and the information that might underpin a psychological analysis, however rough, seemed hopelessly inaccessible.

In 1993, however, Palestinian groups started using suicide attacks as a systematic tactic. By the end of September 2001, when the second intifada (called by the Palestinians the *al-Aqsa* intifada) broke out, 31 suicide attacks had already been carried out in Israel and the occupied territories by 36 suicide bombers (in two attacks two suicides exploded themselves together, and one attack was carried out by three suicides). Unlike the situation in Lebanon, the identities of the suicides, their places of residence, and the groups that sent them were known. Both the groups that engineered the attacks, Hamas and the Palestinian Islamic Jihad (PIJ), claimed responsibility for them. They announced the identities of the perpetrators, and often released videotapes showing the suicides proclaiming their intentions. In principle, under these circumstances one could locate the suicides' families and obtain from them information that might shed light on the suicides' motivations, their behaviors before the attacks, and, hopefully, on their personalities.

Before the second intifada, suicide attacks were prepared in and launched from areas under the control of the Palestinian National Authority (PNA)—areas that Israeli forces did not enter, as stipulated by the Oslo Agreements. Handing over the populated areas of the Territories to the PNA hampered Israeli intelligence capability, and PNA–Israel collaboration in forestalling terrorist attacks was partial and intermittent. Very few of the planned suicide attacks were foiled, and very few would-be suicide bombers were captured. Practically all of those captured were held by the PNA. As the suicides came from Palestinian-controlled areas, their families were also located there. Thus, an Israeli researcher could reach neither the living, would-be suicides nor the families of those who were deceased. Until 1997, the information I was able to collect at the Political Violence Research Unit of Tel Aviv University was limited to demographic details available in the media, which included names, ages, and places of residence, but rarely any biographical background.

In 1997, however, I had the opportunity to launch a systematic study of suicides' families with Nasra Hassan, a Muslim woman from Pakistan who had worked for many years in the occupied territories with an international refugee organization. Ms. Hassan was interested in research on political violence, and sought my advice on pertinent topics. She accepted my suggestion to run a study designed to gain systematic knowledge on suicide bombers, through interviews with their families and friends. While I was primarily interested in scientific evidence that could support or refute a variety of hypothetical explanations of suicide terrorism, Ms. Hassan's own focus was on the Islamic context of these "martyrdom" operations. Using a questionnaire I had devised as a base, she inserted additional aspects. She also added new information to my 1993-1996 list of the names and places of residence of the majority of the suicide bombers. Over the next couple of years she managed to interview the families of nearly all Palestinians who had carried out suicide attacks in the period of 1993-1998. Data on 34 of these suicides (out of a total number of 36 suicides throughout the period under consideration) were shared with me and form the basis of this chapter. Home visits afforded first-hand impressions of the socio-economic status of the suicides' families, in addition to invaluable descriptions of the suicides by their closest relatives. Ms. Hassan's background, her ability to establish rapport with people of all walks of life and cultural backgrounds, as well as her contacts developed over years of working in the Middle East, were key factors in gaining the families' cooperation in the interviews. She was also permitted to interview in Palestinian prisons a number of jailed candidates for suicide attacks, who had been arrested by the Palestinian security services. This study has been the first systematic effort to investigate suicide bombers through the eyes of their families. It should be pointed out, however, that Ms. Hassan and I do not always agree on the interpretation of the data.[1]

The interview questions covered seven topics: the family's demographic details (parents' age, education, occupation and marital history, number and order of siblings, etc.); the suicide's demographic details (date of birth, education, occupation, etc.); his social milieu (social circle, popularity among his friend, social habits, relations with women, entertainment, political awareness and affiliations); attitudes to religion and changes over time (frequency of prayer, frequency of mosque attendance, belief in paradise, talk about martyrdom, etc.); possible precursors to the decision to carry out the suicide act (influential events, behavioral changes, etc.); persons he admired or who influenced him; personality characteristics (general mood, independence, locus of control, history of mental illness and/or suicidal ideation, ambition, aggressiveness, compassion, spiritual vs. earthly interests).

In analyzing the results, I tried to extract from the interviews information on factors that might influence readiness to carry out a suicide attack. I looked for evidence on prevailing or conceivable explanations of suicide terrorism. Specifically, I checked poverty, education, economic status, religiosity, possible reasons for revenge, traumas, and indications of psychopathology. The findings are detailed below.

As the sample covered nearly the entire population of Palestinian suicides prior to the second intifada, it reflects reality as closely as possible. Table 4.1 shows the distribution of the suicides by organization and area of origin (West Bank or Gaza Strip). About two-thirds of the suicides were sent by Hamas and one-third by the PIJ. Interestingly, all PIJ suicides lived in the Gaza Strip, while Hamas suicides came from both the West Bank and the Gaza Strip—an indication that before the second intifada PIJ terrorist networks in the West Bank had not yet been developed.

**Table 4.1** Distribution of Palestinian Suicide Attackers Before the Intifada, by Organization and Area of Residence

|       | *West Bank* | *Gaza Strip* | *Total* |
| ----- | ----------- | ------------ | ------- |
| Hamas | 15          | 8            | 23      |
| PIJ   | 0           | 11           | 11      |
| Total | 15          | 19           | 34      |

Another interesting fact is that nearly 59% of the suicides came from the Gaza Strip. As we shall see later, this ratio changed radically during the intifada, with the overwhelming majority of the suicides coming from the West Bank. This reversal was due partly to the security fence built by Israel around the Gaza Strip, and subsequent stringent control on passage from the Strip into Israel. The question remains, however, why the number of suicides from the Gaza Strip was greater than that of suicides from the West Bank, despite the fact that movement from the latter into Israel was relatively easy and it had a much larger Palestinian population. By the CIA's *World Factbook* estimates, in 1997 the Palestinian population of the West Bank was nearly 1.5 million, and that of the Gaza Strip stood at nearly one million.[2] Hence, the Gaza Strip, with about 40% of the Palestinian population of the territories, produced about 60% of the suicides.

One explanation for the larger number of suicides from the Gaza Strip before the intifada may be related to the rate of refugees among the suicides. Table 4.2 shows the number of suicides before the intifada according to their group affiliation and location of residence—in a refugee camp, or in non-refugee-camp places of residence.

The table shows that 91% of PIJ suicides lived in refugee camps, whereas the majority of Hamas suicides (53%) lived in non-refugee-camp residences. According to the National Palestinian Census of 1997, refugees made up 41.4% of the total population of the occupied territories, but their percentage of the general population was much higher in the Gaza Strip (65.1%) than in the West Bank (26.5%).[3] As the PIJ operated at that time in the Gaza Strip rather than in the West Bank, it would be reasonable to expect the majority of the group's suicides to be refugees. Still, it is notable that the rate of refugees among PIJ suicides (91%) was considerably higher than their rate in the Gaza Strip overall. In fact, the rate of refugee camp residents was high among Hamas Gaza Strip suicides as well (75%), though not as high as among the PIJ. Overall, as Table 4.3 shows, the proportion of refugee camp residents was much higher in the

**Table 4.2**  Suicides by Group and Refugee vs. Non-Refugee-Camp Residence

|  | Refugee camp | Non-refugee camp | Total |
|---|---|---|---|
| Hamas | 8 | 15 | 23 |
| PIJ | 10 | 1 | 11 |
| Total | 18 | 16 | 34 |

**Table 4.3** Number of Refugee Camp Residents by Region

|  | West Bank | Gaza Strip | Total |
|---|---|---|---|
| Refugee camp | 2 | 16 | 19 |
| Non-refugee camp | 13 | 3 | 15 |
| Total | 15 | 19 | 34 |

Gaza Strip (84.2%) than in the West Bank (13.3%). However, in both areas the number of suicides from refugee camps exceeded the proportion of camp residents in the general population.

Over the years, many refugee families moved from refugee camps to better housing in cities and towns. Only 49% of those registered as refugees in the Gaza Strip and 26% of registered refugees in the West Bank live in refugee camps.[4] The number of people registered as refugees (using the United Nations Relief and Works Agency terminology) or having "refugee status" (PNA terminology) is thus much higher than the number of actual refugee camp inhabitants. The combined PNA and UNRWA statistics indicate that the proportion of refugee camp dwellers in the general population in the Gaza Strip is about 31.9%, and in the West Bank 6.9%. In both the Gaza Strip and the West Bank, the rate of refugee camp dwellers among the suicide bombers is thus far higher than their proportion in the general population. In each area the rate of camp-dweller suicides is 2–3 times their proportion in the population.

Furthermore, the influencing factor seems to be not "refugee status," i.e., being a descendent of a refugee family, but living in a refugee camp. Using the broader category of "refugee status" instead of "refugee camp dweller" would only add one suicide bomber to the "refugee" category as shown in Table 4.4 (in one other case, only the suicide's mother was of refugee origin, and the suicide was tallied as "non-refugee").

Why is the rate of refugee camp dwellers so high among Palestinian suicide bombers? An immediate explanation would be the greater resentment

**Table 4.4** Number of Suicides by Group Affiliation and Refugee Status

|  | Refugee status | Non-refugee status | Total |
|---|---|---|---|
| Hamas | 9 | 14 | 23 |
| PIJ | 11 | 0 | 11 |
| Total | 20 | 14 | 34 |

refugees presumably feel toward Israel. As the data suggest, the source of this hatred is not the memory of the historical uprooting from the family's home in 1948, but a life of unremitting misery in the poverty stricken, run-down refugee camps. A related explanation is that the radical groups' greater infrastructure and influence in refugee camps facilitated local operation and recruitment.

## Basic Demographic Characteristics

As demographic characteristics of the total population of Palestinian suicides were covered in the previous chapter, here I provide just a sketch of the 34 suicides whose families were interviewed.

All 34 suicides were males. No females were recruited for suicide attacks before the second intifada, as a matter of policy in both Hamas and PIJ at that time. The suicides' mean age was 22.6 (range: 18–38). Thirty-one were single (91.2%), and two of the married suicides had children (the wife of one was nine months pregnant). None of the single suicides was engaged to be married. Their education ranged from partial elementary school to a university degree, with an average level higher than among the general Palestinian population (see previous chapter). One had only partial elementary school training, 3 had full elementary school education, 17 had full high school education, and 13 were enrolled as students in institutes of higher education (including religious colleges).

Nasra Hassan assessed the family's economic status at the time of the interview in the suicide's home. Of the 34 families, three were assessed as very poor, nine as poor, seven as lower-middle-class, 12 as middle-class, and three as wealthy. Thus, despite the high proportion of refugee-camp residents among the suicides, neither personal poverty nor lack of education can be considered as factors contributing to the willingness to carry out a suicide attack. Nevertheless, the suicides' militancy was conceivably prompted by what they viewed as a community problem rather than personal wretchedness.

## Religion

Another frequent explanation for the propensity to suicide terrorism has been religiosity. Numerous writers have maintained that religious fanaticism is a main factor in driving people to suicide terrorism. This section delineates only the results of the Palestinian families' study; an analysis of the role of religion in suicide terrorism will be offered in Chapter 9.

The majority of families—23 out of 34 (67.6%)—characterized their sons as very religious; 10 families (29.4%) described them as "ordinarily religious" and only one family said that their son was "just a little religious." As most Palestinians are religious, and the families' evaluations are subjective by nature, in order to assess whether a suicide's religiosity was exceptional in his immediate milieu, we also asked how religious he was compared to his family. Nineteen suicides (55.9%) were characterized as "more religious than other family members." It turns out, then, that the majority of suicides came from religious or very religious families, and for more than half, their religiosity was outstanding in the family. Although most Palestinians are religious, these figures are higher than the rate of practicing Muslims in Palestinian society which, according to one survey, stood at 80% among males (Heiberg and Ovensen, 1994). These findings lend support to the notion that, at least in the Palestinian case, religion has been a contributing factor to the inclination to carry out a suicide attack.

*Possible Motives for Revenge*

It has often been alleged that suicide terrorists are motivated by the desire to avenge personal suffering. In the family study, we tried to find out whether the suicide had been exposed to any of several forms of suffering that might provide such a motive. These included the death of a next-of-kin or a close friend in the context of the struggle against Israel, being jailed, wounded or beaten, or having family members in jail.

Only one suicide had lost a close family member (brother) at the hands of Israeli forces. However, 15 suicides had lost friends in the struggle, and six had lost more than one. Not all of the dead friends were killed by Israeli forces; some had committed suicide attacks themselves, and some were killed in "work accidents" while preparing explosive devices. By the families' reports, 16 suicides had been wounded or beaten in clashes with IDF forces, six of them two or three times. Eighteen suicides (52.9%) had been detained or jailed for periods ranging from a week to three-and-a-half years—usually for several months. Ten had been arrested twice, and two had been jailed three times. Most families of those who had spent time in jail claimed that their sons had been tortured during interrogations—beaten, forced to sit in painful positions, or deprived of sleep. Asked whether the prison experience changed their son's demeanor, half of the families noted no difference after his return home. Nine of the suicides' families, however, described various changes in their sons' behavior: quieter (five cases), more hateful towards Israel (five cases), and more religious (three cases). Five families noted that their sons had started talking about *istishhad* (martyrdom) or paradise after returning from jail. The influence of the jail experience can be attributed to the trauma and to hatred of the Israeli jailers—but also to the intense indoctrination and collective pressure of the prisoners' organizations inside jail. Palestinian security prisoners maintain a very tight internal control, including intensive ideological indoctrination. Subjected to this influence, some youngsters who entered prison as callow street enthusiasts may have committed themselves to the idea of self-sacrifice.

The families indicated that prior to their last deadly mission, 27 of the 34 suicides (79.4%) were involved in various intifada activities against Israeli forces; in 19 cases, this was described as intense involvement. These data tally well with the information on the high number of suicides who had been jailed, beaten, or wounded—all but two were described by their families as deeply involved in the struggle. The families were usually not privy to the details of their sons' underground activities, but were generally aware of their affiliations with insurgent groups. According to family members' comments, 27 of the suicides (79.4%) had been active in Hamas or PIJ before they embarked on their suicide missions.

The emerging overall picture suggests that one of the suicides' characteristics is high-level political militancy. Nevertheless, these results should be viewed in the context of Palestinian circumstances during the first intifada. Unlike the second intifada, the first was characterized by mass demonstrations, stone-throwing and street clashes with IDF soldiers. Most Palestinian youngsters participated in these almost daily events in the Gaza Strip, and in Palestinian cities and villages throughout the West Bank. Trying to curb these disturbances, IDF soldiers used tear gas, and rifle butts, as well as rubber and plastic bullets, and conducted mass arrests of violent demonstrators, who were usually sentenced to a few months in jail. Atran (2004c) and Horgan (2005, p. 101) cited a study by Brian Barber, in which 900 Palestinian youngsters were asked about their activity and experiences during the first intifada. A great majority of the males in the sample—81%—reported throwing stones at Israeli forces and settlers; 87% delivered supplies to organizations' activists, 63% were shot at, and 66% suffered physical assault.[5] Thus, the portrait of the suicide bomber before the second intifada may not be all that exceptional in the context of Palestinian society at the time.

As far as the families could tell, the decision to carry out a suicide attack was not prompted by any special personal event such as loss of a close friend or family member, or a humiliating encounter with Israeli forces. The father of one suicide, for example, expressed his bewilderment at the lack of any triggering event, saying, "Even the [political] situation was quiet, normal" (referring to the easing of tensions at the end of 1993, in the wake of the Israeli-Palestinian Oslo Agreement). The decision was apparently not an impromptu reaction to a specific stimulus but had been brewed over a long time. The perpetrating groups declared that in several cases the suicide attacks were revenge for Israeli provocations, such as the murder of 29 Muslim worshippers at the Patriarch's Tomb in Hebron by Baruch Goldstein, a Jewish settler, on February 25, 1994, after which Hamas announced it would carry out five suicide attacks in revenge. Following the assassination of PIJ leader Fathi Shikaki on October 26, 1995, PIJ vowed to take painful revenge. Yet, suicide attacks carried out in the wake of these events were the result of the organizations' decisions rather than the suicides' individual shock, rage, indignation, or burning wish to avenge a personal loss. The families of the suicides who had carried out the attacks following these events did not say that their sons had displayed sudden agitation or depression after these events. The mental process these young men underwent before they became ready to carry out a suicide attack was presumably completed well before the organization decided to send them on their missions.

The families' answers in the interviews show that 47% of the suicides had talked about *istishhad* and 44.1% had often talked about paradise (35.3% had talked about both). These apparently high rates may indicate suicidal ideation, but in the absence of a control group of ordinary Palestinian youngsters, we cannot determine how common these topics were in conversations among Palestinians of their age during the mid-to-late 1990s. Yet the suicides often mentioned *istishhad* in a rather personal manner, as a statement of intent rather than a general discussion of current events. For example, the mother of one suicide said that her son used to approach her and say: "Look, your son is a *shahid!* When you hear of my *shahada* (martyrdom) do not tear your clothes or pull your hair . . . When they bring you my body, thank Allah, saying: O Allah, you have honored us in [my son's] martyrdom. I am an asset for you on this earth as well as in death."[6] Another suicide used to dismiss his mother's suggestions that he should get married, saying that he would be a *shahid*. Still another used to prod his mother: "Come, have a photograph taken with me before I do *istishhad*."[7] Suicidal ideation was also often expressed in nonverbal behavior. One suicide, who used to say to his mother as she was praying, "Pray for *shahada* for me," also collected newspaper articles and photographs of *shahids*.

Talking about *istishhad* and paradise was slightly more common among suicides who had served time in Israeli prison, 61.1% of whom used to talk about these topics compared to 50% of those who had not been imprisoned. They were also more common among those with a record of intensive involvement in intifada activity (63%) than among those who had not been active in the intifada (42.9%). By his brother's testimony, one suicide started talking about *istishhad* more than two years before he undertook his suicide mission and after his release from prison, where he had become affiliated with the PIJ. In the two months prior to his suicide act, his preoccupation with the subject intensified, and news about suicide attacks prompted him to say he would carry out the perfect suicide operation.[8]

## Behavior in the Last Days

Even though a significant number of the suicides had talked about *istishhad*, the families had almost never been aware of their sons' intentions to carry out a suicide attack. For example, one suicide asked his widowed mother to forgive him on the evening before his suicide operation. She suspected he was going to carry out a high-risk mission, but was not aware of its immediacy or precise nature. Still another told his sister-in-law, two days before he set out on his last mission: "In the future, I'll be in paradise, playing and laughing, enjoying myself, while all of you will be weeping." She did not take his statement seriously.[9] Only one brother of a suicide said he had been privy to the plan.

The majority of suicides, 20 out of 34, stayed home until the operation (five of them did not sleep at home on the last night). Some did not stay home in the days preceding the suicide attack—in a few cases apparently because they wanted to avoid emotions that would undermine their resolution, and in other cases because they were wanted by the Palestinian or Israeli authorities, who were keeping a close watch on their homes. Yet at times, even some of these men made an effort to pay a last visit to their families shortly before they set out on the deadly mission. For example, one suicide, who was on the wanted list of the Israeli security services and stayed away from home during the four months preceding his suicide attack, slipped quietly into his home on the morning of the operation and bid his family farewell. They did not realize that this was his final departure.

Asked whether in the days preceding the suicide attack they could identify signs in their sons' behavior that could retrospectively be seen as indicating his intention, members of 16 families did note such extra-ordinary behaviors. Two types of behavior were discerned: acts associated with preparation for the mission, and those related to the final departure from the family. The first type included getting a haircut and buying new clothes, both for tactical reasons (to avoid drawing attention with a shabby appearance) and to die in a clean state. The second type included having one's photograph taken at a photographer's studio as a memento for the family, buying candy for the family's children, or giving away personal belongings to friends. On the evening before his lethal mission, one suicide prayed in every room of his family home. This ritual is sometimes observed by Muslims prior to long trips, such as a pilgrimage to Mecca. Another suicide slept in the last ten days before his suicide not in his own room but in his mother's. This 23-year-old man had also been saving money for an eventual marriage, but some time before his death he began spending his savings on clothes, books, and cassettes of Quran recitations. Several days before his death mission he paid off all his debts to various shops, as Islamic tradition stipulates admission to paradise on payment of debts.[10] A week before his suicide attack, another man gave small Qurans to his sisters. To his favorite sister, he also gave a cassette on death and how the family of Prophet Muhammad had acted after his death. On his last night, he went to that sister's home, woke up her children, kissed them and said goodbye.[11] Still another suicide visited relatives during the last two days of his life. Furthermore, he asked his younger brother, with whom he had quarreled, to forgive him, and gave him some money. On the last night, he slept at his elder brother's home. On the morning of the attack he put on a new suit and a necktie, gave his nephews sweets, and left forever.

In at least one case, the change in the suicide's behavior before the operation was the opposite of a farewell. One father of two young chil-dren, with whom he often played in the evenings, ignored them on the evening before he committed his suicide attack. After the event, his family interpreted his unusual behavior as a reflection of his fear that playing with the children might undermine his readiness to die. Another instance of antagonistic nonverbal communication was displayed by a suicide who, on the morning of the attack, played a cassette of religious music very loudly at his parents' home and refused to turn it down despite his brother's requests. He then left for his death as if he were going to his ordinary daily business.

Some suicides provided no clue to the extreme act they were about to carry out, even though they stayed home in the last hours before going to their deaths. For example, one spent the morning of the attack at home, reading quietly. He left a couple of hours before the attack, casually saying goodbye. Nor did he leave a last letter for his family—the only farewell note the family received was the suicide's videotaped message to the public, recorded by Hamas, which was given to them by two masked operatives on the evening after the attack.

About one-third of the suicides (13 out of 34) left a last message for their families, either at home or with the organization that sent them on their missions. In the latter case, members of the group would bring the last letter (and often also the videotape of the suicide's announcement of his intention to carry out the attack, which was customarily made by the organizers shortly before the attack and distributed to the media). In the letter, the suicide usually urged his family not to mourn him, as shown in the following excerpt:

> . . . I decided to join Izz ad-Din al-Qassam and we will meet in Paradise.
> I beg you my father, ask my mother and sisters not to weep, but to rejoice
> and sing. Do not put on black in mourning.[12]

One suicide left a rather succinct note to his mother, with whom he was very close. After his death, the family found out that he had inscribed a few words on the inner side of a door, hidden by hanging clothes: "Mother, I am leaving. Be happy. After death, Allah's Paradise."[13]

Whether they stayed at home on the eve of their suicide attack or not, some of the suicides left no last message for their families, nor did they make any gesture to indicate their final departure. While not bidding farewell personally before the operation suggests both the need for secrecy and fear of an emotional confrontation with loved ones, who may try to stop the candidate from committing his act, not leaving a last message to be given to the family post-mortem is strange. Imagine the married man with a 4-year old boy, a 3-year old girl, and a wife in the last days of pregnancy: one morning he leaves home without a hint as to his imminent suicide, and without any explanatory message to his wife, children, and parents.

It seems natural that a person about to die would feel the need to say goodbye to his family and apologize for the pain that he is going to cause them—and, in fact, most suicides did leave a last message. Presumably, those who left no message differed from the others in mental state or family relations, but the interviews were not sufficiently exhaustive to reveal these factors. Consider, for example, the case of M.W., who neither bid his family farewell nor left any written message behind. Two days before his suicide, however, he had his portrait made in his uncle's photo studio against the backdrop of al-Aqsa mosque, holding a Quran in his hands, as a memento for his family. After his death, the family had the photograph retouched, showing their son holding his own severed head in his hands. What kind of parent–child relationship lay behind this bizarre gesture? The interview did not reveal it.

## The Suicide's Personality

The interviews did not provide sufficient information for an in-depth psychological analysis. Despite the families' willing cooperation, their descriptions of their "martyred" sons were likely skewed by the wish to present them in a positive light. It is therefore possible that at least some of the suicides had a morbid streak that the interviews failed to detect. In any case, no indications were found for psychotic episodes, hospitalization on mental grounds, or conditions that required psychotherapeutic treatment. Nor was there evidence of involvement in common criminal behavior— the families reported that those suicides who had been arrested were detained because of their militant political activities. Six suicides had lost a father and one had lost a mother in childhood, at ages ranging from 2 to 10 years, but both parents of most suicides were still living at the time of the suicide attack. All suicides came from typical Palestinian families with a large number of siblings, ranging from 4 to 14 (mean: 8.8). Of the 33 families where the suicide's birth order was known, in six cases the suicides were the first or second child (18.2%), and nine were the last or next to last (27.3%).

Twenty-eight families provided a rough portrayal of their deceased sons' personalities, yet no single personality type emerged from these descriptions. Fifteen (53.6%) were described by their families as introverted, loners, quiet, non-gregarious, and inhibited,[14] nine (32.1%) were depicted as leader types, and three (10.7%) as sociable extraverts. Although these descriptions should be viewed with great caution, the relatively high proportion of introverts is interesting.

## The Suicide's Heroes

Most youngsters have heroes they admire and want to resemble. These heroes can be fictional figures from movies or literature, admired family members, historical personalities, or current public figures, such as political leaders, actors, singers, athletes, or scientists. One's choice of heroes presumably says something about one's beliefs and ambitions. Twenty families named several personalities admired by their sons. All the heroes mentioned were various representatives of militant Islam.[15] The most common were the *Sahaba*, Muhammad's companions who fought with him in the wars against the infidels and are praised in the *Hadith* (post-Quranic traditions) for their piety and bravery in battle. Thirteen families mentioned the *Sahaba* individually or as a group as their son's heroes. Prophet Muhammad was cited by 11 of the 20 families. A later Islamic hero–Salah ad-Din (Saladin), a great military leader of the 12th century who defeated the Crusaders and founded the Ayyubid dynasty in Egypt and Syria–was mentioned by three families. Only a few families mentioned 20th century figures. Three mentioned Izz ad-Din al-Qassam, the Palestinian rebel who fought against the Mandatory British forces and the Jews, and was killed in 1935, and whose name Hamas adopted for its military arm. Also mentioned by three different families were Hassan al-Banna, the Egyptian radical Islamic ideologue who founded the Muslim Brotherhood in 1928 and Sayyed Qutb, a Muslim Brotherhood theoretician who preached fundamentalist militant Islam and was hanged in Egypt in 1966. One family mentioned Yahya Ayyash, ("the Engineer"), who organized suicide attacks in the 1990s and was killed by Israeli forces.

Except for Hassan al-Banna and Sayyed Qutb, not only did these heroes represent militant Islam, they were all associated in Muslim collective memory with bravery in war, willingness for self-sacrifice that eventually paid, and great military leadership. Some of these heroes, such as Musab Ibn Umayr and Abu Ubaydah ibn al-Jarrah, were also noted for defying their families. According to the *Hadith*, Musab Ibn Umayr was chained by his mother for joining Islam, and later fought against his own non-Muslim tribesmen, in a battle in which his brother was taken prisoner by the Muslims. Musab advised his comrades to tie his brother tightly, because his mother was rich and they would be able to get a hefty ransom for him.[16]

Abu Ubaydah ibn al-Jarrah was known not only as one of Muhammad's early followers, but also because in one battle he killed his own father, who was fighting against the Muslim army (Abdul Wahid Hamid, 1995).

## Hobbies

Nineteen of the 25 families who could describe their deceased sons' hobbies mentioned various forms of physical activity, including martial arts (10), soccer, (12), weight lifting, gymnastics, running, and swimming. Fourteen families noted that their sons liked reading, and all of them said that the reading material consisted of Islamic literature—the Quran, Hadith, and Islamic poetry. Many suicides spent most of their free time in the neighborhood mosque. Especially in the Gaza Strip, but also in many West Bank villages, mosques served not only as places of religious worship, but also as venues for social gathering and activities, including sports.

## Sample of Biographical Sketches

The following sketches of some of the suicides discussed in this chapter may provide the reader with a more concrete perception of their personalities and interpersonal relations. These sketches are based entirely on their families' accounts.

### A.S.

A.S., 22 years old at the time of his suicide attack, was the first child of a middle-class family. His parents and siblings described him as very kind and polite. He did not do well in school and dropped out of elementary school after the third grade—a rather unusual occurrence among children of Palestinian middle-class families. The family attributed his failure in school to lack of scholastic aptitude ("he was a good Muslim but was not interested in studies"), yet it is unclear whether there was also a background of behavioral disorder or organic problem. He used to work with his father as an apprentice carpenter, but spent much of his time on the street, and his mother used to send his father to bring him home in the evening. Sometimes he worked with his father in Israel, and on several occasions sabotaged machinery and other property. He was very active during the first intifada, and when he was arrested twice and held for a couple of months, the family paid fines to release him. After his second arrest the family arranged for him to get married to his cousin, hoping this would keep him out of trouble. He was married four years but had no children before his death (another unusual situation among Palestinians), suggesting infertility problems. His mother dubbed him "virgin." Apparently, he was a dominant figure in his social circle and domineering toward his younger siblings. When he received his salary, he lined up his siblings and handed out money; he also chided and hit them for failing to pray on time. Toward his father, however, he was quite obedient. Once, after participating in a demonstration, his father slapped him in the face in the presence of his wife and mother, yet he reacted submissively. He was more religious than his family and talked several times about his wish to be a martyr.

## M.W.

M.W., 18 years old at the time of his death, was the fourth child of a large family of 11 siblings. In a photograph he looked thin and short. His family described him as very quiet, obedient, and considerate. His mother said that he was unhappy: "Life was hard for him." Having failed in the examinations, he did not finish high school. This must have disappointed his father, who was a teacher. He liked soccer, and built cages where he held birds that he caught. He was not active in the intifada—he had never been arrested or involved in clashes with Israeli forces. Neither was he overtly interested in martyrdom or paradise. The family is religious, although not fanatic, and M.W. was as religious as the other family members. He was recruited for the suicide attack by his cousin, whom he admired and to whose influence he was susceptible.

## L.A.

L.A. was 22 years old at the time of his death. His parents divorced when he was a child. His father and brothers moved to a Persian Gulf state, but L.A. chose to stay behind and live with his grandparents. His mother remarried but he had no relationship with her, even though they lived in the same village. He studied computer science and was a good student. His grandparents described him as a very quiet and solitary young man. He was involved in the first intifada, but never arrested or injured. Much more religious than the rest of the family, he sometimes stayed at the mosque until midnight and then prayed the whole night at home. He did not talk about martyrdom in the presence of his grandparents, but after his death they heard that during Friday prayer at the Mosque he had asked God loudly to admit him to paradise.

## The Families' Reactions

Almost all families expressed both deep sorrow over their sons' suicide operation, and pride in it. The usual explanation for the grief was that no parent wants to lose a child—but some families stated that the political circumstances (before the intifada) did not justify such action. In one case the suicide's father implicitly criticized this form of struggle: "If one goes on an operation as a soldier, I wouldn't have prevented my son, but this was not the way."[17] Another father admitted his sadness but justified the act: "Of course we feel sorrow, but we accept the operation and his *istishhad*. Our son didn't kill civilians or children, but Israeli soldiers who were still occupying our land, and it was inside the Gaza Strip."[18]

Would the family have prevented their son from carrying out the suicide mission if they could have? Some families equivocated, saying that they would not be able to stop their son if he was determined to become a martyr. Most families, however (61.8%), clearly said, often very emphatically, that they would have done everything in their power to prevent him from carrying out his plans. One mother gave a typical answer: "Of course. He was my son, I would have done anything possible. He is in my heart, I still feel him in my heart. Weeping has ruined my eyes."[19] The father of another suicide was very proud of his son's operation: "This huge, very successful operation couldn't have been a human operation or carried out by human beings alone. It required so much planning, deep inside Israel . . . It was definitely with Allah's help. Allah wanted the operation to succeed." But despite his admiration and his certainty that it had been Allah's will, when asked if he would have stopped his son from doing it, if he could have, he answered bluntly: "I would have stopped him by force!" And the mother concurred.[20] The mother of one suicide was highly supportive of militant activities and during the first intifada she used to bring stones to the street boys to throw at Israeli soldiers. She admired her son's bravery, yet when asked if she would have stopped him from carrying out the suicide attack, she answered: "If I had suspected his plans, I would have locked the doors and the windows and wouldn't have let him out."[21] She said that she was still weeping over his loss. The parents of another suicide were even firmer, with the mother saying that she would have gone to the police if there had been no other way to stop him.[22] The emotional conflict and cognitive dissonance between, on the one hand, support of the armed struggle and pride in their son's role in it, and, on the other hand, the deep grief over his loss, were sometimes expressed in criticism of suicide attacks as futile. One father said: "Personally, I believe in jihad, but even though I'm proud of my son, individual acts and operations don't achieve their goal. That goal will be achieved by a large Muslim army. If I had known, I would have prevented him. It's not easy to lose a son for an individual act that will not achieve the goal."[23] The father of a Hamas suicide was skeptical: "Allah wanted *istishhad* for [my son]. I wouldn't have been able to prevent him . . . Even if I had known, what could I have done? Lock him up? For how long? One Day? Two days? He would have done it anyway. No father would knowingly allow this, but for how long can a father keep a son locked up? One can't exercise control all the time. I would have tried to keep [my son] at home, to calm him down, I would have told him that the IDF would demolish our home [if he did this], but he would have dismissed all these reasons."[24] One mother offered the most dramatic image of pain and longing: "Of course I would have tried to stop him! I would have cut open my chest with a knife, put him inside my heart and sewed him up tight inside, to keep him safe inside my heart."[25]

Only one family completely rejected the dead son, blaming him and the organization that had sent him (PIJ) for an act that had caused them great trouble and was, in their view, both futile and inconsiderate. This attitude was probably dictated by the father who, unlike the mother, expressed no sorrow but only anger at the son. In an attempt to erase the suicide son from the family's memory, the parents removed all his belongings and photographs from the house, did not attend the funeral, nor did they ever visit his grave. The father explained: "Because we are very, very angry at what he did. How could he have done this to his family? He did it without asking us, telling us, or seeking our advice. And without any aim or purpose. We wanted him to complete his education, do a doctorate, be a successful member of the community." The father maintained that visiting the grave would be "un-Islamic [because] he committed suicide. My son betrayed us, he destroyed the family." Describing her feelings about her son's death, the mother said: "[It was] the very worst day in my life. However, it is from Allah. What is gone is gone. I hope and pray that the remaining sons will survive and flourish. I'll always be sad, until the day I die. Then I will meet [my son] and ask him: Why, why did you leave me alone? Why did you do this? I'm your mother, I carried you for nine months, I gave birth to you, and now you have abandoned me." The father said that had he known of his son's plan, he would have turned him in to the PNA police. His criticism of the PIJ, which had sent his son on the suicide mission, was very harsh and sarcastic: "They, with the big beards, they hunt and hurt small children. Surely these clerics deserve paradise more than the rest of us. Why give paradise to the youngsters? Why don't they themselves hurry to paradise in the same way? Or send their own sons? Why not offer paradise to someone from their own family? It's all deception and treachery. They hunt simple boys, they have no right to do this. If the Prophet Mohammad was the imam of the *mujahidin*, he trained them for battle, not like this. Let us be killed in an honorable manner, not for extremists. Let there be an operation for peace, not suicide."[26] Another father did, indeed, convince his son to turn himself in to the PNA police, as he was wanted for militant activity. The son and three of his friends spent six months in a PNA jail, then escaped, and soon thereafter all four carried out suicide attacks.

Unlike the parents, siblings (and cousins, who were occasionally also interviewed) were generally less critical of the suicide and expressed less intense feelings. Still, most said they would not carry out suicide attacks themselves, explaining that the political circumstances (before the intifada, during the peace process) did not warrant such an operation. Yet they may also have been swayed by personal considerations. A cousin of one suicide said: "As part of my conviction, yes, I could [do it], but I wouldn't under the present circumstances because I support my family."[27]

In an interview given to the Islam Online website, Salah Shkhadeh, at the time commander of Hamas' military arm Izz ad-Din al-Qassam Brigades, said about choosing candidates for suicide attacks: "We verify that the young man complies with his parents' wishes . . ." (MEMRI, 2002). But given the families' responses in the interviews, this claim does not reflect the reality.

*Endnotes*

1. Ms. Hassan's has continued her research, in the context of Islam, on Muslim suicide bombers and the factors on which their sponsoring groups, in particular trainers and planners, base their operational decisions. She recently informed me that she has so far gathered data on hundreds of suicide bombers from many parts of the Arab and Islamic world, which she plans to publish in the near future.

2. The CIA *World Factbook* (1997). Available at: http://www.umsl.edu/services/govdocs/wofact97/country-frame.html (accessed May 11, 2005).

3. Palestinian National Bureau of Statistics (1997). *Final Results of the First Palestinian Census, Table of Palestinian Population by Refugee Status, Region, and Sex.* Available at: http://www.pcbs.org/_PCBS/census/phc_97/phc_t7.aspx (accessed: December 18, 2005).

4. UNRWA (2005). *Refugee Camp Profiles.* United Nations Relief and Works Agency Statistics of Palestinian Refugees. Available at: http://www.un.org/unrwa/refugees/camp-profiles.html (accessed December 18, 2005).

5. At the time of writing this chapter, Barber's study was scheduled to be published by Palgrave Macmillan under the title, *Youth as Social Movers: Adolescents and the Palestinian Intifada.*

6. S.S., interview on November 1, 1997.

7. A.S., interview on June 27, 1997.

8. R.O., interview on August, 1997.

9. H.H., Interview on June 28, 1997.

10. K.K., interview on June 24, 1997.

11. R.K., interview on June 25, 1997.

12. A.A., interview on July 7, 1997.

13. M.R., interview on August 6, 1997.

14. This description fits well the findings of the psychological study of would-be suicides (see Chapter 5). In that study, 60% of the would-be suicides were assessed as having a dependent-avoidant personality style.

15. Similarly, in a study in which 35 incarcerated Middle Eastern terrorists—most or all of them *not* suicide bombers—were interviewed, Post, Sprinzak and Denny (2003, p. 172) found that the boyhood heroes of the Islamist terrorists were "religious figures, such as the Prophet, or the radical Wahabi Islamist Abdullah Azzam." However, the heroes of members of secular groups were revolutionaries such as Che Guevara and Fidel Castro.

16. See: Islam Online (2004). Muslim Profiles: Musab Ibn Umayr, Part II. Available at: http://www.islamonline.com/cgi-bin/news_service/profile_story.asp?service_id=922 (accessed January 14, 2006).

17. R.Z., Interview on July 7, 1997.

18. H.H., Interview on June 28, 1997.

19. A.R., Interview on June 28, 1997.

20. A.S., interview on June 27, 1997.

21. S.M., interview on June 28, 1997.

22. M.R., interview on August 6, 1997.

23. M.W., interview on July 12, 1997.

24. E.A., interview on July 1, 1997.

25. R.K., interview on June 25, 1997. See also Hassan, 2001.

26. A.S., interview on June 30, 1997.

27. Interview on July 7, 1997.

# 5

# A Controlled Study of
# Would-Be Suicides

THE FAMILY INTERVIEWS DESCRIBED in the previous chapter provided important data on the suicides' backgrounds, including demographic details and some rough clues on their possible motives for carrying out the suicide attacks. They did not, however, offer direct and detailed information on personality characteristics, motivation for agreeing to carry out a suicide attack, and behavior in connection with the mission. Such information can be obtained from the suicides themselves. Yet, as completed suicides cannot be subjected to interviews and tests, the obvious alternative is persons who were caught before they could accomplish their mission.

Interviews of captured would-be suicide bombers raise several questions, among them whether the would-be suicides are, indeed, an accurately representative sample of the actual suicides. Those who failed to carry out the mission and were caught by the authorities arguably differ in personality and motivation from those who killed themselves, whether they did or didn't reach their target. The only captured would-be suicides who are genuinely representative of the completed suicides are those who tried to activate their explosive charge but whose devices malfunctioned. In such cases, the assailant obviously did everything in his or her power to complete the mission and should be psychologically regarded as a completed suicide. Those caught before they tried to detonate the explosive device offer a less clear picture. It is not certain that, had they reached their destination, they would indeed have carried out their mission, as the possibility of a last-moment change of mind cannot be dismissed. Furthermore, since the would-be suicides have to be interviewed in jail, incarceration may affect their responses in psychological interviews and tests. Furthermore, their responses may be skewed by their desire to impress the interviewers favorably. Bearing all this in mind, captured would-be suicides are nevertheless the best and only accessible representatives of suicide bombers.

Over the years, would-be suicide bombers have been occasionally interviewed by the media. Yet, interesting as these interviews may have been, they cannot replace a professional psychological inquiry. Because suicide bombers' characteristics and motives may vary across cultures and political contexts, I planned to carry out an international study that would subject would-be suicides to standard interviews, questionnaires and tests. Such a study would reveal which characteristics are universal and which are culture or context specific. Unfortunately, difficulties in accessing would-be suicides and limited financial resources have left Israel thus far the only country where would-be suicide bombers have undergone this kind of inquiry. Since 2002, I have headed a series of studies in which Palestinian would-be suicide bombers, a control group of non-suicide terrorists, and local group leaders who organized suicide attacks, were interviewed and tested in prison by clinical psychologists as well as by specialists on Palestinian affairs who were highly familiar with Palestinian society. This chapter describes the controlled study of the would-be suicides. The organizers' study is presented in the following chapter.

## The Would-Be-Suicides Sample

During the second intifada, Israeli security forces arrested a large number of persons who had intended to carry out a suicide attack. Most of these would-be suicides were arrested at various stages of preparation, before they were launched on their missions. As discussed above, a major concern about the use of would-be suicides as representatives of completed suicides was the degree of certainty that they would have indeed carried out the suicide attack if they could have. For the sample of would-be suicides, an attempt was therefore made to select suicide candidates who had been caught as close as possible to the completion of their mission. At the time this sample was selected, in mid-2002, we could identify four would-be suicides who had reached their destination and actually tried to activate the explosive device they were carrying. One, for example, named Sabri here,[1] boarded a bus with the intention of exploding the bomb inside. When the bus driver asked him where he wanted to go, he did not answer, as he did not speak Hebrew. At this point, the driver noticed electrical wires and a switch protruding from Sabri's handbag and suspected he was a suicide bomber. He flew at him, shoved him outside the bus, and tried to pin him down. Sabri tried to press the switch but the charge failed to explode. Another would-be suicide, Ghazi, arrived by taxi in an Israeli town, carrying an explosive charge in a handbag. He walked around for some time, looking for a proper target—as crowded a place as possible—while keeping his hand in the handbag on the charge's switch, ready to activate it. A suspecting police patrol ordered him to take his hand out of the bag and to approach them. Ghazi approached as ordered, but kept his hand in the handbag on the switch. About three feet from the police officers, he pressed the switch but the bomb failed to detonate.

Another 11 suicide candidates carrying explosive devices had been arrested on their way to their target, but did not try to activate the device when they ran into the security forces. Their inclusion in the sample was based on general descriptions of the circumstances of their capture in an attempt to assess, however imprecisely, their determination to complete the mission. Only in the interviews did some reveal that they had decided to abort the mission before they reached their targets. Hesitation, however, does not necessarily result in abandoning the mission, an issue to be discussed later in this chapter and the next.

Samir, who belonged to the second group, approached a PIJ operative and volunteered to carry out a suicide attack. When several weeks had passed since his first contact with the organizer of the attack (the local PIJ leader), Samir kept pressing to be sent on the mission as soon as possible. He was eventually dispatched with two guides whose task was to get him from his West Bank city to the Israeli border and then to the Israeli city of Haifa, where he was supposed to set off an explosion in a disco. At the border, however, they could not find a car and a driver with a permit to enter Israel. As it was late in the evening, the guides suggested spending the night in a village near the border and trying to find a car the next morning, but Samir objected and insisted on carrying out his suicide attack that night. A couple of hours later, one of the guides found a car and a driver, but soon after crossing the border they were apprehended by Israeli soldiers. Samir described their capture:

> The explosive charge was with us in the car. The Israelis got information that I was getting in a car near the village. Suddenly, we saw that the road was blocked by two cars facing each other and we thought it was a road accident. We had to stop, and as soon as we did, Israeli soldiers jumped on us from behind and grabbed us. I could not press the switch because the explosive charge was in a closed box. As they charged at us by surprise, I had no time to get it out and press the switch.

As in the previous case, Rafik, a resident of the Gaza Strip, also volunteered to carry out a suicide attack. He offered himself to an operative of the al-Aqsa Martyrs Brigades (Fatah), whom he knew, and was told to wait. In the following weeks, he persisted with his request and was given the same answer. Finally, he told the Fatah operative that if the group didn't send him soon on a suicide mission, he would contact another organization—Hamas or PIJ. Soon afterward, he was teamed up with another Gazan whom he knew, and was told that they would carry out a double-suicide attack in the Israeli city of Beer Sheva. They received suicide belts and instructions how to use them, and were dispatched for the mission. As all direct passes from the Gaza Strip to Israel were well guarded, they were told to first cross the border into Egypt, where they would meet an Egyptian officer who was supposed to help them cross into Israel for a bribe of $3,000. They were then driven to the Israeli-Egyptian border, where the driver showed them an eight-foot-high concrete wall they were supposed to climb. On the other side, on Egyptian territory, people were waiting for them. The two did not like the situation: the wall was high and exposed to Egyptian and Israeli patrols, and the explosive charges were heavy. They were afraid they might be shot while attempting to climb over the wall. They called the organizer of the attack on their cellular phone and told him of their reservations, and he ordered them to return to Gaza. On their way back, they were caught by an Israeli patrol. In the interview, Rafik admitted that he was afraid and blamed himself for lack of resolve, but had it not been for the obstruction on the way, the two might have reached their target and exploded their devices.

Another criterion for selection was the organizational affiliation of the would-be suicides. Assuming that the perpetrating groups may have attracted or intentionally chosen different types of people, we selected the would-be suicides' sample to include people sent on missions by the three main groups that engineered suicide attacks. Five were sent by Hamas, six by PIJ, and four by the al-Aqsa Martyrs Brigades (Fatah). All were arrested during the intifada.

## The Control Group

Two interconnected questions underpin our study: What features do suicide terrorists share? And how do they differ from non-suicide terrorists? To find out whether the would-be suicides in our sample had psychological traits that distinguished them from other (non-suicide) terrorists, we had to compare them to a control group. In selecting the control group, we tried to find persons imprisoned for terrorist activity, who resembled the would-be suicides as much as possible in age, marital status, education, organizational affiliation, and time served in prison, so as to rule out possible effects of these variables on the results of the psychological tests. With these criteria in mind, thirteen prisoners were selected for participation in the control group. They had been tried and jailed for a variety of security-related offenses, ranging from membership in a terrorist group to weapons training, armed assaults, and attempted murder. Like the would-be suicides, all were arrested during the intifada.

## Psychological Interviews and Tests

Four clinical psychologists fluent in Arabic conducted the psychological interviews. Every participant in the would-be suicides, control, and organizers' groups was interviewed individually by one psychologist, who also administered the psychological tests. The tests included the Rorschach Inkblot Test, Thematic Apperception Test (TAT), House–Tree–Person Drawing Test, and a shortened version of the California Personality Inventory (CPI), which included 300 items.[2] Four senior psychologists, specializing in diagnosis, evaluated the tests. The interviewers and the diagnosticians worked jointly on the final assessment of each case.

With the exception of one organizer, all prisoners asked to participate in the study agreed to be interviewed. Almost all also agreed to take the whole battery of psychological tests. One control participant refused to take any tests, and one of the would-be suicides could not take the tests because of severe vision impairment. These two participants were excluded from the personality assessment statistics. Two of the suicide group refused to fill out the CPI questionnaire on account of fatigue (the CPI was the last test administered in the series). The Rorschach test of one suicide was excluded due to insufficient number of responses, and the CPI of four control-group participants were dropped because of extremely low consistency between answers or an inordinate effort to please (scales Identical and Good Impression, respectively). Still, there was enough material for a psychological assessment of 15 suicides, 12 controls, and 14 organizers of suicide attacks. (The latter will be discussed in the next chapter).

*Reliability Check*

Since the psychologists who conducted the interviews and administered the tests knew to what group the participant belonged, we took into account the possibility of experimenter bias. The interview reports and tests results of all the suicide and control-group participants were therefore given for independent assessment to a senior expert in psychological diagnostics, who was unfamiliar with the participants' group affiliation. His assessment of the participants' personality characteristics was then used as an external measure of the reliability of the original diagnoses. Inter-rater reliability levels corresponded to standard requirements in psychological assessment: 81% agreement for the general clinical diagnosis of ego strength and personality style, 77% for suicidal tendencies, 85% for depressive manifestations, and 92% for psychopathic symptoms.

# Results

*Demographic Characteristics*

As explained above, the members of the control group were selected to match the would-be suicides in demographic characteristics as much as possible. However, at the time of selection, accurate information was obtained only on age and marital status. The demographic characteristics of the control participants should therefore be considered a random representation of all Palestinians who serve time in an Israeli prison for security-related offenses, except in characteristics influenced by age and marital status such as education and employment, which are therefore not random. The demographic characteristics of the two groups are shown in Table 5.1.

As Table 5.1 shows, the suicides and controls were identical in age and marital status. In both groups, the average age was about 19.5 years, and none had ever been married (one would-be suicide was engaged). The suicides' educational level was higher than that of the controls, as more were high school graduates (53.4% compared to 33.3%). Their families' economic level was also higher: only 20.0% of the suicides came from poor families compared to 50% of the controls, and two-thirds of the suicides described the economic situation of their families as "average," compared to one-third of the controls. However, the employment distribution of the two groups was very similar: in both groups, blue-collar workers constituted nearly 60%, students about one third, and the rest were unemployed.

**Table 5.1** Comparison of Demographic and Background Characteristics of the Suicide and Control Groups

| Characteristics | Suicide group (N=15) | Control group (N=12) |
|---|---|---|
| *Age* | | |
| Mean | 19.5 | 19.4 |
| Range | 15-23 | 15-23 |
| *Marital status* | | |
| Single | 100.0% | 100.0% |
| Married | 0 | 0 |
| *Education* | | |
| Partial elementary | 13.3% | 8.3% |
| Full elementary | 0 | 25.0% |
| Partial high school | 33.3% | 33.3% |
| Full high school | 46.7% | 25.0% |
| Partial university | 6.7% | 8.3% |
| Full university | 0 | 0 |
| *Family economic status* | | |
| Low | 20.0% | 50.0% |
| Middle | 66.7.0% | 33.3% |
| High | 13.3% | 16.7% |
| *Employment* | | |
| Blue Collar | 60.0% | 58.3% |
| Student | 33.3% | 33.3% |
| Unemployed | 6.7% | 8.3% |
| *Refugee camp dweller* | 20.0% | 41.7% |
| *Refugee family* | 33.3% | 41.7% |
| *Father alive* | 86.7% | 83.3% |
| *Mother alive* | 100.0% | 91.7% |
| *Religiosity* | | |
| Very religious | 20.0% | 25.0% |
| Ordinarily religious | 80.0% | 58.3% |
| Little religious | 0 | 8.3% |
| Not religious | 0 | 8.3% |
| *Religiosity compared to family* | | |
| More religious than family | 33.3% | 25.0% |
| Same as family | 60.0% | 58.3% |
| Less religious than family | 6.7% | 16.7% |

(*Continued*)

**Table 5.1** Comparison of Demographic and Background Characteristics of the Suicide and Control Groups (*Continued*)

| Characteristics | Suicide group (N=15) | Control group (N=12) |
|---|---|---|
| Organization member | 53.3% | 66.7% |
| Previous resistance activity | | |
| Violent armed | 26.7% | 33.3% |
| Violent unarmed | 13.3% | 25.0% |
| Non-violent | 6.7% | 25.0% |
| None | 53.3% | 16.7% |
| Previous arrests | 0% | 25.0% |
| Extended family members killed | 33.3% | 41.7% |
| Time served in prison before the interview (months) | 7.5 | 13.0 |

The rate of refugee camp dwellers and membership in a family of refugee origin were higher among the controls than among the suicides (41.7% vs. 20.0% and 41.7% vs. 33.3%, respectively). This factor alone cannot, therefore, explain the willingness to carry out a suicide attack. As noted in Chapter 4, the proportion of refugee camp dwellers was higher among suicides than in the general Palestinian population. If the small sample of non-suicides in this study is a genuine representation of "ordinary" (non-suicide) Palestinian terrorists, this finding may suggest that the proportion of refugees is higher among those engaged in insurgent activity in general, but refugee-camp dwelling is not specifically associated with greater inclination to carry out a suicide attack.

A comparison between the suicides and the control group in terms of religiosity yielded mixed results which, taken together, do not support the notion that Palestinian suicide bombers are more religious than non-suicide terrorists. Although the overall rate of religious people was somewhat higher among the suicides (100%) than among the controls (83.3%), more controls (25%) than suicides (20.0%) described themselves as "very religious." The rate of those who described themselves as more religious than their families was higher among the suicides (33.3%) than among the controls (25%), yet most participants in both groups said that they were as religious as their families.

While all suicides were recruited, prepared and dispatched by a terrorist group, not all had been members of the group before they embarked on their mission. The rate of terrorist group members was insignificantly higher among the controls than among the suicides (66.7% vs. 53.3%, respectively). An examination of the type of insurgent activity in both groups revealed, however, that a large proportion of the would-be suicides (53.3% compared to 16.7%) had not been involved in any kind of insurgent activity before they agreed to carry out the suicide attack. This also explains why none of them had been arrested prior to their attempted suicide attack (compared to 25.0% of the controls).

## How Representative is the Sample?

An important question is whether, on the basis of demographic features, the would-be suicides' sample can be regarded as representative of all Palestinian terrorist suicides. The sample's participants were, on the average, more than two years younger than the completed suicides at the time of the second intifada (19.6 and 21.9 years, respectively). There was also a slight difference in marital status, which was presumably affected by age difference: whereas 90.6% of the completed suicides during the intifada were single, all would-be suicides in the sample were single. Another difference was in the rate of refugee camp dwellers: during the second intifada, their proportion in the would-be suicides sample was 18.7%, somewhat lower than among completed suicides (25.46%). Data on other demographic characteristics of completed suicides during the intifada are insufficient to allow sound comparisons. Regarding some characteristics, the partial data available on the completed suicides may be misleading due to possibly biased media reporting. A case in point is educational level. These data are available for only 35.5% of the intifada suicides. A very high proportion of these (60.0%) have been reported as college students or graduates. This rate is much higher than the rates found in both the families' study, which provided accurate data on the pre-intifada completed suicides, and the sample of the intifada would-be suicides. While the younger age of the would-be suicides sample may at least partly explain this difference, reporters may have tended to mention the educational level of suicides more often when these were college students or graduates. When demographic data on the completed suicides are available for only a few cases, the sample's data are presumably a better estimate. The noted differences between the would-be suicides sample and the completed suicides are therefore immaterial. The question is, then, whether these demographic differences are related to disparities in personality and motivation, which might explain why the would-be suicides failed to accomplish their mission. Although methodologically the study provides the best available approximation of the characteristics of completed suicides, it does not propose a definite answer to this question.[3]

## Personality Characteristics

None of the participants in the would-be suicides group and the control group was diagnosed as psychotic, and none of them had a record of hospitalization in a mental institution. Yet contrary to the numerous claims (e.g., Silke, 2003; Sageman, 2004, p. 83; Pape, 2005, pp. 218–219) implying that suicide terrorists lack distinct personality characteristics, the analysis of the clinical interviews and psychological tests of the would-be suicides revealed several common features that differentiated them from the control group. A majority of the would-be suicides (60.0%), as opposed to only 16.7% of the controls, were diagnosed as dependent-avoidant. The characteristics of a dependent personality are a pronounced lack of self confidence, difficulty in making decisions independently, reliance on others' opinions, reluctance to express disagreement out of fear that this may result in disapproval and rejection, and willingness to carry out unpleasant tasks to please others (American Psychiatric Association, 1994, p. 665). An avoidant personality is characterized by timidity and fear of criticism, of being shamed or ridiculed (American Psychiatric Association, 1994, p. 662). Both dependent and avoidant personality types belong to "Cluster C" in the DSM IV and have a high comorbidity rate. Four of the would-be suicides (26.7%) were characterized as impulsive and emotionally unstable. This personality type (which belong to "Cluster B" in the DSM IV) was predominant in the control group (66.7%). Characteristically, these people are emotionally volatile, their mood fluctuating between melancholy and hyperactivity. Their behavior is impulsive and unpredictable, often self-damaging, and they tend to display rage outbursts. The two groups thus differed in the predominant personality type of their participants.

The groups differed significantly also in other important aspects. Whereas six of the would-be suicides (40.0%) displayed *suicidal tendencies*, no symptoms of suicidality were found in the interviews and tests of the control group. Eight of the would-be suicides (53.3%) but only one (8.3%) of the controls had *depressive tendencies*. Three of the would-be suicides were also diagnosed as having post-traumatic stress disorder (PTSD), but none of the control group participants displayed this syndrome. Depressive tendencies were manifested as sadness, sometimes tearfulness, lack of vitality, slowness, and distracted attention. The TAT responses of these participants were dominated by feelings of loneliness, distress, helplessness, and sadness. For example, in response to Card 3BM—which shows the figure of a faceless man or woman sitting on the floor, leaning against a cot or bed, with a handgun on the floor nearby—one of the would-be suicides (Zuheir) provided the following description:

> This woman suffered a lot from hard life and from her home and family events and she's now in a tough situation. She's depressed and bored and she's trying to find a solution to [her] problems or end her life. Perhaps her husband beat her up and she's suffering hunger. If her situation improves in the future she'll have painful memories, and if her situation doesn't improve, she'll be in pain until either the pain or her life will end.

In response to another card, 6BM, which shows two figures standing in a room—a gray-haired woman looking out a window and a young man in a suit, holding a hat in his hand and looking down, both apparently sad or troubled—the same participant said:

> This youngster had been through hard times and his mother is angry and annoyed with him and herself. They are in a tough situation of anger and hard feelings that, in the future, will give them both a nervous breakdown and make them unable to cope even with small problems. In the future, life will be difficult with no improvement and no progress toward other solutions.

Another significant difference between the groups was related to psychopathic tendencies, which were completely absent among the would-be suicides, whereas three of the controls (25%) were assessed as having them. All three were also assessed as impulsive and emotionally unstable.

Table 5.2 summarizes the main differences between the would-be suicides and the control group.

A more detailed analysis of the psychological assessment can be found in Merari, Diamant, Bibi, Broshi and Zakin, (2010). In general, as a group the would-be suicides differed significantly in their personality characteristics from non-suicide terrorists. This difference suggests that certain types of people are more likely to be attracted to suicide terrorist missions. Most were socially marginal youngsters with a keen sense of social failure. Shy and withdrawn, they lacked self-confidence and feared rejection, were

**Table 5.2** Personality Characteristics of Suicides and Controls

| Group | Personality Characteristics | | | | |
| --- | --- | --- | --- | --- | --- |
| | Avoidant-dependent | Impulsive-unstable | Suicidality | Depression | Psychopathic tendencies |
| Suicide | 60.0% | 26.7% | 40.0% | 53.3% | 0 |
| Control | 16.6% | 66.7% | 0 | 8.3% | 25.0% |
| Significance of difference | | 0.014 | 0.053 | 0.014 | 0.04 |

eager to please, and tended to avoid conflicts. The following two examples are representative of this type:

> *Hamed, 21 years old at the time of his arrest, was sentenced to 22 years in prison for his attempted suicide attack. In the interview he seemed shy, polite, and eager to please. Born in a village near Jerusalem, he was the 11th child in a family of six sons and six daughters. His father, 67 years old at the time of Hamed's arrest, was a retired hospital janitor and his mother was a housewife. Both parents had no schooling at all. Hamed's mother is the father's second wife—the father divorced his first wife, the mother of Hamed's two elder sisters. Three sons and five sisters are married. Hamed was neither married nor engaged. Hamed and his unmarried siblings—two brothers and one sister—lived with the parents; the married siblings lived in their own homes. Hamed described his family as ordinary: "neither up nor down," and the atmosphere at home and family relations as "normal." Asthmatic since the age of 10, Hamed described himself as a quiet boy who preferred to stay home and play alone or with his sisters rather than associate with other children, explaining that he was too lazy to go out and therefore played with other children only at school. Occasionally, he used to walk alone in the wadi (dry river bed) in the vicinity of his home. By his account, he was a good student in elementary school, where he had a few friends and good relations with the teachers. In high school, however, his performance deteriorated: "I preferred to watch television and such. I should have made a greater effort but I have not done it. I was angry; it annoyed me, my parents were also angry at me." Having failed several examinations, he dropped out from high school in 12th grade. Between his dropping out and his arrest, Hamed worked in several places as an apprentice electrician. He claimed he had no*

*connections with girls except for his sisters. Asked what were the events that influenced him most, Hamed mentioned his failure at school and failing to carry out the suicide attack, and his subsequent arrest.*

*On the basis of the psychological tests, Hamed was assessed as an avoidant personality. Anxious, shy, and withdrawn, he had very low self-esteem, was rigid and needed to please, yet lacked social competence and refrained from social relations unless he was certain he was wanted. No suicidal tendencies were found.*

*Hamed's description of his motives to carry out the suicide mission sheds more light on his personality. Initially, when asked what made him undertake the suicide mission, he answered simply: "My goal was to go to paradise so as to be with the 72 virgins" (although he described himself as "ordinary" rather than very religious). Later, however, he said: "I also wanted to be famous, to be seen on a poster, and I wanted my family to get money after my death, so that their economic condition would improve." Hamed also said that his decision was influenced by the example of early Islamic heroes and recent famous shahids, whom he wanted to resemble.*

*For Hamed, a socially marginal youngster who felt inferior, incompetent, and a disappointment to his family, the act of suicide seemed a magnificent, instantaneous leap to fame and admiration. Pressing a switch would turn him into a national hero, a source of pride and a benefactor to his family, for his sacrifice would bring them social respect and economic rewards.*

*Sabri, 16 years old at the time of his attempted suicide attack, was born in a West Bank village, the seventh child in a middle-class family of 11 children. Although he agreed to be interviewed, his behavior seemed reserved and apprehensive. Unlike other participants, he refused to drink or eat the fruit offered to him. He described himself as ambitious and trying hard to excel in school to match the academic success of two elder brothers who had university degrees. The dominant influential figures were his father and one elder brother, who stressed the importance of education and good behavior. He avoided bad company and made a point of associating with quiet and humble classmates. He was well liked by his teachers, who nicknamed him haboub (the kind one). He kept his distance from girls "like the distance between heaven and earth" and never masturbated, as such activities are forbidden. Separations, however brief, from his close family members were traumatic for him. With tears in his eyes, he recalled how sad he had been when his brothers had left home for academic institutions, and the sorrow when his father had been hospitalized for a couple of weeks following a road accident. His first encounter with death was when an elder brother of his childhood friend and classmate was "martyred." In the interview he talked at length about the agony he had felt seeing his friend's sorrow—"my friend's tears froze my own tears in my eyelashes." He emphatically said that his friend's grief prompted him to volunteer for a suicide attack, "to console my friend and cheer him up," and insisted that his friend's suffering was the main motive for his decision. Before his decision to carry out the suicide attack, Sabri's religiosity was rather moderate. He prayed at home and sometimes skipped prayers, usually attending the mosque once a week. After his decision to carry out the suicide attack he grew more devout, praying often at the mosque and making sure not to miss any prayers.*

*On the basis of the clinical interview and the tests, Sabri was assessed as emotionally highly dependent with a very strong drive to please. The tests revealed a depressive tendency and rigid obsessive thinking characterized by an all-or-none approach, but no noticeable suicidal inclinations. The pathological need to gratify others, which rested on an extremely rigid code of behavior that can be termed obsessive altruism, prompted him to volunteer for a suicide attack.*

As noted above, 26.7% of the would-be-suicides group was assessed as impulsive and emotionally unstable personality types. The following case is an example:

*Rafik, 21 years old at the time of his arrest, was born to a Gazan family. Both parents had university education. Rafik was the youngest of six siblings. Rafik's mother was his father's second wife. The first wife had seven children. Rafik described himself as a loner since his childhood:*

*"As a child I was a recluse . . . I had no friends in school. I had very few relationships—if I was with one or two, that was enough. And it has been like this until now. I don't like to talk much with people. I'm not afraid, but embarrassed. And it's especially hard for me to talk with women. If a woman talks to me, I blush. With my father I talked normally, but with my mother I only talked a little. I felt embarrassed to talk to her and ask her for things. When I wanted something, I asked my father . . .. With my brothers and sisters, I didn't communicate much. Something like 'good morning,' 'good evening,' something light. Since I liked to be alone, I had a room of my own. Most of the time I locked myself in my room and watched television. The youngest sister is closest to me.*

*I am afraid for her—even of the wind. She is the only one [of the siblings] who is close to me. Sometimes, when I am very nervous and no one can talk to me, then if somebody says 'hi' to me I can beat him up. On the other hand, when I see a small child crying, I may cry with him. I have these kinds of extremes. In elementary school I only had one friend from first grade to sixth grade. We were more than brothers—real friends."*

*Later, Rafik's family moved to another place and he kept in touch with his friend daily by telephone and letters.*

*"Then I made another friend—my father. We used to go out together. If there were problems, I would go to him and he'd come to me. We talked, did things together, not like father and son but like friends. For example, I used to smoke, and at first I was embarrassed to smoke in his presence, but when we became friends we shared cigarettes. But he died. I tried to make other friends after he died, but it was hard for me. In Gaza only liars can live and I cannot live like that. All Gazans are like that, except, perhaps, a hundred people. The mosque was the best place for me, going there, praying. After that, I was more with people from my family, come and go, like that."*

*Rafik described himself as volatile from childhood. He used to respond violently even to slight provocations. For example, when he was about 10 years old he threw a tray full of glasses of hot tea at his father, causing him a burn.*

*His father's sudden death of a heart attack at the age of 78, when Rafik was 20, was a very hard blow to him. Rafik took his father to the hospital, shook him, refused to accept his death, threatened to kill the doctor.*

*"After his death I did not want to go out. I thought, 'who would I be with, with whom would I talk without him?' I thought of committing suicide by cutting my veins, and had my mother not come into my room at that time, I might have done it."*

*He consulted with a Muslim cleric, who told him that suicide was forbidden. He then decided to join the ranks of the militant organization and, soon afterward, volunteered to carry out a suicide operation. He also mentioned that in prison, four days before the interview, he considered committing suicide with painkillers he had stocked.*

*On the basis of the interview and tests, Rafik was assessed as impulsive and unstable with a suicidal tendency.*

Impulsive personality types, such as Rafik, constituted a minority of the would-be suicides group but two-thirds of the control group participants. The following example describes this type of control group participant.

*Mujahed, 18 years old at the time of his arrest, was born in Hebron. He was serving an eight-year sentence for attempted murder. On his own initiative, he went to Tel Aviv, where he stabbed a random Israeli man with a knife. This attack was his first terrorist activity. Although politically affiliated with Hamas, he had not participated in the group's violent activity and had carried out the terrorist attack individually.*

*Mujahed was the youngest among his family's five children. His father was a laborer and his mother a housewife. They hardly pressured him toward academic achievements, nor did they expect much of him in this area. Before the second intifada, his father worked in Israel and was usually absent from home during the week. Mujahed was an unruly boy in school, often involved in brawls and violent incidents. In ninth grade, he was expelled from school for disobedient and troublesome behavior, yet his interrupted formal education notwithstanding, he had a broad range of interests and general knowledge. Especially interested in political, social, and cultural issues, he was an avid consumer of newspapers and television. His political opinions were highly influenced by the writings of militant Islamic thinkers, of whom he mentioned Yusuf al-Qaradawi, Sayyid Qutb, and Hassan al-Banna. Yet despite his deep religiosity and observance of all five daily prayers at the mosque, his behavior was not ascetic. He used to frequent cafés, smoke narghile with friends, and had a girlfriend—something from which a truly devout Muslim would abstain. Not prompted by any specific event, he decided to carry out the attack on the spur of the moment. He claimed he had not carried it out to become a shahid, although he thought his chances of getting killed were very high.*

*On the basis of the interview and test results, Mujahed was assessed as an emotionally unstable personality type, impulsive, with an intense aggressive drive, insufficient internal control, and immature masculine identity. A psychopathic tendency was also detected, but no indications for suicidal or depressive tendencies.*

## Is There a Typical Suicide Bomber?

A fundamental difference between the would-be suicides and the controls was the former's willingness and the latter's unwillingness to carry out a suicide attack.

Hypothetically, in certain cultural, social and political circumstances, all or almost all youngsters might be willing to become suicide bombers. In those circumstances, ending up as a suicide bomber would entail a strong element of chance. Personality characteristics would be immaterial or, at least, a relatively negligible factor. Evidently, this is not the case.

One of the questions that control group participants were asked was: "Have you considered carrying out a 'martyrdom operation' yourself?" Eleven out of the 12 control group participants answered firmly "No." Only one said he had considered it. Asked why they had not considered carrying out a suicide attack, the control participants offered variations of the belief that a suicide act did not suit them personally: "I am incapable of doing it"; "I cannot see myself dead"; "I simply am not interested"; "this is no way to die"; and "I don't have enough faith." Suicides, therefore, differ from those who, under the same circumstances, are willing to kill but would not carry out an act of self-destruction to kill their enemies.

The demographic and psychological data presented above suggest that various types of people may end up as suicide bombers. Nevertheless, these data converged on a predominant type of suicide bomber. Most of the would-be suicides were shy, socially marginal, followers rather than leaders. Many were loners and outsiders, with a history of failure in school, and harbored the feeling of having disappointed their parents. More than one third had suicidal tendencies, which may have played an important role in their willingness to become "martyrs." As a group, their personality features were markedly different from the controls.

An interesting support for these conclusions can be found in an interview with the mother of a suicide bomber who exploded in the Sbarro pizzeria in Jerusalem in August 2001. In the interview, reported by Joyce Davis (2003), the mother provided an unusually frank description of her son, Izz ad-Din al-Masri, who had carried out the attack:

> He didn't really socialize with people, even among the neighbors. He was the only one of my sons who would never talk to any of the women. He would just say from afar *salamu aleikum* (peace be upon you) and that would be it. He wouldn't even look at people, he wouldn't interact with people (p. 128).

However, Al-Masri was apparently very much attached to his mother: "He always was very worried about me, especially my health . . . I had just found out that I had diabetes and he would always eat with me to make sure that I was eating the right things" (p. 129). Al-Masri probably felt that he was a failure. His mother "made it clear that [he] was not the brightest of her children." He was not a good student at school but "somehow got through it." His mother said that their neighbors were surprised at his operation. "They all thought he was a simpleton who could never succeed at doing anything" (p. 129).

This description fits very well the main profile of a suicide bomber found in the present study: an avoidant-dependent personality type, socially marginal and downgraded by the people around him, who finds an opportunity to soar to importance and fame by becoming a *shahid*. As hinted by his mother, al-Masri probably had a suicidal tendency as well: "He worshiped the afterlife. He wanted to be there" (p. 131).

The importance of personality in the making of suicide bombers is further underscored by the fact that aside from personality characteristics, this study did not support background features that might be perceived as explanations for the willingness to carry out a suicide attack. On the whole, the suicides were less militant than the controls, as shown by their lesser involvement in armed-struggle activities. They did not have more personal reasons for taking revenge, they were not more religious, nor poorer. The next section offers a more detailed look into their motives and behavior related to the suicide mission.

## The Suicide Mission: The Candidates' Attitudes and Behavior

In addition to undergoing psychological interviews and tests, the would-be suicides were also interviewed by specialists on Palestinian affairs who had detailed first-hand knowledge of the terrorist groups. These interviews were designed to bring to light the would-be suicides' motives for undertaking the mission, the process they went through from recruitment to execution, and the factors that affected their behavior. The interviews were conducted in Arabic and based on a prepared questionnaire. The findings of these interviews are described below.

### Recruitment

Eight of the would-be suicides (53%) volunteered for the mission on their own initiative. The others were solicited by a recruiter of one of the organizations to undertake a suicide mission. Of the eight volunteers, five had already been affiliated with the organization and approached their contact person in the group with their suicide initiative. The other three got in touch with a person they knew as a militant group operative in their neighborhood or workplace. For reasons explained in the next chapter, the group's consent was usually delayed by days or weeks. The volunteers were often eager and kept pressing to be sent immediately on their mission. Samir described his recruitment:

"I spoke with someone from PIJ. I worked with his brother in the same clothing store. I kept begging him to let me do the operation, because he thought that I was not serious. When he was convinced that I was serious, he gave me the explosive charge and explained to me how to use it."

Typically, both the volunteers and those solicited for the task who had not been group members, were not particular about the organization they would soon serve. Hamed said: "I became a Hamas member by chance, because this group's representative came to me before Fatah representatives."

Four of those solicited had been affiliated with the organization before they were approached for the suicide mission, but three of them had not been involved in any resistance activity before consenting to carry out the suicide attack.

Three of the seven youngsters solicited by the organization agreed on the spot. Three of the other four thought it over for a week or two before they gave their consent, but the fourth candidate vacillated for four months. The recruiters did not usually try to convince the candidates to carry out a suicide operation. Yet sometimes they did exert pressure, as in the case of Salah, with whom the recruiting efforts amounted to an aggressive sales campaign. The process started when a neighbor of Salah, a Fatah al-Aqsa Martyrs Brigades operative, suggested to Salah that he join the group. Salah agreed, and from then on the recruiter met with him daily for an evening walk, during which the operative frequently talked about suicide attacks against Israel. Later, the operative arranged a meeting between Salah and a senior commander in the organization, who asked him whether he would agree to carry out an operation inside Israel. Salah agreed, but said that he had no experience in using firearms. The commander then suggested carrying out a suicide attack. Salah refused, saying that he did not want to die. After the meeting, the recruiter told him that if he would carry out a suicide attack, the group would give his family $25,000. Salah said he would consider the offer, but the recruiter interpreted his response as consent. A few days later, he told Salah that the organization wanted to launch the operation. Although Salah answered he was not ready yet, he was invited to meet with several operatives who asked him again to carry out a suicide attack. He said he agreed in principle, but was not yet ready to do it. Several more meetings took place before Salah said that he was ready. By his account, he finally decided to undertake the mission after sitting alone in the mosque, meditating, and reading Quranic verses on martyrdom. Not surprisingly, in the psychological tests, Salah was assessed as having a dependent personality. His case demonstrates how a person essentially reluctant to carry a suicide action agreed nevertheless because he found it hard to turn down the requests of those whom he perceived as authority figures. He enjoyed and was flattered by his relationship with the recruiter and felt obligated to comply with his wishes.

Some of those who agreed to carry out a suicide attack were initially reluctant but found it hard to refuse, as they felt that turning down the request would mark them as cowards or at least as unpatriotic. Majed was an 18-year-old youngster of a well-to-do family in a West Bank town. His father was a partner in a small family-owned bus company. Majed described his family as religious but not fanatic. None of the immediate family members was involved in militant activity. He was a good student in high school and after graduating, he decided on academic studies in electronics abroad. While in the process of preparing the paperwork for traveling, he was approached by A.B.—a commander of Izz ad-Din al-Qassam (Hamas' military arm) in his town, whom he knew slightly—who asked him to join the organization and carry out a suicide attack. In the interview, Majed said that he had not liked the idea, but did not know how to say no. "I was confused because of our previous acquaintance and I did not know how to avoid him. I was stressed and thought a lot about how to refuse his request." He therefore agreed, hoping that the suicide mission would not be implemented before he would leave town to study abroad and be off the hook. A.B., however, moved fast. Two weeks later, he sent Majed on a reconnaissance trip on the road to Jerusalem, where his eventual suicide attack was supposed to take place. A few days later, another member of the cell carried out a suicide attack in Jerusalem. Majed was told that he would be next in line. He was videotaped reading his will (prepared by A.B.) and was told that he would be dispatched for his suicide attack within two days, but he was arrested on the next day.

Majed was diagnosed as dependent-avoidant. Characteristically for this personality type, he found it so difficult to refuse requests of authority figures out of fear of losing their approval, that he was willing to accept a mission he both feared and abhorred. For the youth of his town, A.B., the recruiter, was a revered figure, admired for his boldness in challenging the Israeli army. Given Majed's personality characteristics, he found it very hard to reject the recruiter's demand.

In response to the question, "What was your feeling after you made the decision to undertake the operation?" five would-be suicides described their mood as "elated" or "ecstatic," and three as "determined." Not surprisingly, six of these eight volunteered on their own initiative. Two volunteers, however, said they had felt fear and confusion. Why, then, did they offer themselves as suicides nonetheless? Presumably, these socially marginal youngsters, carrying a sense of failure and disappointment to their families, felt that volunteering for a mission considered by their community the utmost form of heroism would at once raise their social status (as well as their self image). Only one of those solicited into the mission by a group's recruiter described his feeling after the decision as "elated"; another described his mood as "indifferent"; and a third reported detachment, "as if it was not happening to me." However, most of those recruited by the organization (five out of eight) described feelings of fear, confusion, stress, and hesitation.

## Motivation

Several questions in the interviews addressed the motivation to carry out a suicide attack. The participants were asked what were their own motives for undertaking the mission, and what, in their view, were those of other Palestinians who had carried out suicide attacks. Following an open-ended question on the motivation for suicide attacks, they were asked to assess the influence of several possible motives including the occupation, revenge for personal loss or suffering, religious belief, the wish to go to paradise, economic benefits to the family, and mental condition (being tired of life). Regarding other suicides' motives, some participants said that everyone has his own reasons for agreeing to carry out a suicide mission; most, however, attributed their own motives to others as well. Table 5.3 summarizes the suicides' descriptions of their own motives.

All participants mentioned more than one motive, indicating that the decision to undertake a suicide mission is a result of accumulation and/or interaction of several factors. Still, a dominant, more emphatically expressed motive that overshadowed the others could be discerned in the answers of most would-be suicides.

**Table 5.3** The Would-Be Suicides' Self-Described Motives

| Motives | Very high | High | Low | Very low |
|---|---|---|---|---|
| Nationalistic (occupation) | 9 | 2 | | 1 |
| Personal revenge | 5 | 2 | 2 | 3 |
| Religious | 5 | 1 | 1 | 2 |
| Paradise | 7 | 2 | | 2 |
| Economic gain for family | 3 | | | 5 |
| Glory/fame | 1 | | | 1 |
| Previous *shahids* | 4 | | 3 | 2 |
| Mental condition (wish to die) | 4 | | | |

THE NATIONALISTIC MOTIVE   The term "nationalistic motive" is used here to denote an amalgam of sentiments expressed by the suicides, with emphasis on general resentment of the occupation and often underscoring its specific manifestations. The nationalistic motive was often expressed in terms of the wish to take revenge for the suffering of Palestinians in general (to be distinguished from personal suffering). Yet most examples the respondents gave were related to conditions and events during the second intifada rather than to the basic situation of being under occupation. The importance of the intifada circumstances was clearly expressed by Nimer, who had worked in Israel before the intifada. Asked whether he would be willing to carry out a suicide attack in the places where he worked, he said:

> Before the intifada I would not do it, but during the intifada I would, because before the intifada there were no killings and bombings and there were work opportunities—that is, life was normal. But after the intifada started, conditions changed: the killings, the economic situation, people having no income.

In describing the sources of their motivation, most respondents voiced anger about the destruction, economic hardships, and humiliation at roadblocks. Yet their strongest emotions concerned the killing of civilians, which they had seen on television. Several respondents said that their decision to carry out the suicide attack was prompted by televised images of killed children, which they believed Israel did intentionally. This distorted perception was promoted by heated Palestinian media and official propaganda. In shaping the would-be suicides' mindset and emotions, objective facts did not matter; what mattered was what the prospective suicides believed (Palestinian public attitudes will be discussed in Chapter 7).

Asked, "What made you undertake the [suicide] operation?," Ramzi gave a typical answer:

> The main reason for me—I saw on television how a mother and her four children were killed in Ramallah by the Israelis. They were killed and their bodies were shattered to pieces, and they were killed as they were walking harmlessly on the road. After that I attended a funeral of a *shahid* I did not know (everybody goes to *shahids'* funerals because in Islam you are blessed if you do). During the funeral, a man talked to me. He asked me if I was willing to do a martyrdom operation. I was very angry about the woman and her children and also about the *shahid* whose funeral I was attending, so I agreed to do the operation.

In several cases, the decision was prompted by a specific event the would-be suicide had witnessed. For example, Jamal said that the main reason for his decision was the intifada in general and particularly the April 2002 battle in Jenin's refugee camp. As his village was close to the camp, he was able to see the fighting and destruction.[4]

PERSONAL REVENGE   A cursory examination of the would-be suicides' background hardly revealed any reason for personal revenge. Only one had served time in an Israeli jail before his suicide mission, only one was wounded, and none complained of having been beaten in clashes with Israeli forces. None lost a parent or sibling, although five reported that a second-degree relative had been killed (two uncles, two cousins, and one brother-in-law). While three had brothers in an Israeli jail, this is a dubious reason for taking revenge by committing suicide, and none of the would-be suicides presented it as such. Ten of the would-be suicides had friends or acquaintances who had been killed—four of them had friends or acquaintances who had committed a suicide attack—but acquaintance with fallen youngsters was probably not exceptional during the second intifada.

Still, several would-be suicides indicated personal revenge was important in their willingness to carry out the mission. Most of these listed it as one of several other motives, and one would-be suicide described it as the only reason. Nabil said that before the intifada, he had worked in Israel and saved money. He had planned to get married, build a home, and raise children. When the intifada broke out and the Israeli authorities applied more stringent criteria in allowing Palestinians to enter into Israel, he was detained and interrogated. As he had no work permit in Israel, he was told that he had to go back to the West Bank unless he agreed to cooperate with the Israeli secret service as an informer. He refused and felt deeply insulted by this episode. His hatred and wish to take revenge grew further when his cousin, a Hamas operative, was killed by Israeli forces. He saw his cousin's body in the hospital and wept. This event, he said, was the immediate reason for his consent to die by killing Israelis. His cousin's funeral—a very emotional event with the features of mass hysteria—was attended by many people, and he, like the other mourners, felt intense rage. During the funeral, he was approached by a Hamas operative, who suggested avenging his cousin's death by carrying out a suicide attack. Nabil agreed. "The wish to take revenge grew stronger in me. I felt that my world was ruined. My only motive was revenge, not money or religious gain for my family" (presumably the *shahid's* privilege of being an advocate for his family on the Day of Judgment).

Nabil's somewhat simplistic account of the reasons for his willingness to carry out a suicide attack does not reveal the gamut of his motives. Personality factors certainly played an important role in his decision: a normal person does not commit murderous suicide because he was not allowed to work in a certain place. No doubt, the atmosphere in the Palestinian community at the time of the intifada, which fueled vengefulness and hatred toward Israel, and viewed "martyrs" as the utmost heroic patriots, also profoundly affected his decision. Yet what mattered in Nabil's case was his perception of his personal grudge as the most influential factor in his decision.

Another case of personal revenge was Nimer. He was very close to his uncle, who had been arrested and beaten during the first intifada. After his release from prison the uncle fell ill with cancer, which Nimer attributed to the beatings by the Israelis. "This uncle was very dear to me, almost like my father." During the second intifada, one of his brother-in-law's brothers was killed by Israeli forces and two others were arrested. His account suggested a post-traumatic state:

"The death of my brother-in-law's brother brought it all back to me—my uncle's death, the sights I saw on television—and I began thinking of doing something in revenge and joining them in paradise . . . my brother-in-law's brother was killed in Nablus by a missile and I went there and saw his body burned and covered with stones. Of course I attended his funeral and got very emotional there. It can happen to anyone."

Asked, "How did you make your decision to commit *istishhad*?" he said:

"Actually I did not decide to be a *shahid*, but to take revenge. When I decided to take revenge, I did not know how [to do it]. When I met the person [the PIJ operative] I did not tell him that I wanted to do a martyr-dom operation. Rather, I told him that I wanted to do a revenge operation. He suggested that I would do a martyrdom operation and I said, 'O.K.' Even after I agreed, I did not understand the meaning of it. I thought that it might be planting a bomb or a shooting attack."

Personal revenge was also an important contributing factor in the case of Ali. By his account, as a teenager during the first intifada, he was involved in stone throwing and similar activities against Israeli forces. He described himself as an unruly child whose parents worried about his behavior and therefore sent him to live with his uncle to remove him from the bad influ-ence of the neighborhood kids. He later calmed down, worked regularly, and led a relatively quiet life. At the age of 18, however, when he was on his way to work and found himself trapped in the midst of Palestinian youngsters who attacked an IDF patrol, he was shot and wounded by Israeli soldiers. He described this incident as a turning point that honed his political awareness and inflamed his hatred toward the occupation. After his recovery, he joined Fatah, participated in several attacks, and several months later volunteered to carry out a suicide attack. He indicated that his determination increased further after his brother-in-law had carried out a suicide attack.

Another case in which personal bitterness became an important factor was that of Murad, who suffered from degenerating vision. He had served time in Palestinian and Israeli prisons for Hamas membership and activity, and his eye condition worsened, albeit it had not started in prison. He attributed his deteriorating eyesight to neglect by the prison authorities and was very bitter about it. He felt he would rather die than live as a handicapped man, and the option of dying while taking revenge on the Israelis appealed to him. His recruiter, who had known him from prison where they had spent time together, was aware of his grudge, and many of their conversations at the time of recruitment revolved around Murad's vision problem.

RELIGION AND PARADISE    Palestinians are generally religious. Most pray daily—often all five required prayers—and attend the mosques frequently. One survey (Heiberg & Ovensen, 1994) found that 80% of Palestinian males were religiously observant and 24% were classified as "religiously activist." As noted above, all the would-be suicides defined themselves as "religious" or "very religious." However, only six said that religious motivation (in the sense of fulfilling an Islamic duty or fighting a religious war against the Jews) had figured "very high" or "high" in their decision to carry out the attack. More-over, unlike the nationalistic motivation, which the participants usually expressed very emphatically, the religious motivation was not mentioned spontaneously, and those who rated it high did so only in a confirming response to the interviewer's specific question: "Yes, that too." Interestingly, none of the would-be suicides sent by Hamas attributed great importance to religion, whereas 50% of those sent by PIJ and 75% of those sent by Fatah did. This further attests to the relative unimportance of religion in the suicides' motivation: one would expect that those affiliated with Hamas, a group that has presented the struggle in both religious and nationalistic terms, advocating suicide operations as a religious duty, would attribute a far greater importance to religion as a driving force in their decision. The fact that Hamas and PIJ suicides attributed less importance to religious motivation than Fatah members also suggests that recruitment by a specific group was arbitrary, as the religious groups did not employ religious faith and devotion as selection criteria.

All suicides, with no exception, claimed they believed in paradise. Asked what they expected would happen to them after their death in the operation, some offered quite concrete and simplistic "textbook" descriptions, although each stressed somewhat different parts of the Islamic tradition. Ramzi, for example, said: "My soul would leave my body and go to Allah. I would marry 72 virgins in paradise and live there in a big house. On the day of resurrection of the dead, I would be able to ask Allah to forgive 70 of my family members, especially those who were not religious." Samir answered: "I expected to be in paradise and do there whatever I like, to be close to Allah and do everything one can do there. When you get to paradise, your potency grows 72-fold to allow you to handle the 72 virgins who are waiting for you." Salah's answer, however, implied concern about his body's condition after his death:

> I would get to paradise and my body would remain intact despite the explosion. I heard from clerics that *shahids'* corpses remain intact in the grave . . . the body of an *istishhadi* [suicide] who was killed in 1997 in Afula was shown on the Internet. It hadn't changed.

Despite their firm belief in paradise, most would-be suicides did not mention the desire to get there as the reason for wanting to carry out the attack. Nabil expressed it clearly: "I expected to be in paradise and that's it. In paradise there would be the palaces, virgins, etc. But this was not my goal. What I wanted was revenge." For most would-be suicides, paradise was a strong ancillary factor, but only for a few the primary motivation.

While "paradise now" was not the drive for carrying out the mission, getting there was a very nice fringe benefit of the "martyrdom operation." In fact, only one participant, Hamed, said that his main motivation for undertaking the operation was his wish to go to paradise and marry the 72 virgins (and he also regretted that, the mission having failed, he would have to marry only one wife). Ali expressed a more typical approach: "By *istishhad* one gains twice: killing one's enemies and going to paradise." For Samir, paradise was a facilitating element that mitigated his worries about his family and justified the suffering his action would cause them:

"I had no hesitation about my decision to carry out the martyrdom operation. Although I love my parents and I knew they would miss me, I also knew I would meet them in paradise, because I firmly believe we shall all meet there."

Interestingly, not all were certain about their place in paradise as *shahids*. Murad, a Hamas member, had doubts: "Actually I don't know whether the *shahids* are in paradise. I don't know. They are in heaven, but I don't know whether they are in fact in paradise." Skepticism was also expressed by Jamal who, when asked "What did you think would happen to you after your death?" answered: "God knows. It's in the hands of Allah. If I go to paradise or not—this is in the hands of God. It's unclear to me whether I would be accepted as a *shahid* or not."

For at least three participants, Zueir, Walid, and Ali, paradise was no factor at all. They said that they would have done the mission even if they had known that they would end up in hell. To the question "What did you expect would happen to you after death?" Zuheir answered: "I didn't expect anything after death. I wanted to get rid of my life in this world. That's it!" Walid gave a very similar answer: "I didn't expect anything after death." Both Walid and Zuheir were diagnosed as suicidal. Their primary motive was to stop the pain life was causing them rather than to reach a desirable place or serve a political purpose. In this sense, they fit classical descriptions of mental pain as the reason for ordinary suicide (Shneidman, 1989; Bongar, 2002).

SUICIDALITY    Walid and Zuheir are examples of the few cases in which the main motive to become a *shahid* was the wish to die for personal reasons. Like Judaism and Christianity, Islam forbids suicide. By common tradition, people who commit "ordinary" suicide (*intikhar* in Arabic) go to hell, where they are doomed to repeat forever the acts by which they took their lives (Rosenthal, 1946). Although statistics on suicide rates in Muslim countries are lacking,

existing data suggest very low rates, especially in Arab countries (World Health Organization, 2003). Still, in Muslim societies there are people who, for personal reasons, would rather die than live. For a suicidal Palestinian youngster, carrying out a suicide attack and becoming a *shahid* would clearly be a better way of taking his life than merely committing suicide. Thus, in some cases the sending group serves as an improved version of Robert Louis Stevenson's "suicide club." The advantage of martyrdom over ordinary suicide lies not only in the community's approval, but also in the suicide's ability to justify his act to himself—he believes that dying as a martyr will get him to paradise, whereas by simply killing himself, he will end up in hell.

As noted above, clinical interviews and psychological tests revealed that six would-be suicides had suicidal tendencies. In some cases, the tests were even hardly necessary for detecting the suicidal propensity, because the participants expressed and explained their wish to die quite openly in the interviews. The following two biographical accounts provide vivid examples of this type of would-be suicide.

Walid, the seventh child of 10 in a poor family who lived in a West Bank village, was 19 years old when he volunteered for the suicide operation. His father was a construction worker and his mother a housewife—both simple people with only elementary education. Since early childhood, he had been treated very harshly by his father. His first memory was being hit hard by his father when he was less than three years old because he was afraid to go near the sheep the family kept in their yard. His father's heavy-handed rearing practice continued throughout his childhood and adolescence. In the interviews, he said several times that since early childhood he had wanted to die because of his father's mistreatment. Presumably, he also suffered from sexual abuse, because he said that there were also "very personal and private reasons" for his wish to die, which he would never be able to tell anybody. He did not do well in school and described himself as a fairly secluded boy. He said that although he had often wanted to commit suicide, he had not done it because suicide is forbidden in Islam. He explained his volunteering for a suicide attack by his wish to die because of his "troubles" with his father, who had made his life intolerable, but also because of the economic situation and his feeling that death had become a common phenomenon during the intifada. He said he had attended the funerals of *shahids* in his village, but did not feel sorrow about their death. Rather, he eagerly waited for his turn and felt as though he wanted to speed up his death by volunteering for a suicide mission. In explaining his motivation, he said: "I wanted to end my life and rest." He did not have fantasies about

paradise and virgins, but as a Muslim believer he accepted his religion's version.

Zuheir's autobiographical monologue speaks for itself:

Until my arrest at the age of 15, I lived with my family and my life came down to walking from home to school and back home, and this is the whole story of my life . . . As a teenager, my eyes opened up and I saw how my friends were going on trips, to the swimming pool, and having a good time in cafés. I wanted very much to be like them, but these pleasures were absolutely forbidden to me. At home I was obliterated. I had no say. My father forbade me to do these things because he was afraid I would drift, especially that I would join one of the organizations. He wanted me just to study, study, and study. He forbade me to play and didn't allow me to play computer games or to go out with friends. In school, I had good relations, especially with the teachers, because I was a good student and my grade average was 94%. True, my father provided me with food and clothing, but he didn't give me any spending money so I wouldn't hang out in the streets. The truth is that my relationship with my parents was very bad. Both my father and my mother hurt me. They used to beat me hard, with the broomstick too, and insulted me with harsh words. I envied my friends who had nice clothes and went around with money in their pockets, which they earned during the summer vacation. My parents forced me to wear clothes I didn't like and didn't let me leave the house except for school. All in all, my life was very, very, very miserable. My parents hit me almost daily, every time they thought I misbehaved. They claimed people told them that I behaved badly outside home. I didn't know who told them such things and my parents used to beat me also without any reasons [crying]. My pleadings didn't change their humiliating attitude. This was my life and I reached such a state of despair that I wanted to kill myself. I used to stand in front of Israeli tanks, hoping they would shoot me. I tried it more than once, but it didn't work. I didn't know anymore what to do. I developed a mental complex from thinking a lot whether to commit suicide or not. Then I met people who offered me the chance to carry out an act of *istishhad* [martyrdom]. I had been thinking for a long time about an opportunity to die, and when these men showed up, I said to myself that this was a good opportunity to enjoy a few days with the money they gave me, buy nice clothes, and have a short haircut as I liked before I die and rest from my life [crying again]. Actually, I needed someone who would stand by me and defend me. I simply needed someone who would say to me: 'good morning' and 'have a good sleep,' and would ask me: 'How do you feel?' And 'do you need anything?' I thought hard and decided to accept their offer to carry out an act of *istishhad* not because I belonged to the organization but to realize my wish to die. I therefore agreed, and what happened, happened, and I ended up in jail. The truth is that I like my life in prison much better than my life with my parents. The end of my prison term is approaching and I hope that my relationship with my parents will improve and that they will treat me with respect. If not, I shall run away from home and live on the street or I shall do anything to end my life. I am a person who was deprived of parental love. I don't know anymore what to do. I am a deserted and lonely person. I have no friends and nobody to whom I can open my heart. This is the story of my life. Help me if you can.

Personal motivation was also reflected in the respondents' view of other suicide bombers' motivation. Thus, asked about his view of the others' motivation, Walid said: "The *istishhadi* [martyr] is not going to paradise to marry 72 virgins. The idea is that he is going to die and get rid of his life."

In the case of Walid, as in several others, suicidality was the single most important factor in the decision to volunteer for the suicide attack, but it matured to a suicidal act in interaction with factors related to the political circumstances and social atmosphere. A "martyr's" death not only provided Walid with the legitimacy to carry out an otherwise forbidden act, but was also encouraged by his society. Paradoxically, for at least some of the suicide bombers, the definition of suicide terrorism should be reversed; instead of "killing oneself for killing others," it should read "killing others for killing oneself."

ECONOMIC REWARD    Much has been written about the monetary rewards that suicides' families have received after their sons' deaths and their possible influence on youngsters' willingness to volunteer for suicide missions. Families received money from several sources, including the militant groups, the Palestinian Authority, and charities. Before his fall, Iraq's Sadam Hussein gave $20,000–$25,000 to suicide bombers' families. One might think, then, that this financial aid would spur Palestinian youth to become suicide bombers (Krueger & Maleckova, 2002, Ricolfi, 2005, p. 113).

The great majority of the would-be suicides denied that their willingness to carry out a suicide attack was partly motivated by a promised economic reward to their families. Three, however, said that the hope for economic improvement in their family's condition was a "very high" factor in their decision, and two said that they would have handed themselves in to the Israeli authorities for a sizable monetary reward and the promise of amnesty. Walid, for example, when asked about motivation, said: "Most important is money." He, too, said he thought his family's economic condition would improve after his suicide attack: "They would be angry with me for a while, but later they would accept it and enjoy the money." As noted above, one would-be suicide (Salah) only agreed to carry out the suicide mission after he was promised that the organization would pay his family $25,000 after his death.

## Preparations

After recruitment, preparations for the mission were surprisingly brief, usually involving two or three meetings of the candidate with group operatives in charge of organizing the mission. In most cases, the time from recruitment to dispatching the would-be suicide to the target was quite short: 40 days on average. In five cases, the candidate was sent within a week and in four others in less than a month. Although comparable precise data on suicides before the second intifada are unavailable, in the pre-intifada period the preparation process was apparently longer. Preparation time was curtailed, as a longer process increased the risk of detection by Israeli intelligence and pep talks may have been superfluous in the prevailing atmosphere in the Palestinian community during the second intifada. The media and sermons at mosques and funerals provided sufficient motivation and legitimacy. Under these circumstances, the would-be suicides rightly took the religious authorities' and public support of their intended action for granted. Eleven participants (73%) said they would not have agreed to undertake the mission had they known that religious authorities were against it, and 80% said they would not have done it against the wish of the Palestinian public.

With the exception of one candidate, coaxed for a long time by his recruiter into undertaking a suicide mission, the would-be suicides did not undergo any mental preparations or ideological indoctrination by the organizers. Preparations addressed merely the operational aspects of the mission, i.e., behavior on the way to the target, selecting the target, and activation of the explosive charge. In all cases, these meetings (as well as those during the recruiting process) were conducted by the group's military operatives rather than by religious or political figures. In one case, however, the candidate sought the opinion of a cleric with whom he had studied in the past.

Operational instructions were no less general. There were no rehearsals, and no detailed information was provided on the intended targets.

Except a few cases, no precise targets were specified, and the would-be suicide was simply told to explode on a bus packed with passengers or in a crowded place. Instructions concerning behavior on the way to the target and at the site of attack were also general. In one of the two cases where two suicides were to carry out a joint attack, the two candidates did not know each other. They first met on the day before the operation and were instructed on the activation of the explosive belts. They were told to explode consecutively, but the organizer left it up to them to decide who would explode first and what the time interval between them would be. As in most other cases, the precise site was left to their discretion. In the other planned double suicide attack, the candidates knew each other before the operation and received equally nebulous instructions.

In more than two thirds of the cases, the brief preparation culminated in a videotape of the candidate reading a last statement, an event meant to confirm the candidate's determination to execute his mission and to mark his departure from life. The videotape was almost always made in the last 24 hours before the operation but, in a few cases, two or three days earlier. Although the videotaping was meant to be a ceremonial event, it was always done in shabby surroundings—usually in the home of one of the organization's operatives involved in the preparations—and conveyed improvisation and haste. The candidate was given a weapon (usually a rifle) to hold in one hand and a Quran in the other, and read a brief statement as he was being filmed by one of the group's operatives. In all but one case, the statement had been written by the organizers, although in a couple of cases the candidate added a few words of his own. The fact that the candidates' last testaments were not their own creation suggests that they were unsophisticated youngsters with a rather limited ability to articulate an ideological message, but also that they did not feel a strong urge to say something to the world they were about to leave forever.

It is indeed interesting that only one of the would-be suicides left a letter for his family, and only four said farewell in some way—one of them left a photograph of himself for his mother, and gave his belongings to his brothers—although all stayed at home before going on their suicide mission. Hamed offered a typical description of the last day before the operation:

> I was videotaped reading my testament. A.H. [the organizer] wrote it. I held a Quran in one hand and a Kalashnikov [in the other hand] and presented myself as someone about to do a martyrdom operation. I didn't write letters to anyone. No one of my family knew about it. I didn't write

about leaving my belongings to anyone. I had no debts to return. I didn't say farewell to anyone. There was no special event or prayer to mark it, just the videotaping.

## Feelings on the Day of Operation

Those would-be suicides who were truly determined to carry out the operation reported joy and elation. Samir described his feelings as follows: "On the day of the operation, I felt great joy. I had no thoughts of regret and was completely content with my decision. I was happy because I knew that if the operation succeeded, I would go to paradise."

Ten of the 15 would-be suicides (66.7%), however, expressed conflict and distress. They attributed their hesitation to fear of death and concern about their families. For example, Hamed said:

On the day of the operation, I felt longing for my family. I was sad, because I knew that I was leaving them, even though I hadn't told them anything because I knew they would object to my *istishhad* [martyrdom]. Nevertheless, I decided to carry out the operation and didn't let my feelings interfere with it.

Nabil, who had actually tried to activate the charge, offered the following description:

I felt fear and worry. It's not easy to commit suicide. It was something strange to me, I couldn't imagine myself doing this operation. I hadn't thought of it before. I was very worried that my family would suffer, in the sense that they would feel they lost me and would be sad because I left them. My family wanted to see me married and raising children.

Jamal expressed similar sentiments:

When the matter reached a practical stage, I got frightened. Man is weak. I started thinking of my parents and family—there was also the threat of demolition of [*shahids'*] homes; I didn't want my family to suffer as a result of my action. I didn't think of a heavenly reward that God would give me and my family following the operation.

Three of those who reported hesitation were assessed as suicidal. In itself, suicidality is obviously no guarantee for determination to commit the action. Suicides have second thoughts, and suicidality is not an absolute decision to die. Estimates of the ratio of attempted to completed "ordinary" suicides range between 18:1 and 5:1 (Bongar, 2002, p. 22), and the ratio of those who have entertained suicidal ideas to completed suicides is certainly much higher. ·

For the would-be suicides, the expected family response was by far more important than their friends' responses. Almost all were certain that their families would grieve after their death, with differences only in the assessment of the grief's intensity and its duration. All were also sure that their families would have tried to prevent them from undertaking the suicide mission had they found out about their intention. Indeed, this was the standard reason they gave for not disclosing their plans to their families. The findings of the families' study (Chapter 4) confirm this assessment. Jamal said: "I thought that they [his family] would be sad. How could they be happy?! Their condition couldn't get better [after my death]. Mentally and economically, it's not easy when a family member dies."

## *Growing Fear on the Way to the Target*

Participants' accounts showed clearly that fear and hesitation climaxed after the candidate was dispatched, when he was already on his way to the target. Rafik described the progressive change in his feelings as follows:

Q: What did you feel on the day of execution?
A: Initially, very strong determination. But halfway, my nerves grew weaker. My thoughts started going astray.

Q: What did you think would happen?
A: I thought of many things. My family, friends. When you hesitate, Satan is at work, and if you succeed in overcoming Satan and continue the operation, you'll be received [admitted] by God.

Q: Do you mean Satan got in?
A: Satan got in and didn't get out. I hesitated at the last moment.

Q: So you're saying that you did have the intention?
A: I had the intention but there was fear, Satan, and I didn't have enough time to prepare myself, only a month, whereas a *shahid* needs at least two or three months to prepare himself.

Q: What happened that made you change your mind?
A: On that day I was in shock and decided to go back. I was caught on the way back.

It should be noted that Rafik volunteered to carry out a suicide attack on his own initiative, insisted that his intention was firm, and kept pressing his superior in the group to be sent on the mission. As time went by and he was not sent, he threatened to contact another group if the organization did not send him soon.

Rafik's operation was planned as a double suicide attack. His partner in the mission, Ali, described a similarly progressive fear on the way to the target. He too had volunteered on his own initiative and said he had felt determined throughout the preparations. "Even in the morning of the operation, I was very brave in my mind." But he started hesitating "from the minute I put on the explosive belt . . ... I thought how frightening the belt was, that I was going to explode into pieces. I was thinking of my family and friends, *but the situation was stronger than me*" (emphasis added). This feeling of commitment—"the situation"—kept him going for a while, but "the more I kept going, the more I hesitated."

Ramzi also said he had started hesitating on the way to the target, when he reached the Israeli border. He remembered his mother (his father had died when he was four years old) and thought how she would grieve if he died. Furthermore, he was troubled by the thought that his family's home might be demolished in retaliation for his operation. He decided to abort the mission when he and his guide, who was to get him to the target, arrived at an Israeli Arab village on the border. There they looked for a taxi to take them to Tel Aviv, where the attack was supposed to take place, but they couldn't find any and had to wait. It was at that point that Ramzi decided to return home. He needed this breathing spell, this lapse in the pace of events, to start rowing against the strong current that had been carrying him since his initial consent to become a *shahid*. Had he and his guide immediately found a taxi to take them to Tel Aviv, Ramzi might have continued on his deadly mission to the very end.

Another interesting interruption in the process, which resulted in the candidates' decision to call off the mission, was told by Jamal, who was to carry out a double suicide attack in an Israeli city. A guide brought the two prospective attackers to a mosque in a West Bank Arab village bordering with Israel, where they were supposed to disguise themselves as Druze clerics, put on the explosive belts, and find a taxi to take them to their target. At the mosque, however, they were told that the Israeli army had imposed a curfew and they had better hide as long as it lasted. While waiting in the mosque, they started talking to each other and decided to abort the mission. Jamal described the change of heart as follows:

> Initially, before we set out, I thought of nothing except the operation itself, how I wanted to do it. I focused only on the way I was going to do it [and

thought of] nothing else. My partner and I didn't talk much to each other; we just got acquainted. In the village mosque, we started talking and reached the conclusion that we wanted to abandon the operation, mainly because of our fear and the concern about our families. I started thinking about my life and my future. We called N.J. [the Hamas organizer of the attack] and told him that we wanted to return. He asked us to go on, but I told him that we wanted to leave the mission altogether and he accepted our decision. The reason for our decision was that we got frightened at the execution phase. My fear got stronger and stronger. I was not 100 percent firm and convinced.

These self-descriptions tally very well with what we know about people's behavior in threatening and conflicted situations. Dollard and Miller's (1950) classical studies on behavior under conflict showed that when a certain goal is both attractive and frightening, the strength of both the drive to approach the target and the drive to run away from the target increase as a function of the target's proximity (approach gradient and avoidance gradient, respectively). However, the avoidance gradient is steeper than the approach drive. Hence, when the target is still far away, the drive to approach it exceeds the drive to avoid it, but as the target gets closer, the drive to run away surpasses the drive to approach. Yet an individual's actual behavior depends, of course, on the relative intensities of his drives to approach and avoid a certain target. An individual with a high enough approach drive and a low avoidance drive may reach the target, whereas an individual whose avoidance drive is from the start stronger than his approach drive may not make any move toward the target. The important point in suicides' behavior on the way to the target is that if they experience fear, it is likely to grow as an inverse function of the distance from the target, i.e., the closer the target, the greater the fear. Studies by Breznitz (1984) indicate the rate by which fear increases as the target is getting nearer. In a series of experiments in which participants were told that they would get an unavoidable painful electric shock, Breznitz measured the participants' fear by both their introspective reports and objective physiological measures (heart rate and Galvanic Skin Response). He found that when realization of the threat seemed imminent, fear grew at an exponential rate.

## Pretexts for Aborting the Mission

Hesitant suicides had to cope with a formidable dilemma. Their fear of death gathered momentum as they approached the target, yet aborting the mission would stain them as cowards in the eyes of their senders and friends and, equally important, in their own eyes. Finding an excuse for aborting the mission, as flimsy as it may be, was therefore an obvious solution. A couple of participants described this escape outlet frankly. Talal said he had felt confused and uncertain as soon as he had agreed to undertake the suicide mission and, as the operation approached, he was increasingly hesitant. The last night before the operation, he felt that his decision had been hasty and he made up his mind to abort it. He was willing to surrender to Israeli security forces on the way to the target, but was afraid the soldiers might shoot him. Contemplating an excuse for aborting the mission, he planned to hide the explosive charge, return home, and tell the organizer that the Jews suspected him so he had to get rid of the explosive belt.

Another case in point was Nimer, who was brought by a guide to the outskirts of an Israeli Arab village bordering with the West Bank and told to take a taxi by himself to a nearby Israeli city, where he was supposed to carry out his attack. He was equipped with an explosive belt and an assault rifle. In the interview, he said that as he had entered the Arab village, he thought people were looking at him suspiciously and he therefore decided to hide the explosive charge. At that time, his dispatcher called him on the cellular phone he was carrying and, having heard his story, told him that there was no going back. Shortly thereafter, when Nimer saw a police patrol approaching, he fired a couple of shots at the police car, but then his weapon jammed, he said. He tried to run away but was caught. Asked by the interviewer: "Could you have had second thoughts?" Nimer answered:

> Perhaps. I changed my mind. I said to myself that in the last three years I worked and helped my family and I also didn't say farewell to my family . . . I decided to shoot [instead of using the suicide belt] because there was a chance that I would survive. I told [the dispatcher] over the phone that I had been discovered, when in fact I regretted undertaking the mission.

Nimer seemed to have been torn between fear of dying and commitment to carry out a suicide attack. He solved his dilemma by taking the middle road: he made a token gesture of assault by firing a few shots at a police patrol, thus saving his self-respect and the respect of his organization and community.

Not always did growing fear exceed determination and commitment. Nabil said that on the day of the mission, before he set out on his way he felt great fear. But asked whether he considered aborting the mission, he answered: "On the day I agreed to carry out the operation, that was it.

There was no way back." Indeed, he had done everything he could to complete his mission. He was taken by a guide to Jerusalem and, on the way, listened to Quranic verses on his Walkman. In Jerusalem he boarded a bus packed with passengers and pressed the explosive belt's switch, but the charge failed to go off. He tried again and again, his behavior and expression eventually raising the suspicion of passengers, who also noticed electric wires protruding from his pocket. Some passengers tried to talk to him in Hebrew, which he did not understand. They alerted the driver, who drove the bus at high speed, continually honking the horn, to a nearby police roadblock, while passengers were trying unsuccessfully to remove Nabil's hand from his pocket and restrain him. At the roadblock, several police officers and soldiers boarded the bus and, after a long struggle, succeeded in subduing Nabil, who was fighting back, kicking and biting in frenzy. Asked in the interview to describe his feelings when he boarded the bus, Nabil answered: "A strange feeling. Fear. Not believing what was happening to me. I did not know whether I was pressing the switch or not. Even now I don't know whether I pressed it or not. I was dazed. It was like a trance." Nabil testified that he had been afraid from the moment of recruitment and throughout the preparation process. Yet his sense of commitment, after having consented, was stronger and kept him on track. Like the would-be suicides described above, and in line with the universal characteristics of human behavior under threat, his fear increased after he was dispatched for the attack and the frightening event grew nearer. He tried to cope with this conflict situation by distracting himself with Quranic recitations and shutting his mind off to disturbing thoughts. His description of his mental condition when he boarded the bus and his actual behavior suggest that the intense conflict and anxiety plunged him into a dissociative state, characterized, among other things, by amnesia.

MUTUAL INFLUENCE IN A JOINT SUICIDE MISSION  The use of multiple suicides in the same operation raises an interesting question. Most Palestinian suicide attacks have been carried out by single assailants: out of 185 attacks only 16 involved two or more suicide attackers. Worldwide, however, some of the most notorious attacks have been carried out by multiple suicides. These include the September 11, 2001 attacks in the United States, as well as other attacks by al-Qaeda-affiliated groups in Morocco, Turkey, Indonesia, and the United Kingdom. In Sri Lanka, the Tamil Tigers have often used multiple suicides, especially Sea Tigers' attacks on Sri Lankan Navy vessels. Chechen rebels have also used multiple assailants in a relatively high proportion of their suicide attacks. In the context of suicides' hesitation, the question arises how a joint attack affects the individual's determination. In the Palestinian sample of would-be suicides reported here, three participants were sent to carry out an attack with a partner and all decided to abort the mission. This finding is counterintuitive: a joint suicide mission is expected to create a mutual commitment that would bolster the determination of each partner. However, the partnership seemed to undermine the participants' determination. The direction of multiple team influence on individual members' determination presumably depends on several factors, including previous acquaintance, the nature of the team's interpersonal relations, and the determination of the dominant person in the team.

## Retrospective Attitude to the Failed Mission

Some would-be suicides did not express any regret for undertaking the mission, whereas others viewed it as a result of an impetuous decision. Yet none said that he would repeat his attempt if he could. They usually accepted the failure as proof that Allah did not want them to do it; that is, Allah's will justified their failure. This attitude fits dependent personality style and an external locus of control. Hamed, for example, said:

> I thought I would go to paradise and live there forever. It didn't happen and I went to prison, which for me is like hell. Still, in no way would I try again to carry out an operation. I'll go to paradise some other time. I don't want to try it again also because I think now of my family's sorrow had I died. Therefore, since I'm alive, I have to return to my family and live an ordinary life, without longing for paradise. From now on one woman, if I find one willing to marry me, will be enough for me. I have given up the other 71 girls I was supposed to meet in paradise.

Nabil, whose prime motive was revenge rather than paradise, viewed his suicide attempt as a grave mistake. "I would not repeat it. I feel I made a great mistake. I ruined my life with my own hands."

As might be expected, most suicidal participants did not express remorse for their attempted suicide attacks. Although none of them said he would repeat the attempt if he could, some viewed their future in rather uncertain terms. For example, Zuheir, who had suffered from parental abuse, said that he would like to continue his studies and work, "to experience life," but it all depended on his parents' attitude to him. The response implied that he might try suicide again if his parents' behavior did not change, although he did not say that he would make another attempt to carry out a suicide attack.

Although these responses may have been skewed by prison conditions and, especially, by the participants' wish to give the impression that they no longer present a danger and should therefore be considered for early release, they impressed the interviewers as a genuine reflection of the participants' feelings at the time.

## Definite vs. Uncertain Suicide Bombers

As explained above, the would-be suicides group included four participants who had tried to activate the explosive device and 11 others who had been caught on their way to the target and did not press the switch either because the charge was not within their reach, or because they chose not to set it off. While those who tried to activate the device may be rightfully considered genuine suicides, those who failed to do so might have ultimately decided to abort the mission and therefore should not be regarded as proper representatives of completed suicides. Furthermore, several would-be suicides who failed to activate the explosive device said in the interviews that they had wanted to abandon the mission. Although at least some of them might have completed the mission had the circumstances not provided them with an excuse to abort it, this eventuality is by no means certain. It is thus interesting to compare the characteristics of those who actually tried to activate the explosive device (definite suicides) with those who did not (uncertain suicides). This comparison is shown in Table 5.4.

Although the numbers of participants in both subgroups (and especially in the definite suicide subgroup) are too small to allow firm conclusions, several differences in characteristics are big enough to warrant attention.

Regarding demographic characteristics, the definite suicides were less educated (none completed high school, compared to 72.7% of the uncertain suicides); none lived in a refugee camp or was born to a refugee family, compared to 27.3% and 45.5.7%, respectively, of the uncertain suicides; and a much higher proportion were more religious than their families (75% compared to 18.2%).

Personality characteristics show interesting differences. All definite suicides were assessed as a dependent/avoidant personality, whereas only 54.5% of the uncertain suicides belonged to this category (36.4% were classified as impulsive/unstable and 9.1% as "unclear"). A lower proportion of the definite suicides (25%) were assessed as suicidal, compared to 45.5% of the uncertain subgroup.

**Table 5.4**   Comparison Between Would-Be Suicides Who Tried to Activate the Charge and Those Who Did Not

| Characteristics | Tried (N=4) | Did not try (N=11) |
|---|---|---|
| **Demographic** | | |
| *Age* | | |
| Mean | 19.25 | 19.47 |
| Range | 16–23 | 15–23 |
| *Education* | | |
| Partial elementary | 25% | 9.1% |
| Full elementary | 0 | 0 |
| Partial high school | 75% | 18.2% |
| Full high school | 0 | 63.6% |
| Partial university | 0 | 9.1% |
| *Family economic status* | | |
| Low | 0 | 27.3% |
| Middle | 100% | 54.5% |
| High | 0 | 18.2% |
| *Employment* | | |
| Blue Collar | 50% | 63.6% |
| Student | 50% | 27.3% |
| Unemployed | 0 | 9.1% |
| *Refugee camp dweller* | 0 | 27.3% |
| *Refugee family* | 0 | 45.5% |
| *Religiosity* | | |
| Very religious | 25% | 18.2% |
| Ordinary religious | 75% | 81.8% |
| Little religious | 0 | 0 |
| Not religious | 0 | 0 |
| *Religiosity compared to family* | | |
| More religious than family | 75% | 18.2% |
| Same as family | 25% | 72.7% |
| Less religious than family | 0 | 9.1% |
| **Psychological** | | |
| *Personality type* | | |
| Dependent/avoidant | 100% | 54.5% |
| Impulsive/unstable | 0 | 36.4% |
| Unclear | 0 | 9.1% |
| Suicidal | 25% | 45.5% |
| Depression/PTSD | 50% | 54.5% |

*(Continued)*

**Table 5.4** Comparison Between Would-Be Suicides Who Tried to Activate the Charge and Those Who Did Not (*Continued*)

| Characteristics | Tried (N=4) | Did not try (N=11) |
|---|---|---|
| *Mission related* | | |
| *Sending group* | | |
| Hamas | 50% | 27.3% |
| PIJ | 50% | 36.4% |
| Fatah | 0 | 36.4% |
| *Organization member* | 50% | 54.5% |
| *Previous resistance activity* | | |
| Violent armed | 25% | 27.3% |
| Violent unarmed | 0 | 18.2% |
| Non-violent | 0 | 9.1% |
| None | 75% | 45.5% |
| *Volunteered for the mission* | 75% | 45.5% |
| *Hesitated* | 50% | 72.7% |
| *Mean no. of days from recruiting to dispatching* | 24 | 50 |
| *Videotaping* | 75% | 70% |
| *Double attack* | 0 | 36.4% |
| *Escorted to the border* | 25% | 100% |
| *Escorted inside Israel* | 25% | 71.4% |

Other noteworthy findings are related to previous resistance activity and mission-related behavior. While 54.6% of the uncertain suicides were involved in some resistance activity prior to their suicide mission, three of the four definite suicides had no record of previous resistance activity. A larger proportion of the definite suicides volunteered for the mission on their own initiative (75% compared to 45.5%), and a smaller proportion of them reported hesitation (50% of the definite compared to 72.7% of the uncertain suicides). The definite suicides were dispatched for the suicide attack faster than the uncertain suicides (24 vs. 50 days on average, respectively). Surprisingly, a much higher proportion of the uncertain suicides were escorted on their way to the target. Assuming that the presence of escorts acted to augment the candidate's commitment, this finding may be interpreted as suggesting that, in most cases, the uncertain suicides' failure to complete the mission was facilitated by external circumstances beyond their control rather than by their overt change of mind. It is possible, of course, that a greater determination on their part would, at least in some of the cases, have resulted in their death.

## The Findings in Context

The above data on the would-be suicides' motives may confuse the reader, as no single across-the-board motive can account for all the participants' willingness to carry out a suicide attack. They claimed they had been motivated by several causes and exhibited variations in the blend of motives and the relative weight of each. For many, national revenge was the main factor; for some it was suicidality; still others mentioned personal revenge or money for their families. Important as these individual motives may have been in driving the candidates to their deadly mission, it is noteworthy that the great majority of the would-be suicides—with the only possible exception of one or two heavily suicidal participants—would not have assumed a self-destructive mission for the reasons they stated had it not been for the atmosphere in the Palestinian community at that time. The death of a beloved uncle, the wish to improve the family's economic situation, to gain a promised place in paradise, or to fight the occupation, would not prompt an ordinary youngster to take his life had public opinion not encouraged and glorified this act as the highest form of patriotism. Fighting the occupation or any other kind of perceived wrongs has motivated millions of people in all cultures to resort to violence, though not to commit suicide in the process. From the sending organization's point of view, the advantages of using suicide attacks are clear: in several ways, this is the most effective terrorist tactic. Individual fighters, however, normally prefer to stay alive and continue fighting rather than kill themselves for the cause. It was social encouragement of these particular acts—suicide attacks—that infused the stated motives with their power and legitimacy; without public support, they would probably have seemed bizarre to the suicides themselves.

Nevertheless, most Palestinian youth do not volunteer for suicide missions, although they experience the same conditions. All are exposed to the same television broadcasts and sermons, thousands have lost relatives, and most Palestinians believe that "martyrdom" guarantees a place in paradise. Community atmosphere and the motives expressed by the would-be suicides in the study are therefore effective only in interaction with certain personality characteristics described in the first part of this chapter. The clinical findings suggest that in most cases—those characterized as dependent-avoidant—the crucial personality element in this interaction is the youngster's vulnerability to external influence. For some suicides, however, the interaction of social encouragement and personality traits has a synergistic nature. This seems to apply to both the suicidal candidates and the impulsive-unstable participants. Yet whatever the nature of the interaction, neither of these two elements—public atmosphere and personality characteristics—is alone sufficient to create a suicide bomber.

*Endnotes*

1. To protect the privacy of the study's participants, I identify them by fictional names.
2. The Rorschach Inkblot Test, the Thematic Apperception Test (TAT), and the House–Tree–Person Drawing Test are widely used projective techniques designed to assess personality characteristics and detect psychopathology. The California Personality Inventory (CPI) is a self-reporting personality questionnaire.
3. In an interesting study, Benmelech and Berrebi (2007) compared the age and education of Palestinian suicide bombers who succeeded in completing their missions during the second intifada with those that failed. They found that whereas the mean age of 42 failed suicide bombers was 18.8, the mean age of 106 successful suicide bombers was 22.0. The average education level of successful suicide bombers was also significantly higher than that of failed bombers. It should be noted that these authors defined failed bombers quite broadly, to include those who "1) failed to detonate their explosive devices, 2) looked suspicious and were apprehended or killed by civilians, policemen, or soldiers, 3) panicked and blew themselves up before they reached the target, or 4) chickened out" (p. 234). See: Efraim Benmelech and Claude Berrebi (2007). "Human Capital and the Productivity of Suicide Bombers," *Journal of Economic Perspectives*, *21*,(3), 223–238.
4. In March 2002, Palestinian attacks reached a peak, resulting in the death of 135 Israelis. More than a dozen suicide attacks in Israeli cities took place that month, culminating in an attack in a hotel in Netanya, in which a suicide bomber killed 30 people, including children and old people, who were celebrating Passover. These attacks were organized by terrorist cells in the West Bank. In response, in early April, Israeli forces entered the West Bank in an effort to arrest or kill terrorist operatives. The fiercest battle was fought in Jenin's refugee camp, where Palestinian militants ambushed IDF forces and barricaded themselves in civilian homes. The Israeli forces refrained from using artillery, so as to minimize the number of civilian casualties, but used bulldozers to destroy houses in which Palestinians fired at them. In a battle that lasted several days, 23 Israeli soldiers and nearly 30 armed Palestinians were killed. Palestinian officials and media claimed that Israeli forces massacred many hundreds of civilians in the refugee camp (claims ranged from 500 to 3000 dead). However, a United Nations commission of inquiry determined that there had been no massacre. This commission estimated the number of Palestinians killed at 52, more than half of them armed fighters (United Nations, Report of the Secretary-General prepared pursuant to General Assembly resolution ES-10/10, 2002. Available at: http://www.un.org/peace/jenin/ (accessed: April 4, 2006.).

# 6

# Palestinian Organizers of Suicide Attacks: Psychological Characteristics and Decision Making

O NLY A FEW OF the 2,937 suicide bombers around the globe in the period of 1981–2008 were not sent by organized groups, and acted completely on their own. That is, individual initiative and execution of a suicide attack has been extremely rare. As Kramer (1991, p. 34) correctly observed, "while 'self-martyrs' sacrificed themselves, they were also sacrificed by others." The role of the group—and, specifically, of organizers of suicide attacks—is, therefore, crucial in understanding the making of a suicide bomber, and the organizers' personalities and decision making are central elements in terrorist suicide. This chapter presents a systematic study of Palestinian organizers of suicide attacks that was undertaken in 2005[1].

## Sample

The organizers selected for this study were senior regional commanders of Palestinian militant groups responsible for suicide attacks in Israel and the Occupied Territories, who are serving prison terms in Israel. Since several people were involved in the preparation of each and every suicide attack under discussion, the term "organizer" calls for clarification. As the study focused on the decisions involved in carrying out a suicide attack, and on the personalities of the men who made them, we sought out those who headed and supervised the process from the decision, through the preparations, to the suicide's dispatch to his mission. Usually, albeit not always, this person headed the military arm of the organization in the city or the region at that time (e.g., the Jenin or Tul Karem commander of PIJ or Hamas).

The participating organizers had been sentenced to long prison terms, ranging between 18 years and 35 cumulative life sentences. At the time of the interviews they had already been in prison for an average of 35.6 months (range: 9–118 months).

Compared to rank-and-file members of the groups, who had no reservations about participating in the interviews and undertaking psychological tests, the organizers were much more cautious. The first organizer refused to cooperate unless three other members of the prisoners' leadership, including their elected leader (*Emir*) agreed to join the discussion. He insisted that the decision about participating in the study had to be taken jointly by the four of them. I therefore summoned the other prisoners; three were Hamas commanders and the fourth was a Fatah organizer of suicide attacks, and also a member of Fatah prisoners' leadership. Together with Jonathan Fighel, a member of the research team, I explained to them the study's aims. I told them that the study was designed to investigate the personality characteristics, motivations, and decision-making of commanders and rank-and-file members of insurgent groups—especially, although not exclusively, those fighting for national liberation. I explained that we were particularly interested in what makes people sacrifice themselves for a cause, what motivates them to carry out suicide missions, and how they are selected and prepared for these missions. I also said that we were interested in their traits as leaders, their interaction with their subordinates, and the way they coped with problems they had to confront. I added that this was the first study of its kind, but I hoped that researchers in other countries would carry out similar studies, so as to discover to what extent there are similarities in personality characteristics of insurgent groups' leaders and members across different cultures and contexts. A discussion developed following my introduction. The three Hamas leaders (all of them had academic degrees) asked many questions about my credentials and background, who were the other researchers on the team, and about the nature and course of development of national liberation movements. One of the organizers asked to see a sample of my publications (which I delivered to him a few days later). After a couple of hours of lively discussion, the four leaders decided to cooperate with the research team. Their consent insured the cooperation of the other organizers on our list.

A hypothesis underlying the sample selection was that there might be systematic differences between the militant groups, and between various regions within the occupied territories, in attitudes toward suicide operations and the various aspects of preparing them. I surmised, furthermore,

**Table 6.1** Distribution of the Organizers' Sample by Group and Region

| | *Organization* | | | |
|---|---|---|---|---|
| *Region* | *Hamas* | *PIJ* | *Fatah* | *Total* |
| Samaria | 3 | 4 | 3 | 10 |
| Judea | 2 | 1 | 1 | 4 |
| Total | 5 | 5 | 4 | 14 |

that there may be a difference in these respects between the second intifada and the pre-intifada period. An attempt was therefore made to obtain representation of the three main Palestinian groups that launched suicide attacks (Hamas, PIJ, and Fatah) and within each group of the main regions of the territories—namely, Samaria and Judea (the northern and southern parts of the West Bank, respectively), and the Gaza Strip—as well as of organizers before and during the intifada. However, these requirements could be met only partially. Of the fourteen organizers who participated in the study, five were Hamas members, five PIJ, and four belonged to Fatah. Ten of the sample's organizers operated in Samaria, four in Judea, and none in the Gaza Strip. The pre-intifada period was represented by only one organizer, a Hamas member from Samaria. Table 6.1 summarizes the organizers' distribution.

Most participants had been involved in organizing several suicide attacks. The organizers' indictments and court verdicts provided detailed descriptions of their terrorist activity. On the basis of these data the total number of successful or attempted suicide attacks prepared by the organizers was calculated as 52, an average of 3.7 per organizer in the sample (range: 1–9). Table 6.2 shows the number of successful and failed suicide attacks organized by each participant.

As shown in Table 6.3, there were marked differences between the groups with regard to the mean number of total attacks (both successful and failed) per organizer, as well as in the mean ratio of successful vs. failed attacks.

The table shows that the average number of attacks carried out by a Hamas organizer was half that of a Fatah organizer and a little more than a third of a PIJ organizer. Interpretation of the rate of prepared suicide operations requires, however, consideration of the period for which the organizer was engaged in this activity. These data were found in the organizers' indictments, which listed their terrorist activity by date, allowing calculation of the time span between his first involvement in preparing a

**Table 6.2** Successful and Failed Suicide Attacks Organized by the Study's Participants

| Organizer | Organization | No. of successful suicide attacks | No. of failed suicide attacks |
|---|---|---|---|
| Amjad | Fatah | 1 | 6 |
| Taher | PIJ | 1 | 0 |
| Isma'il | PIJ | 3 | 4 |
| Fares | PIJ | 7 | 2 |
| Kamal | Fatah | 1 | 1 |
| Mustafa | Hamas | 1 | 1 |
| Ra'ed | Fatah | 2 | 0 |
| Amar | Hamas | 1 | 0 |
| Hassan | PIJ | 0 | 6 |
| Awad | PIJ | 0 | 3 |
| Atalla | Hamas | 2 | 0 |
| Na'if | Hamas | 2 | 0 |
| Yasser | Hamas | 2 | 1 |
| Azam | Fatah | 2 | 3 |
| Total | | 25 | 27 |

suicide attack and the day of his arrest. Indeed, Hamas organizers had spent, on the average, shorter periods in suicide bombing activity than their PIJ and Fatah counterparts, yet this specific difference does not account for the entire difference between the groups' rates of organizing suicide attacks. The mean number of attacks per organizer per month of activity (bottom row in the table) shows that, on average, Hamas organizers had indeed carried out suicide attacks at a slower pace (0.38 attacks per month compared to 0.58 and 0.50 for PIJ and Fatah, respectively). The slower pace was presumably a function of more meticulous preparation. This conjecture is supported by the fact that the ratio of successful to failed

**Table 6.3** Successful vs. Failed Suicide Attacks by Group

| Group | Hamas | PIJ | Fatah |
|---|---|---|---|
| Mean successful attacks per organizer | 1.6 | 2.2 | 1.5 |
| Mean failed attacks per organizer | 0.4 | 3.0 | 2.5 |
| Mean total attacks per organizer | 2.0 | 5.2 | 4.0 |
| Ratio of successful/failed attacks | 4.00 | 0.73 | 0.60 |
| Mean duration of activity per organizer (months) | 5.6 | 9.0 | 8.0 |
| Mean no. of attacks per organizer per month | 0.38 | 0.58 | 0.50 |

attacks for Hamas organizers was more than five times higher than for PIJ, and more than six times higher than for Fatah.

## Interviews and Tests

With the exception of one PIJ member, all organizers who had been asked to participate in the study agreed. They were interviewed in prison individually and subjected to the same psychological interviews and tests and diagnostic process as the would-be suicides (Chapter 5). An additional interview was designed to learn about the organizers' decisions on the preparations for and management of suicide attacks, and the factors that affected them. These interviews were also conducted individually and in Arabic. Each participant was interviewed by one of four specialists on Palestinian affairs, who were well acquainted with Palestinian society and the militant groups.

## Demographic and Psychological Characteristics

The average age of the organizers at the time of arrest was 27.6 years (range: 21–36). It differed somewhat across groups, but the range within each group was rather wide. The mean age of Fatah organizers was 25.2 (range: 21–31), for Hamas 27.2 (range: 22–36), and for PIJ 29.0 (range: 21–35). Half of the organizers were single. Of the seven who were married, six had children (1–3). Three organizers (21.4%) had partial high school education, five (35.7%) had graduated from high school, three (21.4%) had partial university education, and three (21.4%) had a university degree. However, there were conspicuous differences in education between the groups. Whereas all Hamas organizers had at least partial university education (three had university degrees and two were students), none of the Fatah organizers had university education—two had completed high school, and two had only partial high school education. PIJ organizers fell in the middle: three had completed high school, one had only partial high school education, and one was a university student.

In their personality characteristics, the organizers differed markedly from both the would-be suicides and the control group participants (see Chapter 5). The ego strength of most organizers (78.6%) was assessed as high, implying that they were well adjusted, could control their behavior, and coped well with external pressures and internal conflicts. In comparison, the ego strength level of the majority of the would-be suicides (66.7%) was assessed as intermediate. This difference was statistically significant (for more details, see Merari, Diamant, Bibi, Broshi and Zakin, 2010). None of the organizers had suicidal tendencies and none displayed post-traumatic symptoms, although three (21.4%) had symptoms of depression. One was diagnosed with psychopathic tendencies. Unlike the would-be suicides, the organizers as a group had leadership abilities; they were assessed as dominant, self-confident, and resourceful. They were socially more perceptive and better able to assess situations conceptually.

Beyond their common features, the organizers differed in demeanor and personality. Some were well educated and inclined to talk about ideological issues and the philosophy of the struggle. Others were street-smart types, who had risen to their command positions from the ranks, filling vacancies created by the arrest or killing of their predecessors. They also differed in their attitude to the interviewers: some were talkative and cooperated willingly, whereas others were more guarded and laconic.

## Unwillingness to Carry Out a Suicide Operation

A salient difference between the organizers and the would-be suicides was in the formers' unwillingness to carry out a suicide attack themselves. Nine organizers said frankly that they were reluctant to kill themselves in a "martyrdom" attack. Awad (PIJ) replied: "No. It's very difficult. Every man has different character and traits. I was destined to organize [suicide attacks] and others were destined to perform martyrdom operations. I am willing to fight but not to die in a suicide attack. For me life is something basic." Another organizer, Yasser (Hamas), said: "I wouldn't be willing to carry out a martyrdom operation. Every one has his role; I was an organizer and another's role was to carry out a martyrdom attack." Presumably, the recognition that one is sending others to make the utmost sacrifice while being reluctant to do it oneself must generate great psychological distress, unless the person in question is utterly cynical and manipulative. Yet the organizers displayed no signs of mental torment about this issue. None expressed remorse or sorrow over either the innocent victims of the attacks, or the youngsters they had sent to die in the process. Most of those who claimed to be unwilling to carry out a suicide attack personally solved the problem merely on a cognitive level. Taher (PIJ) said: "I wasn't ready to do it myself. I sent others because they wanted to do it; I didn't persuade them to do it." Others maintained that they were also in danger of death at the hands of Israeli forces, ignoring the difference between living in risk of being killed by the enemy, and the certain self-inflicted death of the young-sters they had sent. Fares (PIJ) said in this vein: "No. I didn't want go on a martyrdom operation. I was constantly exposed to death by the Israelis and I was living on borrowed time, but the thought of being a martyr didn't cross my mind. Dying by Israeli soldiers or in a martyrdom operation is the same; I'd be a *shahid* anyway." A recurrent theme in the explanations was that their role as organizers was more important than carrying out a suicide attack. Thus, Ra'ed (Fatah) said: "I didn't want to do it myself. I thought I could contribute more as a cell leader. In this role I could also be killed." One organizer (Kamal, Fatah) hinted at the emotional pressure that plagued him despite his rationalization. By his testimony, initially he did not want to carry out a suicide attack himself, but following complaints from families of youngsters he had sent to their deaths, he decided to carry out an attack himself but was arrested before he could implement his decision.

The five organizers who stated they were willing, in principle, to go on a suicide attack, justified their abstention with their more important roles as commanders. Amar (Hamas) said: "I was ready, but I was not asked to do it. My role was to make explosive charges." (In response to a question, he said that he had not offered himself as a suicide bomber.) Hassan (PIJ) and Na'if (Hamas) gave similar responses.

The organizers were also asked whether they would be willing to send a family member on a suicide attack. Two declined to answer, and of the remaining 12, seven said they would be willing to do it, and one evaded the question, saying that it was not a matter of sending a family member, as there had already been a suicide bomber from his village and, this, he thought, was enough for one village. Mustafa, who admitted that he was not ready to do it himself, answered with regard to sending a family member: "I have no problem with that; my ideological background accepts it. There is no discrimination between myself and others; it is justified until the occupation is over." Four organizers said they would not send a family member. Isma'il (PIJ) explained that he would not be able to act against the special emotional bonds with his family.

Actually, in some Palestinian suicide attacks (not merely those prepared or executed by the participants of the studies reported here) organizers did send suicides from their extended family or clan (*hamula*), but rarely did they send a close family member, and in only one case did an organizer send his younger brother on such a mission. In this exceptional instance, the younger brother volunteered on his own initiative, presumably moti-vated by the wish to live (or rather die) up to the expectations of his admired brother. The older brother made the explosive belt, put it on his younger brother, and participated in the will-reading ritual. The brother was sent to explode in Haifa but, having reached his target, was overcome by fear and aborted the mission on the pretext that the explosive charge failed to detonate.[2]

Despite the organizers' explicit unwillingness to kill themselves for the cause, their insurgent activity clearly exacted from them a high personal price that they readily accepted. Asked whether they would continue their activity even if their families suffered as a result, all said that they would. Four noted that their families' homes had actually been demolished.

## Preparing a Suicide Attack

### The Decision

The decision to carry out a suicide attack had been nearly always made at the organization's local echelon. This is clear in the case of Fatah's al-Aqsa Martyrs Brigades which, during most of the intifada, had no central leadership and were merely a cluster of loosely connected local gangs. Yet even Hamas and PIJ, which did have a national political and military leadership, allowed local echelons at the city or regional level to conduct operations as they chose, as long as they were within the organization's general policies. General policy guidelines dictated whether or not to carry out attacks at a given moment (e.g., to declare *hudna*—cease-fire—or to escalate the armed struggle), but the decision on specific attacks has been in the hands of the local command of the organizations. All organizers said that the local command had made the decision to carry out suicide attacks (rather than use other tactics) and had chosen the timing and target. To the question of who had made the decisions to carry out suicide attacks, some organizers replied simply: "I did." Others answered more generally: "The organization's command in the area, taking into consideration the political situation" (Amjad, Fathah); "The regional command is free to act, within the organization's policy" (Isma'il, PIJ); "The local commander, according to the general instructions and directives of the [national] headquarters" (Atallah, Hamas). The difference between the anarchic Fatah and the hierarchical Hamas and PIJ stood out in the organizers' answers to the question whether they would have suspended suicide attacks had the political leadership of their organization decided to do so. As shown in Table 6.4, all Hamas organizers and four out of five PIJ organizers said they would obey the political leadership's decision. One Hamas organizer (Mustafa) said: "I follow the Organization's

**Table 6.4** Organizers' Willingness to Obey Their Organizations' and PNA Orders to Suspend Suicide Attacks

|  | *Hamas (N=5)* | | *PIJ (N=5)* | | *Fatah (N=4)* | |
| --- | --- | --- | --- | --- | --- | --- |
| Willingness to obey: | Yes | No | Yes | No | Yes | No |
| Organization's order | 5 | 0 | 4 | 1 | 1 | 3 |
| PNA order | 0 | 5 | 2 | 3 | 2 | 2 |

directives to the letter; in Hamas there are no breaches like this." A PIJ organizer (Fares) said: "Military operations stem from the organization's general directives and general policy guidelines." Three of the four Fatah organizers, however, said they would not obey the organization's directive and would make their own decisions. Two of them viewed themselves as organizationally autonomous, uncommitted to any higher leadership, although they formally operated under the banner of Fatah's al-Aqsa Martyrs Brigades.

All Hamas and most PIJ organizers were loyal to their own organizations rather than to the PNA government. Asked whether they would stop suicide attacks if ordered by the PNA, all Hamas organizers and three of five PIJ organizers said they would obey only their organization's orders. Interestingly, Hamas organizers rejected PNA authority more blatantly than PIJ members. One PIJ organizer (Hassan), for example, said (concerning his response to a PNA order): "I would consult with the political leadership of the organization and act according to its directives." This response implies preference of PIJ leadership over PNA authority, but does not totally reject or delegitimize the latter. Another PIJ organizer, (Isma'il), gave an almost identical response. The answers of Hamas organizers, on the other hand, smacked of contempt toward the PNA: "Only Hamas leadership and headquarters issue instructions; the PNA has no authority. The PNA issues declarations but in practice cannot protect the people" (Amar); "The PNA's instructions do not oblige me; I have no commitment to nor connection with the PNA" (Atallah). A Fatah organizer explained his refusal of PNA orders by the absence of organizational linkage to and sponsorship by the PNA: "I disobeyed the PNA's instructions because they didn't finance me" (Kamal).

In their description of the factors affecting the decision to carry out a suicide attack, all organizers stressed operational considerations, such as the availability of explosives and a candidate for the suicide attack, and the ability to reach a target (several organizers mentioned curfews and roadblocks as examples of impediments). These factors implied that capability rather than changes in motivation determined the frequency of attacks. Half of the organizers, however, said that the timing was also a function of the perceived need to respond to Israeli actions. In this vein, Atallah, a Hamas member, gave a typical description of the determining factors: "[The timing is determined] first and foremost by operational capability and in the second place by considerations regarding the need to respond to Israeli actions, such as assassinations, entry into Palestinian cities, etc. Sometimes political considerations are also taken into account."

### Recruiting a Candidate for the Suicide Mission

Most organizers insisted that all the recruits for suicide attacks offered themselves on their own initiative, and that the organization did not actively seek candidates for suicide attacks. Only 25% of the organizers who answered this question, who belonged to all three organizations, admitted that some candidates, albeit a minority, were recruited by the group. These claims contradict the data of the would-be suicides' study, which showed that 46.7% of the participants had been approached by a group operative and asked to undertake a suicide mission. Furthermore, an analysis of the indictments and verdicts of 61 candidates recruited by the organizers in this study, which include descriptions of their terrorist activity, reveals that in 35 cases with a clearly identified recruitment process, 54% of the candidates volunteered on their own initiative and 46% were solicited by an organization's recruiter. This ratio is almost identical to the would-be suicides' accounts, and is much higher than the organizers' descriptions. Presumably, the organizers' responses on this issue were influenced by their wish not to be seen as manipulators of naïve youngsters. The disparity may also be related to the interpretation of the terms "solicited" and "volunteered." In their search for prospective suicide bombers, the recruiters may have approached youngsters known in the community to have expressed willingness for "martyrdom" operations (regardless of their real intention). From the recruiter's viewpoint he was approaching a "volunteer," whereas the candidate himself felt he had been solicited, since the recruiter had initiated contact. In any event, claims of a much higher number of willing candidates than the availability of suicide belts are apparently untrue. In many cases the organizers actively sought out candidates for suicide attacks and met with several refusals before they found willing youngsters. The following two cases illustrate the difficulties in recruiting candidates.

Amjad obtained an explosive belt but needed a suicide. He approached a candidate who, he had heard, was willing to carry out a suicide attack. At their meeting, the candidate agreed, but asked to say farewell to his parents. He went home and never returned. In an attempt to find a replacement, one of Amjad's recruiters located a youngster who expressed willingness to carry out a suicide attack. The organizer met him, and the youngster agreed but wanted to think more about it. Later that night he called the organizer and said that he had changed his mind, but would try to find a replacement. Several hours later he called again, saying that he could not find a replacement and therefore would do it himself, but only after his sick mother had recovered. After consultations, the organizer decided that the candidate was unreliable and severed contact with him.

Isma'il, then a bombmaker and second in command of PIJ's military arm in Jenin, prepared a car bomb for use by a suicide attacker (Isma'il had later become the leader of the local organization, following the death of his predecessor). There was thus a car bomb but no suicide yet. The local PIJ commander therefore asked his assistant A.F. to find one. A.F. asked another operative, B.Y., if he knew of a suitable candidate. B.Y. advised him to ask still another operative, S.K., who arranged a meeting between A.F. and A.K., a teenager whom he knew to have expressed the wish to carry out a suicide attack. The youngster indeed agreed to carry out the attack and, after preparations that included driving lessons, set out on his mission with Isma'il, who was supposed to accompany him to the Israeli border. On the way, however, the booby-trapped car (carrying 200 kg. of explosives) broke down, and they slowly made their way back. During the night the car was fixed, but the candidate's family had meanwhile discovered his plan and persuaded him to renege.

Half of the organizers said that the candidates are sometimes recruited by the organizer himself. Five others, however, said the organizer should not do the recruiting. There were no differences between the groups in this respect, and the diverse opinions apparently reflect the individual organizer's personal experience, style of leadership, and conditions of operation.

THE ORGANIZERS' VIEWS OF THE RECRUITS    The organizers' preferences for suicide candidates' characteristics were primarily dictated by operational considerations, but also reflected social awareness.

All organizers preferred young recruits, although there were differences regarding the exact age group. Some organizers preferred 17 to 18-year-old youngsters, since they are more eager and unencumbered by family obligations, whereas others preferred people in their 20s, because they are more mature. Only three organizers mentioned a minimum age—15 or 17 years.

The organizers expressed clear preference for unmarried candidates. Almost all also noted that they would not recruit an only son, or a young-ster whose family had already lost a member in the struggle. Half of the organizers claimed that they would not recruit a man who is the main provider for his family. These limitations may stem from the assumption that those concerned about their families are more likely to abort the mission, but also from moral considerations and the wish to maintain an ethical image in the community.

In their description of the social background and motives of the pro-spective suicides, most organizers stated that the candidates came from all social strata. Four of them, representing all three groups, said that most suicides were poor, simple, and unsophisticated, mainly refugee camp dwell-ers, although some came from well-to-do families. This description does not quite fit the findings of the study of would-be suicides (Chapter 5) but, interestingly, it was the perception of some of the organizers.

Asked about the recruits' desirable characteristics, six organizers (two of them Fatah members) mentioned religious belief as an important requirement. The candidate should be "determined, ready to sacrifice him-self for Allah, the religious element is predominant" (Mustafa, Hamas); "The shahid must be religious, willing to sacrifice himself" (Ra'ed, Fatah); "First and foremost—a firm belief in paradise, conviction in the Palestinian national struggle, and in the need to fight the occupation" (Atallah, Hamas). An equal number of organizers gave primacy to nationalist moti-vation, some of them connecting it with religious commitment. A Hamas organizer, Na'if, said: "The promise of paradise and the belief that the shahid will get there is very important, but it is not enough in itself. There must be a strong nationalist motivation and belief in the need to act against the occupation." Another Hamas organizer (Yasser) expressed an interesting opinion: "The true motivation of the candidates is nationalist. Nationalism is the essential motivation. There is no religious reason that in itself drives a man to carry out a suicide operation. Religion reinforces and helps the nationalist motivation. It is a political drive with religious backing." This observation is congruent with the previous chapter's conclusions about the promise of paradise as a contributing motive. Almost all organizers agreed with this assessment. Asked what prompted Palestinian youth to volunteer for suicide missions, all mentioned Israeli actions during the intifada as the main cause. Religious belief was brought up only by some as an additional factor. Only two organizers (Hamas and PIJ) viewed paradise and "love of martyrdom" as the primary cause. Ra'ed 's description was typical: "The feeling of confinement, the killing, all these inflame hatred and contribute to the willingness to volunteer [for suicide action]."

Several organizers emphasized characteristics that facilitate the suicide's ability to pass Israeli security checkpoints and reach the target undetected: "The candidate should be serious and mature, with the looks and behavior that would enable him to get into Israel" (Isma'il, PIJ).

Security considerations and the need to avoid detection by Israeli intelligence had an important role in selecting the candidates. In this regard, almost all organizers viewed previous membership in the organization as a disadvantage. Taher (PIJ), for example, said: "We prefer a man who had not been involved in resistance activity, someone who lives in a place far from the organizer and the recruiter, so that the connection between them would not be discovered." Similarly, Ra'ed (Fatah) said: "Usually, the istishhadeen [martyrs] are not members of the organization, because the security forces know those who are members and this may jeopardize the operation." And Kamal (Fatah): "It's better if the candidate is not a member of the organization and unknown to the Israeli authorities, so that he can pass the roadblocks smoothly." Two organizers, however, thought that previous membership in the organization was desirable. Mustafa (Hamas), for example, said: "It's better if they have a background of membership in the organization; it shows that they have high [ideological] awareness."

The organizers were also asked about reasons for rejecting a candidate. Aside from the family conditions mentioned above, most organizers said they would not take mentally unstable candidates, suicidal people who want to die for personal reasons, and criminals. Five organizers said they would not recruit a hesitant candidate. Three organizers—one of each organization—said they would not recruit a woman for a suicide mission.

CHECKING THE CANDIDATE   All the organizers said that youngsters who want to volunteer for a suicide operation contact someone known in their neighborhood as an organization operative (some organizers used the expression, "known as wanted by the Israeli security forces"). Since Israeli intelligence boasts many arrests of organization members in general, and of those involved in suicide attacks in particular, one may assume that the groups would exercise extreme caution in recruiting people who offer themselves, out of fear that they may be agents of Israeli intelligence trying to expose the group's network of operatives active in organizing suicide attacks. However, four organizers said that they had no means of checking the candidate's background and they simply relied on their impressions of him during the meeting. Most organizers did conduct some inquiry, asking in the neighborhood about the candidate and his family. One Hamas organizer (Amar) noted that in the Gaza Strip the organization ran a security department that conducted these checks, but the conditions in the West Bank did not enable maintenance of central departments of this kind, and every local organizer had to do the job himself. A Fatah organizer (Azam) said that to check a candidate's background, he used his contacts in a PNA intelligence organization where he had worked in the past.

The candidate's motivation was examined in conversations with the recruiter and later with the organizer. The main purpose was to assess commitment to the mission and screen out those who were likely to change their minds. A couple of organizers said they used to test the candidate's dedication by seemingly trying to convince him to drop the idea. Fares (PIJ) said: "The main examination was a test of the sincerity of the candidate's intention. The method was to try to convince him not to do the operation. This way it is possible to see whether the candidate is truly determined to do the operation whatever it takes."

All the organizers said that the final decision on recruiting the candidate was made by the organization's regional head, i.e., by them.

### Reinforcing the Candidate's Commitment

For security reasons, candidates for suicide attacks were prepared individually, even for joint attacks.

Only one organizer (Hassan, PIJ) said that some meetings with the candidate were designed to prepare him mentally for his mission. The discussion focused on religious issues, on previous shahids, their qualities, the respect they earned after their deaths, and their high status in paradise, as well as on the esteem and treatment the organization and the community would lavish on the candidate's family. All other organizers claimed it was unnecessary to boost the candidates' motivation, as they were already highly motivated when they volunteered for the mission. This assessment of the candidates' mental readiness does not quite tally with reality. In fact, an analysis of these organizers' indictments revealed that of 61 suicides prepared by them, 36% aborted the mission. Nor does this assessment correspond to the data of the would-be suicides study, which showed a high rate of hesitation among them. Yet, the organizers' reports on the absence of meetings for mental preparation seem to genuinely reflect the situation during the second intifada, when most organizers did not invest much time and effort in the mental preparation of candidates. Afraid to be detected by Israeli intelligence agencies, they tried, as a rule, to make the preparation period as short as possible and, therefore, kept the number of meetings to the bare minimum (usually two or three), and devoting those primarily to operational instructions. The organizers invariably claimed that the candidates met only those involved in the operational preparation, rather than people from the religious or political echelon. Even in this time-pressured, operations-oriented preparation, it is clear that at least some organizers felt the need to reassure the candidate—if not to convince him—and to alleviate his concerns. These talks were presumably held during the recruitment phase and interwoven with the operational preparations. Apparently, the candidates were deeply concerned about what would happen to their families' after their deaths, particularly regarding the expected demolition of their families' homes. Almost all organizers said the candidates were promised that the organization would rebuild their families' homes, and provided examples of suicides whose families had been taken care of.

ATTITUDE TOWARD HESITANT CANDIDATES   All organizers said that hesitant candidates were nonexistent or very rare. This observation does not tally with the would-be suicides' self-descriptions that were discussed in Chapter 5 (66.7% said that they hesitated even after they had volunteered or agreed to undertake the mission). Nor does it match the analysis of the organizers' indictments and verdicts, which, as noted above, showed that more than one third of the candidates recruited had abandoned the mission. This disparity may be attributed to the organizers' reluctance to be perceived as convincing hesitant youngsters to commit suicide. Still, in many cases the organizers may have been truly unaware of the candidates' hesitations, as the latter presented a heroic façade in their meetings with the locally revered leaders who had invited them to join the struggle.

All but one organizer claimed they were opposed to convincing hesitant candidates on the grounds that those who hesitate were unreliable and likely to jeopardize the operation. A Hamas organizer (Atallah) added that it was impossible to convince people to kill themselves if they are not ready to do it. Only one organizer (Yasser, Hamas) said he had tried to persuade wavering candidates. Yet despite the organizers' claims, at least some candidates must have expressed conflict and uncertainty, and the organizers therefore tried to alleviate their concerns and bolster their determination. This assessment is buttressed by the organizers' description of how they handled the candidates' worries about the possible demolition of their families' homes by the IDF in retaliation for their attack. Most organizers said the candidates were assured that the organization would help their families to rebuild their house. Nevertheless, the testimonies of the hesitant would-be suicides described in Chapter 5 indicate that this promise did not suffice to relieve their concerns in most cases, and the families' responses described in Chapter 4 clearly show that in practically all cases they would have done anything to stop their sons from carrying out a suicide attack.

The organizers were concerned about the attitudes of the candidates' families before, but less after, completion of the operation. Of ten organizers who answered the question how they would handle family opposition to their sons' intended suicide mission, eight said categorically that the operation must be cancelled immediately if the suicide's family learns about it, as the family would try to prevent it at any cost—including contacting the PNA or even the Israeli authorities. Amjad (Fatah), for example, said that one father, who discovered his son's intention to carry out a suicide attack, turned him in to the PNA. The organizer noted that in his opinion, the father was ready to surrender his son to the Israeli authorities had he been unable to stop him otherwise. All the organizers maintained they had made no attempt to persuade the families, as they believed such attempts to be futile. Azam (Fatah) thought that the mothers were the pivot of family opposition, and thought that a mother who supported her son's suicide was insane. The organizers did not seem emotionally bothered about sending a youngster to his sure death against his family's will; their only concern was operational success.

Indeed, some organizers experienced several cases in which a family found out about the plan and was able to foil it. In one case Amjad tried to recruit M.F., a youngster who, he heard, was willing to carry out a suicide operation. When he met him, M.F. refused but said he had a friend, M.A., who would be willing to do it. M.A., 17 years old, indeed agreed, was prepared, videotaped, given 1000 NIS ($250) for travel expenses, and dispatched to carry out the suicide attack in Jerusalem. He returned that evening, however, saying that the money was not enough for the trip. He received more money and spent the night at home, planning to go again on the mission next morning. Meanwhile his father discovered the plan (his son may have told him as a way out), forced him to stay home and pummeled the friend who had recruited him.

Only one organizer said he had visited the family after the operation. Avoidance of a meeting with the suicides' families may stem from the need to keep the operatives' identity secret, in particular because an irate family may want to take revenge. It also may stem from the emotional difficulty of facing the grieving family. Yet, a couple of organizers displayed blatant detachment from personal responsibility. Awad (PIJ), for example, said: "I had no connection with the family. I did not feel responsibility. The PIJ took care of them. The responsibility is with the martyr himself. He decides to undertake the mission. I do not convince him [to do so]."

THE WILL  The practice of videotaping a candidate for a suicide attack dates back to the pro-Syrian Lebanese groups in the mid-1980s. Palestinian groups have used this practice ever since they started the suicide-attacks campaign in 1993. As explained in the previous chapter, in this ritual the candidate was videotaped reading a last statement, holding a weapon in one hand and the Quran in the other, against the backdrop of the organization's flags, posters and slogans. The videotape is usually released to the media immediately after the operation.

All the organizers viewed the videotaping first and foremost as propaganda, intended for the Palestinian audience (an example to follow), for the Israeli audience (to spread fear) and the world at large (a show of Palestinian desperation and determination). Atallah (Hamas) provided a comprehensive description of the purpose: "Every insurgent movement needs to communicate its message to the enemy and to the insurgent community. The aim is to influence both the enemy and the people, to encourage others to follow suit and to deter the enemy, to publicize in the world the Palestinian problem and the reasons for the operation. With regard to the enemy, it is intended to deter and demonstrate that the Palestinians are willing to sacrifice their lives for their freedom." Several organizers mentioned additional purposes of the videotape: to publicize the perpetrating organization and to commemorate the suicide. Five organizers said that the videotaping ritual strengthens the candidate's motivation and constitutes a point of no return: "The videotaping is actually a contract between the candidate and the organizer" (Na'if, Hamas); "The videotaped reading of the testament creates a situation of commitment to complete [the mission]. There is no way back!" (Azam, Fatah).

Most organizers claimed that the candidate is involved in writing the testament; only a few said that it is dictated by the organization (the groups did not differ in this regard). This claim contradicts the would-be suicides' testimonies, all of whom but one said that their testaments had been written by the organizers (see Chapter 5). As in other cases, the organizers' version may have been prompted by the wish to underscore the candidates' role in the process, so as not to be perceived as manipulators of unsophisticated youngsters.

As the last act of securing the candidate's commitment, the testament ritual is performed very close to dispatching the candidate on his mission. Almost all organizers said that the videotaping was usually done the day before the candidate was dispatched, and sometimes on that very day. These reports are congruent with the would-be suicides' accounts.

Most organizers were aware of cases in which the candidate refused to be videotaped, and some met with personal refusals. Three organizers explained such refusals as a sign of modesty—reluctance to be regarded as someone seeking fame— and one thought that in the case he had encountered, the refusal stemmed from lack of resolve, because the candidate perceived the videotaping ritual as an irrevocable commitment (Kamal, Fatah). All but one organizer said that although the videotaping served the organization's interest, the ritual is not a must. Often, those who refuse to be videotaped agree to be photographed by a still camera.

## Operational Decisions and Instructions

A SINGLE OR MULTIPLE ATTACK? Eight of the 52 suicide attacks (15.4%) prepared by the studied organizers were designed as double attacks, in which two candidates were sent to explode at the same time and place. Six of the eight double attacks (75%) failed, a higher rate of failure than in the case of single attacks (51.9%). Each organizer who had prepared a double suicide attack did so only once, that is, the eight double attacks were prepared by eight different organizers who represented all three militant groups. In the interviews, they were asked about their preferences for single or double attacks. Most claimed that multiple suicide attacks had a greater psychological effect because they cause more casualties and demonstrate the organization's capability. Only one advocate of multiple attacks noted the effect of mutual strengthening of the suicides' determination in such missions. Those opposed to multiple attacks saw them as a waste; one of them argued they lacked operational justification, and merely flattered the organizer's ego in his competition with other operatives.

Only one organizer saw an advantage in the previous acquaintance of partners to a multiple suicide attack. The others argued that the candidates should meet only in the final phase of the preparations, shortly before their dispatch for the mission. To justify their preference they adduced security issues and the need for compartmentalization. One organizer, however, reported that in his experience, a previous acquaintance had acted negatively—the dominant partner of the suicide team was afraid and influenced the other to abort the mission. Half of the participants displayed a rather improvisational approach: they did not attend to details of the attack, avoided nominating the leader of the team, and claimed that the suicides themselves should decide who explodes first, at what distance and time interval from the other.

SELECTING THE TARGET   The city to be attacked was almost always selected by the organizer, with the precise location often left to the suicide's discretion, although in several cases it was predetermined before dispatching him, especially when he, or the guide assigned to bring him to the location of the attack, was familiar with the city. The suicides were usually instructed to explode in a crowded place and aim at killing as many people as possible. Most organizers—12 out of 14—openly admitted that the suicides were instructed to kill civilians at random. Amar (Hamas) for example, described the target as "a crowded place, congested with people, [so as to cause] a maximum number of casualties." Some organizers, however, paid lip service to moral considerations, stating that the first preference was to attack military targets, civilians being a second choice. Only two organizers, both Fatah members, described the choice of targets using patently false propaganda—namely, that the selected targets were military or violent settlers who shoot at Palestinians. Yet both organizers were responsible for suicide attacks against random civilians in Israeli cities. All organizers said that accessibility was a primary consideration in selecting the target. Kamal tersely summed up the selection criteria as "capabilities and accessibility," Taher described them as "an easy target, ability to reach it," and Atallah said, "first and foremost—operational considerations and accessibility." None mentioned moral constraints.

THE GUIDE   In most cases the suicide was escorted by one or more persons on his way to the target. The data on the would-be suicides described in the previous chapter showed that two-thirds of them were escorted to the border, and more than 50% were escorted all the way to the target within Israel. The guides to the border were usually organization members privy to the operation, who participated in various stages of its preparation. They were familiar with the area and knew the locations of IDF roadblocks and ways to circumvent them.

At the border, however, the suicides usually took a taxi (often ordered ahead of time) driven by an Israeli Arab who specialized in carrying illegal workers, or by an inhabitant of the territories with a permit to enter Israel. In most cases, albeit not all, the driver inside Israel was unaware that he was driving a suicide to his target. In several cases one of the organizer's assistants was driving a car ahead of the car in which the candidate was riding, to make sure the road was clear of military patrols and improvised roadblocks. In a few cases, women escorted the suicide to reduce suspicion by Israeli security forces.

The escorts' role was not merely to guide the candidate to his target; they were an extension of the organizer's control over the suicide, with their presence reducing the likelihood that the candidate would change his mind. They were also the organizer's long arm, maintaining communication with him by cell phone for instructions if problems arose on the way.

BEHAVIOR ON THE WAY TO THE TARGET    Problems on the way to the target were commonplace: sudden curfews, roadblocks, military patrols, and—more often than could be expected—mechanical failure of the car. At the border, where the suicide usually was to meet an Israeli taxi driver, the latter sometimes failed to show up. In the interviews the organizers invariably said that in case the suicide could not reach his target he should return to base and wait for another opportunity. Yet if he was already within Israel, he was expected to choose another target and explode. The same rule applied to cases in which the suicide was stopped by security forces and could not escape. In this event, he was expected to explode rather than surrender. Three organizers said that the suicide should explode himself even if he could escape. A different potential problem, however, involved the suicide's increasing hesitation after his dispatch. All the organizers maintained that in this eventuality the suicide should return home. Hesitant suicides who aborted the mission are not punished—but are not sent again, as they are assumed to be unreliable and a security risk.

The organizers were, of course, aware of the high likelihood of interferences on a suicide's way to the target. Most did not want to leave the decisions entirely to the suicides, and therefore saw fit to retain communication with them via cellular phone after dispatching. Only three said that after dispatching they avoided all communication with the suicide. Aware of the security risk involved in communicating with the suicides, the organizers tried to minimize it in various ways, including the use of code words and hints, equipping the suicides with previously unused telephones, and forbidding communication after the suicide crossed the border. Two organizers, however, said that they had instructed the suicide (or the guide) to call the last minute before the attack, assuming that the risk of exposure at this time is immaterial, because the time was too short for the Israelis to prevent the attack.

## Dropping Out

Supplementary data were found in the organizers' indictments, which detailed their attempts, both successful and failed, to recruit candidates for suicide attacks. Altogether, the sample's organizers had tried to recruit 61 youngsters for 52 suicide operations (some of the planned attacks involved more than one candidate). For 55 of the 61 recruits, the indictments allowed assessment of whether the candidate abandoned the mission or not, although in many cases the mission was aborted due to factors unrelated to the candidate's determination. The data show that 35 candidates (64%) persevered in the mission (26 of them actually carried it out) and 20 (36%) abandoned it at some stage. The groups displayed considerable differences in candidate dropout rates: whereas in PIJ and Hamas it was less than one-third (27% and 31%, respectively), in Fatah the rate was about twice as high—56%. As preparation procedures were quite similar across groups, this difference may be attributed to the lower selectivity of Fatah organizers in recruiting candidates, despite the fact that PIJ organizers recruited a much larger number of candidates than either Hamas or Fatah, as shown in Table 6.5.

Six of those who dropped out simply failed to show up at scheduled meetings, or otherwise severed contact with the group's operatives without notifying the recruiters or organizers about their decision. The reasons given by those who explained their withdrawal from the mission related mostly to family objection or concern about the family. Some of those who aborted the mission after they had already been dispatched, however, resorted to technical problems as an excuse. A few said that they had hidden

**Table 6.5** Number of Recruited Candidates and Dropout Rate for the Samples' Organizers, by Group Affiliation

| Group | PIJ | Hamas | Fatah | Total |
|---|---|---|---|---|
| No. of candidates recruited | 32 | 13 | 16 | 61 |
| Dropout rate | 27% | 31% | 56% | 36% |

the explosive charge because Israeli security forces were active in the area, but later could not find it, and one said that the charge had failed to explode although he had tried to activate it.

There was a significant difference between the dropout rate of volunteers and those solicited by an organization's recruiter. Based on a careful analysis of the indictments, I could determine in only 35 cases whether the candidate volunteered or was solicited for the task. Of these, 19 volunteered and 16 were solicited. While the dropout rate was 16% among the volunteers, it was 56% for those who were solicited. These results are hardly surprising. Even if some volunteers still hesitated, as we have seen in the previous chapter, the assumption is quite reasonable that they were initially more motivated.

The indictments data also support the analysis of fear and conflict development discussed in the previous chapter on the basis of the would-be suicides' self-reports. As I suggested, fear grows and conflict intensifies as an inverse function of the distance from implementation of the mission, i.e., the closer the moment of death the greater the fear, hence the hesitation. The indictments data show that the dropout rate indeed rose dramatically as death drew closer. Figure 6.1 shows this point graphically.

Figure 6.1 shows clearly that the dropout rate increased as the time of the mission approached, rising steeply in the final phase, when death was imminent. Of the 20 candidates who initially agreed to undertake the mission but decided to abandon it, only one dropped out after he had given his consent to the recruiter but before he met the organizer ("1st meeting"

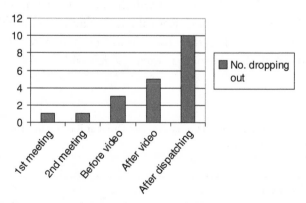

**Figure 6.1**  Number of candidates deserting the mission by stage of preparation.

in the chart), and another during his first meeting with the organizer ("2nd meeting" in the chart). Three candidates dropped out after they had already met the organizer but before they were subjected to the videotaping ritual ("before video" in the chart). As noted in the previous chapter, this ritual usually took place very shortly before dispatching, and the candidate was told that he would go on the mission the next day or on that very day. With the suicide mission thus much closer and more real than before, five candidates dropped out in the brief time span between the videotaping and dispatching ("after video" in the chart). Fear rose sharply and peaked after dispatching, when the candidate was already traveling to his death. It was at this time—within just a few hours—that the largest number of candidates succumbed to overwhelming fear and aborted the mission ("after dispatching" in the chart). Thus, although the period between recruiting and execution usually lasted weeks, 75% of the dropouts jumped off the boat in the last day or two, most of them (50% of all dropouts) in the very last hours.

Is there a point of no return?[3] In my lectures and writings on the subject (e.g., Merari, 2000; Merari, 2005) I described the videotaping ritual as such. Yet the newer data presented in this book show that while the video-taping may, indeed, reinforce commitment, in a significant number of cases it does not diminish fear, which presumably increases—at least in some candidates—all the way to the target. In fact, a few candidates reached the target and only there, at the last moment, refrained from pressing the switch. One such case was R.M., who had been sent by Mustafa (Hamas). R.M. was initially scheduled to participate in a double attack with his cousin. He consented but later changed his mind on the pretext that his sister was in the United States, and he wanted to wait for her return before going on the mission. The cousin therefore carried out the suicide mission alone, exploding on a bus in Tel Aviv. The death of his cousin may well have left R.M. with feelings of guilt; it may have also shamed him socially. He therefore agreed to carry out another suicide attack, despite his fear. He was hastily instructed on how to operate an explosive belt, videotaped, and dispatched on the same day. The organizer instructed him that should he be stopped at a security roadblock, he must immediately explode the charge, even if his escort, a Hamas operative, would be killed too, as a result. He was driven by the escort to the target, a restaurant in Tel Aviv, where the escort left him on his own. R.M. approached the restaurant but at the door was stopped by a security guard who suspected him. Ignoring his instructions, R.M. turned and ran away but was caught soon.

Would R.M. have set off the charge on his body had he not been stopped at the restaurant door? Possibly, but we cannot be sure. At this moment of extreme conflict a very thin line presumably separated dying from surviving, and any external stimulus could have made the difference.

However, in some hesitating candidates there may be a moment of reconciliation with the mission, after which they manage to quell their fear, so that the avoidance gradient described in the previous chapter ceases to rise at some point along the way. The case of Nabil described in the previous chapter suggests that this process may indeed occur in some suicides. Nabil, who said that he had been afraid all the way, described himself as entering an altered state of consciousness when he boarded the bus on which he tried to explode.

At the other end of the motivation continuum were a number of suicides eager to explode as soon as possible. One suicide sent by Isma'il, for example, volunteered on his own initiative, was videotaped and dispatched to carry out an attack inside Israel. He did not make an effort to look for a crowded place; instead, he entered a home on the outskirts of a small village and exploded, killing a 65-year-old woman and wounding her three grandchildren. Another suicide, also a volunteer, was sent by the same organizer to carry out a suicide attack in an Israeli city. On his way he arrived at an Israeli village on the border early in the morning, entered a grocery store and exploded killing the 63-year-old shop owner who was there alone. In the absence of psychological data on these suicides it is impossible to determine what their mental condition was at that time. Nevertheless, their behavior suggests that they first and foremost sought their own death.

## Conclusion

How reliable were the organizers' answers? In general, their frankness was impressive. Many, albeit not all, details in their answers on the preparations could be checked against, and tallied well, with the descriptions of their activity in the indictments. The organizers also answered candidly some questions that may have threatened their self-perception and projected image—in particular the question on their willingness to carry out a suicide attack. Their sweeping admission of their reluctance to do it themselves presented them in an unflattering light, but attested to their candor. Digressions from the truth were related mainly to issues that challenged their moral integrity. They denied, for example, the practice of convincing youngsters to carry out suicide attacks. In this regard, the testimonies of the would-be suicides and the analysis of the indictments provide a more accurate picture.

Despite the differences in the ratio of successful to failed attacks shown in table 6.3, the organizers' accounts did not reveal systematic differences between the groups with regard to policies and methods of recruitment, preparations for the suicide attack, target selection, and instructions for conduct on the way to the target. Even in areas that should, conceivably, reflect the groups' diversity—such as attitude to religion, which could affect the selection of candidates and their mental preparation—the variance within the groups was greater than between the groups. This surprising finding may attest to the decentralized management of suicide attacks, even in the politically centralized Hamas and PIJ. Variations in management style (e.g., the degree of centralization and personal involvement in details) stemmed from individual differences between the organizers rather than from their organizational affiliation. Hence no "Hamas style" or "Fatah style" of organizing a suicide attack. The organizers faced the same problems and difficulties—such as hesitation, family opposition, and interruptions on the way to the target—and tailored their solutions according to their personal leadership abilities. The differences in the rate of success between the groups and between organizers within each group may be due to factors that were not detected in the interviews. Thus, although all the organizers explicitly viewed the candidates' motivation as a crucial factor, some were presumably better judges of character than others. Similarly, even though all the organizers were aware of the need for strict secrecy about the preparations, their conduct presumably varied. The fact that Hamas organizers were better educated than those of the other two groups may be somehow related to these differences.

*Endnotes*

1. Parts of this chapter have been published recently in *Terrorism and Political Violence* (Merari, Fighel, Ganor, Lavie, Tzoreff & Livne, 2010).
2. With regard to foreigners who volunteered to join al-Qaeda in Iraq, Felter and Fishman (2008, p. 57) found a connection between the agent of recruitment and the willingness to become a suicide bomber. By their findings, the rate of volunteers for suicide missions was high among those recruited by an acquaintance, a neighbor, an organization activist, or through the internet (ranging from 57.8% to 100%), but relatively low among those recruited by a family member (18.2%).

3. Lester and Lester (1971, p. 23) commented wisely: "Death is a gradual process and no one moment can be identified as the time when it occurs. From the viewpoint of suicidology, the question of when physical death occurs is less important than the individual's subjective experience of death. He may consider himself 'as good as dead' when his body is still functioning, or he may expect his consciousness and awareness to continue beyond bodily death."

# 7

# Public Atmosphere

As an act ostensibly meant to serve the community (the nation, an ethnic group, or the followers of a religion), suicide attacks are greatly influenced by the attitudes of the communities from which they emerge. Public opinion affects suicide attacks at both the group and the individual levels. These two avenues of influence are discussed in this chapter. Like other aspects of suicide terrorism, data on Palestinian public attitudes to suicide terrorism (as well as to other aspects of the armed struggle) are by far richer than in other places where campaigns of suicide terrorism have taken place.

For this reason the Palestinian arena will be used as the main case in point in the following discussion.

## The Influence of Public Attitude on Groups' Decisions to Use Suicide Attacks

Terrorist groups that have used suicide attacks are not indifferent to the opinions and attitudes of those they view as their constituency – the population whose interests they claim to serve, and from whom they recruit their members. In choosing tactics and targets, the group tends to act within the boundaries of its constituency's approval. Terrorist groups differ in their sensitivity to their constituency's attitudes, and even more so in the definition of what they perceive as their constituency. But all of them are tuned, to some degree, to the opinions held by their reference community (the community they are fighting for) regarding their actions. In many cases, this community is a national group or a large ethnic segment within which the insurgents live—a situation that augments public opinion's influence on their decisions. This is true of nationalist groups such as the Palestinian Hamas, PIJ, and Fatah, the Lebanese Hizballah and the Syrian Social Nationalist Party (SSNP),[1] Chechen rebels, the Taliban in Afghanistan, and the Kurdish PKK. Members of these groups have lived within the communities in which they grew up, have shared the community's hardships and joys, and have believed that the community granted them the license to operate. For groups that fight for an international ideology such as religion, on the other hand, the reference group may be an imagined community of like-minded people scattered around the globe.[2] Militant Islamists who have traveled to Afghanistan and, more recently, to Iraq, to fight against the infidels belong to this category, as do the groups that carried out the attacks in Madrid (March 11, 2004) and in London (July 7, 2005). Still, even given the same circumstances, some groups are more attentive to public sentiment than others. In the Palestinian arena, Hamas has been more sensitive to public opinion than PIJ. In several periods since the Oslo Agreement of 1993, the latter has carried out suicide attacks even at times when Hamas had suspended them on grounds that the Palestinian public would not support such attacks.[3]

Evidence showing the influence of public opinion on terrorist groups' decisions whether or not to carry out suicide attacks was found in the study of organizers described in Chapter 6. Asked if they would cease suicide attacks if they knew the Palestinian public would oppose them, 80% of the organizers said yes. One of the Hamas organizers said: "If I knew for sure that the public opposes suicide attacks I would stop them immediately. I am sure that Hamas would not continue suicide attacks contrary to the wish of the [Palestinian] public." A PIJ organizer said: "Our actions are popular resistance. They are supported by the public. If the public opposed suicide attacks I would not carry them out. An organization must rely on broad popular support." Three of the five PIJ organizers who participated in the study said that they would not act contrary to public sentiment. Thus, the field echelon of PIJ commanders, who lived among their people and were directly exposed to public responses in their neighborhood, seemed to be more attentive to public opinion than the organization's top leadership, which issued orders from Damascus.

## The Influence of Public Opinion on Individuals

Suicide bombers are part and parcel of their community's social milieu and their immediate peer circle. The willingness to undertake a suicide mission is, therefore, greatly influenced by public attitude. It is easy to understand that when everybody says that suicide bombers are national heroes—when their posters are covering the walls, when audio tapes and CDs with songs praising their valor are sold in every street corner, when television, radio stations and newspapers are recounting the stories of their bravery—many youngsters would find it rather appealing to join their ranks. But in a situation where the majority of the community is opposed to terrorism in general, and to suicide attacks in particular, very few would find this option attractive. An ordinary youngster in a Palestinian city or village during the second intifada, approached by a terrorist group's recruiter with the offer to carry out a suicide attack, may or may not agree—but in any event he would not find it a crazy, criminal, or offensive idea. On the other hand, in the Muslim neighborhood in Leeds, where the London suicide bombers came from, an average youngster approached with this offer would most likely be appalled and probably contact the police. This, in a nutshell, explains why suicide bombings are rather frequent in Israel and Sri Lanka, but rather rare in Western Europe, despite large Muslim populations in many European cities. A poll conducted within the Muslim community in Britain a year after the July 7, 2005 suicide attacks in London, which had been carried out by Muslim British citizens, found that 13% of the respondents thought that the suicide bombers should be regarded as "martyrs" and 7% maintained that "suicide attacks against civilians in the UK can be justified in some circumstances." However, as the *Times* noted, the majority of the Muslim community "want the Government to take tougher measures against extremists within their community," and the number of British Muslims who said that they would be proud if a close family member joined the police – 35% of the respondents—was much higher than the number of those who said that they would be proud if a family member decided to join al-Qaeda (2%).[4] Similar attitudes to suicide attacks were found among Muslims living in the UK and in several other European countries, in a Pew Research Center poll conducted in 2006. Fifteen percent of the Muslims sampled in the U.K., 16% of those in France and Spain, and 7% of those in Germany, thought that suicide bombing against civilian targets, in order to defend Islam from its enemies, is often or sometimes justified. However, most of the respondents in all European countries sampled, 64% in France, 69% in Spain, 70% in the UK, and 83% in Germany, said that suicide attacks against civilians were never justified.[5]

The effect of massive public support for the individual willingness to volunteer for suicide attacks is not only in the political and moral justification of the act itself. Refusing an offer to undertake a suicide mission or, sometimes, to volunteer for such a mission, jeopardizes the individual's social status among his peers, as well as his self-image, by marking him as a coward, unpatriotic, or both. Concerning the atmosphere in the Tamil community in Sri Lanka, Gunawardena (2004, p.13–14) noted:

> There are many other factors which come into play in the individual's deci-sion in becoming a suicide terrorist. Societal and peer pressure, social stigma by the dishonour brought about by refusal to become one and the 'societal conditioning' of Tamil Society all contribute. Self-sacrificial service became a norm rather than an exceptional act and an outward display of their com-mitment to the leader, the organisation and to the cause.

Ricolfi (2005, p. 113) noted that the places of origin of Palestinian suicides tended to cluster geographically and socially, suggesting that sui-cide bombers are influenced by peer pressure and emulation. As an exam-ple, Ricolfi noted that eight out of 11 players in a Hamas-associated football team from Hebron carried out suicide attacks.[6]

## Fluctuations in Palestinian Public Opinion

Palestinian public attitudes to suicide attacks since the Oslo Agreement of September 1993 can be tracked through reliable public opinion surveys. The Center for Palestine Research and Studies (CPRS) in Nablus, headed by Dr. Khalil Shikaki, is one of the main polling institutions that have run systematic surveys in this period. CPRS conducted frequent polls, using representative samples of the Palestinian population in the West Bank and the Gaza Strip, in the period of 1993–2000. After July 2000, Shikaki con-tinued his surveys at the Palestinian Center for Policy & Survey Research (PSR) in Bir Zeit. Reliable public opinion surveys of the Palestinian popu-lation in the West Bank and the Gaza Strip have also been carried out since 1993 by the Jerusalem Media and Communication Center (JMCC), another Palestinian polling institution. Still other polls have been con-ducted by the Development Studies Programme (DSP) at Birzeit University. Appendix 1 lists the results of 82 polls conducted from September 1993 to January 2009, which included questions concerning Palestinian public attitudes to armed attacks against Israeli targets in general, and to suicide attacks in particular.

In general, findings of the surveys conducted by different pollsters are similar and show the same trends. Thus, taken together, they can be used as a joint source for monitoring Palestinian society's attitudes to suicide attacks. Figure 7.1 shows the average quarterly percentages of support for suicide attacks in public opinion surveys conducted by Palestinian poll-sters in the period from August 1995 to September 2006, the quarterly number of suicide attacks at that time, and the combined quarterly number of actual and foiled suicide attacks in the period of September 1993 to December 2004.[7]

Specific questions concerning attitudes to suicide attacks were not asked in Palestinian polls before August 1995. The questions taken into account for analyzing public opinion trends included those explicitly asking about attitudes to suicide attacks, and those that asked about atti-tudes to attacks against Israeli civilians inside Israel.

Questions asked in the Palestinian polls used various phrasings in ref-erence to the violent activity of the Palestinian groups. In many polls, questions referred specifically to suicide attacks (as a form of attack in gen-eral, or in reference to a particular attack). Other questions, however, referred to "armed attacks," "military operations," or "military resistance." Comparison of polls which used different wording should, therefore, be done with caution. In one case, where different wordings were used in the same poll—one of them referring to "military operations against Israeli targets" and the other to "suicide bombing operations"—a difference in the rate of support was indeed found. The difference, however, was not large: 39.8% supported "military operations" and 32.7% supported "suicide bombing operations."[8] An even smaller difference in the responses to these two phrasings in the same poll—less than 2%—was found in another JMCC poll, in which 73.6% of the respondents supported "military operations against Israeli targets" and 72.0% expressed support for "suicide bombing operations against Israeli civilians."[9] Presumably, because suicide

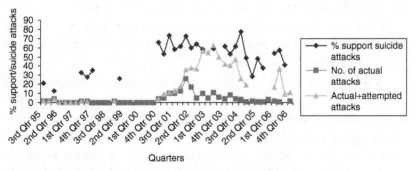

**Figure 7.1** Palestinian public support for suicide attacks (% of respondents), and the number of actual and attempted suicide attacks per quarter, 1995–2006.

attacks have been the most spectacular form of terrorism used by the Palestinian groups after the 1993 Oslo Agreement, for many people – Palestinians as well as others – the armed struggle was spontaneously associated with this particular form of attack.

In general, the wording "armed attacks against Israeli civilians inside Israel," which has been used often in the PSR polls, can be taken to mean suicide attacks, because inside Israel (as distinct from the occupied territories), suicide attacks have been the main tactic used by the Palestinian groups. Furthermore, the distribution of responses to this wording closely corresponds to the distribution of responses to the wording "suicide attacks."

A significant portion of the Palestinians has supported suicide attacks throughout the period of 1995–2006. Even before the outbreak of the second intifada, support for suicide attacks ranged from 5.3%[10] to 35.5%.[11] The mean rate of support for suicide attacks across the eight polls conducted before the second intifada was 23.9%. Thus, nearly a quarter of the Palestinians supported suicide attacks against Israeli civilians inside Israel at a time when the peace process was making progress and was endorsed by a majority of Palestinians. As soon as the intifada started, support for suicide attacks almost tripled; in April 2001 it stood at 73.7%.[12] The average rate of support in the first phase of the intifada (September 2000 through March 2002) was 67.1%: two-thirds of the Palestinian population supported suicide attacks against Israeli civilians inside Israel. In late March 2002, in the wake of a sharp rise in suicide attacks and a corresponding increase in Israeli civilian casualties, Israel launched the "Defensive Shield" operation, during which Israeli forces reoccupied Palestinian cities and towns in the West Bank. Following the operation, the rate of support for suicide attacks somewhat declined, with an average of 62%.[13] A much greater drop in support took place after the death of Arafat (November 11, 2004). In the two years after that event the average rate of support was 45.6%.

Taken in the context of their contemporary events, the polls make it possible to draw some inferences about the factors influencing the Palestinian public's attitude to suicide attacks.

A systematic difference in Palestinian public attitudes can be detected with regard to the type of target. Without exception, support for attacks against soldiers and settlers has been considerably higher than support for attacks against civilians inside Israel. While support for attacks inside Israel has fluctuated in accordance with the political situation, support for suicide attacks against Israeli soldiers and settlers has remained very high throughout the entire period. Even before the second intifada, at the time when the peace process was making progress and the Palestinian authorities generally tried to prevent the Hamas and PIJ attacks (albeit with limited decisiveness), public support for attacks against Israeli soldiers and settlers was remarkably high. Thus, in a CPRS poll conducted in August 1995, only 24.3% of the sample supported "Hamas and Islamic Jihad's suicide operations against Israeli targets" and a mere 18.3% supported "armed attacks against Israeli civilian targets," while 67.6% supported "armed attacks against Israeli army targets" and 69.2% supported "armed attacks against Israeli settlers."[14] Support for attacks against soldiers and settlers grew even higher during the second intifada. In a PSR poll conducted in December 2001, 58.2% supported "armed attacks against Israeli civilians inside Israel," whereas 92.3% supported "armed attacks against Israeli soldiers in the West Bank and the Gaza Strip" and 92.1% supported "armed attacks against Israeli civilian settlers in the West Bank and the Gaza Strip."[15] Other polls showed similar differences.[16]

## Factors Influencing Support for Suicide Attacks

The notion that support for suicide attacks among Palestinians is negatively related to support for negotiations with Israel and with optimism about the future seems intuitively reasonable. As Figure 7.2 shows, however, this negative relationship is not perfect. Even at the height of the second intifada, when support for suicide attacks was higher than 70%, about half of the Palestinians supported negotiations with Israel and about 40% expressed optimism. Thus, although optimism and support for negotiations with Israel declined during the intifada by about 50% compared

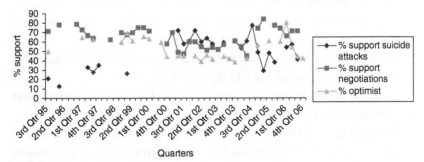

**Figure 7.2** Support for suicide attacks compared with support for negotiations with Israel and with optimism among Palestinians, 1995–2006.

to the pre-intifada period, for a large proportion of the Palestinians support for suicide attacks has not, presumably, been a result of desperate pessimism.

Several demographic factors appear to influence the attitudes to suicide attacks in the Palestinian society. Support is usually (albeit not always) greater in the Gaza Strip than in the West Bank.[17] This difference may be related to the finding that support for suicide attacks is higher in refugee camps than in cities and villages. The percentage of refugees is much higher in the Gaza Strip than in the West Bank.[18] As shown by the findings of the study of suicides' families (Chapter 4) and would-be suicides (Chapter 5), the representation of refugee-camp residents and sons of refugee families among suicide bombers was higher than their corresponding rates in the general population. Nevertheless, this trend was reversed at times when residents of the Gaza Strip, but not those of the West Bank, had an interest in reducing the level of militancy, or had expectations for improvement in the political situation in the immediate future. Thus, in a poll conducted in March 1996—when the Gaza Strip was already under autonomous Palestinian rule, but most of the West Bank was still under Israeli occupation—23.8% of the West Bank residents sampled supported suicide attacks, compared to only 16.8% of the Gaza Strip residents.[19] Similarly, a poll conducted in March 2005, after the announcement of Prime Minister Sharon's plan to withdraw Israeli forces from the Gaza Strip and dismantle all Israeli settlements there, found a lower rate of support for suicide attacks in the Gaza Strip than in the West Bank.[20]

Young people tend to support suicide attacks more than older people. This trend is hardly surprising, as younger people generally tend to radicalism and militancy more than older people. Indeed, the great majority of suicide terrorists have been less than 30 years old.

People who have some university education (students or university graduates) tend to support suicide attacks more than people who have little or no education.[21]

A surprising finding is that women have been found to be somewhat more supportive of suicide attacks than men.[22]

Support for suicide attacks has been consistently and markedly higher among people who identified themselves as Hamas supporters than among Fatah supporters.[23] This finding seems to suggest that Islamic radicalism is an important factor in the atmosphere which gives rise to suicide attacks. Indeed, a JMCC poll found that the rate of support for suicide attacks was higher among Muslims than among Christians in the Palestinian community.[24]

Yet, in Palestinian public perception Hamas represents radical, uncompromising nationalism at least as much as it represents Islamic militancy.

Interestingly, in a study conducted in Lebanon on the attitudes to suicide attacks of Lebanese Muslims and Palestinian refugees living in Lebanon, Haddad (2004) found trends that are by and large similar to those observed in the polls of Palestinians in the occupied territories. Among both Lebanese and Palestinians, women showed higher support for suicide attacks than men. In the Palestinian sample, support for suicide attacks was higher among residents of refugee camps, and in both the Lebanese and Palestinian samples the most important determinant of support for suicide attacks was attachment to "political Islam," i.e., Islamic militancy.

In some of the polls, support for suicide attacks has been influenced by recent events, which had aroused an emotional urge to take revenge for casualties inflicted by Israeli security forces.[25]

A noteworthy finding is that support for specific suicide attacks is consistently (and conspicuously) higher than support for the general notion of suicide attacks as a method. Thus, in a poll conducted by PSR shortly after a suicide attack in a restaurant in Haifa (October 4, 2003), in which 21 people were killed, 74.5% of the respondents expressed support for that attack, whereas in the same poll only 54.4% supported "armed attacks against Israeli civilians inside Israel."[26] A similar difference was found in a PSR poll conducted a few weeks after a suicide bombing attack in Beer Sheva (August 31, 2004): while 77.4% of the respondents supported that specific suicide attack, only 53.4% supported "armed attacks against Israeli civilians inside Israel."[27] In still another example, support for a specific suicide attack in Tel Aviv on April 17, 2006 was considerably higher (69.4%) than support for the general notion of armed attacks against Israeli civilians inside Israel (56.1%).[28] The only exception to this rule is a poll conducted in March 2005, in which only 29.1% of the respondents expressed support for a specific suicide attack, which had taken place in Tel Aviv a couple of weeks earlier.[29] Although no question was asked in that poll concerning support for suicide attacks in general (or attacks against Israeli civilians inside Israel, as the question was often phrased in PSR polls), the rate of support for the specific attack was much lower than the rates of support for specific attacks found in other polls. The rate of support for the Tel Aviv attack was also considerably lower than the rates of support for suicide attacks in general, which were found in polls both before and after the March 2005 poll. The reason for this systematic difference is not quite clear; hypothetically, however, it can be explained by the notion that the reaction to concrete suicide attacks reflects immediate emotions of joy for causing the enemy pain.

## Public Support is a Necessary but Not Sufficient Factor for Large-Scale Suicide Campaigns

The foregoing analysis leaves little doubt that the community's attitude to suicide attacks has a strong influence on the volume of suicide attacks generated by the community members. Nevertheless, in itself public opinion cannot generate suicide attacks on a large scale; even when suicide attacks are supported by a majority of the public, other factors must exist to move people from abstract support to actually engaging in this behavior. A series of polls conducted by the Pew Research Center have shown that large segments of the population in several Muslim countries justify suicide attacks against civilians to defend Islam from its enemies. Thus, in a poll conducted in 2005, 57% of the respondents in Jordan, 39% in Lebanon, 25% in Pakistan, and 15% in Indonesia justified suicide attacks.[30] In some of the countries higher rates of support for suicide attacks were found in earlier polls.[31] In a similar vein, high rates of support for suicide attacks against Westerners in Iraq were found in these countries.[32] Thus, the rates of support for suicide attacks in some of the Muslim countries are as high as the rates of support for suicide attacks among Palestinians at the height of the second intifada. Yet, they have carried out a very small number of suicide attacks against Western targets in their own countries. Some of the militant Islamists in North African and Middle Eastern countries have found their way to Iraq and have carried out suicide attacks there. However, the number of Jordanians and Lebanese among them has apparently been rather small, despite the sizable support in these countries for suicide attacks in Iraq. Paz (2005) analyzed the obituaries of Islamic militants, most of them foreigners who traveled to Iraq to fight in the framework of "al-Qaeda in Mesopotamia" against the American-led coalition and were killed there. These obituaries had been published in al-Qaeda affiliated websites. Most of the 154 "shahids"—61%—were Saudis, with 10.4% Syrians, 7.1% Kuwaitis, and 8.4% indigenous Iraqis. Only four of the shahids (2.6%) were Jordanians and two (1.3%) were Moroccans. Thirty-three of the 154 shahids carried out suicide attacks; only one of them was from Morocco (3%) and none from Jordan. Later studies obtained similar results. Thus, Hafez (2007a), who also used Islamic websites as a source, found that only four out of 124 suicide bombers in Iraq were Jordanians. Felter and Fishman

(2007; 2008), who analyzed captured al-Qaeda records that detailed the background of about 600 foreign volunteers who had come to Iraq to fight in the ranks of al-Qaeda in the period between August 2006 and August 2007, found that Moroccans comprised 6.1% and Jordanians 1.9% of the foreign volunteers. These studies show that public support for suicide attacks is, in itself, insufficient for generating actual suicides.

The difference between the rates of participation in suicide attacks of Moroccan and Jordanians on the one hand, and Palestinians, Sri Lankan and Chechens on the other hand, shows that an abstract ideological support of suicide attacks can move a few to actually volunteer for such attacks, but in the absence of other factors it is insufficient for motivating a large number of youngsters to give their lives for what they consider a just cause. Three other conditions must exist for generating a massive suicide campaign, namely: (1) A feeling that the struggle involves existential interests of the community; (2) support and encouragement of suicide attacks by generally accepted social agents, such as the media and figures of authority; and (3) an organization that transforms the raw readiness to actual behavior by recruiting the suicides and preparing the mission.

## Perception of Existential Interests at Stake

In almost all cases where a massive campaign of suicide attacks has taken place, the community which generated these attacks (or a sizable segment of it) felt that its existential interests were at stake. These interests have not necessarily been liberation from a foreign occupation by a democratic state, as Pape (2003; 2005) has claimed. Indeed, the Tamils, Palestinians, Kurds, and Chechens have fought for independence—but in other places, such as in Pakistan and many of the attacks in Iraq, the suicides have been motivated by sectarian interests. To motive many people to take an active part and making sacrifices, the conflict must have direct relevance to the community. People have opinions on many political, social, and religious issues, and some of these opinions are rather strong. They may firmly support or object to globalization, capitalism, communism, or any given religious belief, and they may express their support in a variety of ways, such as signing petitions and contributing money. But as long as the issue at stake does not directly affect their lives, they do not wish to risk their lives for the cause they advocate. This latter situation characterizes the attitude to suicide attacks held by members of Muslim communities that are not directly involved in an acute conflict.

## The Critical Role of the Organization

Public support for suicide attacks has a great influence on the number of potential volunteers for such missions, but the actual implementation of these attacks is done by organized groups. The terrorist organization molds the diffuse public feelings of humiliation, hatred, and thirst for revenge, and channels them into a concrete form of action. The urge to hurt the enemy does not necessarily lead to a suicidal action; only the organization directs the volunteer to this form of attack. With the exception of only four cases, all suicide terrorist attacks have been organized by groups, not by private individuals on their own whim.

# Support for Suicide Attacks by Mainstream Agents of Influence

In a book based on first-hand impressions of Palestinian society, Ann Marie Oliver and Paul Steinberg (2005), who lived a long time among Palestinians in Gaza and the West Bank, described the Palestinian public's attitude to suicide attacks as follows:

> Support for suicide bombings went far beyond the military wings of the nationalist and Islamist movements. Parents dressed their babies and toddlers as suicide bombers and had them photographed in local photography studios. Children marched with suicide belts around their chests. University exhibitions included one that recreated an actual suicide bombing carried out in the Sbarro restaurant in Jerusalem, replete with pizza slices and bloody body parts. The Palestinian Authority named popular soccer tournaments after martyrs belonging both to Fatah and the rival Hamas, with even the suicide bomber who blew himself up during an Israeli family celebration of Passover, killing thirty of them, thus honored. On public TV, the Palestinian Broadcasting Corporation aired videos of men being lured away by the *hur*, the beautiful virgins of Paradise promised to martyrs, as if they were commercials or public service announcements. If the term *cult* did not suggest a fringe phenomenon, we might begin to speak of a cult of martyrdom; as it is, the devotees of death on all fronts have become too numerous and too diverse for us to do so any longer. (p. xxiii).

Indeed, in Palestinian society, suicide attacks have been established as a praiseworthy act, a generally admired expression of patriotism and sacrifice. All social agents of influence have shared this attitude, thus creating an overwhelming impact on people's opinions. Palestinian inhabitants of the occupied territories of all ages and walks of life have been swamped with news, sermons, artwork and teaching that have glorified the shahids and praised their sacrifice. Praise for suicide bombers has not been limited to media outlets representing the militant groups; mainstream newspaper editorials and PNA government television broadcasts have voiced the same sentiments. As Margalit (2003) noted, "Once a suicide bomber has completed his mission he at once becomes a phantom celebrity. Visitors to the occupied territories have been struck by how well the names of the suicide bombers are known, even to small children." Glorification of shahids is embedded in the Palestinian education system and thus becomes a basic element in the formation of values of future generations. A study of 29 textbooks published in the school year 2004–2005 by the Palestinian National Authority's Ministry of Education for 5th and 10th grades, found that these books were replete with phrases exalting shahids and the glory of martyrdom.[33] Praise for martyrdom operations was introduced not only in Islamic education and history textbooks, but also in a matter-of-fact manner by using phrases glorifying shahids as syntactic examples in grammar textbooks.

## Praise for Shahids in Non-Palestinian Media

Palestinians' support for suicide attacks has been reinforced by the approving attitudes of public opinion in other Arab countries, which constitute the broader social, cultural and political milieu for the Palestinians. Many religious and secular opinion leaders in Arab countries have expressed support for suicide attacks, giving the Palestinian people a feeling that they are not crazy fanatics. Support for suicide attacks among radical Islamic circles and their media organs in various Arab countries is not surprising and can be taken for granted. The fact that this support has permeated much broader echelons of society, however, is less obvious and arguably more important. In Egypt, for example, an editorial of *Al-Akhbar*, a government-sponsored daily, wrote following a Palestinian suicide attack on passengers in a bus station inside Israel:

> [The operation] was the only effective answer to the [feelings of] bitterness and pain in our reality. This operation proved that the Palestinian individual is still capable of breaking through all forms of siege and oppression, when he is armed with steadfastness and the justice of his cause, and capable of reaching the depths of the Zionist entity in order to strike at it.[34]

Support for Palestinian suicide attacks was also expressed by Dr. Lutfi Nasif, a columnist for the Egyptian government daily, *Al-Gumhuriya*. He suggested that these attacks were praiseworthy because they spread fear among Jews who had immigrated to Israel and would help drive them out of the country, as well as deter others from coming. Therefore, in his words, "We salute all the Shahids and are sorry for their departure, but the freedom tax must be paid, even if it is expensive . . . ."[35]

The same sentiments in a more virulent form were expressed in another Egyptian government newspaper, *Al-Akhbar*, by the columnist Bahjat Ibrahim Al-Dsuqi, who wrote that "the rats who came from the US, Europe, and Russia will flee." He also opined that "whoever blows himself up as a revenge against the enemies is a Shahid of the highest rank of Martyrdom, because he has sold his soul and bought Paradise. We are not afraid of [sacrificing] thousands of Martyrs."[36] Another *Al-Akhbar* columnist, Walid Badran, also thought that suicide attacks would drive Israeli Jews out of the country unless they reached an agreement with the Palestinians.[37]

Following the first suicide attack by a Palestinian woman, Wafa Idris (January 27, 2002), the Egyptian media was swamped with praise. Ahmad Bahgat, a columnist for the leading Egyptian daily Al-Ahram, a generally respected newspaper, wrote:

> Wafa revealed the meaning of the Palestinian personality; she revealed the heroism of the Palestinian woman and turned from a living creature walking on the Earth to a symbol that went down in history, the trace of which cannot be eradicated. As a nurse, her work was like that of the merciful angels. She cared for the sick and injured, and rescued the wounded. And behold, she expanded the sphere of her work from saving individuals to saving the Palestinian nation.[38]

Another *Al-Gumhuriya* columnist, Abd Al-Wahab 'Adas, wrote: "She gave, for the first time, a different example of women's heroism . . . Wafa's pure spirit will join in waving the flag of Palestine above the dome of Al-Aqsa. Wafa Idris engraved her name with pride, with strength, and with honor . . . on the conscience of every Muslim Arab."[39]

The attitudes of Egyptian writers to suicide attacks are of particular interest because of Egypt's dominant cultural and ideological influence in the Arab world, and because of its relative freedom of the press. However, favorable positions concerning suicide attacks have also abounded in Arab media in other countries. For example, following a suicide attack at a Tel

Aviv disco, in which 22 Israeli teenagers were killed (June 1, 2001), Dr. Ali 'Aqleh 'Ursan, head of the Syrian Arab Writers Union, wrote:

> Whoever denounces the operations of the Shahids joins the Arab politicians who apologize for the legitimate struggle. However, these do not represent the conscience of the nation, nor do they influence the public... It is the blood that writes history, and the black ink cannot soil the golden pages written in the blood of the Shahids, on their way to liberate Palestine, the Golan, and South Lebanon.[40]

Justification of suicide attacks through dehumanization of the victims characterizes the commentary by Hamad Al-Majid, a columnist for the London-based Arabic weekly *Al-Sharq Al-Awsat*, who described the victims as "a riffraff of Zionists whose killing has brought happiness to any bereaved Palestinian mother and remedy to every injured family in Jerusalem . . . We wish that just like the Zionist airports were filled with those vagabond homosexuals on their way in, they will be filled once again on their way out, without anyone feeling sorry for them."[41]

## Religious Authorities

Palestinian religious authorities have unanimously extolled suicide bombers (as well as other *shahids*). Praise for *shahids* and encouragement of martyrdom has been expressed not only by clerics associated with the militant Islamic groups but by those appointed by the PNA as well, such as the Mufti of the PNA, Sheik Ikrima Sabri,[42] the Chief Mufti of the PNA Police, Sheik Abd Al-Salam Skheidm,[43] and many others.[44]

As Paz has pointed out, the legitimacy of Palestinian suicide attacks against Israeli civilians has spread beyond the Palestinian arena and gained a consensus in the Islamic establishments of the Arab world.[45] A leading figure among the Islamic authorities who has supported suicide attacks has been Sheikh Yusef al-Qaradhawi. Qaradhawi, an Egyptian Islamic cleric who has lived and taught in Qatar for many years, has been one of the most influential religious authorities in the Islamic world in recent years, and especially in the Middle East. His weekly program on Al-Jazeera television has exposed him to a vast Muslim audience. His *fatwas* (religious rulings) endorsing Palestinian suicide attacks have been widely publicized and often quoted. In a *fatwa* dated March 22, 2004, for example, he stated: "The martyr operation is the greatest of all sorts of jihad in the cause of Allah. A martyr operation is carried out by a person who sacrifices himself, deeming his life [of] less value than striving in the cause of Allah, in the cause of restoring the land and preserving the dignity."[46] In an earlier interview, Qaradhawi justified killing Israeli civilians as follows:

> Israeli society is militaristic in nature. Both men and women serve in the army and can be drafted at any moment. [On the other hand] if a child or an elderly is killed in such an operation, he is not killed on purpose, but by mistake, and as a result of military necessity. Necessity justifies the forbidden.[47]

Qaradhawi has been associated with the Muslim Brothers, a radical Islamic movement founded in Egypt in 1928, which has, among other things, spawned the Palestinian Hamas.[48] As such, his support for suicide attacks may not be surprising. However, support for suicide attacks has also been expressed by mainstream religious authorities in several Arab countries, especially Egypt. Cairo's al-Azhar University—which Gilles Kepel (1993), one the best scholars on Islamic movements in Egypt, described concisely as "the highest authority of Islam in Egypt; government controlled to some extent and therefore criticized by the Islamicist movement" (p. 276)—has been the home of several enthusiastic supporters of suicide attacks.

The top Egyptian cleric of al-Azhar University, Sheikh Muhammad Sayyed Tantawi, initially opposed suicide attacks against civilians, ruling that "the suicide operations are of self-defense and a kind of martyrdom, as long as the intention behind them is to kill the enemy's soldiers, and not women or children."[49] Later, however, apparently under pressure from other high-ranking Egyptian clerics, he modified his position, stating that martyrdom (suicide) attacks were the highest form of jihad, urging Palestinians of all factions to intensify them, and saying that attacks against women and children were legitimate as long as the Israeli occupation continued.[50]

Other high-ranking religious authorities in Egypt who have endorsed Palestinian suicide attacks have included, *inter alia*, Sheikh Ali Abu Al-Hassan, Chairman of the Religious Ruling Committee at al-Azhar University,[51] Egypt's Mufti,[52] Sheikh Dr. Ahmad al-Tayyeb, who was later appointed President of al-Azhar University,[53] and his successor in the position of Egypt's Mufti, Dr. Sheikh 'Ali Gum'a. In an interview with the Egyptian newspaper *al-Haqiqa* in July 2003, Gum'a said:

> The one who carries out *Fedaii* [martyrdom] operations against the Zionists and blows himself up is, without a doubt, a *Shahid* because he is defending

his homeland against the occupying enemy who is supported by superpowers such as the U.S. and Britain.[54]

## Academic Authorities

Academic authorities constitute another source of influence on public attitudes. Academics in several countries have joined the media and the religious establishment in expressing support for suicide attacks. In Egypt, for example, Dr. 'Adel Sadeq, chairman of the Arab Psychiatrists Association and head of the Department of Psychiatry at 'Ein Shams University in Cairo, has said in an interview with *Iqraa*, a Saudi satellite television channel:

> . . . The psychological structure [of the perpetrator of a suicide attack] is that of an individual who loves life. This may seem strange to people who see the human soul as most sublime. They are incapable of understanding [the suicide attack] because their cultural structure has no concepts such as self-sacrifice and honor. These concepts do not exist in a number of cultures, and therefore they offer stupid interpretations, attesting to ignorance . . . But we know this well, because our culture is one of sacrifice, loyalty, and honor . . .
>
> When the martyr dies a martyr's death, he attains the height of bliss . . . As a professional psychiatrist, I say that the height of bliss comes with the end of the countdown: ten, nine, eight, seven, six, five, four, three, two, one. And then, you press the button to blow yourself up. When the martyr reaches 'one,' and then 'boom,' he explodes, and senses himself flying, because he knows for certain that he is not dead . . . It is a transition to another, more beautiful world, because he knows very well that within seconds he will see the light of the Creator. He will be at the closest possible point to Allah . . . None in the [Western] world sacrifices his life for his homeland. If his homeland is drowning, he is the first to jump ship. In our culture it is different . . .
>
> There are no Israeli civilians. They are all plunderers. History teaches this . . . I am completely convinced that the psychological effect [of the attacks] on the Israeli plunderer is [the realization] that his existence is temporary . . . They have become completely convinced that their existence in this region is temporary . . . Remove the Apache [helicopter] from the equation, leave them one-on-one with the Palestinian people with the only weapon [for both sides] being dynamite. Then you will see all the Israelis leave, because among them there is not even one man willing to don a belt of dynamite . . .[55]

Dr. Ibrahim Abrash, a lecturer on politics at the Rabat University in Morocco, asserted that Palestinian suicide attacks are legitimate from the point of view of international law and should not be regarded as terrorism.[56]

Dr. Muhammad Kamal Al-Din Al-Imam, a Lecturer on Islamic law at the Alexandria University Faculty of law, justified the killing of Israeli civilians by suicide bombers: "The [Israeli] society as a whole attacks the land of Palestine. They are all armed, they are all part of a military force, they are all recruited. They came from various countries in order to occupy someone else's land. Can someone who committed such a crime be treated as a civilian?!!" Al-Imam even suggested that it is permissible to kill Muslims along with the "heretics" if there is no other way of killing the enemy.[57]

## Other Voices

These descriptions rightly convey the impression that the most important agents of influence in the Palestinian society—namely, the media, the educational system, and religious authorities, those that form public opinion—have not only supported suicide attacks but glorified this behavior as the utmost form of patriotism. Yet, there have also been other voices in Palestinian society and in the Arab world that have criticized this phenomenon, even during the heat of the second intifada. MEMRI recorded the uneven debate on suicide attacks in a series of publications. Interestingly, however, in most (albeit not all) cases even those who opposed suicide attacks justified their opposition by utilitarian rather than moral arguments (on the ground that the attacks arouse anti-Palestinian sentiments in the world).

One of the critics in the Palestinian community was Yassir Arafat himself, Chairman of the PNA. In a speech in May 2002, he declared that suicide attacks against civilians are "unacceptable," because they alienate the international community from the Palestinians.[58] Other high-ranking Palestinian critics of suicide attacks have included Abd Al-Razzaq Al-Yahya, at the time Interior Minister,[59] former Minister for Parliamentary Affairs, Nabil Amru,[60] and Mamduh Nofal, at the time Arafat's Advisor on Military Affairs.[61] Others, such as Bassam Abu Sharif, have advised that suicide operations be limited to attacks against soldiers and settlers in the occupied territories while refraining from attacks against civilians inside Israel.[62]

In June 2002, following the escalation in suicide attacks inside Israel in the wake of the Defensive Shield operation during the al-Aqsa intifada, when Israeli forces re-entered Palestinian cities in the West Bank, 55 prominent Palestinians published a call to stop suicide attacks. The statement did not criticize all suicide attacks, only those directed against Israeli citizens inside Israel; thus, suicide attacks against Israeli security forces in Israel and the territories as well as attacks against Israeli civilians in the Territories were apparently considered acceptable. The call did not criticize suicide attacks against civilians on moral grounds. Rather, it argued that suicide attacks were damaging to Palestinian interests because they exacerbated the conflict, strengthened the right wing in Israel and "provide excuses" for the Israeli government to continue the war against Palestinian cities and villages.[63] A somewhat modified call with 315 signatories was published two days later. The modified version added a strong condemnation of "all measures implemented by the Israeli repression against our people, including the policy of incursions, assassinations, and siege, and stress that the occupation is the basis of the tragedy to which our people is subject and that resistance is a right and an obligation."[64]

Outside the Palestinian Territories, Dr. Abd Al-Hamid Al-Ansari, former dean of the Shari'a (Islamic law) and Law Faculty at Qatar University, observed that "Today, no one blows himself up among women and children, in a restaurant, in a hospital, or on a subway except for Muslims, who continue to do so, terrorizing people." The association between suicide attacks and Islam damages Islam's image. Al-Ansari argued that Islam forbade killing women and children, and that those who commit suicide are condemned to hell. He criticized Qaradhawi's fatwas, which allowed suicide attacks against civilians in Israel and Iraq, calling them a "fatal breach" of Islamic law, concluding that "These fatwas are a moral and ideological mark of shame, which we must purge from our Islam."[65]

*Endnotes*

1.  The Syrian Social Nationalist Party (SSNP), a pro–Syrian Lebanese group, carried out 10 suicide attacks against Israeli forces and the Israeli–sponsored South Lebanese Army in Lebanon during the years 1985–1987.

2.  The affiliates of this kind of *international* imagined community have less in common than members of a national group who live in the same country, to whom Benedict Anderson (1991) referred as an "imagined community." Still, they share a firm conviction in a certain ideology or religion and a strong feeling of collective deprivation.

3.  Hamas suspended suicide attacks from late August 1995 to February 1996, because the group's political leadership felt that the Palestinian public would not favor such attacks at the time that the peace process was proceeding reasonably well. A public opinion survey conducted in August 1995 by a Palestinian research organization, the Jerusalem Media and Communication Center, showed that only 24.3% of the Palestinians supported suicide attacks at that time, while 62.2% opposed them. Hamas resumed suicide attacks after Israel killed Yahya Ayyash, a mastermind of suicide attacks (known as "The Engineer"). Ayyash was regarded as a national hero throughout the Palestinian community and Hamas leadership reckoned that under

those circumstances the public would not only accept massive revenge but expected it. Hamas also suspended suicide attacks during the two–year period from November 2004 to November 2006, at a time when Palestinian public support for such attacks declined, whereas PIJ continued suicide attacks throughout that period.

4. Times Online, July 4, 2006, available at: http://www.timesonline.co.uk/article/0,,22989–2254764,00.html, accessed January 29, 2007. The poll was conducted for the Times of London and ITV.

5. The Great Divide: How Westerners and Muslims View Each Other. The Pew Global Attitudes Project, results of survey released on June 22, 2006. Available at: http://www.pewglobal.org, accessed on January 31, 2007.

6. Although Ricolfi's point concerning peer influence is correct, his observation that "A tiny number of refugee camps around the West Bank towns of Hebron, Nablus, and Jenin supply the great majority of martyrs" (p. 113) is somewhat exaggerated. Only 22 of the 129 suicide bombers in the period of 1993–2006, whose homes were in the West Bank, lived in refugee camps.

7. The number of foiled suicide attacks was taken from data published by the Intelligence and Terrorism Information Center at the Center for Special Studies (http://www.terrorism-info.org.il/malam_multimedia//ENGLISH/COUNTER-TERRORISM-DATA/PDF/E_1B.PDF, accessed on January 16, 2010)." These data covered the period of October 2000 to December 2004.

8. JMCC Poll No. 19, April 1997, available at: http://www.jmcc.org.

9. JMCC Public Opinion Poll No. 44, March 2002, available at: http://www.jmcc.org. The more general question was phrased as follows: "Do you support the resumption of the military operations against Israeli targets as a suitable response within the current political conditions, or do you reject it and find it harmful to Palestinian national interests?" (73.6% supported and 20.0% opposed). The more specific question was phrased as: "What is your feeling towards suicide bombing operations against Israeli civilians, do you support it or oppose it?" (72.0% strongly supported or somewhat supported, and 21.7% strongly opposed or somewhat opposed).

10. JMCC Poll No. 14, March 1996. Available at: http://www.jmcc.org

11. CPRS Poll No. 29, September 1997. Available at: http://www.pcpsr.org.

12. JMCC Poll No. 40, April 2001.

13. In March 2002, shortly before the onset of the "Defensive Shield" operation, 72% of the Palestinians stated that they supported, or strongly supported, suicide attacks against Israelis (JMCC Poll No. 44, March 20–23, 2002). But in May 2002, about one month into the operation, the level of support dropped to 52% (PSR Poll No. 4, May 15–18, 2002). It is perhaps indicative that in the latter poll support for suicide attacks was higher in the Gaza Strip (59%) which was not affected by the Israeli operation, than in the West Bank (47%), whose cities and villages directly suffered from the Israeli forces' incursion.

14. CPRS Public Opinion Poll No. 19, August–September 1995, available at: http://www.pcpsr.org/survey/cprspolls/95/poll19a.html. In the weeks preceding the poll two suicide attacks were carried out by Hamas and Hamas operatives were arrested by the PNA.

15. PSR Public Opinion Poll No. 3, December 19–24, 2001. Available at: http://www. pcpsr.org.

16. For example, PSR Public Opinion Poll No, 4, May 15–19, 2002; PSR Poll No. 6, November 14–22, 2002; PSR Poll No. 7, April 3–7, 2003; PSR poll No. 11, March 14–17, 2004; PSR Poll No. 14, December 5, 2004.

17. See, for example, PSR poll No. 4 (May 2002), PSR Poll No. 9 (October 2003), PSR Poll No. 13 (September 2004), PSR Poll no. 17 (September 2005), PSR Poll No. 20 (June 2006), and PSR Poll No. 21 (September 2001).

18. See explanatory text in CPRS Poll No. 13 (November 17–19, 1994).

19. CPRS Poll No. 22, March 29–31, 1996.

20. PSR Poll No. 15, March 10–12, 2005.

21. See, for example, CPRS Poll No. 19 (August 1995), PSR Poll No. 4 (May 2002).

22. CPRS No. 19, August 1995, PSR Poll No. 9 (October 2003, PSR Poll No. 13, September 2004.

23. See, for example, PSR Poll No. 4 (May 2002), PSR Poll No. 9 (October 2003), PSR Poll No. 13 (September 2004), and PSR Poll No. 15 (March 2005).

24. JMCC Poll No. 8 (August 1995). In this poll, 26.0% of the Muslims but only 9.8% of the Christians supported "the continuation of Hamas and Islamic Jihad's suicide operations against Israeli targets."

25. The explanatory text of PSR poll No. 20 (June 2006) notes:
    "It is worth mentioning that this poll was conducted during the period in which Israeli shelling of the Gaza Strip led to a high number of casualties among Palestinian civilians at a Gaza beach and in populated areas. But while findings show a significant increase in support for violence against Israelis based on emotional drivers, a significant drop has been registered in this poll in the percentage of those who believe that armed confrontations have helped Palestinians achieve national rights in ways that negotiations could not from 69% last March to 54% in this poll." Available at: http://www.pcpsr.org.

26. The specific question was: "With regard to the bombing operation in the Maxim Restaurant in Haifa, which led to the death of 20 Israelis, do you support or oppose this operation?" (74.5% of the respondents said that they "strongly supported" or "supported" the attack, and 21.8% said that they "strongly opposed" or "opposed" it). The general question was: "Concerning armed attacks against Israeli civilians inside Israel, I . . ." (54.4% supported or strongly supported such attacks and 43.2% opposed them). See: PSR Public Opinion Poll No. 9, October 7–14, 2003, available at: http://www.pcpsr.org.

27. PSR Public Opinion Poll No. 13, September 23–26, 2004, available at: http://www. pcpsr.org. The question relating to the specific suicide attack was: "With regard to the latest bombing attack in Beer Shiva in Israel early in this month which lead to the death of 16 Israelis, do you support or oppose this attack?" (77.4% of the respondents said that they "strongly supported" or "supported" the attack, and 19.7% said that they "strongly opposed" or "opposed" it). The general question was: "Concerning armed attacks against Israeli civilians inside Israel, I . . ." (53.8% supported or strongly supported such attacks and 44.3% opposed them).

28. PSR Public Opinion Poll No. 20, 15–18 June, 2006, available at: http://www.pcpsr. org. The question relating to the specific suicide attack was: "A bombing attack took place in Tel Aviv last April leading to the death of 11 Israelis. Do you support or oppose this bombing attack?" (69.4% of the respondents said that they "strongly support" or "support" the attack, and 26.6% said that they "strongly oppose" or "oppose" it). The general question was: "Concerning armed attacks against Israeli civilians inside Israel, I . . ." (56.1% supported or strongly supported such attacks and 42.0% opposed them).

29. PSR Public Opinion Poll No. 15, March 10–12, 2005, available at: http://www. pcpsr.org. The question was: "Two weeks ago a bombing attack took place in Tel Aviv leading to the death of four Israelis and the injury of 50 others in front of a night club. Do you support or oppose this attack?"

30. See: Where terrorism finds support in the Muslim world. Pew Research Center, available at: http://pewresearch.org/obdeck/?ObDeckID=26, accessed on June 11, 2006. The poll's question was: "Some people think that suicide bombing and other forms of violence against civilian targets are justified in order to defend Islam from its enemies. Other people believe that, no matter what the reason, this kind of violence is never justified. Do you personally feel that this kind of violence is often justified to defend Islam, sometimes justified, rarely justified, or never justified?" The rates of support for suicide attacks are the percentages of respondents who maintained that suicide attacks were often or sometimes justified.

31. For example, in Morocco the rate of support for suicide attacks was 40% and in Pakistan it was 41% in 2004, in Lebanon it was 73% in 2002. Pew poll, op. cit.

32. According to the 2005 Pew poll (op. cit), rates of support for suicide attacks against Westerners in Iraq were: Morocco – 56% (66% in 2004), Jordan – 49% (70% in 2004), Lebanon – 49%, Pakistan – 29%, Indonesia – 26%, and Turkey – 24%.

33. Meridor, N., a study of textbooks in the Palestinian education system, distributed by the Intelligence and Terrorism Information Center at the Center for Special Studies, Israel, April 16, 2006. Available at: http://www.terrorism-info.org.il/malam_ multimedia/English/eng_n/pdf/as_nm_e.pdf. Accessed: November 30,, 2009.

34. MEMRI Inquiry and Analysis Series No. 54, quoting Al Akhbar (Egypt), April 24, 2001. Available at: http://memri.org/bin/articles.cgi?Page=subjects&Area=conflict& ID=IA5401 Accessed: Jan 11, 2004.

35. MEMRI *Inquiry and Analysis Series – No. 66*, July 27, 2001, quoting Al–Gumhuri-yya (Egypt), June 2, 2001. Available at: http://memri.org/bin/articles.cgi?Page= subjects&Area=conflict&ID=IA6601, Accessed: Jan. 10, 2004.

36. MEMRI *Inquiry and Analysis Series – No. 66*, July 27, 2001, quoting Al–Akhbar (Egypt), June 1, 2001. Available at: http://memri.org/bin/articles.cgi?Page=subjects &Area=conflict&ID=IA6601, Accessed: Jan. 10, 2004.

37. MEMRI *Inquiry and Analysis Series – No. 66*, July 27, 2001, quoting Al–Akhbar (Egypt), June 3, 2001. Available at: http://memri.org/bin/articles.cgi?Page=subjects &Area=conflict&ID=IA6601, Accessed: Jan. 10, 2004.

38. MEMRI *Inquiry and Analysis Series – No. 85*, February 14, 2002, quoting *Al–Ahram* (Egypt), February 3, 2002. Available at: http://memri.org/bin/articles.cgi?Page=archi ves&Area=ia&ID=IA8302 Accessed: Dec. 12, 2005. Ibrahim Nafi', Editor–in–Chief of *Al–Ahram*, also expressed understanding (albeit not enthusiasm) for Wafa Idris'

suicide attack. He wrote: "She decided to end her fresh young life at a moment of a profound sense of oppression such as no people had suffered as the Palestinians do. But before that, she decided that her death would reverberate so as to draw attention to the tragedy created by the Israelis, with their airplanes and tanks against a defenseless people." (MEMRI *Inquiry and Analysis Series No. 85*, February 14, 2002, quoting *Al–Ahram* (Egypt), February 5, 2002. Available at: http://memri.org/bin/articles.cgi?Page=archives&Area=ia&ID=IA8302 Accessed: Dec. 12, 2005).

39. MEMRI *Inquiry and Analysis Series – No. 85*, February 14, 2002, quoting *Al–Gumhuriya* (Egypt), January 31, 2002, as cited in *Al–Quds Al–Arabi* (London), February 2, 2002. Available at: http://memri.org/bin/articles.cgi?Page=archives&Area=ia&ID=IA8502, Accessed: Dec. 12, 2005.

40. MEMRI *Inquiry and Analysis Series – No. 66*, July 27, 2001, quoting Al–Usb'u Al–Adabi (Syria), June 9, 2001. Available at: http://memri.org/bin/articles.cgi?Page=subjects&Area=conflict&ID=IA6601, Accessed: Jan. 10, 2004.

41. MEMRI *Inquiry and Analysis Series – No. 66*, July 27, 2001, quoting Al–Sharq Al–Awsat (London), June 5, 2001. Available at: http://memri.org/bin/articles.cgi?Page=subjects&Area=conflict&ID=IA6601, Accessed: Jan. 10, 2004.

42. MEMRI Inquiry and analysis Series No. 61, June 25, 2001, quoting *Voice of Palestine Radio*, May 25, 2001. http://www.memri.org/bin/articles.cgi?Page=countries&Area=palestinian&ID=IA6101, accessed January 10, 2004.

43. MEMRI Inquiry and analysis Series No. 61, June 25, 2001, quoting *Al–Hayat Al–Jadida(PA)*, September 17, 1999. Available at: http://www.memri.org/bin/articles.cgi?Page=countries&Area=palestinian&ID=IA6101, accessed January 10, 2004.

44. See: MEMRI Inquiry and Analysis Series No. 25, February 24, 2000, MEMRI Inquiry and Analysis Series No. 61, June 25, 2001, and MEMRI Special Report No. 20, August 22, 2003. All these reports can be found at http://www.memri.org.

45. See: Paz, R. Qaradhawi and the World Association of Muslim Clerics: The new platform of the Muslim Brotherhood. PRISM Series of Global Jihad, No. 4/2 – November 2004. Available at: http://www.e–prism.org/images/PRISM_no_4_vol_2_–_Qaradhawi.pdf, accessed: January 25, 2005.

46. Available at: http://www.islamonline.net/fatwa/english/FatwaDisplay.asp?hFatwaID=68511, accessed January 30, 2005.

47. MEMRI Inquiry and Analysis No. 53, May 2, 2001, quoting *Al–Ahram Al–Arabi* (Egypt), February 3, 2001. Available at: http://www.memri.org/bin/articles.cgi?Page=archives&Area=ia&ID=IA5301, accessed January 10, 2004.

48. See: The Qaradawi Fatwas. Middle East Quarterly, Summer 2004, Volume XI, No. 3, available at: http://www.meforum.org/article/646, accessed: January 20, 2007.

49. MEMRI Inquiry and Analysis Series No. 53, May 2, 2001, quoting *Sut Al–Ama* (Egypt), April 26, 2001. Available at: http://www.memri.org/bin/articles.cgi?Page=archives&Area=ia&ID=IA5301, accessed January 10, 2004. See also: MEMRI *Inquiry and Analysis Series – No. 65*, quoting Ruz Al–Yussuf (Egypt), May 18, 2001. Available at: http://memri.org/bin/articles.cgi?Page=subjects&Area=conflict&ID=IA6501 Accessed: Jan. 10, 2004.

50. MEMRI Special Dispatch Series No. 363, April 7, 2002, quoting http://www.lailatalqadr.com/stories/n040401.shtml, April 4, 2002 (an al–Azhar University website).

Available at: http://memri.org/bin/articles.cgi?Page=archives&Area=sd&ID=SP36302, accessed: February 25, 2004.

51. MEMRI Inquiry and Analysis Series No. 83, quoting *Afaq Arabiya* (Egypt), January 30, 2002, as cited in *Al–Quds Al–Arabi* (London), January 31, 2002. Available at: http://memri.org/bin/articles.cgi?Page=archives&Area=ia&ID=IA8302 Accessed: Dec. 12, 2005. *Afaq Arabia* is an Egyptian Muslim Brotherhood's mouthpiece.

52. The *Mufti* is a top religious–legal advisor, appointed by the government, whose role includes issuing religious rulings (*fatwas*), usually in response to questions.

53. MEMRI Special Dispatch Series No. 363, April 7, 2002, quoting al–Azhar website http://www.lailatalqadr.com/stories/p4040401.shtml, April 4, 2002, available at: http://memri.org/bin/articles.cgi?Page=archives&Area=sd&ID=SP36302, accessed: February 25, 2004.

54. MEMRI Special Dispatch Series No. 580, October 1, 2003. Available at: http://www.memri.org/bin/articles.cgi?Area=sd&ID=SP58003, accessed February 20, 2007.

55. MEMRI *Special Dispatch Series – No. 373*, April 30, 2002, quoting *Iqraa TV* (Saudi Arabia/Egypt), April 24, 2002. Available at:: http://memri.org/bin/articles.cgi?Page=archives&Area=sd&ID=SP37302, Accessed: November 25, 2005).

56. MEMRI Inquiry and Analysis Series No. 66, July 27, 2001, quoting *Al–Quds Al–Arabi* (London), May 25, 2001. Available at: http://memri.org/bin/articles.cgi?Page=subjects&Area=conflict&ID=IA6601, accessed: Jan. 10, 2004.

57. MEMRI Inquiry and Analysis Series No. 65, quoting *Al–Liwa Al–Islami* (Egypt), June 14, 2001. Available at: http://memri.org/bin/articles.cgi?Page=subjects&Area=conflict&ID=IA6501, accessed: Jan. 10, 2004.

58. MEMRI Inquiry and Analysis Series No. 100, July 4, 2002, available at: http://memri.org/bin/articles.cgi?Page=subjects&Area=conflict&ID=IA10002, accessed on Jan. 10, 2004, quoting the Palestinian al Ayam of may 16, 2002 report of Arafat's speech.

59. MEMRI, op. cit., quoting *Al Hayat Al Jadida* (PNA), June 14, 2002.

60. MEMRI, op. cit., quoting the Palestinian daily *Al Quds*, May 29, 2002.

61. MEMRI, op. cit., quoting *Al Hayat Al Jadida* (PNA), *June* 9, 2002. Interestingly, in the 1970s Mamduh Nofal was the head of operations of the Democratic Front for the Liberation of Palestine. In that capacity he oversaw the hostage taking operation in which about 100 high school children were taken hostage in the northern Israeli town of Ma'alot and 20 of them were killed. In later years Nofal has moderated his position and became a supporter of political action and negotiation rather than armed struggle.

62. MEMRI, op. cit., quoting *Al Sharq Al Awsat* (London), May 2, 2002. Bassam Abu Sharif was the Popular Front for the Liberation of Palestine (PFLP) spokesman in the 1970s–mid 1980s, who in 1986 joined Fatah and served as Arafat's political advisor.

63. MEMRI Special Dispatch Series No. 393, June 25, 2003, quoting *Al–Quds* (Palestinian Authority), June 19, 2002. Available at: http://memri.org/bin/articles.cgi?Page=subjects&Area=conflict&ID=SP39302, accessed: Jan. 11, 2004.

64. MEMRI, Special Dispatch Series No. 393, June 25, 2003, quoting *Al–Quds* (Palestinian Authority), June 21, 2002. Available at: http://memri.org/bin/articles.cgi?Page=subjects&Area=conflict&ID=SP39302, accessed: Jan. 11, 2004.

65. MEMRI Special Dispatch Series No. 968, August 25, 2005, available at: http://memri.org/bin/articles.cgi?Page=archives&Area=sd&ID=SP96805, accessed February 20, 2007.

# 8

# Suicide Terrorism in the Light of Suicide Theory

A REASONABLE STEP IN TRYING to understand terrorist suicide is to explore the scholarly literature on suicide in general. Indeed, self-destruction is a key element in terrorist suicide, and a vast body of knowledge has been accumulated on factors that influence people's willingness to commit suicide.

The literature on suicide is enormous. Scholars have tried to understand it for thousands of years, and modern social and medical scientists have added their considerable share to the effort. A casual search through "Google scholar" in August 2009 under the key word "suicide," yielded about 802,000 items. Presumably, even scholars who have devoted their entire careers to the study of this behavior have read only a small fraction of the thousands of books and tens of thousands of articles on the subject. For the purpose of this study, I scrutinized only the main theories and approaches in this area. As this theoretical journey was undertaken to better understand the specific phenomenon of terrorist suicide, the next obvious step was to examine whether the theoretical insights square with the facts of terrorist suicide. The results of this inquiry are described in this chapter, which opens with a general, albeit selective, survey of theories of suicide, then checks their compatibility with the empirical data on terrorist suicide.

While numerous disciplines have contributed to the study of suicide, sociology and psychology have been at the forefront of research. Sociology studies suicide as a social phenomenon, looking for factors that explain changes in suicide rates in a specific society over time, or differences in suicide rates between societies. Psychology, which focuses on the individual, traces personality characteristics or individual life experiences that affect the tendency to commit suicide.

## Sociological Theories

The French sociologist Emile Durkheim laid the foundations of modern suicide research in his classic book *Le Suicide*, published in 1897, in which he treated suicide as a phenomenon determined by social rather than individual factors. Having identified three main types of suicide—egoistic, altruistic, and anomic—as well as mixed types prompted by a combination of the main factors, he succinctly described the three types of suicide:

> Egoistic suicide results from man's no longer finding a basis for existence in life; altruistic suicide, because this basis of existence appears to man situated beyond life itself. The third sort of suicide . . . results from man's activity lacking regulation and his consequent suffering. By virtue of its origin we shall assign this last variety the name of anomic suicide. (Durkheim, 1951, p. 258).

Durkheim's theory points to *social integration* as the key factor in both egoistic and altruistic suicide. Low social integration is conducive to egoistic suicide, whereas altruistic suicide is common in societies with high social integration. As several suicidologists have pointed out (e.g., Lester & Lester, 1971; Maris, Berman, & Silverman, 2000), Durkheim did not define precisely the meaning of integration, but later researchers elaborated it. For Durkheim *egoistic suicide* was the outcome of the individual's insufficient social integration in either the community (macro level) or the family (micro level). Suicide is generally more frequent in less cohesive societies. According to Durkheim, this factor accounts, then, for the lower suicide rates in Catholic compared to Protestant societies, as the latter are more individualistic. The family's micro-society also plays a role in egoistic suicide. Suicide is less common in societies where the family provides a cohesive social structure for the individual (Durkheim, 1951). While the level of social integration is a relatively stable structural characteristic of society, it is also subject to the temporary influence of events that reinforce or sap its cohesiveness, such as wars.

Durkheim attributed *altruistic suicide* to highly cohesive and rigorous societies. Self-inflicted death is in line with the social rules of behavior in certain circumstances, because this is what the person is expected to do. Hence, altruistic suicide is the product of two factors: a high degree of obedience to social rules and circumstances in which these social rules warrant suicide. In Durkheim's words:

> The individual kills himself at the command of his conscience; he submits to an imperative. Thus, the dominant note of his act is the serene conviction

derived from the feeling of a duty accomplished . . . When altruism is at a high pitch . . . the impulse is more passionate and unthinking. A burst of faith and enthusiasm carries the man to his death. This enthusiasm itself is either happy or somber, depending on the conception of death as a means of union with a beloved deity, or as an expiatory sacrifice, to appease some terrible, probably hostile power. (Durkheim, 1951, p. 283).

Durkheim distinguished three forms of altruistic suicide: obligatory, optional, and acute. Obligatory suicide exists in certain societies where social norm or custom prescribes suicide in specific situations. Typical examples of this kind are the suicides of wives after their husbands' death (e.g., the now rare practice of *sati* in parts of India), or of servants after their masters' death. Optional altruistic suicide occurs when suicide is considered a merit but is not obligatory, as in the Japanese Samurai custom of *seppuku* (popularly known as *hara-kiri*). Acute altruistic suicide is prompted by the desire to die in order to merge with a deity as the ultimate expression of a religious belief. Durkheim found typical examples of this last type of altruistic suicide in what he regards as "lower societies." In his view, some of the Christian martyrs also belong to this category. "Though they did not kill themselves, they sought death with all their power and behaved so as to make it inevitable" (1951, p. 227).

Durkheim viewed suicide in the military as a form of altruistic suicide. To support his claim, he used statistics of several countries, showing that the suicide rate was higher among officers and noncommissioned officers than among enlisted men, higher among volunteers than among conscripts, and much higher among reenlisted volunteers. The rate also increased with the duration of service, and was highest among elite troops. Durkheim attributed suicides in the army to the ambience of obedience typical of military service—"a soldier's principle of action is external to himself; which is the quality of the state of altruism" (p. 234). He hardly explained, however, why persons in the military would want to commit suicide in the first place, and, especially, how committing suicide served the call of duty. The data on suicides that he used to support his claim pertained to suicides in peacetime rather than in combat. Thus, at the time they committed suicide the military persons were not required by duty to do so; on the contrary, the authorities probably perceived their suicide as a breach of duty. Durkheim described the events that precipitated suicide in the military as follows:

Influenced by this disposition, the soldier kills himself at the least disappointment, for the most futile reasons, for a refusal to leave, a reprimand, an unjust punishment, a delay in promotion, a question of honor, a flush of momentary jealousy or even simply because other suicides have occurred before his eyes or to his knowledge (pp. 238–9).

It is hard to see how these reasons serve the needs of the homeland, the military, duty, or any other ideal, social structure, or supreme authority that the soldier might cherish. Durkheim's term *altruistic suicide* means, therefore, suicide driven not by the perceived benefit to society but by social norms as perceived by the individual who commits suicide.

The third type, *anomic suicide*, is a function of Durkheim's concept of *social regulation*, i.e., the extent to which society controls the needs, expectations, and behavior of its members. Anomic suicide occurs when societal regulation of people's lives is slackened. Typical situations that increase suicide rates include economic crises, political changes and, on the micro-social level, divorce. Durkheim viewed most circumstances conducive to this type of suicide as temporary rather than as a structural attribute of society. Thus, anomic suicide is caused by a *change* in social control rather than by an absolute low degree of social regulation—that is, not by lack of social regulation in the person's life, nor by poor economic, political, or social conditions, but rather by a sudden change in the social regulation of the individual's life. Thus, suicide rates rise not only during a decline in economic conditions but also when the economy suddenly improves. Durkheim noticed an increase in the suicide rate not only as a concomitant of economic growth, but also following "positive" political changes, such as the expansion of Prussia in 1866.

For Durkheim, the causes of anomic suicides lay in the incongruity of perceived economic and social status needs, aspirations, and capabilities. Nevertheless, the suicide rate increase across a broad spectrum of private and social situations suggests that the cause of anomic suicide may be less specific—namely, the destabilization of old life styles and habits, and the difficulty of adjusting to new rules of conduct. Alvarez (1990, p.114) offers a succinct generic description of this kind of suicide: "He kills himself because, for better or worse, his accustomed world has been destroyed and he is lost." In current psychological terms, one may hypothesize that anomic suicide rates are higher among those with an external rather than internal locus of control.

Durkheim (1951) mentioned briefly—in a mere footnote—a fourth type, which he termed *fatalistic suicide*. The opposite of anomic suicide, this category is typical of situations in which overwhelming oppressive social regulation generates a sense of hopeless suffocation by external control. In this category Durkheim includes oddly diverse conditions: slavery and living under "excessive physical or moral despotism" on the one hand, and very young husbands and married childless women on the other hand (p. 276). Yet he believed that this type of suicide was rather rare and, therefore, unimportant at the time.

Beyond the main types of suicide he postulated, Durkheim was aware of the complexity of suicide and the great variety of its forms. A composite type of particular interest for the study of politically motivated suicide is the *anomic-altruistic suicide*:

> One and the same crisis may ruin a person's life, disturb the equilibrium between him and his surroundings and, at the same time, drive his altruistic disposition to a state which incites him to suicide. Such is notably the case of what we have called suicide of the besieged. If, for example, the Jews killed themselves en masse upon the capture of Jerusalem, it was because the victory of the Romans, by making them subjects and tributaries of Rome, threatened to transform the sort of life to which they were accustomed and because they loved their city and cult too much to survive the probable destruction of both (pp. 288–9).

This schematic description leaves many questions unanswered but it provides a clue to where Durkheim might have placed suicidal terrorism in his theoretical system.

At first sight, terrorist suicide seems to be a typical case of Durkheim's altruistic suicide, as the act of self-destruction is allegedly carried out in the service of the suicide's society. Several authors have, indeed, tagged it as such (Maris et al., 2000, p. 242; Pape, 2005, Chapter 9; Weinberg, Pedahzur & Canetti-Nisim, 2003; Leenaars & Wenckstern, 2004; Biggs, 2005; Gambetta, 2005). Further probing, however, would challenge the aptness of this description, or at least reveal underlying complexities. Durkheim used the concept of altruistic suicide to characterize societies, not individuals. To formulate it, he looked at suicide rates in various societies and attributed the differences between them to divergent characteristics of these societies. He did not examine directly the motives of the individuals who committed suicide but inferred them from the characteristics of their respective societies. For example, in labeling suicides in the military as "altruistic," Durkheim relied on his observation of military norms, such as obedience. He viewed altruistic suicide as a stable rather than situational feature of a particular society. The societies in which it occurs are highly "integrated," that is, very cohesive, and therefore, strongly affect their members' behavior. The society may be a culture, a nation, or the military microcosm. Hence, to apply Durkheim's concept of altruistic suicide to terrorist suicide means to attribute these suicides to the traits of the societies or micro-societies in which they occur—a religion, an ethnic community, or a terrorist group. Terrorist suicide, however, has been practiced in very diverse societies. Not only are Lebanese Shi'ites, Lebanese Sunnis, secular Lebanese, Palestinians, Egyptians, Armenians, Marxist Kurds, and Tamil Hindus notorious for politically motivated suicide, so are German communists, Irish Catholics, Vietnamese Buddhists, and American Protestants who have killed themselves for an ideological cause. The crucial factor is arguably not the larger social unit—the ethnic group, religious group, or nation—but the micro-society of a terrorist group itself, which provides the social milieu that generates self-sacrificial suicide in accordance with Durkheim's altruistic variety. These highly cohesive, rigorous social structures create rules of conduct and behavior ethics that members are expected to follow. Yet the vast majority of terrorist groups, regardless of their structure, have not resorted to suicide attacks at all. Furthermore, there is no evidence that terrorist groups that impose a particularly strict discipline and a tight structure have resorted to suicide tactics more than the looser groups. On the contrary, among the Palestinian groups, the Popular Front for the Liberation of Palestine (PFLP) has a tighter structure and discipline than Fatah. Yet the PFLP has carried out only a few suicide attacks, whereas Fatah has carried out many. Moreover, as discussed in Chapter 5, a large number of Palestinian suicides had not been members of the group before they agreed to carry out a suicide attack on its behalf.

In addition, as described by Durkheim, altruistic suicide is meant to save the individual's honor rather than to help society. His examples from the military are not suicidal attacks in battle. Rather, they are cases in which a person's feelings or self-dignity are hurt—refused leave, an insult, refused promotion and the like. In Durkheim's terms, the archetypal altruistic suicide is the Japanese custom of *seppuku* (hara-kiri). Terrorist suicides are quite different, as they are claimed to be committed in the service of society rather than as a reaction to personal shame. In this sense, they are similar to the Japanese World War II kamikaze phenomenon, rather than to hara-kiri. Among Palestinian suicide bombers, cases in which a man volunteered to carry out a suicide attack to atone for shameful behavior or tarnished reputation (e.g., suspicion of collaborating with the Israeli authorities) have been rare; none were found among the suicides described in Chapters 4–6.

## Epidemiological Aspects

SOCIODEMOGRAPHIC FACTORS   Beyond their descriptive importance in drawing up the boundaries of the suicide phenomenon, demographic attributes of suicides also help understand the phenomenon's underlying causes. Over the years, much information has been accumulated on a variety of demographic factors associated with the rate of suicide. Chapter 3 detailed the demographic characteristics of suicide bombers. The main findings concerning ordinary suicides are listed here.

*Gender.* Suicide rates are known to be much higher among males, although suicide *attempts* are considerably higher among females (Bongar, 2002; World Health Organization [WHO], 1993, 2003; Jacobs et al., 1999; Maris et al., 2000). With the exception of China (WHO, 2003; Maris et al., 2000), these findings are generally consistent across nationalities and ethnic groups, as well as age groups. The differences are attributable in part to the potentially more lethal methods used by men.

*Age.* Suicide rates generally increase steadily with age (Lester & Lester, 1971; Miller & Paulsen, 1999; Moscicki, 1999, Maris et al., 2000). However, the direct relationship between age group and suicide rate may be limited to Western cultures at certain times. Iga (1993) quoted data on suicides in Japan showing that until 1980, suicide rates in the 20–24 age group were considerably higher than in older age groups. Similarly, among African American and Native American males, suicide rates are highest in the 20–29 age group (Moscicki, 1999). Age also affects the ratio of attempted to completed suicides. In most countries the ratio is highest in the young age group of 15–24 (i.e., a relatively high number of attempts and small number of complete suicides). In other countries the ratio is highest in the 25–34 age group. The ratio declines steadily with the older age groups (Pritchard, 1996).

*Marital status.* In general, suicide rates are lower among married persons than among singles, divorcees, or the widowed. Among young people, however, suicide rates are higher among the married (Lester & Lester, 1971; WHO, 1993; Jacobs, Brewer, and Klein-Benheim 1999).

*Socioeconomic level.* Durkheim (1951) postulated higher suicide rates among upper social strata. More recent studies, however, showed an inverse relationship between socioeconomic status and suicide rate (Stack, 2000).

## The Influence of Religion

Variations between the rates of suicide in countries with different dominant religions, or among different religious groups in the same country, have prompted researchers to examine the influence of religious affiliation on suicide. Durkheim believed religion to be an important factor in the rate of suicide because it affects social integration. In Catholic practice, the relations between individuals and their congregations are much tighter than in Protestant communities. Hence, suicide rates are lower in Catholic than in Protestant countries. Interestingly, Durkheim did not ascribe these lower rates to the stricter Catholic position on suicide. Yet, the attitude of religion to self-destruction may significantly sway a person's willingness to commit suicide.

Pritchard (1996) disputed the direct effect of religion on suicide, pointing out that Catholic Hungary held (at the time) the world record for suicide, and Catholic Austria competed with Finland for second place. Still, he agreed with Stack's 1992 study, which shows that suicide is affected not by religious culture as such, but by a person's church attendance. Pritchard attributed this factor to the social support that church attendance provides, serving as an effective antidote to loneliness. However, church attendance may also indicate the person's depth of belief in religious principles. Thus, in Hungary and Austria, where suicide rates are high, most people formally belong to the Catholic Church but do not live by its principles—as suggested, among other things, by their scarce church attendance. In Italy and Spain, on the other hand, where people take Catholicism seriously and follow its rules, suicide rates are very low. In other words, religion seems to have a two-pronged effect on the propensity to commit suicide. First, it affects the extent to which people feel lonely and miserable. As part of the community, religious institutions are a social milieu that provides social support, whose intensity and effectiveness are influenced by the characteristics of the religion. Catholic institutions are usually more involved in the community than Protestant institutions, and seek a more active relationship between the individual and the congregation. Nonetheless, the nature and intensity of social support are influenced also by other cultural characteristics of the community. Thus, the relationship between the individual and the community is more intensive in Italy than in Austria or Hungary. Second, a religion's position on suicide directly bears on the rate of suicide. Some individuals, however lonely and miserable, presumably would not commit suicide if their religion forbids it under threat of severe punishment in the afterlife, and if their families would suffer embarrassment and humiliation.

There is an important difference between these two functions of religion in terms of its effect on suicide. Religious institutions have no monopoly on social support, even where such institutions constitute the central social framework. There are always other social associations, such as labor unions, political organizations, and—most important—the family. Religion does, however, hold a monopoly on its believers' moral attitudes toward suicide. Moreover, in societies where religion provides the main ethos and moral code, its principles affect the general social attitude to suicide and, therefore, the conduct of nonbelievers as well.

Nevertheless, the importance of religious attitude to suicide is, of course, limited. Minois (1999) points out that during the Middle Ages in France, men and women of all social echelons committed suicide despite unqualified condemnation and threat of severe punishment by religious and civil authorities. This shows that even absolute condemnation does not prevent suicide altogether. At the other end of the permissibility spectrum, in Japan, where religion and social customs do not consider suicide a sin (Iga, 1993), the rate is similar to that in Germany and lower than in Switzerland, Belgium, Austria, and France (WHO, 1993).

Since more than 90% of terrorist suicides around the world in the 1981–2008 period were carried out by Muslims, we are especially interested in suicide among this population. Clearly, Islam objects to suicide (Rosenthal, 1946; Palazzi, 2001). Statistics on suicide rates in Islamic countries are lacking, but available data show very low rates, especially in Arab countries (WHO, 2003). Although the published low rates of suicide may in part reflect underreporting, the data consistency suggests that suicide rates among Muslims are, indeed, considerably lower than among members of other religions. In a comparative study in Israel, suicide rates among Muslims were lower than among Jews (Levav & Aisenberg, 1989). Thus, the great share of Islamic terrorists among suicide bombers worldwide stands in stark contrast to Islam's attitude to "ordinary" suicide and to suicide rates in Islamic countries. This contrast seems to stem at least in part from the support that suicide attacks, termed "martyrdom operations," have enjoyed among many Islamic clerics, who have used religion as a facilitator rather than inhibitor of this particular form of suicide (other explanations for the high proportion of Muslims among suicide bombers will be discussed in Chapters 9 and 10).

## Contagion

As most terrorist suicide attacks have occurred in clusters ("campaigns") at certain places over a period of time, suicide contagion or imitation, which has attracted the attention of sociologists, seems relevant to our topic. This phenomenon reflects the inspiration and encouragement given to some by a model suicide event. The suicide who triggers a spate of imitations is usually a famous figure, and thus more readily serves as a model for identification than an anonymous person. The model suicide's fame also guarantees broad media coverage of the event, thus potentially influencing a large number of people. In a classic study on suicide contagion, Philips (1974) found that the suicide rate in the U.S. rose by 12% in the month following Marilyn Monroe's suicide (August 1962). Copycat suicides may also result from imitation of fictional models in literature and movies. Anecdotal reports suggest that following the publication of Goethe's *The Sorrows of Young Werther* in 1774, whose romantic hero committed suicide, there was a wave of suicides by youngsters across Europe.

Durkheim (1951) took notice of contagion, but believed its effect was negligible compared to the fundamental factors that determine suicide rates (i.e., social integration and regulation):

> In short, certain as the contagion of suicide is from individual to individual, imitation never seems to propagate it so as to affect the social suicide-rate. Imitation may give rise to more or less numerous individual cases, but it does not contribute to the unequal tendency in different societies to self-destruction, or to that of smaller social groups within each society. Its radiating influence is always very restricted; and what is more, intermittent. Its attainment of a certain degree of intensity is always brief. (p. 140).

Durkheim assumed that those likely to be influenced by a model suicide were inclined to commit suicide anyway, and the model's influence in most cases merely affected the timing rather than the act itself: "The thought of an act is not sufficient to produce a similar act itself in an adult, unless he is a person himself specially so inclined" (p. 140). Still, Durkheim thought that the danger of imitation increased when the model act was not rejected or, worse, approved by society. Regarding suggestions to prohibit information on suicides to prevent imitation, Durkheim maintained that it was not the information itself, but the attitude toward the act, that might provoke imitation:

> Actually, what may contribute to the growth of suicide or murder is not talk-ing of it but how it is talked of. Where such acts are loathed, the feelings they arouse penetrate the recital of them and thus offset rather than encourage individual inclinations. But inversely, when society is morally decadent . . . example becomes truly dangerous not as example but because the revulsion it should inspire is reduced by social tolerance or indifference. (p. 141).

There is some disagreement among suicidologists on the potency of the contagion effect. A joint workshop conducted by the U.S. National Institute of Mental Health, the Centers for Disease Control and Prevention, and the Substance Abuse and Mental Health Services Administration in October 2003 determined that "there is a proven relationship between fictional and non-fictional media portrayal of suicide and suicidal contagion".[1] Still, reviewing the literature on this subject, Jobes, Luoma, Hustead and Mann (2000) noted: "However, although many studies have suggested that media reports of suicide may spark copycat suicidal behav-iors, much of this research has been plagued with methodological prob-lems as well as some inconclusive findings." (p. 551).

Application of this notion to terrorist suicide seems to warrant the assumption that the large number of suicide attacks in a certain country and time (say, Palestinian attacks during the second intifada or Tamil Tigers attacks before the 2002 ceasefire agreement) can be at least partly attributed to some youngsters' inclination to imitate previous suicides, similar to the spate of suicides in the wake of Marilyn Monroe's or other celebrities' deaths. This may well be true, although spontaneous political suicides carried out by individuals without assistance by an organization, have usually had relatively few imitations—far below the number of sui-cide attacks in organized campaigns in places such as Lebanon, Sri Lanka, Israel and Iraq. Jan Palach, the Czech student who burned himself to death in a Prague public square in January 1969 in protest against the Soviet Bloc invasion of Czechoslovakia, had very few imitators. His funeral turned into a mass protest against the Soviet occupation, but despite the great publicity and public identification with his act, only six other people imitated his example in the four months that followed his death (Biggs, 2005, p. 182).[2] Similarly, despite widespread opposition to the Vietnam war in the 1960s, only seven Americans burned themselves over a period of eight years following the example of Alice Herz, an 82-year-old peace activist, in March 1965.[3] In Vietnam, several Buddhist monks imitated the self-immolation of Thich Quang Duc, who burned himself to death in 1963, in protest against the oppression of Buddhists by the Diem regime. Most of these suicides took place in 1966, three years after the "model" suicide event. Thus, *spontaneous* political suicides do not quite qualify for the term "contagion."

The disparity between the small number of *spontaneous* copycat polit-ically-related self-immolations and the relatively large number of suicide terrorist attacks is due to the fact that practically all terrorist suicides did not operate on their own, but were sent by organizations. In this sense, terrorist suicide differs fundamentally from ordinary suicide. Nevertheless, the concept of contagion seems highly relevant at one stage in the making of a suicide bomber—people's willingness to offer themselves for these missions. The empirical evidence presented in Chapters 5 and 6 shows that about half of the Palestinian suicides volunteered on their own initia-tive. Their willingness to do so was no doubt influenced by the public atmosphere, as discussed in Chapter 7, whose effect is reminiscent of what Goldman and Beardslee (1999) wrote about adolescent suicide contagion: "It appears that once the taboo of suicide is breached, it becomes a far more accessible and acceptable possibility to vulnerable members of the group or community." (p. 427).

The magnitude of contagion in ordinary suicides, and the influence of public atmosphere on the willingness to volunteer for terrorist suicide, are affected by the same factors. Maris, Berman, and Silverman (2000, pp. 254–255) identified several conditions that facilitate suicide contagion:

- The tendency to imitate the suicide model is greater among those who perceive themselves as similar to the model.
- Imitations increase as a function of publicity (duration and intensity) of the model acts.
- More imitations occur when the model is socially praised and glorified.
- Teenagers are more prone to imitations than adults.

All these factors exist in the case of suicide bombers.

## Psychological Theories

Sociological theories of suicide have generally failed to explain why certain terrorist groups have resorted to suicide attacks and others have not. The number of terrorist groups that have used true suicide attacks, i.e., attacks designed to include suicide of the attackers, is small—about three dozen out of the many hundreds of groups that have operated during the recent three decades. From a sociological point of view, the groups that have used suicide attacks as a tactic would be assumed to differ in either structural or environmental aspects (cultural milieu, political conditions, etc.) from the groups that have not used this tactic. Yet, no such differences have been found.

A basic question that sociological theories are inherently unable to answer pertains to the fact that suicide bombers comprise a tiny fraction of the members even in groups that have used suicide attacks. Inevitably, then, one would attribute qualities to the terrorist suicide other than, or in addition to, commitment to an ideological cause; i.e., some special personal characteristics. This aspect is addressed by psychological theories of suicide.

Since suicide is an individual act, sociological theories are inherently incapable of explaining it directly. Sociologists look for correlations between suicide rates in society, and a variety of factors such as age, social class, living conditions or events, and then offer a hypothetical explanation for their findings. As they use circumstantial evidence, their explanations are necessarily speculative. At best, they can convincingly show that a certain factor, say economic depression, significantly affects the rate of suicide—but they do not and cannot explain why some individuals commit suicide under these circumstances while most do not. A direct rather than circumstantial explanation of suicide must resort to psychological methods—that is, examine the suicide himself and identify both his personality characteristics and the specific circumstances that prompted his act.

Alvarez (1990) summed up the sociological theories of suicide as follows:

> Thus the sociological theories woven around suicide are all to some extent true—though some are truer than others and most are conflicting—but they are also partial and circular. They return constantly to an inner negation and hopelessness which social pressures may bring to the surface but which existed before those pressures and will probably continue even after they are removed (p. 118).

This unflattering opinion does some injustice to sociological studies of suicide. It reflects Alvarez's emphasis on the individual rather than social, human rather than statistical, correlates of suicide: "The real motives which impel a man to take his own life are elsewhere; they belong to the internal world, devious, contradictory, labyrinthine, and mostly out of sight." (p. 123). For understanding these motives psychology is, then, a better tool than sociology.

However, psychological studies of suicide by and large ignore political suicide in general, and terrorist suicide in particular. Even treatises of murder-suicide do not mention this subject or regard it as outside the interest of suicidology, as it is driven by political rather than personal motives (Nock & Marzuk, 1999). Nevertheless, applying the insights on the psychological background of ordinary suicide to terrorist suicides may be an illuminating endeavor.

## The Psychoanalytic Approach

Freud did not write a comprehensive treatise of suicide (Myatt & Greenblatt, 1993) but did occasionally refer to it in his writings. His notions on self-destruction were tracked and summarized by Litman (1996), and his general ideas were further developed by his followers. Essentially, Freud attributed suicide to an ambivalent and conflictual love-hate attitude toward a very significant person with whom one identifies. In a broader sense, this conflict reflects the basic competition between Eros—the drive for life and love—and Thanatos—the drive toward destruction and death—with the latter being the winner. In Maltsberger's (1999) words, "At the heart of the matter lies an unconscious identification of the self with another person who is both loved and hated. Thus it becomes possible to treat oneself, or some part of oneself (typically one's disavowed body), as an alien and an enemy" (p. 73). Alvarez (1990) offered a somewhat different psychodynamic interpretation of suicide, extending Freud's description of melancholia to explain his view on the making of a suicidal mood: "This is the vicious circle of melancholia, in which a man may take his own life partly to atone for his fantasied guilt for the death of someone he loves, and partly because he feels the dead person lives on inside him, crying out, like Hamlet's father, for revenge" (p. 139).

In the etiology of suicide, Zilboorg (1996) emphasized in particular the identification with an important person who died when the suicide was a child. This concept is anchored in the Freudian formation of the superego as a result of identification with parent figures or their fantasized representations, which are incorporated into the child's self. Zilboorg went as far as to maintain that "only those individuals who appear to have identified themselves with a *dead* person and in whom the process of identification took place during childhood or adolescence, at a time when the incorporated person was already actually dead, are most probably the truly suicidal individuals" (p. 71). Yet, the influence of the loss of a parent in childhood on the inclination to commit suicide later in life is a matter of controversy. Barraclough and Hughes (1987) found that parental loss in childhood yielded no significant difference between suicides and nonsuicide controls. Lester (1989), however, found that the loss of a parent between the ages of 6 and 14 is especially common in later suicides. And yet, empirical data derived from the interviews with families of completed suicides (Chapter 4) and with would-be suicides (Chapter 5) did not support Zilboorg's notion. Among the completed suicides only 7 out of 34 lost a parent (at ages ranging from 2–17), and among 15 would-be suicides only two lost a father (at ages 4 and 19).

Karl Meninger (1938) differentiated between three types of suicides, according to main motivation: (1) the wish to die, so as to escape difficulties in life; (2) the wish to kill—suicide as revenge against other people; (3) the wish to be killed—as self-punishment. The wish to die and the wish to kill were well expressed in the interviews with the Palestinian would-be suicides (Chapter 5). Most—if not all—suicides wanted to kill anonymous members of a political entity defined as the enemy, and a few clearly wanted to die. However, Meninger had in mind the psychoanalytic notion of wishing to kill internalized significant individuals who played a critical role in the suicide's psychological development, usually family members, toward whom the suicide felt a mixture of love and hate. This specific notion of the wish to kill was not supported in the clinical interviews with would-be suicide terrorists, although it may be argued that it did not get a fair chance because the interviews were not psychoanalytically oriented.

Almost all terrorist suicide attacks have been carried out by detonating explosive devices the suicide carried on his body or in a handbag. As a result, the suicide's body was badly mutilated. This particular form of self-destruction calls attention to the suicide's attitude to his or her body. Maltsberger (1993; 1999) noted that many suicides feel alienated from their bodies: "The alienated body may be experienced as troublesome in less disturbed patients (hypochondria, body dismorphic disorder), as unreal, empty, or otherwise defective in others, as possessed by alien presences in psychosis, and as divisible, in certain dissociative states" (1999, p. 74). This attitude to the body is attributed to bodily changes in puberty and reflects blame of the body for "sexual or sadistic feelings." Maltsberger's observation that suicide-prone persons are extraordinarily aggressive tallies with the general psychoanalytic perception of suicide as an expression of self-directed aggression. Subjectively, however, suicidal individuals feel an intolerable mixture of anxiety and depression.

## Hopelessness and Escape from Pain

One of the most influential theories on suicide is Shneidman's. Whereas Freud and his followers have viewed suicide basically as internally directed aggression, Shneidman emphasizes despair. In his view, the wish to commit suicide stems almost always from intense psychological pain caused by frustrated psychological needs. Suicide is the solution of those who view it as the best way to stop the pain. Shneidman's often-cited "ten common-alities of suicide" (1985, pp. 121–149), i.e., factors that exist in all cases of suicide, are:

1. The common purpose of suicide is to seek a solution.
2. The common goal of suicide is cessation of consciousness.
3. The common stimulus in suicide is intolerable psychological pain.
4. The common stressor in suicide is frustrated psychological needs.
5. The common emotion in suicide is hopelessness–helplessness.
6. The common psychological state in suicide is ambivalence.
7. The common perceptual state in suicide is constriction.
8. The common action in suicide is egression.
9. The common interpersonal act in suicide is communication of intention.
10. The common consistency in suicide is with lifelong coping patterns.

Table 8.1. shows that some of the characteristics listed above may, indeed, fit what we know about terrorist suicides, but others do not.

As could be expected, Shneidman's suicide commonalities fit better with those of the would-be suicides described in Chapter 5 who were assessed as suicidal (6 out of 15). Two expressed the wish to die in order to stop mental suffering (against a backdrop of parental abuse). In line with Shneidman's concept, they expressed such intolerable mental pain and

**Table 8.1** Comparison of Shneidman's Commonalities with Suicide Terrorists' Characteristics

| Criterion | Comments |
|---|---|
| Purpose: find a solution | Suicide presented as solution to national rather than personal problem |
| Goal: cessation of consciousness | No support in suicide terrorist data in most cases |
| Stimulus: intolerable pain | No support in suicide terrorist data in most cases |
| Stressor: frustrated needs | National rather than personal needs |
| Emotion: hopelessness–helplessness | No support in suicide terrorist data |
| Psychological state: ambivalence | Supported in suicide terrorist data (many hesitate) |
| Perceptual state: constriction | Fits some suicides on the way to target |
| Action: egression | No support in suicide terrorist data in most cases |
| Interpersonal act: communication of intention | Supported by suicide terrorist data at the group level and sometimes in the family |
| Consistency: lifelong coping patterns | No support (no prior record of attempts) |

hopelessness–helplessness that they did not care what would happen to them after death. The majority of the would-be suicides, however, did not display these emotions. They did not undertake the mission to stop intolerable personal anguish. The goal of their suicidal act was not cessation of consciousness, nor did their decision derive from a mental state of hopelessness–helplessness. It was, rather, a form of empowerment. For the majority of would-be suicides the decisive element in the homicidal–suicidal act was the homicidal part, for which suicide was a tool, while for a minority the homicide part was an excuse to kill themselves. In line with this pattern, most terrorist suicides did not fit Shneidman's "consistency" principle, since they had no record of previous suicide attempts.

Some of the other commonalities listed by Shneidman fit terrorist suicide in a specific way, although here the circumstances differ from those Shneidman presumably had in mind. Behind the terrorist suicide act there were, indeed, frustrated needs—but the frustrations were related to the community's situation rather than to the suicide's interaction with the social milieu. On a deeper personal level, most were motivated to undertake the suicide mission by their wish to please authority figures, or to be perceived as heroes in the community. These motives may be interpreted as a reflection of frustrated (unfulfilled) needs of nurturance and status. Yet, these needs prompted them to give in to external pressure and death was, in most cases, a by-product rather than the desired intrinsic goal. Among terrorist suicides, communication of intention also figured in a special way. The videotaped pre-dispatching ritual in which the suicide candidate reads his last statement is certainly a declaration of intention, yet unlike in the case of ordinary suicides, it is not a call for help but a statement of commitment and devotion, as well as a propaganda tool for the struggle. Yet privately, as described in Chapter 4, several suicides relayed their intentions to their families obliquely, even if provocatively. Most, however, did not give their families a clue.

Two-thirds of the would-be suicides described in Chapter 5 reported hesitation, thus fitting Shneidman's category of ambivalence. Evidence further suggests that some suicides were in a state of constricted perception on their way to the target, focusing on the mission to be performed and shutting themselves off to internal fears. Thus, in the suicide terrorists' experience, constriction was a way of coping with hesitation. The rate of failing the mission was presumably higher among those who were unable to quell their hesitation.

In sum, Shneidman's commonalities partially fit terrorist suicide characteristics. The disparities are related to the basic difference in motivation between ordinary and terrorist suicides: while the former are motivated by the wish to die, for most of the latter their own death serves primarily to kill others.

Farber (1968) underscored the importance of hopelessness in the genesis of suicide. The greater the hope, the less likely is suicide to occur. His concept of hope—the perceived ability to influence and to be satisfied by the world—refers to the individual's expected ability to function within his social milieu, rather than to a general communal situation such as living under occupation. Lester and Lester (1971, p. 45) noted in this regard that suicidal people tend to see not only the present but also the future as negative, expecting to be socially isolated in the future. This observation may well match the mental condition of some but certainly not all would-be suicides.

Despair and hopelessness are also considered key background factors in adolescent suicide. This age group is of particular interest in the context of this book, as most terrorist suicides are persons in their late teens or early twenties.

Myatt and Greenblatt (1993) claim that "adolescent suicide never occurs in the absence of powerful social influences and stressors. Though ultimately suicide is usually a solitary action, its genesis is primarily social in nature" (pp. 195–196). Their model of the road to suicide specifies the following series of factors:

1. Skill deficits (never learned, poor modeling, punishment, etc.)
2. Interpersonal failure (particularly salient during school years)
3. "Learned helplessness" / negative cognitions / feelings of inadequacy (lowering of self-esteem)
4. Hopelessness
5. Further reduction in social behavior and reinforcers
6. Isolation and depression
7. Suicidal ideation/behavior

The emphasis on the importance of social influence in the genesis of suicide is certainly in line with terrorist suicide. Still, the chain of factors described in Myatt and Greenblatt's model is related to the emergence, in some individuals, of the wish to die for personal reasons rather than related to social encouragement to carry out a suicidal act perceived as heroic. In this sense, the model is more applicable to those would-be suicides who were assessed as suicidal, but not to others.

## Risk Factors

Over the years, an immense amount of information has accumulated on factors associated with the risk of suicide. These factors were by and large established statistically, i.e., persons who commit suicide tend to have these attributes. One way of comparing suicide terrorists to ordinary suicides would be, therefore, to check whether the attributes (risk factors) generally perceived as characteristic of ordinary suicides are also present in terrorist suicides.

Suicidologists tend to agree on risk factors. Jacobs, Brewer and Klein-Benheim (1999) mentioned such sociodemographic factors as being male, aged 60 years or older, living alone, being unmarried, not having young children at home, and financial problems. As clinical risk factors they listed "manic-depressive disorder, major depressive disorder, schizophrenia, substance abuse, history of suicide attempts, suicidal ideation, comorbid panic attacks, severe anhedonia, and recent humiliation." (p. 4).

Klerman (1987, cited in Jacobs et al., 1999) differentiated between risk factors for adults and risk factors for adolescents, noting demographic, psychosocial, psychiatric, and "miscellaneous" factors for each group. Risk factors for adults include: *Demographic*: Males; people who are widowed, divorced, or single. *Psychosocial*: Lack of social support; unemployment; drop in social and economic status. *Psychiatric and medical*: Presence of a psychiatric diagnosis, especially major affective disorder; comorbidity; physical illness; family history; psychological turmoil; previous attempts. *Miscellaneous*: Alcohol use or abuse; presence of firearms. Risk factors for adolescents include: *Demographic*: Males more than females; married people more than unmarried people. *Psychosocial*: History of perinatal distress; status of being unwed and pregnant; parental absence or abuse; academic problems. *Psychiatric and medical*: Affective illness, especially bipolar; substance abuse; attention deficit hyperactivity disorder; epilepsy; conduct disorders, impulsivity, explosiveness; family history; disciplinary crisis; humiliation; previous attempts. *Miscellaneous*: Exposure to suicide; presence of firearms and alcohol.

With regard to precipitating factors, Moscicki (1999) summarizes the literature as follows: "Severe, stressful life events, in conjunction with an underlying mental disorder, can precipitate a suicide event in vulnerable individuals. The three most common groups of life stressors that have been identified in completed suicides are conflict–separation–rejection, economic difficulties, and physical illness" (p. 49).

An authoritative report of the United Nation's World Health Organization (1993), which lists major risk factors for suicide, concludes: "The presence of a psychiatric disorder (including alcoholism and drug abuse) represents the strongest risk factor for suicide. It is generally stated that psychological autopsy studies in the U.S. and Europe show that over 90% of patients who succeeded in committing suicide have a psychiatric illness at the time of death, and that two disorders, depression and alcoholism, are associated with 80-85% of suicides" (p. 7).

To demonstrate the incongruence between established profiles of suicide and the typical terrorist suicide, one can compare the risk factors recommended to clinicians for assessing the likelihood that their patients would commit suicide (Linehan, 1999) with the characteristics of Palestinian suicides.

Table 8.2 lists suicide risk factors frequently mentioned in the suicidological literature and compares them with the data on terrorist suicides presented in the family study (Chapter 4) and the would-be suicides study (Chapter 5). The sources listed for the various factors are certainly not exhaustive; they do, however, represent the prevailing view in the literature.

**Table 8.2** Compatibility of Ordinary Suicide Risk Factors with Findings on Terrorist Suicides

| Factor | Sources | Existence in Palestinian terrorist suicides |
| --- | --- | --- |
| Mental illness, esp. mood disorders | Lester & Lester, 1971; Barraclough & Hughes, 1987; Klerman, 1987; WHO, 1993; Jacobs et al., 1999; Linehan, 1999; Miller & Paulsen, 1999; Moscicki, 1999; Tanney, 2000; Bongar, 2002 | Exists in some in a mild form |
| Alcohol and drug abuse | Lester & Lester, 1971; Klerman, 1987; WHO, 1993; Jacobs et al., 1999; Linehan 1999; Miller & Paulsen, 1999; Moscicki, 1999; Lester, 2000; Bongar, 2002 | None |
| Recent severe stressful event (interpersonal loss or conflict, economic or legal problems, moving, humiliation, etc.) | Jacobs et al., 1999; Moscicki, 1999 | No evidence |
| Loss of interpersonal relationship (divorce, spouse death, etc.) | Lester & Lester, 1971; Klerman, 1987; WHO, 1993; Jacobs et al., 1999; Linehan, 1999; Moscicki, 1999 | Rare |
| Sexual abuse history | Klerman, 1987; Linehan, 1999; Moscicki, 1999; Maris et al., 2000 | Rare |
| Jailed | WHO, 1993; Linehan, 1999; Moscicki, 1999; Maris et al., 2000 | Suicide is not committed in jail. Past imprisonment probably increased wish for revenge in some cases |
| Absence of social support | Klerman, 1987; Linehan, 1999 | Some |
| Unmarried | WHO, 1993; Jacobs et al., 1999; Linehan, 1999 | Does not fit risk for young persons |
| No church membership | Linehan, 1999 | Does not fit |
| High family suicide rate | Lester & Lester, 1971; Klerman, 1987; Jacobs et al., 1999; Linehan, 1999; Moscicki, 1999 | No evidence |

*(Continued)*

**Table 8.2** Compatibility of Ordinary Suicide Risk Factors with Findings on Terrorist Suicides (*Continued*)

| Factor | Sources | Existence in Palestinian terrorist suicides |
|---|---|---|
| Access to lethal means | Klerman, 1987; WHO, 1993; Jacobs et al., 1999; Linehan, 1999; Miller & Paulsen, 1999; Moscicki, 1999 | Fits factor |
| Male | Klerman, 1987; WHO, 1993; Jacobs et al., 1999; Linehan, 1999; Miller & Paulsen, 1999 | Fits factor |
| Older age | Lester & Lester, 1971; WHO, 1993; Jacobs et al., 1999; Linehan, 1999 | Does not fit factor |
| Low social involvement | Lester & Lester, 1971; Klerman, 1987; Linehan, 1999 | Fits factor for some |
| Previous suicide attempts | Klerman, 1987; WHO, 1993; Jacobs et al., 1999; Linehan, 1999; Miller & Paulsen, 1999 | Rare |
| Criminal behavior (young men) | Linehan, 1999; Miller & Paulsen, 1999 | Does not fit factor |
| Unemployed | Klerman, 1987; WHO, 1993; Linehan, 1999 | Minority of cases |
| Poor health | Lester & Lester, 1971; Klerman, 1987; WHO, 1993; Jacobs et al., 1999; Linehan, 1999; Moscicki 1999 | Does not fit factor |
| Miniepidemic in community | WHO, 1993; Miller & Paulsen, 1999; Moscicki, 1999 | Fits factor |

The disparity between the psychological profile of ordinary suicides and terrorist suicides becomes clear when we consider the generally perceived risk factors for suicide. Thus, Moscicki (1999) writes:

> The strongest known risk factor and primary context for completed and attempted suicide is the presence of mental and addictive disorders. Psychopathology is necessary for serious suicidal behaviors to occur . . . Psychological autopsy studies have consistently found that over 90 percent of all completed suicides in all age groups are associated with psychopathology . . . The most frequently reported diagnoses are mood disorders, found in both men and women, followed by substance abuse (predominantly alcohol abuse/ dependence), and conduct disorder or antisocial personality. (p. 45).

Moscicki also notes that there is a positive relationship between the severity of psychopathology and the suicide risk, and that "mood and addictive disorders and mood and personality disorders appear to be particularly lethal combinations." (p. 46).

Unlike ordinary suicides, most Palestinian completed and would-be suicides did not display severe psychopathology, and none whatsoever were alcohol or drug abusers (most of the suicides were members of extremist Islamic organizations, which have conducted a fierce struggle against drugs in the Palestinian society, and alcohol drinking is, of course, forbidden for Muslims). In the would-be suicides sample, only two had made minor suicidal attempts. Altogether, they would not be assessed as high-risk for suicide.

## Conclusion

This chapter sought to answer two interrelated questions. First: do existing suicide theories explain suicide terrorism? And second: do suicide terrorists have the same characteristics as "ordinary" suicides? As it turns out, none of these questions has an unequivocal answer. By and large, the ambiguity is due to the great diversity in circumstances, motives, demographic and psychological characteristics of "ordinary" suicides, and to the lesser but still considerable variation in the characteristics and motives of terrorist suicides. As a result, certain aspects of suicide theories and some characteristics of ordinary suicides are partially pertinent to terrorist suicide. Overall, however, this phenomenon differs sufficiently from ordinary suicide to be recognized as *sui generis*.

The basic uniqueness of terrorist suicide is that it is planned and prepared by an organization rather than by the individual destined to die. Both psychological and sociological theories explain the act of self-destruction as a result of individual decision (although the suicide may be influenced by social forces, norms, and events). Terrorist suicide, however, usually appears in waves ("campaigns") that start and end as decided by the perpetrating organizations. As suggested above, Durkheim's concept of optional altruistic suicide may be the closest approximation to the terrorist suicide phenomenon as we know it today. Yet, even this theory regards suicide as an individual rather than organizational act. In fact, terrorist suicide rates are highest in countries where ordinary suicide rates are low.[4]

Contrary to ordinary suicide, terrorist suicide is ostensibly committed for a political rather than personal cause—that is, not out of personal distress or suffering but for the good of the public that the organization (and the suicide) claims to represent. In fact, in the study reported in Chapter 6, Palestinian organizers of suicide attacks have claimed that they reject candidates who want to die for personal reasons.

The fact that terrorist suicide is initiated and prepared by groups rather than by individuals significantly determines the characteristics of the suicides recruited for the mission. In the study of would-be suicides described in Chapter 5, 40% of the participants were assessed as having suicidal tendencies. This finding is important not only because it suggests that a significant minority of candidates may have been swayed by their wish to die for personal reasons, but also because suicidal dispositions were not detected in the majority (60%) of suicide candidates. Does this mean that they did not want to die? Evidently, they were willing to undertake a suicide mission. What, then, made them volunteer, or at least agree, to kill themselves?

The results of the would-be suicides study suggest that the crucial risk factors for this particular type of suicide differ from those for ordinary suicide. As the interviews and tests show, most suicide bombers in our sample did not undertake the mission because they wished to die so as to put an end an intolerable mental pain, but because their personality characteristics made them more susceptible to external influence. Thus, a basic difference between ordinary and terrorist suicide is related to the specific circumstances under which the latter is carried out. Given this difference, some psychological characteristics associated with the decision to commit suicide are particularly significant. For example, a dependent personality is not usually considered a high-risk factor for ordinary suicide.[5] But in the making of a terrorist suicide, when the suicide operation is praised by the community and the candidate is recruited by an authoritative figure, this personality type becomes a critical factor in determining the person's vulnerability (60% of the Palestinian would-be suicide sample described in Chapter 5 were assessed as dependent-avoidant).

In sum, preliminary as it may be, the evidence accumulated thus far suggests that terrorist suicide differs sufficiently from ordinary suicide to warrant its own theoretical framework.

*Endnotes*

1. National Institute of Mental Health (2003). The Science of Public Messages for Suicide Prevention. Washington, D.C., October 22-23. Available at: http://www. nimh.nih.gov/suicideresearch/suicidepreventionoct2003.cfm, accessed on May 24, 2006.

2. According to Biggs (2005), the imitation of ostensibly politically motivated suicides took place in four countries – Hungary, the U.K., the Soviet Union, and Czechoslovakia. He notes, however, that in Czechoslovakia alone there were seven suicides by fire in the two weeks that followed Palach's death, "none apparently with any political motivation" (p. 182).

3. Wikipedia (2006). Alice Herz. Availble at: http://en.wikipedia.org/wiki/Alice_Herz. Accessed: May 24, 2006. See also Biggs (2005, p. 181) and Swerdlow (1993, p. 130).

4. In 2002, the year with the highest number of suicide bombers in Israel, there were 61 Palestinian suicide bombers. This is about 2 suicides per 100,000 population, a higher rate than the "ordinary" figures reported for most Arab countries.

5. Psychological autopsy studies found an incidence of 10–28% of Cluster C personality disorders among suicides (Tanney, 2000, p. 330). In the DSM-IV (American Psychiatric Association, 1994), Cluster C includes avoidant, dependent, and obsessive-compulsive personality disorders.

# 9

# Current Explanations of
# Suicide Terrorism

Attempts to explain suicide terrorism were made as soon as the phenomenon appeared in Lebanon in the early 1980s. Their number soared after the 9/11/2001 attacks in the U.S., a traumatic event that has aroused great concern about this particular form of terrorism and has prompted academics from a variety of fields to apply their professional insights and tools in an attempt to explain this phenomenon.

Most writers on this topic have been aware that suicide terrorism (and terrorism in general) is a complex phenomenon affected by many factors. Usually, however, their explanations have tended to emphasize a particular factor at the expense of others.

The prevailing explanations, which will be examined in this chapter, focus broadly on four main themes. Most emphasize *political grievances* and causes that presumably radicalize the populations from which suicide bombers emerge, and generate in these populations such virulent hatred toward their adversaries that they are willing to kill themselves for the sake of killing their perceived enemies. Other explanations have discussed *utilitarian* considerations of the groups that have perpetrated suicide attacks, stressing the relatively high impact of suicide operations compared to other terrorist tactics. Still other explanations have attributed the phenomenon to *cultural traits*--especially self-sacrifice--that allegedly make certain societies more prone than others to resort to suicide attacks. On the *individual level*, authors have located the motives of suicide terrorists in religious fanaticism, poverty, personal trauma, the wish to take revenge for personal humiliation or loss of relatives, and, of course, psychopathology.

Explanations of suicide terrorism typically entail several problems. Atran (2003a, supporting online material, p. 4) has correctly noted:

> Scholarly explanations of the genesis of suicide terrorism have tended toward rather simplistic reductions to some essential cause or factor. Some of these elements have been more important than others, depending on time and place. All are also characteristic of phenomena other than suicide terrorism. None alone are sufficient to explain its genesis.

Indeed, explanations of suicide terrorism all too often do not differentiate between suicide attacks and other forms of terrorism. Thus, many authors mention factors relevant to the willingness to resort to terrorism in general, but are not specific to the willingness to undertake suicide missions. An explanation of suicide terrorism must account for the willingness not only to take high risks but also to kill oneself in the course of the struggle.

A major methodological limitation of the current explanations of suicide terrorism stems from limited empirical evidence, as authors support their assertions with data culled mostly on Palestinian suicides and (much less) on suicides in Lebanon. These specific empirical data cannot be readily generalized to suicide terrorists in other places. The predominance of Palestinian suicides as a source of detailed information on terrorist suicide is due to several factors. Among these are the salience of the Israeli-Palestinian conflict in the world media, the practice of Palestinian organizations of releasing information about the suicides, and the accessibility to the media of suicides' families and other sources of information in the community, such as public opinion polls and interviews with political leaders of the perpetrating groups. In other places, even if the general background of the conflict and the context of suicide attacks are known, information on the personal backgrounds, psychological characteristics, and motivations of the suicides is too meager to allow any solid conclusions. In countries plagued by suicide attacks, such as Iraq, Afghanistan and Sri Lanka, even the names of most suicide bombers are unknown, let alone their demographic features.

## Political Grievances

By "political explanations" I mean those that attribute suicide terrorism to people's dissatisfaction with their political situation. However, writers who have attributed suicide terrorism to political grievances have usually referred to the more specific political situation of being under occupation. One typical explanation has been offered by Eyad Sarraj, a Palestinian psychiatrist from Gaza, in a statement titled "Why we have become suicide bombers."[1] Sarraj attributes Palestinian suicide attacks to despair accumulated over decades of Israeli occupation, to the inability of Palestinian refugees of the 1948 war to return to their old homes in Israel, and to disappointment at the failure of the peace process, for which he blames Israel. A dominant element in his account is the feeling of daily humiliation experienced under occupation. Mohammed Hafez (2004; 2006) acknowledges the complexity of the phenomenon and the need to address it not only in its political context, but also on the organizational and individual levels—yet, he locates the basic cause of suicide terrorism in a situation in which "groups or communities feel overwhelming threats and victimized by external enemies in the course of political conflict" (2004, p. 1). Aware that only a handful of conflicts have generated suicide terrorism, Hafez does not limit the necessary political background to the occupation, but, like Sarraj, who sets despair at the center, he believes the readiness to resort to suicide attacks is the result of a growing sense of victimization:

> Extreme violence does not develop in a vacuum; it usually follows previous cycles of low-intensity violence that polarize communities and foster feelings of victimization. Societies embrace extreme violence when they perceive overwhelming threats to their security, identity, or national aspirations, and when they see themselves solely as the victims at the hands of unjust authorities. A progression of radicalization must take place before communities agree to support extreme measures. Absent overwhelming threats and feelings of victimization—whether real or perceived—societies are likely to reject extreme violence against ordinary civilians. (p. 13).

With anti-Western suicide terrorists such as al-Qaeda members presumably in mind, Atran (2003a, p. 1536) adds the global and historical dimensions to the context, while emphasizing the same emotional motives that drive suicide bombers, i.e., feelings of injustice and humiliation:

> In the Middle East, perceived contexts in which suicide bombers and supporters express themselves include a collective sense of historical injustice, political subservience, and social humiliation vis-à-vis global powers and allies, as well as countervailing religious hope.

Khalil Shikaki (2004), a widely respected Palestinian pollster, has pointed out specific aspects of the occupation:

> Capitalizing on Palestinians' growing fear and thirst for revenge, Islamist groups such as Hamas and the Palestinian Islamic Jihad (PIJ) gained public favor with suicide bombings and violence against Israelis. Average Palestinians were feeling more and more threatened by Israeli-imposed checkpoints, curfews, and sieges of Palestinian cities and towns; by the separation barrier being built deep in the West Bank; and by continued Israeli land confiscation and settlement construction.

Writing about the Tamils, Joshi (2000) has offered a similar view of the perception of extreme oppression and hopelessness as the root cause of suicide terrorism. He describes the background for the willingness of Tamils to carry out suicide attacks as follows: "Their willingness to assume this role is born of a sense of frustration at the lot of the minority Tamils in Sri Lanka. Army intimidation is a fact of daily life for many Tamils, while young Tamils can look forward to only the bleakest economic prospects."

Kalyvas and Sánchez-Cuenca (2005) have argued that the necessary, albeit insufficient, condition for suicide terrorism is political repression and economic misery: "Unless repression is great and/or the surrounding (rather than individual) economic deprivation severe, the proper motivations leading to participation in SMs [suicide missions] are unlikely to emerge." (p. 231).

Several authors have suggested that suicide attacks have served not only as a means to remedy situations perceived as oppressive and unjust, but also as a way to regain the lost honor and self-respect of communities that feel humiliated by a superior enemy (e.g., Silke, 2003; Reuter, 2004; Blum, 2005; R. Hassan, 2004). Such extreme form of violence and sacrifice empowers those who feel belittled, disadvantaged, and oppressed, helping them regain their self-respect. This notion is similar to Franz Fanon's (1965) idea that violence has a cathartic value for oppressed peoples. Fanon, a psychiatrist from Martinique involved in the Algerian struggle for independence (1954–1962), offered a psychological view of the role of violence in the struggle for independence of oppressed people. In his famous book *The Wretched of the Earth*, he maintained that violence is a necessary—indeed essential—part in the process of psychological redemption of peoples that feel oppressed, humiliated, and valueless due to their protracted experience of repressive occupation.

It is not surprising that the perpetrating groups themselves also mention oppression, unjust deprivation, and humiliation as crucial to their decision to resort to suicide attacks. Leaders of Palestinian groups usually proffer explanations of this kind. Still, suicide attacks have not always been carried out under circumstances that can be readily described as a humiliating occupation, suffering, despair, and hopelessness. For example in 1983, when the first suicide attacks against the multinational force took place in Lebanon, Husayn Musawi, one of the founding leaders of Hizballah, justified them by claiming that the peacekeeping multinational force was waging war on the Muslims in Lebanon (Kramer, 1990). Hizballah's spokesman Sayyid Ibrahim al-Amin stated that the attack on the Marine barracks was a response to American aggression, because the United States had "transformed Lebanon into a military test laboratory for their advanced weapons." (Kramer, 1990, p. 142). Although these claims were obviously false, the suicide attacks were no doubt motivated by a political reason— namely, the fear of Hizballah and its state sponsors, Syria and Iran, that the presence of the multinational force would hamper their influence in Lebanon. Nonetheless, the presence of the small multinational force in Lebanon could not be perceived as an oppressive occupation by any stretch of the imagination.

Bin Laden's "Declaration of Jihad against the Americans Occupying the Land of the Two Holy Sanctuaries," issued on August 23, 1996, provides the ideological basis for al-Qaeda's attacks—in particular, suicide attacks—on the United States. At the core of this message, which urges Muslims around the world to wage war against the United States, is the claim that Muslims are victims of Western oppression:

> It is no secret to you, my brothers, that the people of Islam have been afflicted with oppression, hostility, and injustice by the Judeo-Christian alliance and its supporters. This shows our enemies' belief that Muslims' blood is the cheapest and that their property and wealth is merely loot. Your blood has been spilt in Palestine and Iraq, and the horrific images of the massacre in Qana in Lebanon are still fresh in people's minds. The massacres that have taken place in Tajikistan, Burma, Kashmir, Assam, the Philippines, Fatani, Ogaden, Somalia, Eritrea, Chechnya, and Bosnia-Herzegovina send shivers down our spines and stir up our passions. All this has happened before the eyes and ears of the world, but the blatant imperial arrogance of America, under the cover of the immoral United Nations, has prevented the dispossessed from arming themselves. (Lawrence, 2005, p. 25).

In a message released by al-Jazeera in December 2001, Bin Laden justified the suicide attacks of September 11, 2001 on the U.S. as follows:

> The events of 22nd Jumada al-Thani, or Aylul [September 11] are merely a response to the continuous injustice inflicted upon our sons in Palestine, Iraq, Somalia, southern Sudan, and other places, like Kashmir. The matter concerns the entire *umma* [Muslim nation]. People need to wake up from their sleep and try to find a solution to this catastrophe that is threatening all of humanity. (Lawrence, 2005, pp. 148–149).

As al-Qaeda's suicide attacks demonstrate, actual suffering of the perpetrators and being personally subjected to humiliation and despair is not a necessary condition for the willingness to resort to suicide terrorism. However, what matters is arguably not objective reality (whatever it may mean) but people's perceptions of it. While most readers of this book probably think that describing Saudi Arabia as being under American occupation is a distortion of reality, for the perpetrators of the 9/11 attacks it may have been the truth. Yet in some cases, there is no reason whatsoever to assume that suicide attackers are motivated by subjective feelings of oppression and humiliation. In Pakistan, where Sunnis constitute the ruling majority, militant Sunni groups carried out 14 suicide attacks in a campaign against the Shiite minority[2] in the period from July 2003 to December 2008.[3] These attacks were motivated by the radical Sunnis' belief that the Shiites are heretics and must be forced to adopt the Sunni version of Islam or perish.

In Iraq, besides suicide attacks against coalition forces and the newly created Iraqi army and police, a massive campaign of suicide attacks has been conducted by militant Sunni groups (mainly al-Qaeda in Iraq) against the Shiite community. More than 160 suicide attacks, some involving multiple suicide bombers, were carried out between January 2004 and December 2008 against civilian Shiite targets such as mosques, funeral mourners, weddings, pilgrims, Shiite community facilities, political leaders, and the random public in Shiite neighborhoods. These attacks, which left over 3,200 people dead and more than 6,000 wounded, were motivated by the ancient Sunni hatred for the "heretic" Shiites, but also by the intention to destabilize the country by fomenting a sectarian war that would derail the pacification process. Even if the attacks are viewed as a side effect of the American occupation that has divested the Sunni minority from its previous dominant position in the country, they were carried out against fellow Iraqis of a rival sect that cannot be considered an occupying force.

The Sunni suicide campaigns against Shiites in Pakistan and Iraq show that oppression is not a necessary condition for choosing this extreme form of terrorism. Of course, they do not contradict the claim that suicide terrorism is motivated by political objectives. This claim, however, does not add much to our understanding of the roots of suicide terrorism. Actually, the notion that suicide attacks (and any terrorism, for that matter) are related to a political context is a truism, as it is embedded in the very concept of political terrorism—which is, by definition, politically motivated violence. The recognition that terrorism is politically motivated does not help us explain suicide attacks as a special form of terrorism. Furthermore, the claim that suicide terrorism is on the rise when people feel oppressed, deprived, threatened, and humiliated is, in itself, insufficient for explaining the phenomenon. Only a small number of the many political conflicts around the globe have generated suicide terrorism, and these have not necessarily been the most devastating. Thus, no suicide attacks have been recorded in Darfur, where an estimated number of between 50,000 and 400,000 people have been killed since 2003 by the Sudanese government and its supported militias. Neither were such attacks recorded in East Timor following oppression and massacres carried out by Indonesian forces and militias, nor have suicide attacks taken place in response to the Rwanda genocide or following the massacres and ethnic cleansing in Bosnia. *Hence, suicide terrorism seems to be triggered by other factors besides political grievances, grave as they may be.*

The fact that grievances are not a sufficient explanation for suicide attacks did not escape some writers. Silke (2003), for example, has suggested several exacerbating conditions that prompt groups to resort to suicide attacks, among them a longstanding bloody conflict. He noted that at least some organizations, e.g., the PKK, have opted for suicide attacks when they suffered defeats. In a similar vein, I wrote:

> Under what circumstances does a group, Islamic or not, decide to resort to suicide attacks? Asking members to kill themselves is an extreme step, which is contradictory to basic psychological tendencies. For this reason, it is logical to expect that only under extreme circumstances would a group be willing to resort to this extreme way of fighting. Extreme circumstances are situations in which, by the group's perception, its main cause or its organizational existence are in grave danger. (Merari, 2005).

Interestingly, suicide in the context of conventional war (rather than a terrorist campaign) has also been attributed to desperate situations, where an imminent danger of defeat called for extreme measures. This has been a common explanation for the Japanese decision to resort to kamikaze attacks en masse in October 1944, when the U.S. offensive in the Philippines was perceived by the Japanese military leadership as a crucial danger of inevitable defeat in the war (Hoyt, 1999). Hill (2005, p. 42), who notes that Russia and Germany also used suicide during World War II (though on a much smaller scale than the Japanese kamikazes), writes: "As was the case with Japan, such measures were usually adopted by countries facing unusually desperate circumstances."

## Utilitarian Explanations

Whereas political grievances explain suicide terrorism as an emotionally motivated practice, other explanations have focused on the utilitarian aspect of the phenomenon, i.e., the intention to achieve strategic goals. This approach defines suicide terrorism as a rational, goal-directed tactic rather than in terms of the emotions associated with grievances that a given community perceives as legitimate.

Utilitarian explanations of suicide terrorism are related, of course, to the organization's motivation rather than that of the individual. This view is generally justified, because suicide attacks are an organizational enterprise. As almost all have been planned and orchestrated by terrorist groups, they should be viewed primarily as a group's calculated tactic rather than as the product of an individual's emotional, impromptu urge (Merari, 2002). As several authors have argued (e.g., Sprinzak, 2000; Atran, 2003a, 2004b; Harrison, 2003; Pape, 2003, 2005; Hafez, 2004; Hoffman & McCormick, 2004; Gupta & Mundra, 2005), resorting to suicide attacks is a rational choice by the perpetrating organizations.

In explaining why terrorist groups resort to suicide attacks, writers have focused on two interrelated aspects of their utility: tactical advantage and strategic results. Many authors have noted that for the perpetrating organization, suicide attacks have several tactical advantages compared to other terrorist methods (e.g., Merari, 1990; Ganor, 2001; Luft, 2002; Stern, 2003; Cronin, 2003; Atran, 2003a, 2004b; Hoffman, 2003; Hoffman & McCormick, 2004; Hafez, 2004; Gupta & Mundra, 2005): they cause a large number of casualties, generate extensive media coverage, and instill fear among the target public. The suicide bombers constitute a kind of smart bomb, because they can select their target according to predetermined criteria, such as the victims' number, type, and accessibility.

The suicide's willingness to die increases the likelihood that an attack will take place even if the bomber is discovered on his way to the target and cannot reach his original destination. Another advantage for the perpetrating organization is that it need not prepare an escape route for the attacker. Furthermore, the attacker's death eliminates the risk that he or she may be arrested and talk under interrogation.

## Strategic Objectives

Many authors have referred to the strategic objectives of suicide attacks as an explanation of the perpetrating groups' decision to adopt this form of terrorism. However, these objectives do not differ from those of non-suicide terrorist activity, and hence cannot be regarded as specific causes of suicide terrorism—even if, tactically, suicide attacks are more effective and extreme. Therefore, the claim that suicide attacks serve the strategic goals of the organizations that carry them out does not contribute significantly to the understanding of the phenomenon. For example, Gambetta (2005, p. 260) noted that "all SMs [suicide missions] are carried out by the weaker side in conflicts characterized by a marked asymmetry in the balance of military force." A similar observation was made by Pape (2005), who termed suicide attacks "a strategy for weak actors" (p. 27). In fact, long before suicide terrorism emerged as a systematic tactic, scholars have recognized that terrorism in general (not only suicide attacks) is a strategy adopted by insurgents fighting against the far superior force of the states they challenge (Schmid, 1983; Schmid & Jongman, 1988). Crenshaw (1990), for example, suggested that insurgent groups resort to terrorism not only because they are weak compared to the governments they challenge, but because their weakness precludes them from using other strategies of insurgency (e.g., guerrilla) that require a large number of participants.

According to Pape (2003, 2005), the strategic goal behind suicide terrorism is quite specific: "At bottom, suicide terrorism is a strategy for national liberation from foreign military occupation by a democratic state." (2005, p. 45). As a generalization, this simplistic formula is clearly incorrect. For example, al-Qaeda does not quite fit the description of an organization for national liberation, and has carried out suicide attacks against Western targets around the globe, as well as against Saudi targets. Motivated by a religious *and* political ideology, al-Qaeda fights primarily both Western cultural and political influence. The group has demanded the expulsion of

American forces stationed in Saudi Arabia and other Arabian Peninsula countries, but these forces cannot be regarded as occupiers by any stretch of imagination—certainly not by the definition of occupation used by Pape, namely, "foreign occupation involves the exertion of political and military control over territory by an outside group" (2005, pp. 45–46). Although most (albeit not all) suicide attacks have been carried out in the context of fighting against a perceived occupation, Pape ignores the fact that most of the conflicts that have generated terrorism over the recent decades—usually without suicide attacks—have been conducted for the purpose of ostensible national liberation or ejection of foreign forces. Fighting an occupation is therefore not specifically associated with suicide attacks. Furthermore, nothing specific in the fight against a foreign occupation invites suicide attacks more than would, say, social or religious causes. History shows that people are willing to die for their religious belief no less than for their country.[4] Moreover, organizations that led social revolutions did not recoil from sacrificing their members for the cause.[5]

## Intergroup Competition

Several authors (Cronin, 2003; Hafez, 2004; Bloom, 2004, 2005; Ricolfi, 2005; Gupta & Mundra, 2005) have suggested that one of the reasons terrorist groups resort to suicide attacks is their competition with rival groups over popular support. Presumably, since suicide attacks demonstrate determination and willingness to sacrifice oneself, and due to their dramatic nature and high media value, groups wish to carry them out to gain public support by establishing their leading status in the struggle. Yet, empirical evidence suggests that the competition factor is of marginal importance. In most suicide campaigns (e.g., Sri Lanka, Chechnya, and the Kurdish struggle in Turkey) there was no competition; the insurgency has been carried out by one group only. In the Palestinian case, on which most writers base their claims, presumably rival groups (Hamas, PIJ, Fatah, and PFLP) have cooperated in numerous instances to prepare joint suicide attacks. In most cases, intergroup cooperation has taken place at the regional or local command level, where local leaders of the militant groups often know each other and willingly help the other group in preparing and implementing an attack. In at least 18 cases (9% of the total number of Palestinian suicide attacks since 1993) the suicide attack has been carried out jointly by two or more groups that have assisted each other with logistical support, such as providing a suicide belt or a guide to the target.

## How Important is the Success of Suicide Campaigns?

Pape (2003, 2005) has claimed that at least some of the appeal of suicide attacks lies in their achievement of a strategic objective, which is, in his view, the expulsion of a foreign occupying force from a territory:

> Moreover, over the past two decades, suicide terrorism has been rising largely because terrorists have learned that it pays. Suicide terrorists sought to compel American and French military forces to abandon Lebanon in 1983, Israeli forces to leave Lebanon in 1985, Israeli forces to quit the Gaza Strip and the West Bank in 1994 and 1995, the Sri Lankan government to create an independent Tamil state from 1990 on, and the Turkish government to grant autonomy to the Kurds in the late 1990s. In all but the case of Turkey, the terrorist political cause made more gains after the resort to suicide operations than it had before. (Pape, 2003, p. 343).

Indeed, as has been noted by many writers, suicide attacks are usually a more lethal form of terrorism. However, with the exception of the withdrawal of the multinational force from Lebanon in 1984, Pape's examples are wrong. Contrary to his claim, the partial withdrawal of Israeli forces from Lebanon in January–May 1985 was not prompted by suicide attacks but by other types of terrorist attacks, which were much more numerous and caused a much greater aggregate number of casualties. Actually, effective Israeli security procedures led to a dramatic drop in the number of Israeli forces' casualties after 1983 (see Table 2.3). Thus, the single suicide attack against Israeli forces in 1983 resulted in 36 Israeli fatalities, but no fatalities were caused by the single suicide attack that was carried out against Israeli forces in 1984. In the first five months of 1985, before the Israeli withdrawal to the security zone of South Lebanon, there were five suicide attacks against Israeli forces and the Israeli-sponsored South Lebanese Army, which resulted in 14 fatalities—less than three deaths per attack on average.[6] All in all, in the three years before May 1985, the total number of Israeli fatalities in Lebanon (including Israeli soldiers killed in the 1982 war in clashes with Syrian and PLO forces) reached 1217, of which only 50 were caused by suicide attacks.[7] The assumption that suicide attacks were the cause for the Israeli withdrawal is therefore not supported by the facts. Furthermore, the final Israeli withdrawal from Lebanon in May 2000 was also not influenced by suicide attacks but by other types of terrorist and guerrilla operations that caused a small but steady number of casualties per year. The withdrawal took place long after suicide attacks against Israeli forces in Lebanon had practically ceased, due

to successful Israeli preventive procedures that convinced the leadership of
the perpetrating groups that they did not cause Israel sufficient damage.
Of the 41 suicide attacks in Lebanon, only three were carried out after
1995, resulting in a total of two fatalities. In fact, as Kramer (1990) noted,
as early as 1985, fifteen years before Israel's final withdrawal from Lebanon,
Hizballah's spiritual leader, Mohammad Hussayn Fadlallah, realized that
suicide attacks failed to achieve their intended results and ruled that under
these circumstances they were to be stopped. In Fadlallah's words:

> We believe that suicide operations should only be carried out if they can
> bring about a political or military change in proportion to the passions that
> incite a person to make of his body an explosive bomb . . . But the present
> circumstances do not favor such operations anymore, and attacks that only
> inflict limited casualties (on the enemy) and destroy one building should not
> be encouraged, if the price is the death of the person who carries them out.[8]

Pape is equally wrong about the effect of Palestinian suicide attacks.
He claims that Hamas suicide attacks during the peace process were motivated by the organization's wish to hasten Israel's withdrawal from
Palestinian cities in accordance with the Oslo Agreement, and that Hamas
suspended suicide operations in the second half of 1995, at a time when
Israel "accelerated the pace of withdrawal" (2005, p. 41).[9] The facts are
quite different from Pape's description. As several writers (e.g., Sprinzak,
2000; Schweitzer, 2000; Bloom, 2005, p. 24), have already noted, Hamas'
objective was to abort rather than expedite the peace process (which necessarily implied stopping all Israeli interim withdrawals).[10] Suicide attacks
carried out by Hamas did, in fact, contribute to the demise of the peace
process, and as such were successful from Hamas' point of view, albeit
contrary to Pape's. Several times following suicide attacks carried out by
Hamas, the Israeli government postponed withdrawals from parts of the
occupied territories as stipulated by the agreements with the PLO. Hamas'
temporary suspension of suicide attacks in the second half of 1995 and
again in March 1996 was not the result of Israel's partial withdrawals, as
Pape claims. It was enforced mainly by severe steps taken by the Palestinian
National Authority against the Hamas leadership and organizational infrastructure, under strong Israeli and American pressure. Hamas political
leaders in the Gaza Strip were arrested and humiliated, and the organization's offices were closed down. Under these circumstances the group's
leadership decided that continuation of suicide attacks was not worth the
damage to the organization.

Furthermore, the Hamas political leadership suspended suicide attacks at that time because it felt that its militancy was losing Palestinian popular support. In 1995–6 the prevailing view among Palestinians was that Hamas' attacks (especially the spectacular suicide attacks inside Israel) were counterproductive, because they led Israel to stall promised withdrawals and to impose a variety of sanctions such as roadblocks and restrictions on the admission of Palestinians laborers into Israel, which caused the Palestinians considerable hardship. In March 1996, following resumption of suicide attacks, support for Hamas declined to 5.8% (compared to 16.6% in August 1995) and in May 1996, Palestinian public support for suicide attacks fell to an all-time low of 21.1%.[11] Despite the opposition of the military wing commanders and of the radical Hamas leadership in exile, the local political leaders were able to impose their decision to suspend suicide attacks temporarily.[12]

Perhaps the most blatant distortion of history among Pape's examples of suicide terrorism successes, is his claim that Israel released Hamas spiritual leader Sheikh Ahmad Yassin from prison under pressure of Hamas suicide attacks (2005, p. 65). In fact, Yassin was released by Israel as a gesture to King Hussein of Jordan, following Israel's embarrassing failed attempt to assassinate Hamas leader Khaled Mash'al in Amman, on September 25, 1997. Two Israeli Mossad agents involved in the attempt were arrested by the Jordanian police, and Jordan threatened to put them on trial and to sever diplomatic relations with Israel. Given harsh public criticism across the Arab world, the release of Sheikh Yassin was meant to help the Jordanian government justify its decision to release the captured Israeli agents. It had nothing to do with appeasing Hamas (Halevy, 2006; Mishal & Sela, 2000, p. 111). A detailed description of the Israeli-Jordanian negotiations that led to Yassin's release from prison can be found in Efraim Halevy's (2006) memoirs (Halevy acted as Israel's emissary to Amman during the crisis).

In sum, the attempt to explain suicide terrorism by the strategic objectives of the perpetrating organizations is insufficient, as it does not tell us why some organizations resort to suicide attacks whereas other terrorist groups, with similar objectives, refrain from using this tactic. As mentioned above, suicide attacks do have several tactical advantages over other terrorist methods. Yet the question remains why some groups use them, whereas other groups fighting for a similar cause do not.

Suicide attacks are just one among a plethora of tactics available to terrorist groups, such as car bombs detonated by remote control or timing device, roadside explosive charges, and armed assaults—tactics commonly used in conflict areas such as Iraq, Afghanistan, Chechnya, and Israel. Like other tactics, suicide attacks are meant to serve the political–strategic objectives of the insurgent groups. These objectives explain the terrorist groups' use of violence, but not their choice of suicide attacks rather than other available terrorist methods. Why, for example, have the Tamil Tigers and Palestinian groups used suicide attacks, whereas the Basque ETA and the Irish PIRA, also groups that have fought for national liberation, have not? The group's strategic goal does not provide an answer to this question. There must be, therefore, other reasons behind this phenomenon.

## Culture and Religion

Suicide terrorism involves both self-destruction and killing others. With regard to the latter element, the role of religion hardly needs any explanation. Throughout history people have killed others in the name of religious beliefs. Killing oneself, however, is another matter. All three great mono-theistic religions, Judaism, Christianity and Islam, have traditionally forbidden suicide, although they all sanctified the willingness to die in defense of the faith, as long as death is inflicted by the enemy rather than by the martyr himself (or herself). The authorization—indeed, glorification—of self-destruction for killing the enemy, issued by radical Islamic clerics, is a recent departure from orthodox Islam. Despite its recency, religious justifi-cation is generally considered one of the main motivational constituents of suicide terrorism, at least in the case of Muslim suicide bombers.

Hypothetically, there are two ways in which a culture (including reli-gion) may prompt groups and individuals to carry out suicide attacks. One pertains to cultural values and customs that dictate under what circum-stances a person may or should commit suicide or let himself (or herself) be killed. The other, specifically related to religion, affects people's beliefs and expectations about what happens after death. Authors who have viewed Islam as a major component in the making of suicide terrorists have attrib-uted great importance to the Islamic belief that the *shahids* go straight to paradise (e.g., Hoffman, 1998, pp. 98–100; Ganor, 2001; Hassan, 2001).

Suicide terrorism was started in an Arab country (Lebanon) by a mili-tant Islamic group (Hizballah). As of the end of 2008, nearly 95% of the suicide attacks around the globe have been carried out by groups that orig-inated in Muslim societies, and about 70% by groups from Arab countries. The prevalence of Muslims, especially Arabs, among suicide attackers has led many scholars to assume that the propensity to carry out suicide attacks is affected by certain cultural traits typical of Muslims in general, and Arabs in particular. The assumption that suicide attacks are influenced by cultural traits has been supported by the historical example of World War II Japanese kamikazes, whose willingness to carry out suicide attacks has been attributed to Japanese tradition and education (Ohnuki-Tierney, 2002; Inoguchi & Nakajima, 1958; Christoph Reuter, 2004; Hill, 2005).

Numerous authors have attributed to culture, and especially to religion, a central role in the emergence of suicide terrorism. Hafez (2004, p. 1) wrote:

> At the level of society, suicidal violence is embraced and venerated when three conditions are met: (1) prevailing cultural norms and mores encompass belief systems, symbolic narratives, and historical traditions that justify and celebrate martyrdom; (2) legitimate authorities promote or acquiesce to extreme violence; and (3) groups or communities feel overwhelming threats and victimized by external enemies in the course of political conflict.

Writers (e.g., Crenshaw, 2001; Silke, 2003; Strenski, 2003) have often maintained that suicide terrorism tends to take place in societies that support martyrdom and self-sacrifice. Some scholars, however, have specifically attributed suicide terrorism to Islamic traditions. Long before Islamic suicide bombers became the widespread phenomenon we know today, Maxell Taylor (1988, p. 110) wrote about suicide attacks in Lebanon: ". . . the behaviours which we find so difficult to understand (suicide bombing, for example) have their origins in the kind of religious practice which characterises Islamic fundamentalism, and especially Shi'iteism." (p. 110). Taylor later wisely expanded his explanation to encompass other cultural characteristics: "The Shi'ite terrorist, like the Kamikaze, belongs in a social, historical, religious and mystical context that legitimizes and sustains such behaviour." (p. 114). In Taylor's view, however, the most important cultural factor that contributes to terrorist suicide is societal control and members' conformity. Taylor thought that the same factor was also instrumental in both the chain suicides of IRA and INLA members in Maze Prison in 1981 and the suicide in prison of the German Red Army Faction (better known as the Baader-Meinhof group) members in the 1970s: "Both contemporary Shi'ite society, and the Japanese society of the time, show many attributes of intense control, with restrictions on extra-societal influences. In many respects they are as 'psychologically' closed as the prisons which sustained both the Baader-Meinhof and the IRA suicides" (1988, p. 120).[13]

Raphael Israeli (1997, p. 107) also attributes suicide terrorism to Islamic influence: "Turning to an Islamic frame of reference for a definition, and perhaps a diagnosis, would then appear imperative if we are to comprehend the underlying motives of this sort of unparalleled mode of self-sacrifice." Paz has expressed a similar view (2001, p. 88):

> This combination of religious and social elements in Islamic societies is the key to understanding what we term 'suicide terrorism,' or what Islamic movements call 'self sacrifice' or 'istishad.' What we actually have here is a combination of religious justification and religious interpretation, together with social factors rooted in the surrounding society.

## The Importance of Honor in Arab Culture

Several authors have suggested that the high importance attributed by Arab culture to the defense of the family and the clan's honor may have a role in the proclivity of Arab youngsters to carry out suicide missions. In traditional Arab culture, the individual is obliged to avenge violated family honor and is willing to pay a high personal price for this emotional satisfaction. A woman suspected of having socially unacceptable relations with a man is often murdered by a next of kin, a brother, a cousin, or her father, because the family's honor is at stake. When a member of the extended family (*hamula*) is killed by a member of another clan, each and every male in the extended family is obliged to take revenge by killing a male of the killer's clan. The only way to avert a tit-for-tat revenge is for the killer's family to approach the victim's family with admission of guilt and an offer of reparations. The offended family usually accepts the gesture and the matter is settled in a feast called *sulha* (forgiveness, reconciliation). This social custom may well be reflected also in the psychological attitude of many Arabs to political conflicts as well. Several years ago I was invited by Professor Herbert Kelman of Harvard University to participate in one of his simulated negotiations between Israelis and Palestinians. Kelman had been running these negotiation exercises for many years. Typically, each side was represented by four persons, who argued for their community's interests and needs in the negotiations. The simulation started by each side presenting the most essential demands in the conflict, those absolutely vital and not given to any compromise. First the Israeli team stated that for Israel, the most existential demand was the security of Israel as a Jewish state; borders, however, were negotiable. The Palestinian participants then presented their most important, non-negotiable demand: they wanted

Israel first to *apologize* for the wrongs it had done to the Palestinians over the many decades of the conflict, and then take remedial steps. To the Israelis this seemed both unjust and unhelpful. We responded that both sides to the conflict have caused suffering to each other over the years, citing examples of Palestinian intransigence such as the refusal to accept the U.N. Partition Plan of 1947 (which Israel accepted) and their waging of war against Israel with the intention of eradicating the young Jewish state. Other examples included the PLO's officially stated goal to destroy Israel throughout the first 25 years of its existence, and numerous instances of Palestinian indiscriminate terrorist attacks and massacres of Jews from 1927 (the "Massacre of the Jews" in Hebron, two decades before the establishment of Israel) up to the recent indiscriminate suicide attacks directed at Israeli civilians. We suggested that instead of blaming each other for wrongs of the past, we'd better look forward and find a way to live together in the future. The Palestinians, however, were adamant: First you must apologize. We Israelis were especially surprised by the Palestinians' emotional and (in our view) unfair approach, not only because all four Palestinian participants were highly educated, intelligent professionals, but also because their personal demeanor was quite pleasant and displayed no hatred or aggressiveness whatsoever. With this deadlock in the negotiation process, we took a break. As we continued our discussion in an informal atmosphere, the two men of the Palestinian group explained to me the importance of the *sulha* practice in Arab tradition as a means of redeeming honor without bloodshed.

In weighing the importance of hurt honor in the motivation of suicide terrorists, we should remember that revenge for national (rather than personal) humiliation and suffering was the most prevalent reason Palestinian suicide bombers gave for their willingness to undertake their mission (Chapter 5). This response may be interpreted as an extension, from the family circle to the national level, of the traditional obligation to avenge hurt honor.

## Japanese Tradition as a Case in Point

An often mentioned example of cultural influence on the willingness to commit suicide is the Japanese tradition of honorable death known as *seppuku* or *hara-kiri*. This example is recurrently used to explain the phenomenon of Japanese kamikaze pilots during World War II.

However, unlike the kamikaze practice, *seppuku* did not entail killing others, but only oneself, because of tainted honor or a violated code of conduct. Despite this difference, the importance of this longstanding tradition in shaping the mentality that underpinned the kamikaze units may lie in instilling the idea that, under some circumstances, voluntary death is a socially admirable virtue. Hill (2005, p. 4–25) offers evidence of many kamikaze cases that were not motivated by the abstract notions of fighting for the Emperor or the honor of falling in battle, but by the more concrete wish to defend their families.

Regarding sacrifice in combat, however, does the Japanese tradition of voluntary death for social reasons essentially differ from that of other cultures? All cultures and national traditions venerate heroic death in battle, and children of all nationalities are raised on historical stories of the noble deaths of national heroes. Unlike in Japan, however, the fallen heroes of the West died in combat but did not kill themselves.

## How Important are Culture and Religion?

Presumably, the scholarly (and media) opinion that religion is crucial to the production of suicide attackers has been reinforced by the claims of the perpetrators themselves. By now, all newspaper readers are familiar with the statements of numerous militant Muslim leaders and activists proclaiming the Muslims' love for death "in Allah's path" and their wish to become *shahids* and get to paradise sooner rather than later. These proclamations have been issued for both internal and external consumption. For the home public, they have been meant to justify by a religious argument the use of human bombs, as well as to recruit volunteers. For the outside world—adversaries and observers—they are part of a psychological warfare intended to instill fear and awe. Do these propagandistic self-descriptions truly reflect the crucial role of religion in the making of Islamic suicide bombers?

Twenty years ago, when Lebanon was the only country where suicide attacks were conducted as a systematic campaign, I wrote: "Culture in general and religion in particular seem to be relatively unimportant in the phenomenon of terrorist suicide." (Merari, 1990, p. 206). In Lebanon, more than half of the suicide attacks were carried out by secular groups. Should this position be revised in 2006, when the great majority of suicide attacks around the world have been carried out by Muslim groups?

For several reasons it is quite clear that religious fanaticism is neither a necessary nor a sufficient condition for suicide terrorism (Merari, 2004; Klyvas & Sánchez-Cuenca, 2005). Religion is not a necessary factor because a significant number of the groups that have used suicide attacks (including some of those bred in Arab countries) have been secular. The majority of the groups that carried out suicide attacks in Lebanon in the 1980s were secular, most of them pro-Syrian organizations (Merari, 1990).[14] These groups have been responsible for nearly two-thirds of the suicide attacks in Lebanon. Contrary to the general perception, Hizballah—the only truly religious group that carried out suicide attacks in Lebanon—has been responsible for only 14 out of 41 suicide attacks in that country. In the Palestinian arena, two of the groups that have jointly carried out about one-third of the suicide attacks in the second intifada are secular—Fatah (whose members carried out suicide attacks under the banner of al-Aqsa Martyrs Brigades) and the quasi-Marxist PFLP. The Tamil Tigers, who have carried out a large number of suicide attacks in Sri Lanka, are a secular group that has espoused some Leninist principles in the past. The Kurdistan Workers Party (PKK, or *Partiya Karkeran Kurdistan*), which has carried out most of the suicide attacks in Turkey, is a Marxist organization, as is the Turkish Revolutionary People's Liberation Party/Front.[15] Furthermore, as the interviews with Palestinian would-be suicides show, six of the respondents (40%), including some of those dispatched by the religious groups Hamas and PIJ, said that their willingness to carry out suicide attacks had not been motivated by religious sentiments at all.

The conclusion that religious fanaticism is not a sufficient factor in the making of a suicide terrorist is an obvious corollary of the fact that only a minute fraction of the immense number of religious fanatics around the globe end up as suicide terrorists. No doubt, millions of Muslims firmly believe that *istishhad* is a religious duty and that *shahids* are rewarded by a sure place in paradise. Yet they do not attempt to fulfill this lofty duty themselves. In 1994, I interviewed a person in jail I shall name "Z" here, who was a seasoned member of Izz ad-Din al-Qassam, the military arm of Hamas. The main purpose of the interview was to obtain information about Z's close friend J, who had fought to the death in a terrorist operation. As Z had known J from childhood, I hoped to glean some details about J's personality. In the course of the discussion, I asked Z: "Where do you think J is now?" "He is in paradise, of course," came the sure answer. "And what is it like for him to be in paradise?" I asked. Z described his friend as serene and happy, spending his time close to Allah, in the company of the prophets and other *shahids*. Given this blissful description, my next question probably seemed rather silly to Z: "Do you think that J was better off when he was on earth, with us, or is he better off now, in paradise?"

Z's answer smacked of contempt: "Of course he is better off now that he is in paradise!" "And what about yourself?" I went on. "Would you also rather be in paradise now?" Z stared at me for a moment, baffled, then said firmly: "Me? No!"

In my lectures I often tell this episode to demonstrate that one can be a militant religious fanatic and even willing to die for the cause, but not ready to kill oneself. Z was no doubt a true Muslim believer. Earlier in our conversation he stated his conviction that Islam would eventually prevail in the world. He deeply believed that *shahids* have a guaranteed place in paradise and that his friend was, indeed, there. His personal record as a member of Izz ad-Din al-Qassam attested to his readiness to pay a high price for his belief, even to risk death in battle. Yet he was reluctant to commit suicide.

Of course, this line of reasoning is not limited to religious fanaticism; it applies to culture in general, as well as to other potentially relevant factors. Many people have killed for a political or ideological cause, but only a relatively very small number have killed themselves intentionally in the process. Hence, in themselves, such factors as culture, religion, or political circumstances are insufficient for explaining the propensity for suicide attacks.

Still, even if culture and religion alone cannot explain suicide terrorism, they are not negligible factors. What seemed true twenty years ago, when Lebanon was the only place where a suicide terrorist campaign was conducted and the data included only some 40 cases, must be reviewed now that much more extensive data are available. Over 2600 suicide attacks in 38 countries show that the great majority of suicide bombers around the globe have come from Islamic, mostly Arab, cultures. To what extent, then, is this fact the result of Islamic (particularly Arab) culture and religious background? To what extent is it the product of a particular set of political circumstances and past experiences (whether objectively true or imagined) that make certain ethnic groups, which happen to be Muslim, more susceptible to the use of suicidal violence? The relevant hypothetical question is whether, under the same circumstances, other cultures—Western, African, or Chinese—would produce suicide attacks at the same rate (if at all) as Islamic cultures do. While there is no empirical basis to allow a firm answer to this question, we can logically assume that culture (including religion) does have a significant influence on the way people perceive and react to situations. A vast social science literature shows that cultural differences do affect human behavior, and there is no reason to assume that such differences, in interaction with certain political conditions, have no influence on the proclivity to resort to suicide attacks.[16] Evidently, culture does not have an all-or-none effect. But some cultures (notably Islamic/Arabic), because of the reasons they adduce for voluntary dying and their attitude to life after death, may very well produce more suicide terrorism than others under the same circumstances.

## Group Processes

Two decades ago Maxwell Taylor (1988, p. 118) wrote about the hunger strikes of Irish and German terrorists in prison:

> It may be that the religious context to such issues rather obscures analysis; the critical factor may not be religion as such, but an environmental context that *both* allows *and* supports it. A characteristic of terrorists like the Baader-Meinhof group and the Provisional IRA is the extent to which they can exercise control over their members. During the period prior to, and during, the hunger strikes, in both groups the prisoners were able to communicate between themselves and outside. The individuals involved were under enormous pressure to conform, and subject to actual, or fear of, intimidation if they failed to do so.

In later years several other authors have recognized the critical importance of group allegiance and pressure in the process of making suicide bombers. Thus, Atran (2003a, supporting online material, p. 10) wrote:

> In sum, both psychosocial (small cells organized under charismatic leadership) and socio-ecological (unattached males in supportive religious and peer groups) factors shape the causal network of interconnected representations, emotions, and behaviors that are broadly characteristic of contemporary suicide bombing.

In reference to the factors that influence recruitment for a suicide mission, Ricolfi (2005, p. 113) notes that the places of origin of Palestinian suicides tend to cluster geographically and socially, suggesting that suicide bombers are influenced by peer pressure and emulation. As an example, Ricolfi notes that 8 out of 11 players in a Hamas-associated football team from Hebron carried out suicide attacks.[17]

In his pioneering work, Sageman (2004) has shown the importance of social networks in the recruitment of young Muslim immigrants, mainly in European countries, to terrorist activity (not necessarily suicide attacks) and the process of radicalization that they undergo. The importance of peer-group influence on the decision to join terrorist organizations was also pointed out by Post, Sprinzak and Denny (2003). Based on interviews with 35 non-suicide terrorists in Israeli prison, these authors also underscored the importance of identification with the group on the individual member's behavior after joining: "As an individual succumbs to the organization, there is no room for individual ideas, individual identity and individual decision making" (p. 176). In my own lectures and writing, I also described group pressure and commitment as a key factor in the production of suicide bombers (Merari 2002; 2005; 2006).

## Explanations Based on Individual Psychology

As already noted, there are good reasons for addressing the political, social and cultural contexts that sway people to engage in terrorism. Nevertheless, contextual factors alone are insufficient to explain why, given the same situation, certain people end up as suicide bombers (or active terrorists in general, for that matter), whereas others do not. As Horgan (2005, p. 101) points out, the number of people who actually carry out violent terrorist operations constitutes only a small percentage of those subjected to the presumed background conditions and triggering stimuli. In the same vein, we can add that only a small fraction of the members of any terrorist group become suicide bombers. Thus, the rarity of suicide attackers seems to warrant the assumption that they have distinctive personality characteristics. Whenever they have operated, they have constituted only a small segment of their fellow terrorists, and certainly a minute fraction of those who shared their ideological convictions. Public opinion polls have shown that at the height of the second intifada more than 70% of the Palestinians supported suicide attacks as a tactic. Yet, only several hundreds of these many hundreds of thousands of supporters agreed to carry out a suicide attack. Similarly, millions of Muslims around the world have approved of suicide attacks against American forces in Iraq. For example, a Pew Research Center poll released in March 2004, found that 31 % of the Turks, 46% of the Pakistanis, 66% of the Moroccans, and 70% of the Jordanians felt that suicide bombings against Americans and Westerners in Iraq were justified.[18] In the same vein, many in these countries viewed Osama bin Laden favorably (Pakistan 65%, Jordan 55%, and Morocco 45%). However, the number of those who carried out suicide attacks in the name of this ideology has not reached 2000.

Most people may be intuitively inclined to attribute the willingness to carry out suicide attacks to the offenders' individual traits. This intuition presumably reflects the notion that there must be something psychologically wrong with, or at least peculiar about, young, physically healthy people who kill themselves willingly. One may easily comprehend (in the sense of perceiving as rational) the killing of others out of personal ambition or for a political cause (e.g., in a war between states, or in the course of a violent uprising), as well as the killing of oneself for a personal reason such as severe physical ailment or mental suffering. But why kill oneself if one wants to kill the enemy? People comprehend and are accustomed to the fact that some soldiers take very high risks in battle, sometimes going on missions with an extremely low chance of survival. As Gambetta (2005, p. 271) argues, the willingness to die for a cause is "neither historically nor anthropologically a surprise." Throughout history, billions of soldiers have probably gone to war knowing that they might be killed. Yet only a very small fraction of them *killed themselves* for the cause. There is, presumably, a fundamental psychological difference between readiness to die in battle, and self-destruction for the same cause. Of course, there is the well-known exception of the Japanese kamikazes of World War II, who did kill themselves. But their suicide operations were conducted within the framework of military units, on the decision of the military command, and are therefore perceived as different from the attack of an individual who volunteers to kill himself outside the pressing framework of a military unit in times of war.

Martyrdom is also quite easy to understand. History offers a roster of people who preferred to die rather than abandon their faith. But Christian and Jewish martyrs did not actively seek death, nor did they commit suicide; they were killed by others. The phenomenon of individuals who commit suicide for a political cause thus seems so exceptional that many assume those who choose to die this way must have some special psychological characteristics.

Several authors have, indeed, suggested that suicide terrorists have psychological traits that make them more likely candidates for these acts. In a paper published in 1990, when suicide terrorism was in its infancy and the scarce data available were limited to the Lebanese case, I argued that because suicide bombers constituted a tiny minority of the terrorists, personality factors seemed to play a critical role in suicidal terrorism, "although the available information does not permit any generalizations concerning personality patterns" (p. 207). In that paper I speculated that suicide bombers are suicidal persons who found it socially convenient to carry out their suicidal act in a context and manner acceptable in their society. In later years, a few scholars have speculatively suggested a variety of personality traits specific to suicide bombers. Aware of the absence of empirical evidence for psychopathology among suicide bombers, Lester, Yang, and Lindsay (2004) nevertheless suggested that suicide terrorists may be suicide-prone and may have authoritarian personality traits.[19] They did, however, view the authoritarian personality pattern as characteristic of terrorists in general, thus failing to explain how it differentiates between suicide and non-suicide terrorists. Volkan (2001) maintained that suicide bombers suffer from identity problems that make them susceptible to external group influence. In his view, such identity problems tend to develop in regressed societies. Lachkar (2002), on the other hand, suggested that suicide terrorists are characterized by a borderline personality disorder which, in her view, is prevalent in Arab culture. Salib (2003) hypothesized that the 9/11 al-Qaeda suicides were a case of *Folie à plusieurs* (madness of many), a situation in which several people share the same delusional idea.[20]

In a response to Scott Atran's paper (Atran, 2003a), Tobeña (2004) listed several personality traits that may play a role in the making of suicide bombers, such as dominance, proneness to risk-taking, fearlessness, aggressiveness, Machiavellianism, narcissism, and obedience.

Gordon (2002, p. 287) claimed that a psychiatric analysis of suicide bombers was unnecessary, as the phenomenon could be explained by political circumstances. Suicide bombers, he wrote, "are not usually mentally disordered and their behaviour can be construed more in terms of group dynamics." He did, however, surmise that "perhaps psychiatric terminology is as yet deficient in not having the depth to encompass the emotions and behaviour of groups of people whose levels of hate, low self-esteem, humiliation and alienation are such that it is felt that they can be remedied by the mass destruction of life, including their own."

Because none of these suggestions was based on a direct psychological examination of suicide bombers, they are all speculative and should be taken as shots in the dark.

## The Prevailing View: Suicide Bombers are Normal

Contrary to what seems to be the public impression, the currently prevailing opinion among scholars is that suicide terrorists are psychologically normal, and explanations of suicide terrorism should, therefore, be sought in areas other than psychopathology. Thus, Atran (2003a, p. 1535) argues that ascribing suicide terrorism to assumed psychopathological characteristics of the perpetrators reflects a "fundamental attribution error, a tendency for people to explain behavior in terms of individual personality traits, even when significant situational factors in the larger society are at work." He maintains that suicide terrorists are "nonpathological individuals," who respond to situational factors in an extreme way.

In a report submitted to the U.S. Congress, Cronin (2003, p.8) claimed: "Research on suicide attacks indicates that most terrorist operatives are psychologically normal, in the sense that psychological pathology does not seem to be present, and the attacks are virtually always premeditated."

In a similar vein, Andrew Silke (2003, p. 94) noted:

> It is a little disconcerting to learn that as with other terrorists, there is no indication that suicide bombers suffer from psychological disorders or are mentally unbalanced in other ways. In contrast, their personalities are usually quite stable and unremarkable (at least within their own cultural context).

Pape (2005, p. 23) wrote:

> Few suicide attackers are social misfits, criminally insane, or professional losers. Most fit a nearly opposite profile: typically they are psychologically normal, have better than average economic prospects for their communities, and are deeply integrated into social networks and emotionally attached to their national communities.

Basel Saleh (2004, p. 3) extended the argument that suicide terrorists do not suffer from psychological disorders and claimed that they do not have any distinctive psychological characteristics at all: "Profiles of the personal characteristics of the suicide attackers failed to disclose any common pattern that can help identify them."

Describing cases of self-immolation carried out in connection with the Vietnam War, Maxwell Taylor (1988, p.106) wrote:

> The individuals concerned (at least those in the West) appeared to be suffering from no known incidence of psychiatric illness and the drama of the means of suicide seems to be more related to context than their psychiatric state. There is no evidence available to suggest that the people concerned were anything other than rational and aware of what they were doing.

## Rationality and Planning Ability

A corollary of the claim that suicide bombers are normal is the view that their decision to carry out a suicide attack is a matter of rational choice (e.g., Sprinzak, 2000; Harrison, 2003; Hafez, 2004; Hoffman & McCormick, 2004; Bloom, 2005). The argument for rationality rests on the notion that the suicide gains something valuable in return for his life, such as a hero's status in his community or a place in paradise. Here, however, the term "rationality" loses much of its conventional meaning. When personal beliefs are introduced into the equation, every human act is rational, even if the calculation is based on mistaken premises. Thus, a paranoid who firmly believes that his greengrocer is contemplating to murder him in collaboration with the state's intelligence agencies is acting rationally when he kills the greengrocer in self-defense.

Some writers have based their conclusion that terrorists are "normal" on the terrorists' ability to plan and carry out complex operations. Hudson (1999, p. 10), for example, wrote: "There is little reliable evidence to support the notion that terrorists in general are psychologically disturbed individuals. The careful, detailed planning and well timed execution that have characterized many terrorist operations are hardly typical of mentally disturbed individuals." At the time Hudson wrote these words, he was right about the absence of solid empirical evidence for terrorist psychopathology. Yet he wrongly assumed that persons who suffer psychological disorders are incapable of planning and executing complex schemes. His assumption probably rested on the image of a "mentally disturbed" person as an acute psychotic. Psychological disorders, however, vary greatly, and the ability to conceive and execute complex tasks depends on the nature, and especially the severity, of the disorder. An acute schizophrenic patient or a person in the depths of depression would not be able to plan and carry out an elaborate scheme of operation; this is not the case with milder forms of mental disorders, which do not impair planning ability or impede the energy to execute plans. History is replete with examples of people with mental disorders who displayed diabolical efficiency in planning and committing crimes on an inordinate scale—Hitler and Stalin are blatant examples. Moreover, the specific task of a suicide bomber does not require the capabilities of a Hitler or a Stalin; it can be carried out by just about anyone. On the positive side of behavior, Nobel Prize winner John Nash is a salient example of ingenious thinking and severe mental disorder coexisting in the same brain.[21] In fact, Nash is not exceptional. Numerous studies have found that the incidence of mental disorders among eminent artists and scientists is considerably higher than in the general population (e.g., Juda, 1949; Martindale, 1972, 1990; Andreasen & Canter, 1974; Andreasen, 1987; Ludwig, 1992, 1995; Felix Post, 1994, 1996; Witztum & Lerner, 2009). Arnold Ludwig (1992, 1995), for example, examined 1004 biographies of prominent 20th century personalities that included scientists, artists and writers, businessmen, and social activists. He found that the rate of people who resorted to psychiatric treatment was twice as high in his sample (26%) than in the general population (13%). Seventy-seven percent of the poets in his sample suffered from a depressive disorder and 18% of them committed suicide.

## Suicidality

In their discussions of psychopathology, some authors have specifically addressed the possibility that suicide bombers may be suicidal (e.g., Lester et al., 2004; Holmes, 2005). In an early article (Merari, 1990, p. 206), I suggested that suicide terrorism is undertaken by people who "wish to die for personal reasons." At that time, the total number of terrorist suicide attacks around the globe was less than 50, almost all in Lebanon. More important, since there were no psychological data on the suicides, my suggestion was clearly speculative. Later on, the interviews with families of Palestinian suicide bombers described in Chapter 4 provided data on the suicides' personal backgrounds. These data, however, did not include a direct investigation of the suicides and could not offer sound information on personality characteristics. On the basis of that information I concluded that most Palestinian suicide terrorists did not display the generally accepted characteristics of "ordinary" suicides (Merari, 2004; 2005). Recently I wrote:

> The profiles of the terrorist suicides gleaned from the interviews did not resemble typical suicide candidates, as described in the literature. By their family members' accounts, 47% of the 1993–1998 Palestinian suicides occasionally said that they wished to carry out an act of martyrdom and 44% used to talk about paradise. However, the young persons who eventually committed suicide had no record of earlier attempts of self-immolation and were not at odds with their family and friends, and most of them expressed no feelings of being fed up with life. In the suicides' notes and last messages, the act of self-destruction was presented as a form of struggle

rather than as an escape. There was no sense of helplessness-hopelessness. On the contrary, the suicide was presented as an act of projecting power rather than expressing weakness. It thus seems that most terrorist suicides in the Palestinian sample were not "suicidal" in the usual psychological sense. (Merari, 2006, p. 109).

Most current writers concur with the view that suicide terrorists are not suicidal. Israeli (1997, p. 97) suggested that "the so-called Muslim fundamentalist 'suicide bombers' have nothing suicidal about them." Margalit (2003) wrote: "From the accounts of them in the press and the statements by those who know them, the suicide bombers are not what psychologists call suicidal types—they are not depressed, impulsive, lonely, and helpless, with a continuous history of being in situations of personal difficulty." Gambetta (2005, p. 269–270) reached a similar conclusion: "All the evidence shows that, in contrast with those who commit suicide, 90 per cent of whom are depressed or have diagnosable mental disorders . . . suicide attackers — just like self-immolators — are not suicidal nor do they display any serious psychopathology, not even those who carry out small-scale missions." Ellen Townsend (2007) reviewed the literature pertaining to the question of the suicidality of suicide bombers, focusing especially on empirical studies (of which she found five, of diverse quality and methodologies). She concluded: "The results of this review strongly suggest that suicide terrorists are not truly suicidal and that attempting to find commonalities between suicide terrorists and others who die by suicide is likely to be an unhelpful path for any discipline wishing to further understanding of suicidal behavior." (p. 47).

Like the opinions on distinctive personality characteristics of suicide bombers, these observations (including my own in past years) have not been based on a systematic, direct psychological examination but mostly on external impressions drawn mainly from media reports. The findings presented in Chapter 5 suggest that a significant minority (40%) of the suicide bombers (at least to the extent that they are represented by Palestinian would-be suicides) does have suicidal tendencies, albeit minor in most cases.

## The Deductive Argument: Terrorists (in general) Are Normal

In the absence of empirical psychological studies on suicide bombers, many authors have dismissed the importance of personality factors, relying on data on non-suicide terrorists. Ricolfi (2005, p. 106), for example, assessed the behavior of Palestinian suicide bombers as follows:

> From a psychological standpoint, the most important finding is that there is no apparent connection between violent militant activity and personality disorders—with the exception of a few rare cases, found for instance among *Rote Armee Fraktion*, the German terrorist group also known as Baader Meinhof. In the great majority of cases, psychiatric evidence indicates that terrorists are perfectly normal individuals. Nor is there any apparent signifi-cant association between the inclination towards militancy (suicidal or other-wise) and particular types of personality.

In a recently published book, Louise Richardson (2006, p. 41) wrote:

> In the most extreme cases, why does someone kill himself as a means of kill-ing others? The most obvious and common explanation is that he is crazy. But terrorists, as I have said, are, by and large, not crazy at all. Interviews with current and former terrorists as well as imprisoned terrorists confirm that the one shared characteristic of terrorists is their normalcy, insofar as we understand the term. Efforts to produce a terrorist profile have invariably failed. Some are introverted, some extroverted; some loud, some shy; some confident, some nervous.

A similar approach has been taken by a number of other scholars, e.g., Atran (2003a), Silke (2006), and Gambetta (2005).

The logic of this approach is, presumably, meant to be deductive: Terrorists are normal; suicide bombers are terrorists; ergo, suicide terrorists are normal. In practice, however, considering the empirical evidence on which this conclusion is based, the logic applied is inductive, because the studies that failed to find abnormality among terrorists in general are very few, inconclusive, and cannot be taken as proof for the general argument.[22]

By and large, the opinion that terrorists do not have a common psy-chological profile (Merari, 1994; Hudson, 1999; Kruglanski, 2002; Atran, 2003a; McCauley, 2004; Horgan, 2005; Richardson, 2006; Kruglanski & Fishman, 2006) rests on the absence of research rather than on direct find-ings. A scientifically sound conclusion that terrorists have no common personality traits must be based on many comparative studies of terrorists from different countries and functions, using standard psychological tests and clinical interviews. As such studies have not been published, the only scientifically sound conclusion for now is that *we do not know* whether terrorists share common traits, but we cannot be sure that such traits do not exist.

Moreover, the search for a *general* terrorist profile across nations and roles may be aiming too high, and may have been counterproductive because it has diverted scholars from asking questions that may be more easily answered. Scholars who have written on the topic of terrorist personality have ignored the diversity of functions covered by the term "terrorist," which can refer to a vast range of activities. Whereas some terrorist group members are in charge of nonviolent tasks such as propaganda, recruiting, smuggling, hiding weapons, forging documents, and other logistical jobs, others carry out violent attacks. Furthermore, there are significant differences between violent tasks, both in terms of the personal risks to the perpetrators and the brutality they entail. Presumably, greater brutality is required for shooting women and children at close range than for placing a bomb in a supermarket and leaving the scene before it explodes. Killing oneself by setting off a suicide belt in the midst of a casual crowd requires still other personality characteristics and another state of mind. Conceivably, the likelihood of finding common traits among people who perform a certain type of terrorist task (notably, suicide attacks) is greater than the likelihood that "terrorists" in general have common traits.

Another source of confusion in the discussion on terrorist personality has been the focus on "abnormality." In assessing the importance of individual psychological traits, most scholars have based their opinion on the apparent absence of signs of "abnormal" behavior—explicitly or implicitly interpreted as psychosis or extreme maladjustment—but ignored the possibility that terrorists may have "normal" personality traits in common.[23]

The focus on insanity is not only unwarranted but also surprising, because most violent common criminals are not psychotic either. There is no reason why we should expect people who commit murder for a political cause to be insane while we know that most common murderers are not. Yet the observation that most murderers are not psychotic should not divert our attention from the possibility that they have some psychological traits that facilitate criminal behavior. Thus, studies have shown a high prevalence of psychopathic tendencies among common criminals (Dolan & Doyle, 2000; Hare, 2001).[24] Contrary to common criminals, suicide bombers are unlikely to display psychopathic characteristics; psychopaths do not sacrifice themselves for the community. Indeed, none of the would-be suicides in the study described in Chapter 5 displayed psychopathic tendencies. Apparently, suicide bombers differ from common criminals. Still, in both cases there is a high rate of certain (different) psychological traits. Had we merely looked for insanity we would have missed these less dramatic characteristics. Normality is a rather elusive term. Are nonpsychotic people who suffer from a personality disorder "normal"? Even if suicide terrorists are not mentally ill, the question remains whether they have psychological traits that make them more prone to carry out suicide attacks than other persons.

In a way, the claim that there are no *universally* common traits shared by terrorists is almost self-evident. Everything we know about human behavior suggests that there is no reason to suppose that *all* terrorists have a certain set of traits, because in other types of behavior we do not find a perfect correlation between a single trait or a set of traits and the behavior in question. In this vein, Hudson (1999, p. 31) argued: "Just as there is no necessary reason why people sharing the same career in normal life necessarily have psychological characteristics in common, the fact that terrorists have the same career does not necessarily mean that they have anything in common psychologically." This is not quite accurate, however. We know that people who have certain traits are *more likely* than others to behave in a certain way. Vocational psychology is based on empirical evidence, which has shown that people who have certain personality characteristics, preferences, habits, and talents are likely to succeed better in certain occupations than others. This does not mean that *all* lawyers, physicians, journalists, or social workers share the same traits. It merely means that, on average, people with these traits are more inclined than others to choose, and more likely to succeed in, certain occupations.[25]

Looking for a single personality type to explain all terrorists may also contribute to a sweeping, premature conclusion that terrorists have no distinctive features. As noted above, it is likely that members of terrorist groups who are in charge of different tasks may also differ in their personality traits. It is also possible, however, that terrorists whose overt behavior is similar (e.g., those who carry out high-risk missions such as armed assault) may exhibit more than one personality pattern. Thus, in the study of would-be suicides reported in Chapter 5, two dominant personality patterns emerged: dependent-avoidant (60%) and impulsive-unstable (26.7%). It is possible, of course, that similar studies conducted in other countries, under different cultural, political, and social conditions, would find other dominant personality patterns.

# Conclusion

To understand the motivation to resort to suicide terrorism, one must take into account the interactive influence of three factors, namely, the political context, group processes, and individual characteristics (Hafez, 2004). These factors are not mutually exclusive; the notion that certain political conditions generate grievances that, in turn, drive people to terrorism, explains why under some conditions people are more willing to use violence than in other circumstances—but it does not explain why only a minority of the people in a given situation become active terrorists, or suicide bombers, for that matter. And, because practically all terrorism is a group activity (nearly all modern terrorist attacks have been carried out by groups rather than by independent individuals), group influence and decision-making processes are also an important element in generating terrorism.[26] Thus, Tobeña's (2004) comment is quite appropriate:

> Research efforts directed at disentangling the critical social vectors of suicidal terrorism are extremely important. They can, however, become even more valuable if individuals are taken into account, rather than rejecting the perspective out of hand just because there is an absence of clear links with psychopathology or the lack of reliable differences between introverts and extroverts.

Finally, as the data in Chapters 5 and 6 suggest, the interaction between personality characteristics and group and public pressure is essential for explaining why some people are willing to become suicide bombers while most others are not.

*Endnotes*

1. Sarraj, E. (N.D.). Why we have become suicide bombers: Understanding Palestinian terror. Washington, D.C.: Mid-East Realities. Available at: http://www.middleeast.org/archives/newslet1.htm (accessed August 19, 2006).
2. According to the CIA *Factbook*, 77% of Pakistan's population are Sunnis and 20% are Shiite. See: https://www.cia.gov/cia/publications/factbook/geos/pk.html (accessed September 19, 2006). The Sunnis hold the senior positions in government service and the military.
3. Examples of suicide attacks carried out by militant Sunni groups against Shiite targets in Pakistan during this period include the following: July 4, 2003, an attack against a Shiite mosque in Quetta, 48 killed and 65 wounded; February 28, 2004, an attack in a Shiite mosque in Rawalpindi, four wounded; May 7, 2004, an attack in a Shiite mosque in Karachi, 15 killed and 215 wounded; May 31, 2004, an attack in a Shiite mosque in Karachi, 24 killed and 34 wounded; October 1, 2004,

an attack in a Shiite mosque in Sialkot, 31 killed and 75 wounded; May 27, 2005, an attack in a Shia shrine in Islamabad, 19 killed and 65 wounded; February 9, 2006, an attack in Hangu against a Shiite religious procession during the Ashura, 27 killed and 50 wounded; July 14, 2006, an attack in Karachi targeted a prominent Shiite cleric, Allama Hassan Turabi, who was killed along with his nephew and two body guards; January 17, 2008, an attack in a Shiite mosque in Peshawar, 12 killed and 25 wounded; July 13, 2008, an attack on a Shia gathering in Dera Isma'il Khan, 4 wounded.

4. The Sunni campaigns of terrorist suicide attacks against Shiite communities in Pakistan and Iraq demonstrate that suicide terrorism is not necessarily a strategy for liberation from occupation by a *democratic state*.

5. Pape's claims have been criticized by several scholars, notably, Atran (2006), Abrahms (2006), Moghadam (2006), and Piazza (2008).

6. Pape (2005, p. 40) mentions a higher number of fatalities caused by suicide attacks in Lebanon: 197 in the period of November 1983 through April 1985, and 156 in the period of June 1985 through June 1986. His count, however, includes non-Israeli fatalities of suicide attacks in Lebanon, which are irrelevant to his claim concerning the effect of suicide attacks on Israeli policy. For example, only 36 of the 88 people killed in the suicide attack on the Israeli Government Building in Tyre on November 4, 1983, were Israelis; the others were casual Lebanese civilians. Likewise, almost all the suicide attacks listed by Pape (2005, p. 254) in the period of July 1985–November 1986 targeted the South Lebanese Army (SLA) rather than Israeli forces. Pape also includes in his list of Hizballah attacks against Israel a suicide attack against a *Lebanese* army post in Beirut, on June 15, 1985, long after Israeli forces evacuated Beirut. That attack resulted in 23 fatalities. It is hard to see what this attack has to do with Hizballah's campaign against Israel.

7. Israeli Defense Ministry statistics, cited in The Lebanon War, YNET News (*Yediot Aharonot* daily), January 8, 2006. Available at: http://www.ynetnews.com/articles/0,7340,L-3284684,00.html (accessed: September 7, 2006).

8. Monday Morning. December 16, 1985. Interview with Fadlallah,, as quoted by Kramer (1990, p. 148).

9. To support his claim, Pape quotes a statement by Mahmud al-Zahar, a Hamas leader, saying that the use of violence should be subjected to cost-benefit calculations. In this same statement al-Zahar said that the group's goal is the complete destruction of Israel and the institution of a Palestinian state in its stead. The statement does not support Pape's claim in any way.

10. Jeroen Gunning, who lived in the Gaza Strip for a long period of time in the course of his research on Hamas, and interviewed Hamas leaders as well as rank and file, wrote that Hamas leaders themselves admitted that the rationale behind Hamas suicide campaigns in the years 1994–1996 was to undermine the legitimacy of the Palestinian Authority and to obstruct the peace process (Gunning, 2008, p. 211).

11. Polls conducted by the Center for Palestine Research and Studies (http://www.cprs-palestine.org).

12. In late February–early March 1996 Hamas carried out a series of four suicide attacks inside Israel, in response to the killing by Israel of Yahya Ayyash, the mastermind of

suicide attacks and a senior leader of Izz a-Din al- Qassam, Hamas' military arm. The killing of Ayyash aroused a wave of Palestinian protest demonstrations, and the Hamas leadership felt that the Palestinian public not only gave it a license to carry out spectacular attacks to avenge the death of Ayyash, but even expected the group to exact a price from Israel.

13. In 1981, 10 members of the IRA and INLA died on a chain hunger strike in Belfast's Maze prison. This case is discussed in Chapter 10. In Germany, several members of the Red Army Faction committed suicide in jail during the 1970s: Holger Meins died on hunger strike on November 10, 1974; Ulrike Meihof committed suicide by hanging in Stammheim jail on May 9, 1976; Andreas Baader, Jan-Karl Raspe and Gudrun Ensslin committed suicide by pistol shots (Baader and Raspe) and hanging (Ensslin) in Stammheim prison on October 18, 1977 (Aust, 1987).

14. Secular groups that have carried out suicide attacks in Lebanon in the 1980s include: The Syrian Social Nationalist Party (SSNP), a pro-Syrian organization, whose agenda called for the annexation of Lebanon by Syria; The Arab Socialist Baath party, a secular pan-Arab party (the ruling party in Syria); the Socialist Nasserite Organization; the Lebanese Communist Party; and two secular Palestinian groups, the Popular Front for the Liberation of Palestine (PFLP) and the Popular Front for the Liberation of Palestine-General Command.

15. The Revolutionary People's Liberation Party/Front, generally known by the acronym of its Turkish name DHKP/C (*Devrimci Halk Kurtulus Partisi/Cephesi*), carried out three suicide attacks in the period of 2001–2003.

16. In this regard, Atran (2003a, supporting online material, P. 10), argued: "Institutionalized creation of intimate social cells of willing believers works to canalize ideas (as might a school) and emotions (as might a church) into proximate causes of actions that lead to attack forms of martyrdom. One's performance in the network of religious and cultural behaviors often has a complex causal determination that involves any number of variously interrelated personal and social selection factors (*S28*). These pertain to the internal environment of individual ideas and emotions, as well as to external conditions of social and physical context."

17. Although Ricolfi's point about peer influence is well taken, his observation that "[a] tiny number of refugee camps around the West Bank towns of Hebron, Nablus, and Jenin supply the great majority of martyrs" (p. 113) is somewhat exaggerated. Only 22 of the 130 suicide bombers in the period of 1993–2006, whose homes were in the West Bank, lived in refugee camps.

18. Pew Global Attitudes Project (2004). A Year After Iraq War: Mistrust of America in Europe Ever Higher, Muslim Anger Persists. Washington, D.C.: The Pew Research Center for People and the Press. Available at: http://people-press.org/reports/ pdf/206.pdf (accessed November 7, 2005).

19. The "authoritarian personality" concept was developed after World War II to explain the personality of followers of the Nazi regime (Adorno, Frenkel-Brunswik, Levinson, & Sanford, 1950).

20. In psychiatry the term *Folie à deux* refers to a situation in which two persons (usually of the same family) share the same paranoid delusion.

21. Although the clinical outbreak of Nash's paranoid schizophrenia occurred after he had made his great mathematical contributions, for which he received the Nobel Prize, the pre-clinical manifestations of the disease probably existed earlier in his life.

22. Published studies that have attempted to conduct systematic *clinical psychological* interviews with terrorists have been carried out in Germany and Italy. In the German study (Jager, Schmidtchen and Sullwold, 1982; Baeyer-Katte, Claessens, Feger, & Neidhart, 1982), active or suspected members of the Red Army Faction were interviewed by a group of researchers. There was a considerable disparity among the researchers with regard to the existence of psychological disorders among the terrorists studied. The study also suffered from methodological problems. For a discussion, see Horgan, 2005, pp. 54–55; Crenshaw, 1986; Taylor, 1988, p. 91). Studies of Italian terrorists (Ferracuti, 1982; Ferracuti & Bruno, 1983) also reached ambiguous conclusions. For a detailed critique, see Horgan (2005).

23. Many authors have quoted Hassan's (2001) claim that "none of them were uneducated, desperately poor, simple minded or depressed" as evidence that suicide bombers are normal. As I noted in Chapter 4, which describes the study I did with Nasra Hassan, the family interviews could not provide sufficient ground for a psychological assessment of the suicides. An accurate description of the psychological findings from these interviews is that no evidence was found for mental illness (as might be indicated, for example, by hospitalization in a mental institution or overt psychotic behavior). Hassan rightly says that on the basis of the family interviews one may assume that the suicides did not display major risk factors of suicide (e.g., severe mental disorders, substance abuse, or previous suicidal attempts). The interviews, however, did not enable finer psychological evaluations, such as the existence of subclinical depression. This kind of assessment can only be obtained in clinical interviews with, and psychological tests of, the suicides themselves, as was done in the study reported in Chapter 5. This study, which found statistically significant psychological differences between would-be suicides and "ordinary" terrorists, does not support Hassan's impressions.

24. For a comprehensive survey of the relationship between personality and psychopathology and crime, see Wilson & Herrnstein (1985), pp. 173–209. These authors' summary of the research findings on individual traits of ordinary criminals seems to fit also the findings on suicide bombers: "People who break the law are often psychologically atypical. This is not to say that they are necessarily sick (although some are), or that atypicality of any sort characterizes every single lawbreaker. Rather, the evidence says that populations of offenders differ statistically in various respects from populations of nonoffenders." (p. 173). Drawing on psychological research into proneness to common criminal violence among youngsters, Huesmann (2002) suggested that terrorists, like ordinary juvenile delinquents, have a "low baseline arousal and show little emotional reaction to observing violence, either because of disposition or due to habituation by repeated exposure to violence in their environment." These traits are typical of a psychopathic personality, often found among common criminals (Wilson & Herrnstein, 1985). Huesmann's observation however, is speculative and does not rest on empirical research on terrorists. In the empirical

study reported in Chapter 5, none of the suicide bombers was assessed as having psychopathic tendencies and only one of the organizers was assessed as such.

25. Interestingly, Alan Krueger, an economist from Princeton University, has justified his interest in terrorism by noting that "participation in terrorism is just a special application of the economics of occupational choice." (Krueger, 2007, p. 11).

26. Many of the 19th and early 20th century anarchist terrorist attacks were conducted by independent individuals, who were not associated with organized groups, although the perpetrators were usually part of a social and intellectual counter-establishment milieu that influenced their thinking and violent activity.

# 10

## Conclusion: An Integrative View of Suicide Terrorism

### The Constituents of Suicide Terrorism

The knowledge on terrorist suicide attacks, which has accumulated in the course of the recent two decades, makes it possible to form a comprehensive—albeit tentative—picture of this phenomenon. The qualification of our knowledge as tentative signifies the fact that most of the direct data on the making of suicide bombers, and on the bombers' personality characteristics, are based on Palestinian suicides. Making firm generalizations pertinent to suicides in other places has to wait for comparative studies.

Suicide terrorism is a complex phenomenon. As Hafez (2004; 2006) has suggested, a comprehensive description of this phenomenon must address its three components: the community setting, the organizational dimension, and the psychological characteristics of the individuals who carry out the attacks. This concluding chapter summarizes the roles of these three dimensions and the way they interact with each other to produce suicide terrorism.

### The Social Environment

Like other forms of terrorism, suicide attacks are politically motivated. They are carried out to satisfy political demands and attain political objectives. The campaigns of suicide attacks by al-Qaeda against Western and Jewish targets in Tunisia, Morocco, and Turkey, as well as the attacks against Shiite targets in Pakistan and in Iraq, show that these demands are not necessarily based on actual oppression, and are certainly not limited to situations of occupation by foreign forces. What matters, however, is that some groups of people believe in these political or ideological goals to the extent that they are willing to kill, and even sacrifice their members, to attain them.

The greater the number of people who believe in the cause, the larger the number of suicide attacks. Although even a small group with only little popular support can carry out an occasional suicide attack, sustaining a large number of attacks requires a large organization and broad support from a public from which candidates for suicide attacks can be recruited. As has already been noted, the great majority of suicide attacks around the globe have been carried out in countries where an acute conflict has radicalized the population as a whole or a significant part of it: Iraq (58.2% of the world's total), Afghanistan (15.2%), Israel (7.1%), Pakistan (5.9%), Sri Lanka (3.9%), Lebanon (1.9%), Russia (1.4%), and Turkey (1.1%). Obviously, broader popular support means a larger number of people who are willing to take an active part in the struggle. Not all those who side with the idea of the struggle are willing to take personal risks for the cause, and only a small minority is ready to die for it. Other things being equal, however, the larger the pool of supporters, the larger will be the absolute number of potential volunteers for suicide bombers. Furthermore, larger terrorist organizations develop the necessary mechanisms for identifying and recruiting these potential candidates, as well as the logistical infrastructure for preparing the attacks, making this terrorist method a mass-production line.

Broad popular support is also important with regard to the legitimization of suicide attacks. When public opinion endorses suicide attacks, and views them as the utmost form of patriotism and heroism, joining the ranks of these heroes seems attractive. In this supportive social atmosphere, youngsters who are unaffiliated with terrorist groups may offer themselves for suicide attacks because they are grabbed by the community's zeal, and because they want to be admired by their peers. Under these circumstances, it is also difficult for a youngster to refuse a recruiter's offer to undertake a suicide mission, even if he is not truly enthusiastic about the idea of becoming a "martyr," for fear that a refusal will mark him as coward or unpatriotic. On the other hand, in a situation where the community opposes suicide attacks, viewing them as immoral or politically damaging, the number of volunteers is likely to be very small because it requires swimming against the social current. A small minority of the suicide attacks has been carried out in situations where the majority of the community opposed them. In these situations, such as the case of the London attacks of July 7, 2005, the suicides were part of a small social circle that endorsed terrorism and brewed together the idea of carrying out a "martyrdom operation." This small group of like-minded people became the suicides' relevant social milieu, the source of collective authority for their behavior (Sageman, 2004; 2005), superseding the opinion of the larger community. Thus, social support is an essential element in the creation of suicide bombers, and the scope of these attacks is directly related to the breadth of this support.

## The Group's Role

The importance of group influence becomes clear when we realize that practically all terrorist suicide attackers worldwide have been prepared and sent by groups, rather than acting alone on their own initiative.[1] The group's involvement has an obvious importance in facilitating the attack by providing the explosive charge, and bringing the assailant to the target. Yet, a determined lone attacker, whose hate is so intense that he (or she) is willing to die to kill an enemy, can carry out an attack on an occasional target with no assistance—even if it is with a less effective weapon such as a hand grenade or a homemade explosive device. The greater importance of the group, however, is not in the logistical facilitation of the suicide attack but in the motivational aspect: instilling the idea of suicide attacks in the community, or at least among a circle of followers, recruiting candidates, and fortifying their commitment to the task.

I first came to realize the importance of group influence on terrorist suicide when I pondered the chain suicide of Irish nationalists in Maze Prison in 1981. Ten members of PIRA (Provisional Irish Republican Army) and INLA (Irish National Liberation Army) died one after another in a hunger strike, in protest against the British government's decision to turn down their demand to be recognized as political prisoners (rather than common criminals). Although this event does not qualify as an act of suicide terrorism, because the hunger strikers did not kill anyone but themselves, it was an act of self-destruction for a political cause and, as such, can teach us much about the psychological mechanisms involved in suicide terrorism. Self-starvation is an extremely demanding way to die, much more difficult than the instantaneous death caused by a self-inflicted explosion. It took the hunger strikers from 46 to 73 days to die. During that time, mothers, wives and priests begged at least some of the hunger strikers to stop their self-destruction (O'Malley, 1990; Beresford, 1994).

The force that made them continue their strike to the very end, ignoring all pressures, must have been very strong. What was this force that sustained their determination? The assumption that all ten were suicidal persons, who happened to be in jail at the same time, is rather implausible. It is also unlikely that they were motivated by religious fanaticism and the promise of a place in paradise.[2] The only way to understand this frightening demonstration of human readiness for self-sacrifice is to look at the influence of the group on its individual members. The chain suicide was a product of a group contract that one could not break. The group pressure in that situation was as strong as the group pressure that led hundreds of thousands of soldiers in World War I to charge against enemy machine gun fire and artillery to almost sure death. And, it was even stronger once the first hunger striker died. From that point on, the contract to die became almost unbreakable, because the person who could release the next in line from their commitment was already dead. This state of mind is expressed well in the words of Liam McCloskey, who ceased his hunger strike on the 55th day, as quoted by O'Malley (1990, p. 85):

> Once you were on hunger strike it would have taken more courage to stop of your own accord than to keep going on because it seemed so much like losing face and backing down when other men died . . . We were caught in our own trap where there were ten men dead and we felt we had to keep going on and look for a way out of it.

The powerful commitment to the other strikers—those already dead and those still alive—was extremely hard to break because of the fear of what members of the reference group (the other prisoners as well as the prisoner's social circle outside prison) would think of you. Stopping the hunger strike meant that people with whom the hunger striker associated, and whose opinions he valued, would regard him as weak, unmanly, and unreliable.[3] No less important, perhaps, was the threat to the self-image, the way the striker viewed himself. The easiest way out of this predicament was an external intervention that would enable the striker to save face and attribute his decision to break his commitment to circumstances beyond his control.

In addition to the ten who died, seven others who started hunger striking stopped short of dying. Four of the seven were fed on their families' orders after they lapsed into a coma, but they did not resume the hunger strike as they regained consciousness. Similarly to the Palestinian suicide bombers, the families played a crucial role in interrupting their road to death, and similarly to the Palestinian organizers of suicide attacks, the IRA organizers of the hunger strike were most concerned with the families' role in weakening the hunger strikers' determination (O'Malley, 1990, pp.122–123).

Group pressure is particularly strong and effective in a prison situation, where inmates live with the same group of people 24 hours a day for a long period of time. Under these conditions, social sanctions for behavior disapproved by the group are very painful and affect the whole spectrum of the punished person's daily activity. Effective sanctions do not have to be physical; the threat of disrespect, scorn and ostracism by the other inmates can be extremely potent in influencing one's behavior. This pressure presumably influenced the inmates' volunteering to join the hunger strike,[4] and made it extremely difficult to drop out once they started.

Group pressure was, presumably, also very strong among the Japanese kamikazes in World War II. Like prison inmates, soldiers live together continually, especially in overseas service in war time. The large number of kamikazes was first and foremost a result of the Japanese military leadership decision to adopt this tactic and use it en masse. However, the massive execution of the kamikaze tactic was impossible had it not for the willingness of the pilots themselves to play their part by giving away their lives. This willingness was in some cases instigated by the volunteers' genuine zeal, but in others it was impelled by direct and indirect group pressure. A vivid description of group pressure to volunteer to become kamikaze pilots was offered by Emiko Ohnuki-Tierney (2002, p.169):

> Once on the base, soldiers were asked to "volunteer" to be pilots. In most cases, all the members of a corps were summoned into a hall. After a lecture on the virtue of patriotism and on the need to sacrifice oneself for the emperor and Japan, they were told to step forward if they were willing to volunteer to be tokkotai [Kamikaze] pilots. It is indeed superfluous to point out how difficult it would have been to stay behind when all or many others stepped forward. Sometimes the officer in charge went through a ritual of blindfolding the young men – a gesture to eliminate peer pressure, asking them to raise their hands to volunteer. But the rustling sounds of the uniforms as they raised their hands made it obvious that many did so, leaving those hesitant without a choice but to volunteer.

Group pressure took also an indirect form, drawing on internalized social and cultural values. On the basis of diaries and letters written by fallen kamikazes, Ohnuki-Tierney (2002, p.169) concluded that "an important reason for volunteering was not peer group pressure as such, but they could not bear seeing their comrades and friends offering their lives while protecting their own."

Group pressure is also strong in cults, especially when their members live together. Presumably, this force was an important factor in the group suicides of Masada, Jonestown, and Waco, discussed in Chapter 2.

In some cases, terrorists allocated for suicide missions live together and are, therefore, subjected to intense group influence such as those described above. The Tamil Tigers reportedly selected the suicides from among their fighting forces, which were organized like a regular army. The selected suicides lived together and trained in special units called Black Tigers (Hopgood, 2005, pp. 60-63).

Cohabitation increases commitment to the group and the effectiveness of group pressure. Yet, commitment to the group is a major factor in sustaining the suicide candidate's motivation even in cases where suicide terrorists are recruited and trained individually, such as in the Palestinian case (Merari, 2004; 2005; 2006). Commitment to the group is established at the recruiting phase, when the candidate gives his consent to undertake the mission. It grows stronger in the course of preparation, in which the candidate meets with the organizers of the attack. In situations where the majority of the population supports suicide attacks and regards the suicides as national heroes, such as among Palestinians, persuading the candidate of the justification of the planned attack is usually unnecessary. But the candidate's meetings with the revered local leader of the militant group, in which the candidate reiterates his wish and readiness to carry out the attack, further strengthen his commitment and make it harder for him to back off. Presumably, it is extremely hard for a socially unimportant youngster to say no to a collectively admired, authoritative figure, because a refusal—and even more so a change of heart—would taint him as a coward in the community's as well as in his own eyes. This commitment was exemplified in the testimony of the suicide bomber Nabil (see Chapter 5), who said that he continued with the mission although he felt great fear, explaining: "On the day I agreed to carry out the operation that was it. There was no way back."

Many groups that have carried out suicide attacks used to record the candidates' last testament on videotape, usually shortly before they were dispatched for the mission. Most Lebanese groups (with the notable exception of Hizballah) have done so in the 1980s. From the start, Palestinian groups have routinely videotaped the suicide candidates, although on some occasions they skipped this practice for lack of video cameras or because the candidate refused to be filmed. Some other militant Islamic groups have also videotaped their suicide attackers. Thus, at least some of the 9/11/2001 suicide hijackers, al-Qaeda suicides in Iraq and Saudi Arabia, Ansar al-Sunna suicides in Iraq, members of the Egyptian al-Jihad who carried out a suicide attack in Pakistan, Indonesian Dar ul-Islam members, and Pakistani Jeish e-Mohammad suicides, had been videotaped before they carried out their attacks. The suicide bombers who carried out the July 7, 2005 attacks in London also left a videotape. The videotaping ritual is often done for propaganda purposes (Hafez, 2007b), but it has also a vital role in fortifying the candidate's resolve to carry out the attack. Once the candidate states on camera his commitment to carry out the attack, opting out becomes almost impossible unless the candidate can justify it to the group and to himself as a result of external intervention beyond his control.

For employing suicide terrorist attacks on a large scale, the larger groups have developed systematic procedures for recruiting and preparing candidates. These procedures are designed to maximize the likelihood that the candidates will not change their minds. Suicide attacks have, however, been carried out also by small, ad-hoc cells, such as the groups which carried out the suicide attacks in Morocco (May 16, 2003), Tunisia (April 11, 2002), and London (July 7, 2005).[5]

The existence of a large organization and a seasoned mechanism for preparing suicide attacks, such as in the cases of Palestinian groups, the LTTE and al-Qaeda in Iraq, is not a necessary requirement for producing suicide attacks. Large groups usually exist in situations where armed struggle is supported by a significant part of the community. When such a group decides to resort to suicide attacks, it therefore has a large number of potential volunteers and usually also employs an aggressive recruitment campaign that glorifies the suicide bombers. Thus, once they reach the decision to use suicide attacks, large groups can do it on a large scale. Yet, even a small ephemeral group can carry out a suicide attack. Presumably, the difference between transient groups of a few members and large organizations is mainly in the recruiting process, and much less so in the social pressure that they exert to keep candidates for suicide attacks on track.

## The Individual Level

As suggested in the previous sections, the group is the critical element in the decision to use suicide attacks, as well as in preparing them, and public atmosphere has a critical influence on the scope of this form of terrorism in a given arena and circumstances. Yet, suicide attacks are carried out by individuals. Are all individuals in a given situation equally likely to become suicide terrorists? As already mentioned, the currently prevailing opinion among terrorism researchers is that suicide terrorists are normal and that they do not have any distinctive psychological features. This opinion, however, stems from absence of evidence to the contrary, rather than from a direct investigation of suicide bombers. The new studies reported in this book (Chapters 4–6) show that suicide terrorists, compared to "ordinary" (nonsuicide) terrorists, do have some typical traits. Although none of the would-be suicides was diagnosed as psychotic, most of them had personality traits which made them more amenable to recruiting for suicide missions. Two main personality patterns were discerned: dependent–avoidant personality (60% of the would-be suicides) and impulsive–unstable personality (26.7%). Dependent–avoidant individuals are more susceptible to external influence, more willing to please, less likely to refuse requests by persons of authority, and are thus more easily influenced by public opinion and group pressure. They also suffer from a feeling of inadequacy, and the demonstrative sacrifice carries the promise of glory and the promise of instantaneously turning a feeling of impotence into a show of power. Generally, these people are followers rather than leaders; characteristically, the leaders are disinclined to commit suicide for the cause.[6]

The other personality type found among Palestinian would-be suicide bombers was the impulsive–unstable pattern. People having this personality style tend to be impetuous, volatile, and self-destructive. With these characteristics in mind, it is easy to comprehend why they volunteer for suicide missions. At the same time, however, they are also unstable and may easily change their minds. This may explain why all would-be suicide bombers in the sample, who evidently tried to activate the explosive charge, belonged to the dependent–avoidant rather than to the impulsive–unstable category.

As noted in Chapter 5, 40% of the would-be suicides displayed suicidal tendencies, meaning that they had an urge to die for personal reasons, unrelated to the ostensible political cause. For these youngsters, "martyrdom," a socially admired death, was an excellent choice in a society that otherwise condemns self-destruction.

My view of suicide terrorism has changed over the years, as more data has become available. In the 1980s I viewed suicide attacks as primarily a product of personality factors (Merari, 1990). Starting from the late 1990s, when some data on recruitment and preparation processes of suicide bombers became available, and in the absence of empirical data on the personality characteristics of suicide bombers, I came to see suicide bombers mainly as a product of group decision and group pressure, a view that I presented in a series of lectures and articles.[7] Only in recent years, on the basis of the direct evidence on Palestinian suicide bombers' personality characteristics and motivations, have I gained more comprehensive understanding of the way in which social milieu, group processes and individual traits interact to produce this strange form of human behavior.

## *What Groups Use Suicide Attacks?*

Despite the continuing spread of suicide terrorism, only a minority of the terrorist groups around the world has so far adopted this tactic. An important question is, therefore, whether these groups have common characteristics that could be identified as factors that have influenced their decision to use suicide attacks.

In the period from 1981 to 2008, 74% of the suicide attacks whose perpetrating organization is known have been carried out by groups whose main agenda is militant-Islamic, and another 12% by groups who espouse a mixture of Islamic and nationalist ideology. Nationalist-ethnic groups, such as the Tamil Tigers and the Palestinian Fatah, that do not adhere to a religious ideology, have carried out only 14% of the attacks.

The share of Islamic groups in suicide terrorism has grown dramatically in recent years. In the 1980s, groups whose main agenda was militant-Islamic carried out only 2.6% of the suicide attacks. Their share grew slightly to 4.7% in the 1990s. In the new millennium, however, they carried out 81.5% of the suicide attacks. These facts clearly show that, at least under the present circumstances, the characteristic of militant Islamism is a strong contributing factor in determining a group's inclination to use suicide attacks although, as explained in the previous chapter, it is neither a necessary nor a sufficient factor. However, the importance of the Islamic factor has still to be explained.

As noted, some authors have attributed the use of suicide attacks by Islamic groups to Islamic traditions and practices, as well as to cultural traits of Islamic societies in general and Arab societies in particular. This view fails to account for the fact that suicide attacks are a new phenomenon that has not been practiced by Islamic societies before the 1980s; furthermore, not all Islamic groups have resorted to suicide attacks, and those that did, have done it over a limited period of time. These facts suggest that the tactic of suicide bombing is a novel fashion and that the political context, as perceived by these groups, may be more important than the group's religious and cultural background.

Under what circumstances does a group, Islamic or not, decide to resort to suicide attacks? Asking members to kill themselves is an extreme step that for most people is contradictory to basic psychological instincts. For this reason, it is logical to expect that only under extreme circumstances would a group be willing to resort to this extreme way of fighting. Extreme circumstances are situations in which, by the group's perception, its main cause or its organizational existence are in grave danger.

This logical hypothesis seems to be supported by empirical facts in some, but not all cases. Hamas, for example, started using suicide attacks in 1993, at the beginning of the Israeli-Palestinian peace negotiations. The peace process was perceived by Hamas as an existential threat, both because it antagonized the very basis of Hamas ideology, and also because it was perceived as a danger to the organizational existence of the group under PLO control. The LTTE started using suicide attacks in 1987, at a time when the group was in retreat under the blows of the Sri Lankan army (Gunaratna, 2000). Likewise, the Kurdish PKK decided to use suicide attacks at a time when the group was in distress, suffering heavy blows from the Turkish army, which resulted in a deteriorated morale among the group's fighters. The group intensified the use of suicide attacks after the capture of its leader, Abdullah Ocalan (Ergil, 2001; Schweitzer, 2001). A back-to-the-wall situation has also been a major factor in the decision of some other groups to resort to suicide attacks, e.g., the Chechen rebels and the Turkish DHKP-C. The latter group staged a couple of suicide attacks at a time when a mass hunger-strike to the death, carried out by its members in Turkish prison (an act of desperation in itself) failed to achieve any effect on the Turkish authorities.

In contrast to these groups, however, the context of suicide attacks carried out by several other groups, notably al-Qaeda and its satellite groups in Indonesia, Saudi Arabia, Morocco, Tunisia and Turkey, cannot be described as a back-to-the-wall situation. Al-Qaeda was not under a devastating American offensive when it decided to carry out the suicide attacks in 1998, 2000, and September 2001. And, despite the American "War on Terrorism," nor did al-Qaeda's affiliated groups in Muslim countries, such as Turkey and Indonesia, face a threatening turn of events, at least in their local habitats, that would prompt them to resort to the most extreme measures in their power. Possibly, the use of suicide attacks by these groups reflects the fact that this terrorist method has become fashionable and a routine trademark of militant Islamic groups. This fashion has set a new standard of operation that obliges these groups. To a large extent, the persistence of suicide attacks on a large scale will be determined by the degree to which this fashion has become an integral part of the Islamic ethos.

## Coping with Suicide Terrorism

Several authors have observed that one of the factors which make suicide attacks an attractive tactic for terrorist groups is the fact that there is no need to make an escape plan for the suicide bomber. Authors have also asserted that suicide terrorists cannot be deterred, because they are not only willing to die but actively seek death. Nevertheless, the brief history of this phenomenon shows that much can be done to prevent suicide attacks, and this form of terrorism can be significantly curtailed if not totally obliterated.

A distinction must be made between situations in which suicide attacks have disappeared because the insurgency that they were part of ended, and situations in which insurgent groups abandoned this method, but continued using other tactics. The fact that suicide attacks cease when the insurgency is over is trivial, of course. The question in this final section of the book is whether suicide attacks can be contained or prevented as a tactic, despite the continuation of the violent struggle (although the question of how to end an insurgency is much more important than the question of how to prevent a certain tactic, such as suicide attacks).

As mentioned in Chapter 2, in Lebanon, Israeli forces were able to drastically curtail the frequency of suicide attacks by adopting simple measures. In Lebanon, the targets for suicide attacks were not random civilians, but Israeli and South Lebanese Army forces. Similar to the situation in Afghanistan two decades later, the attacks in Lebanon in the 1980s were directed mostly against soldiers manning roadblocks, or against Israeli military vehicles on the main roads. After the first attacks, the Israeli army instituted procedures designed to control the approach of civilian vehicles to the roadblocks. Drivers and passengers in the approaching vehicles were directed to stop at a safe distance, get out of the car, and then proceed toward the roadblock on foot, lifting their shirts to prove that they did not carry explosives on their bodies. The cars were then checked by a single soldier, so as to minimize casualties in case the car exploded. To prevent suicide car bombers from ramming Israeli military vehicles on the road, the use of the road by civilian vehicles was minimized and drivers were forbidden to approach Israeli military vehicles while driving. As mentioned in Chapter 2, these procedures resulted in a sharp decline in the number of fatalities as a result of suicide attacks, many of which caused no casualties whatsoever. This was also the reason why Lebanese groups abandoned suicide attacks after 1989. It seems that similar procedures have been followed in Afghanistan. Actually, the low rate of casualties there is quite similar to that in Lebanon after 1984.[8]

The examples of Lebanon and Afghanistan show that suicide attacks are ineffective against prepared, defended targets. Their devastating effect has been in cases where they targeted crowded people in buildings, buses, cafes, or markets. These kinds of targets cannot be defended like a military roadblock in the field, or as a protected government building is guarded. However, Israel's experience is an example that much can be done even in face of a campaign of suicide attacks against random civilian targets. As shown in Figure 2.3, the percentage of foiled suicide attacks rose dramatically from 31.5% in 2001, to 87.6% in 2003 and 87.9 in 2004. This achievement was the result of better intelligence and an improved ability to act upon this intelligence, both factors being a consequence of the presence of Israeli forces in the West Bank, in the wake of the Defensive Shield operation. In the circumstances prevailing in Israel, in which the time between the groups' decision to carry out a suicide attack and the dispatching of the suicide candidate to his destination has been rather short, as were the distances between the launching point and the target, this has been a remarkable achievement. The bits and pieces of information suggesting that a suicide attack was being prepared had to be correctly interpreted very rapidly, and military forces (in the West Bank) and police (inside Israel) had to take action on a rather short notice. This required very smooth coordination between various elements of the intelligence apparatus, as well as between the intelligence organization and field forces. Thus, the presence of the Israeli forces inside the cities and towns of the West Bank, in which most of the suicide attacks were organized, was a necessary precondition for achieving the high rate of success in thwarting the suicide attacks.

In acting upon intelligence which discovered preparations to carry out a suicide attack, Israel faced the problem of incapacitating the perpetrators of the planned attack. Even though Israeli forces were present in the

West Bank, they could not operate freely as a police force would do in a country under normal circumstances. In most cases, arresting the organizers of the attack could only be achieved by a sizable force and a clash with armed members of the militant Palestinian groups. Under these circumstances, Israel resorted to "targeted killing" of militants who were regarded as "ticking bombs," i.e., about to carry out a terrorist attack. Most of the attacks of these operatives have been carried out using missiles fired from helicopters, but some were done by ground forces. The use of precise bombs dropped from aircraft has been extremely rare. Palestinian group operatives involved in the preparation of suicide attacks figured high on the list of targets.[9] Critics of the "targeted killings" viewed them as government-executed assassinations, or at least extrajudicial executions. However, this practice has been used under similar circumstances by other democracies as well, especially the United States. The moral and legal justification of targeted killings in combating terrorism rests on the similarity between an intense terrorist campaign and war, in which it is permissible to kill enemy combatants without warning.[10] Indeed, the second Palestinian intifada, as well as the intense insurgencies in Iraq and in Afghanistan in the first decade of the 21st century, amounted to wars. A different question is whether, regardless of their legal and moral justification, targeted killings have been effective in reducing suicide attacks. Apparently, the answer to this question is complex. In the short run, it is almost self-evident that the elimination of experienced organizers of terrorist attacks has an immediate detrimental effect on the operational capability of the groups in question. In the long run, however, insurgent organizations can replace the deceased commanders, especially in the case of large groups that enjoy substantial public support. It is also possible that targeted killings, especially when they are directed at persons perceived as public heroes, may have a provocative rather than a deterrent effect, although the empirical evidence is not unequivocal. In Israel, the killing of Fatah operatives has, apparently, been instrumental in that group's decision to resort to suicide attacks,[11] and Hamas and PIJ have often publicly vowed to avenge the deaths of their operatives by suicide attacks. Indeed, following the killing of Yahya Ayyash in January 2006, Hamas promised and carried out a series of suicide attacks in Israel. On the other hand, several targeted killings of top Hamas leaders and operatives have not been followed by a rise in suicide attacks. Most significantly, the killing of Hamas' highest leaders, Ahmad Yassin (March 22, 2004) and Abd al-Aziz Rantisi (April 17, 2004) were not followed by a rise in suicide attacks. In fact, Hamas carried out only one suicide attack during the four months following these killings. Assuming that Hamas did not lack motivation to avenge their deaths, the absence of a substantial reprisal can be attributed to either inability to carry out such attacks under the conditions prevailing in 2004, or to fear of further Israeli reprisals. In either case, these assassinations were not followed by negative consequences.[12] Thus, generalizations concerning the long-term effect of targeted killing of terrorist operatives cannot be readily made, as these effects apparently depend on a variety of other factors.

Controlling access to potential targets has been quite effective in preventing suicide bombers from attacking specific high-value facilities. This can be easily achieved in the case of important government buildings, military camps, sensitive infrastructure and industrial compounds, which have limited entry routes and are not open to the public at large. Facilities open to the general public that have nevertheless limited access routes can also be defended effectively, albeit at a large cost, as is the case of security checks at airports. Defending a large, densely populated, geographical area, however, is a different matter. In the specific conditions of Israel, a small country where suicide bombers have come from the even smaller occupied territories, measures designed to control access into Israel have contributed to the capture of would-be suicides on their way to the target. This, however, has been achieved at a costly political and humanitarian price. Many roads, not only those leading into Israel but also between Palestinian towns and villages, have been blocked, so as to channel passage to a limited number of routes. In these open routes, checkpoints have been established, causing Palestinians to waste hours on their way to work, schools, or hospitals.[13] The harassment and humiliation that ordinary Palestinians suffer at the checkpoints have undoubtedly been a major source of animosity toward Israel.

In addition to roadblocks and checkpoints, Israel has created security fences along the borders of the occupied territories, first in the Gaza Strip and later in the West Bank. Although some of the southern parts of the West Bank fence have not been completed as of this writing, the fence has already been a major obstacle for Palestinian groups' efforts to penetrate Israel.[14] In the West Bank, the fence did not follow the 1967 border. In several places it intruded Palestinian territory, so as to encompass Israeli settlements close to the border. Furthermore, in some places it separated Palestinians from their fields, causing them daily inconvenience. Thus, as in the case of roadblocks and checkpoints, the evident advantage of the fence from a security point of view has been achieved at the cost of further consternation on the part of the Palestinian population.

Suicide bombers who escape detection and manage to enter a bustling city are hard to stop. Providing that they are instructed to explode in the midst of random crowd, to cause a large number of casualties (as they usually are), they have plenty of targets to choose from. Nevertheless, even under these circumstances the simple measure of positioning guards at entrances to venues where many people congregate in an enclosed space, such as shopping malls and restaurants, can reduce the number of casualties—because the impact of an explosion in the open air is less than that of an explosion in an enclosed space. Guards at shopping mall entrances cannot behave like soldiers manning a roadblock in a war zone; they cannot order all people approaching them to stop at a safe distance and lift their shirts. A suicide bomber can therefore get close enough to the guard and alongside other people in the vicinity. Indeed, several guards in Israel have been killed in this way. Yet, the number of casualties would have been considerably higher had the suicide bomber been able to enter a building.

Guards can also have a deterrent effect. Most people perceive suicide bombers as underterrable, because they are evidently seeking death. However, as the interviews with would-be suicide bombers described in Chapter 5 show, a majority of the interviewees stated that they hesitated. Furthermore, analysis of the organizers' indictments discussed in Chapter 6 showed that more than a third of the suicide candidates actually aborted the mission after expressing their initial consent. The evidence also shows that fear tended to grow sharply in the last hours before the expected death. Apparently, most of the candidates overcame this fear and carried out the mission, but a significant minority abandoned it despite their commitment. As I suggested, under this acute conflict between fear and commitment, any obstacle may, sometimes, tilt the balance toward a decision to abort the mission. In some cases, therefore, the presence of a guard may make the difference.

The foregoing discussion suggests that suicide attacks can be significantly reduced (albeit not completely eliminated) by tactical countermeasures. The degree of success of these countermeasures depends on the conditions prevailing in the arena of struggle. Some of the measures applied in Israel, including physical barriers designed to impede terrorists' freedom of movement, can only be applied in places where the terrorists originate in geographically small, clearly demarcated areas such as the occupied territories.

They are impractical in places where the terrorists are intermingled in the general population, such as in Iraq and Afghanistan. Positioning guards at entrances to public places, such as shopping malls, concert halls, and restaurants can be done anywhere, but it has an economic cost and causes the public some inconvenience. Because of these constraints, they are likely to be adopted only in the face of an ongoing persistent terrorist campaign.

The use of targeted killing is limited to situations where the struggle takes the form of an all-out war, in which the insurgents enjoy some territorial control over areas that are out of reach for civilian police, such as in Iraq, Afghanistan, and the Palestinian-controlled territories. No law-abiding liberal democratic country can use this measure in lieu of due legal process in areas under its control.

In all circumstances, the main tool in the tactical battle against suicide attacks has been, and will always be, good intelligence work. It cannot be replaced by the massive use of force.

A point to remember is that some tactical measures that are justified for preventing an immediate threat have a more important, longer-range negative impact. Targeted killing operations in which many innocent civilians are killed alongside the intended target generate bitterness and hatred that are likely to produce more suicide bombers. Under the threat of imminent attacks, decision makers are always under public pressure to do everything in their power to prevent the attacks, fearing that they would lose their constituency's support if they fail to do so. They therefore tend to authorize whatever measures necessary to forestall the immediate danger. Despite the pressure of the moment, however, they must remember to weigh the longer-range consequences of the measures they are authorizing. Part of the difficulty of making a wise decision is that the terrorist threat which the government is supposed to prevent is often concrete and immediate, whereas the longer-range adverse consequences of the countermeasures are remote and cannot be readily assessed in physical terms, because they have to do with people's feelings and attitudes.

The importance of tactical measures for preventing suicide attacks notwithstanding, the hearts and minds of the communities which generate the suicide bombers are the main battlefield against suicide attacks (as well as against terrorism in general). Although it is always possible that a small, socially isolated group of people who share a radical ideology would decide to resort to violence, this kind of social aberration may at most carry out a few terrorist acts (including suicide attacks) before its members are killed or captured by the police. Sustaining a prolonged, widespread violent insurgency campaign requires support in large segments of the population. An insurgent movement that loses popular support is bound to wither rapidly. With regard to the specific tactic of suicide attacks, the importance of social support has already been mentioned earlier in this chapter.

Changing the hearts and minds of the population from which terrorists emerge means different things to different people. Some view this objective as an educational, propaganda, and psychological warfare mission. Others think in terms of addressing the grievances that give rise to political violence in the first place. Both of these interpretations entail immense problems, and are extremely hard to achieve. Although even a superficial analysis of this issue would exceed the boundaries of this book, I would like to note that addressing insurgents' grievances practically always creates grievances on the part of other sides to the conflict. Education and psychological operations have a certain value, but can only achieve limited results. In this line of activity, for example, statements by moderate Muslim clerics condemning suicide attacks are often mentioned as a way to convince Muslim youth against undertaking a suicide mission. Some statements of this kind have, indeed, been issued by high-ranking Muslim clergymen and probably had some effect. At the same time, however, radical Muslim clergymen have issued *fatwas* encouraging Muslims to carry out suicide attacks (see Chapter 7). A Muslim youngster who has to choose between the moderate and the radical rulings will probably act in accordance with his political inclination, the influence of his immediate reference group, and his personality characteristics. Education and information are always perceived and interpreted under the influence of the existing political context and social milieu.

Finally, while recognizing the importance of "soft" ways to achieve conciliation, it should also be noted that changing the population's attitude can hardly, if at all, be achieved without the use of force. The recent decline in the Palestinian population's support for suicide attacks (and armed struggle in general) was not achieved because the Palestinians were convinced that suicide attacks against civilians are immoral or religiously forbidden, or because their grievances have been met, however partially. Rather, the change was effected by the Palestinians weariness with the social and economic costs of the continuation of armed struggle, and the loss of hope that this approach would help them achieve their aspirations. Yet, history shows that this kind of lull is only temporary and violence is bound to erupt again sooner or later, unless the period of respite is used for finding a mutually acceptable peaceful solution.

*Endnotes*

1. I know of only four out of the 2,937 suicide bombers in the period of 1981–2007 who acted privately. In the first case of this kind, on February 8, 1995, Khalid Ahmad Mahmud Awad, an Egyptian citizen, burst into the Russian embassy in Rabat, Morocco, carrying a sign with the word "Chechnya." He was speaking incoherently in Arabic, apparently alluding to the safety of his wife in Russia, and threatened the consul with a knife. When the consul escaped to another room, Awad detonated an explosive charge he was carrying and was seriously wounded. In another case, on March 30, 2004, in La Paz, Bolivia, Eustaquio Pichacuri entered the national congress building and went to the visitors' wing. He wore eight sticks of dynamite in a vest and had additional sticks in a backpack. While negotiating with police, he detonated his vest, killing two police officers and wounding ten others. Pichacuri was a laid-off miner and his suicide act was a protest against the lack of early pensions. Picharcuri was not associated with any group. In the third event, on July 25, 2004, in Caoping, (Ebian County) China, a villager by the name of Zhang Mingchun, who had a dispute with the Mingda corporation about compensation for land appropriation, carried out a suicide bombing, killing the Chairman and General Manager of the corporation. In all these cases there was clearly a strong private interest on the part of the perpetrators, although they can be perceived as expressing a broader social or political protest. The fourth case (in which the bomber survived), took place in Jerusalem. On December 28, 2002, Ala'a Karaki, a 20-years-old Palestinian student, tried to explode a car bomb he was driving but the bomb failed to explode. In his interrogation Karaki said that he had become religious six months before the event and decided to carry out a suicide attack on his own to atone for his years of heresy. He said that he was not assisted by any group.

2. The Catholic Church considers suicide as a mortal sin, and all of the Maze Prison hunger strikers were Catholics. In the case of the 1981 hunger strike, however, the Church did not take a firm stand. O'Malley (1990, p. 177) points out that after Bobby Sands's death the Irish bishops issued a statement which said that although the Church teaches that suicide is a great evil, "there is some dispute about whether or not political hunger striking is suicide, or more precisely, about the circumstances in which it is suicide." However, Catholic priests, including the Pope's envoy, Irish-born Monsignor John Magee, tried to convince the hunger strikers to stop the strike.

3. Taylor (1988, p. 118) noted in this regard: "The individuals involved were under enormous pressure to conform, and subject to actual, or fear of, intimidation if they failed to do so."

4. More than 70 prisoners volunteered to join the hunger strike. Interestingly, those who offered themselves did not simply start fasting on their own decision. Rather, they offered themselves to the prisoners' leadership, which examined their candidacy (O'Malley, 1990, p. 76). It is possible that some of the volunteers offered themselves because they felt that this was what the group expected them to do, fearing that refraining from doing so would have a negative effect on their status in the group. Presumably, volunteers of this kind felt relief when they were left out of the strike.

5. Sageman, M. (2005, p. 8) described the group influence on members of jihadist cells as follows: "Their self sacrifice is again grounded in group dynamics. The terrorist is ready to show his devotion to his now exclusive friends, their group, and their cause by seeking death as a way to show his devotion to all of them. In-group love combined with out-group hate is a strong incentive for committing mass murder and suicide."

6. As discussed in Chapter 6, nearly two-thirds of the organizers of suicide attacks stated in the interviews that they were unwilling to carry out a suicide attack themselves, and the remaining organizers said that they might do it, but their role as commanders was more important.

7. For example, in a testimony in the U.S. Congress in 2000, I said: ". . . to put it in a nutshell, suicide terrorism is an organizational phenomenon. This is most important to understand." In that testimony, however, I suggested that in recruiting suicide candidates "an organization makes use of people who are willing to die to begin with," meaning that the groups recruit suicidal people [Merari, A. (2000). Testimony before the Special Oversight Panel on Terrorism of the Committee on Armed Services, U.S. House of Representatives, 106th Congress, July 13]. I expressed this view in many other lectures in the following years, e.g., at the International Security Studies Program lecture Series, Tufts University (January 2002) and at the Institute for Social Research of the University of Michigan, Ann Arbor (February 2002).

8. In Lebanon, in the period of 1985–2000, when security procedures were already in place, the average number of fatalities per suicide attack was 2.4. In Afghanistan, in the period of 2005–2008, the average number of fatalities per suicide attack was 3.7.

9. According to Drucker and Shelah (2005), from the beginning of the 2nd intifada (September 2000) to May 2004, 237 Palestinian operatives were killed in Israeli targeted killing operations and seven others were wounded. In these operations 125 passers-by or unintended victims (family members or other persons who happened to be in the vicinity of the target) were also killed and 585 were wounded. In this period, Israel carried out, on average, one targeted killing operation every five days. According to B'Teselem, an Israeli–Palestinian human rights organization, during the period of September 29, 2000 through December 26, 2008, 233 "Palestinians who were the object of a targeted killing" were killed alongside with 386 unintended Palestinian civilian fatalities (statistics available at B'Tselem's website, http://www.btselem.org/english/statistics/casualties.asp, accessed May 29, 2009).

10. For a thorough discussion of the legal aspects of targeted killings see Heymann and Kayyem, 2005. This book includes a summary of the conclusions of "The Long-Term Legal Strategy Project for Preserving Security and Democratic Freedoms in the War on Terrorism."

11. The targeted killing of Ra'ed Karmi, a Fatah leader in Tul Karem, in January 2002, has often been mentioned as an event that provoked Fatah's al-Aqsa Martyrs' Brigades to resort to suicide attacks inside Israel (see Chapter 2).

12. No significant increase in Hamas suicide attacks was observed also following targeted killings of major Hamas leaders during the height of the second intifada

(e.g., the killing of Ibrahim Maqadmeh on March 20, 2003, and that of Ismai'l Abu Shanab on August 21, 2003), even though at that time Hamas was clearly able to carry out suicide attacks. The absence of a specific response to these targeted killings perhaps reflects the fact that Hamas at that time operated anyway at the peak of its capability.

13. B'Tselem, an Israeli-Palestinian human rights organization, has reported that as of the end March 2009, there were 63 permanent checkpoints on roads connecting Palestinian cities and villages in the West Bank, in addition to 39 checkpoints that are the last control points between the West Bank and Israel (B'Tselem, "Restrictions on Movement: Information on checkpoints and roadblocks." Available at: http://www.btselem.org/english/Freedom_of_Movement/Statistics.asp, accessed: June 9, 2009).

14. Explaining the decline in suicide attacks in Israel by his organization, PIJ leader Ramadan Shalah said in November 2006, in an interview to Hizballah's television station Al-Manar: "There is the separation fence which is an obstacle to the resistance, and if it were not there, the situation would be entirely different." (Al-Manar television, November 11, 2006). Two years later, in an interview to the Qatari newspaper Al-Sharq, Shalah reiterated this statement: "For example, they built a separation fence in the West Bank. We do not deny that it limits the ability of the resistance [i.e., the terrorist organizations] to arrive deep within [Israeli territory] to carry out suicide bombing attacks, but the resistance has not surrendered or become helpless, and is looking for other ways to cope with the requirements of every stage [of the intifada] . . ." (Al Sharq (Arabic), March 23, 2008). Hamas leader Musa Abu Marzuq also admitted that the fence had been a major hindrance to his organization's ability to carry out suicide attacks. Asked by a group of Egyptian intellectuals and politicians why the suicide bombing activity had decreased since the Hamas government came to power, he said: "[carrying out] such attacks is made difficult by the security fence and the gates surrounding West Bank residents" (Abd al-Muaz Muhammad, Ikhwan Online, the Muslim Brotherhood Website, June 2, 2007). All sources were quoted by the Intelligence and Terrorism Information Center at the Israel Intelligence Heritage & Commemoration Center (IICC), March 26, 2008. Available at: http://www.terrorism-info.org.il/malam_multimedia/English/eng_n/pdf/ct_250308e.pdf.

# REFERENCES

Aaronovitch, D. (2005, July 19). Nursing a grievance, blinded by narcissism — such ordinary killers. London: Times Online. Available at: http://www.timesonline.co.uk/article/0,,22369-1699136,00.html, Accessed: January 1, 2006.

Abdul Wahid Hamid (1995). *Companions of the Prophet*. Columbia, MD: MELS Publishing. Available at: http://web.umr.edu/~msaumr/reference/companions/English/ubaydah.html. Accessed: December 22, 2005.

Abrahms, M. (2006). Why terrorism does not work. *International Security, 31*(2), 42–78.

Adorno, T., Frenkel-Brunswik, E., Levinson, D., & Sanford, N. (1950). *The Authoritarian Personality*. New York: Harper.

Altindag, A., Ozkan, M., & Oto R. (2005). Suicide in Batman, Southeastern Turkey. *Suicide and Life-Threatening Behavior, 35*(5), 478–482.

Akhmedova, K. & Speckhard, A. (2006). A multi-causal analysis of the genesis of suicide terrorism: The Chechen case. In: J. Victoroff (Ed.), *Tangled Roots: Social and Psychological Factors in the Genesis of Terrorism*. Amsterdam: IOS Press.

Alvarez, A. (1990). *The Savage God: A Study of Suicide*. New York: W.W. Norton.

American Psychiatric Association (1994). *Diagnostic and Statistical Manual of Mental Disorders, Fourth Edition*. Washington, DC: American Psychiatric Association.

Anderson, B. (1991). *Imagined Communities: Reflections on the Origin and Spread of Nationalism*. London: Verso.

Andreasen, N. (1987). Creativity and mental illness prevalence rates in writers and their first-degree relatives. *American Journal of Psychiatry, 144*, 1288–1292.

Andreasen, N. & Canter, A., (1974). The creative writer: Psychiatric Symptoms and family history. *Comprehensive Psychiatry, 15*, 123–131.

Atran, S. (2003a). Genesis of suicide terrorism. *Science, 299*(7), 1534–1539. Supporting online material is available at: http://www.sciencemag.org/cgi/data/299/5612/1534/DC1/1.

Atran, S. (2003b). The strategic threat from suicide terror. AEI–Brookings Joint Center for Regulatory Studies, Related Publication 03–33, December 2003. Available at: http://www.aei-brookings.org/publications/abstract.php?pid=410. Accessed: December 17, 2003.

Atran, S. (2004a). Soft Power and the psychology of suicide bombing. *Terrorism Monitor, 2*(11), 1–3.

Atran, S. (2004b). Mishandling suicide terrorism. The Washington Quarterly, *27*(3) 67–90.

Atran, S. (2004c). Genesis and future of suicide terrorism. Available at: http://www.interdisciplines.org/terrorism/papers/1/24. Accessed: December 14, 2005.

Atran, S. (2006). The moral logic and growth of suicide terrorism. *The Washington Quarterly, 29*(2), 127–147.

Aust, S. (1987). *The Baader-Meinhof Group: The Inside Story of a Phenomenon.* London: The Bodley Head.

Baeyer-Katte, W., Claessens, D., Feger, H., & Neidhart, F. (1982). *Analysen zum Terrorismus 3: Gruppeprozesse.* Darmstadt: Westdeutcher Verlag.

Balasingham, A. (1983). *Our Theoretical Guide to the National Question.* From Liberation Tigers and the Tamil Eelam Freedom Struggle by the Political Committee of the Liberation Tigers of Tamil Eelam. Available at: http://www.tamilnation.org/ltte/83guide.htm. Accessed: November 28, 2005.

Barraclough, B. & Hughes, J. (1987). *Suicide: clinical and epidemiological studies.* London: Croom Helm.

Benmelech, E. & Berrebi, C. (2007). Human capital and the productivity of suicide bombers. *Journal of Economic Perspectives, 21*(3), 223–238.

Beresford, D. (1994). *Ten Men Dead.* London: Harper Collins.

Bergman, R. (2002). *Vehareshut Netuna* [Authority Given]. Tel Aviv: Miskal-Yediot Ahronot Books and Chemed Books (Hebrew).

Berrebi, C. (2003). *Evidence About the Link Between Education, Poverty and Terrorism Among Palestinians.* IRS Working Paper 477, Princeton University. Available at: http://www.irs.princeton.edu/pubs/pdfs/477.pdf. Accessed: November 9, 2003.

Biggs, M. (2005). Dying without killing: self-immolations, 1963–2003. In: D. Gambetta, *Making Sense of Suicide Missions* (pp. 173–208). Oxford: Oxford University Press.

Bloom, M. (2004). Palestinian suicide bombing: public support, market share, and outbidding. *Political Science Quarterly, 199*(1), 61–88.

Bloom, M. (2005). *Dying to Kill: The Allure of Suicide Terror.* New York: Columbia University Press.

Bongar, B. (2002). *The Suicidal Patient: Clinical and Legal Standards of Care.* Washington, DC: American Psychological Association.

Breznitz S. (1984). *Cry Wolf: The Psychology of False Alarms.* Hillsdale, NJ: Lawrence Erlbaum.

Brown, V. (2008). Foreign fighters in historical perspective: The case of Afghanistan. In: B. Fishman (Ed.), *Bombers, Bank Accounts, & Bleedout: Al-Qaida's Road in and Out of Iraq.* West Point: Combating Terrorism Center. Available at: http://www.ctc.usma.edu/harmony/pdf/Sinjar_2_July_23.pdf.

Clark, D. and Horton-Deutsch, S. (1992). Assessment in absentia: The value of the psychological autopsy method for studying antecedents of suicide and predicting future suicides. In: R. Maris, A. Berman, J. Maltsberger, & R. Yufit (Eds.), *The Assessment and Prediction of Suicide* (pp. 144–182). New York: Guilford Press.

Cordesman, A. and Obaid, N. (2005). Saudi Militants in Iraq: Assessment and Kingdom's Response. Washington, DC: Center for Strategic and International Studies (working paper). Available at: http://www.csis.org/media/csis/pubs/050919_saudimiltantsiraq. pdf. Accessed: February 18, 2008.

Crenshaw, M. (1986). The psychology of political terrorism. In: M. Hermann (Ed.), *Political Psychology: Contemporary problems and Issues* (pp. 379–413). London: Jossey-Bass.

Crenshaw, M. (1990). The logic of terrorism: Terrorist behavior as a product of strategic choice. In: W. Reich (Ed.), *Origins of Terrorism: Psychologies, Ideologies, Theologies, States of Mind* (pp. 7–24). Washington, D.C.: Woodrow Wilson Center Press.

Crenshaw, M. (2001). Suicide terrorism in a comparative perspective. In: *Countering Suicide Terrorism* (pp. 21–29). Herzliya, Israel: The International Policy Institute for Counter-Terrorism at the Interdisciplinary Center.

Cronin, A. (2003). *Terrorists and Suicide Attacks*. CRS report for Congress, Congressional Research Service, The Library of Congress, August 28. Available at: http://fpc.state. gov/documents/organization/24049.pdf. Accessed: June 13, 2006.

Dale, S. (1988). Religious suicide in Islamic Asia: Anticolonial terrorism in India, Indonesia, and the Philippines. *Journal of Conflict Resolution*, 32(1), 37–59.

Davis, J. (2003). *Martyrs: Innocence, Vengeance, and Despair in the Middle East*. New York: Palgrave Macmillan.

DeMause, L. (2002). The childhood origins of terrorism. *Journal of Psychohistory*, 29(4), 340–348. Available at: http://www.primal-page.com/terrorld.htm. Accessed: December 16, 2005.

Dixon, N. (1976). *On the Psychology of Military Incompetence*. New York: Basic Books.

Dolan, M. and Doyle, M. (2000). Violence risk prediction: Clinical and actuarial measures and the role of the Psychopathy Checklist. *British Journal of Psychiatry*, 177, 303–311.

Dollard, J. & Miller, N. (1950). *Personality and Psychotherapy: An Analysis in Terms of Learning, Thinking and Culture*. New York: McGraw-Hill.

Drucker, R., & Shelah, O. (2005). *Boomerang*. Jerusalem: Keter. [Hebrew].

Dupuy, R.E. & Dupuy, T. (1986). *The Encyclopedia of Military History*. London: Jane's Publishing Co.

Durkheim, E. (1951). *Suicide: A study in sociology*. New York: The Free Press.

Elster, J. (2005). Motivations and beliefs in suicide missions. In: D. Gambetta, *Making Sense of Suicide Missions* (pp. 233–258). Oxford: Oxford University Press.

Ergil, D. (2001). Suicide terrorism in Turkey: The Workers' Party of Kurdistan. In: The International Policy Institute for Counter Terrorism, *Countering suicide terrorism* (pp. 105–128). Herzliya, Israel: The Interdisciplinary Center.

Esposito, J. (1998). *Islam and Politics* (4th Ed.). New York: Syracuse University Press.

Esposito, J. (2002). *Unholy War: Terror in the Name of Islam*. New York: Oxford University Press.

Fanon, F. (1965). *The Wretched of the Earth*. New York: Grove/Atlantic.

Farber, M. (1968). *Theory of Suicide*. New York: Funk & Wagnalls.

Felter, J. & Fishman, B. (2007). Al-Qaeda's Foreign Fighters in Iraq: First Look at the Sinjar Records. West Point: Combating Terrorism Center. Available at: http://www.ctc.usma. edu/harmony/pdf/CTCForeignFighter.19.Dec07.pdf. Accessed: January 29, 2008.

Felter, J. & Fishman, B. (2008). Becoming a foreign fighter: A *second* look at the Sinjar records. In: B. Fishman (Ed.), *Bombers, Bank Accounts, & Bleedout: Al-Qaida's Road in and Out of Iraq*. West Point: Combating Terrorism Center. Available at: http://www. ctc.usma.edu/harmony/pdf/Sinjar_2_July_23.pdf.

Ferracuti, F. (1982). A sociopsychiatric interpretation of terrorism. *Annals of the American Academy of Political and Social Science, 463*, 129–140.

Ferracuti, F. & Bruno, F. (1983). Psychiatric aspects of terrorism in Italy. In: I. Barak-Glanz and C. Huff (eds.), *Aggression in Global Perspective*. Elmsford: Pergamon Press.

Fields, R., Elbedour, S. & Hein, A. (2002). The Palestinian suicide bomber. In: C. Stout (Ed.), *The Psychology of Terrorism: Clinical Aspects and Responses* (pp. 193–223). Westport, CT: Praeger.

Gambetta, D. (2005). Can we make sense of suicide missions? In: D. Gambetta, *Making Sense of Suicide Missions* (pp. 131–172). Oxford: Oxford University Press.

Ganor, B. (2000). Suicide Terrorism: An Overview. The International Policy Institute for Counter-Terrorism at the Interdisciplinary Center, February 15. Available at: http:// www.ict.org.il. Accessed: June 16, 2006.

Ganor, B. (2001). Suicide attacks in Israel. In: *Countering Suicide Terrorism* (pp. 134–145). Herzliya, Israel: The International Policy Institute for Counter-Terrorism at the Interdisciplinary Center.

Gazit, S. (Ed.). (1989). *The Middle East Military Balance 1988–1989: A Comprehensive Data Base & In-Depth Analysis of Regional Strategic Issues*. Published for the Jaffee Center for Strategic Studies (Tel Aviv University) by The Jerusalem Post and Westview Press.

Goldman, R. & Beardlslee, W. (1999). Suicide in children and adolescents. In: D. Jacobs (Ed.), *The Harvard Medical School Guide to Suicide Assessment and Intervention* (pp. 417–442). San Francisco: Jossey-Bass.

Gordon, H. (2002). The 'suicide' bomber: Is it a psychiatric phenomenon? *Psychiatric Bulletin, 26*, 285–287.

Goren S., Subasi M., Tirasci Y., and Ozen S. (2004). Female suicides in Diyarbakir, Turkey. *Journal of Forensic Sciences, 49*(4), 1–3.

Gunawardena, A. (2004). LTTE 'Black Tigers': The Sri Lankan Experience. Paper presented at the Suicide Terrorism Research Conference organized by the U.S. National Institute of Justice and the U.S. Department of Homeland Security, Washington, D.C., 25–26 October. Available at: http://www.nijpcs.org/terror/Gunawardena Paper. PDF. Accessed: November 22, 2004.

Gunning, J. (2008). *Hamas in Politics: Democracy, Religion, Violence*. New York: Columbia University Press.

Gupta, D. and Mundra, K. (2005). Suicide bombing as a strategic weapon: An empirical investigation of Hamas and Islamic Jihad. *Terrorism and Political Violence, 17*(4), 573–598.

Haddad, S. (2004). A comparative study of Lebanese and Palestinian perceptions of suicide bombings: The role of militant Islam and socio-economic status. *International Journal of Comparative Sociology, 45*(5), 337–363.

Hafez, M. (2004). Manufacturing human bombs: Strategy, culture and conflict in the making of Palestinian suicide terrorism. Paper presented at the National Institute of Justice Suicide Terrorism Conference, Washington, D.C., October 25–26. Available at: http://www.nijpcs.org/terror/. Accessed: August 19, 2006.

Hafez, M. (2006). *Manufacturing Human Bombs: The Making of Palestinian Suicide Bombers.* Washington, DC: U.S. Institute of Peace.

Hafez, M. (2007a). *Suicide Bombers in Iraq: The Strategy and Ideology of Martyrdom.* Washington, DC: U.S. Institute of Peace.

Hafez, M. (2007b). Martyrdom mythology in Iraq: How jihadists frame suicide terrorism in videos and biographies. *Terrorism and Political Violence, 9*(1), 95–115.

Halevy, E. (2006). *Man in the Shadows: Inside the Middle East Crisis with a Man Who Led the Mossad.* New York: St. Martin's Press.

Hare, R. (2001). Psychopaths and their nature: Some implications for understanding human predatory violence. In: A. Raine and J. Sanmartin (eds.), *Violence and Psychopathy* (pp. 5–34). New York: Kluwer Academic/Plenum Publishers.

Harrison, M. (2003). *An Economist Looks at Suicide Terrorism.* Available at: http://www. securitymanagement.com/ library/Suicide_Harrison0803.pdf. Accessed: June 13, 2006.

Hassan, N. (2001). An arsenal of believers. *The New Yorker*, Nov.19, pp. 36–41.

Hassan, R. (2004). Terrorists and Their Tools - Part I: Suicide Bombings Driven More by Politics than Religious Zeal. Yale Global Online (Yale Center for the Study of Globalization), April 23, Available at: http://yaleglobal.yale.edu/article.print?id=3749. Accessed: June 13, 2006.

Heiberg, M. and Ovensen, G. (1994). *Palestinian Society in Gaza, West Bank and Arab Jerusalem: A Survey of Living Conditions* (Chapter 9). Fafo Institute of Applied Social Science, Report 151. Available at: http://almashriq.hiof.no/general/300/320/327/fafo/reports/FAFO151/index.html. Accessed: April 5, 2006.

Hewitt, C. and Kelley-Moore, J. (2009.). Foreign fighters in Iraq: A cross-national analysis of Jihadism. *Terrorism and Political Violence, 21*(2), 211–220.

Heymann, P. and Kayyem, J. (2005). *Protecting Liberty in an Age of Terror.* Cambridge, MA: MIT press.

Hill, P. (2005). Kamikaze, 1943–5. In: D. Gambetta, *Making Sense of Suicide Missions* (pp. 1–42). Oxford: Oxford University Press.

Hoffman, B. (1998). *Inside Terrorism.* London: Victor Gollancz.

Hoffman, B. (2003). The logic of suicide terrorism. *The Atlantic Monthly*, June. (pp. 40–47).

Hoffman, B. and McCormick, G. (2004). Terrorism, signaling, and suicide attack. *Studies in Conflict and Terrorism, 27,* 243–281.

Holmes, S. (2005). Al-Qaeda, September 11, 2001. In: D. Gambetta, *Making Sense of Suicide Missions* (pp. 131–172). Oxford: Oxford University Press.

Hopgood, S. (2005). Tamil Tigers, 1987–2002. In: D. Gambetta (Ed.), *Making Sense of Suicide Missions* (pp. 43–76). Oxford: Oxford University Press.

Horgan, J. (2005). *The Psychology of Terrorism.* London: Routledge.

Hoyt, E. (1999). The Kamikazes. Short Hills, New Jersey: Burford Books.

Hroub, Khaled (2006). *Hamas: A Beginner's Guide*. London: Pluto Press.

Hudson, R. (1999). *The Sociology and Psychology of Terrorism: Who Becomes a Terrorist and Why?* Washington, DC: Federal Research Division, Library of Congress. Available at: http://www.loc.gov/rr/frd/pdf-files/Soc_Psych_of_Terrorism.pdf. Accessed: December 12, 2005.

Huesmann, R. (2002). How to grow a terrorist without really trying. Paper presented at the Annual Convention of the American Psychological Association, Chicago, August. Available at: http://www.rcgd.isr.umich.edu/roots/Huesmann.HowToGrowTerrorists. pdf. Accessed: June 17, 2006.

Hurwitz, E. (1999). *Hizballah's military echelon: a social portrait* (Tel Aviv: Dayan Center for Middle Eastern Studies, Tel Aviv University.

Iga, M. (1993). Japanese suicide. In: A. Leenaars (Ed.), *Suicidology*. Northvale, New Jersey: Jason Aronson.

Inoguchi, R. and Nakajima, T. (1958). *The Divine Wind: Japan's Kamikaze Forces in World War II*. Annapolis, Maryland: Naval Institute Press.

Israeli, R. (1997). Islamikaze and their significance. *Terrorism and Political Violence, 9*, 96–121.

Jaber, H. (1997). *Hezbollah: Born with a vengeance*. New York: Columbia University Press.

Jacobs, D., Brewer, M, and Klein-Benheim, M. (1999). Suicide assessment. In: D. Jacobs (Ed.), *The Harvard Medical School Guide to Suicide Assessment and Intervention*. San Francisco: Jossey-Bass.

Jager, H., Schmidtchen, G., and Sullwold, L. (1982). *Analysen zum Terrorismus 2: Lebenslauf Analysen*. Opladen: Westdeutcher Verlag.

Jobes, D., Luoma, J, Hustead, L., and Mann, R. (2000). In the wake of suicide: Survivorship and prevention. In: R. Maris, A. Berman, and M. Silverman (eds.), *Comprehensive Textbook of Suicidology* (pp. 536–561). New York: The Guilford Press.

Jones, J. (2008). *Blood that Cries Out From the Earth: The Psychology of Religious Terrorism*. New York: Oxford University Press.

Joshi, C. L. (2000): Sri Lanka: suicide bombers. *Far Eastern Economic Review*, June1. Available at: http://www.feer.com/_0006_01/p64currents.html. Accessed: June 24, 2002.

Juda. A. (1949). The relationship between highest mental capacity and psychic abnormalities. *American Journal of Psychiatry, 106*, 296–307.

Juergensmeyer, M. (2001). *Terror in the Mind of God: The Global Rise of Religious Violence*. Berkeley: University of California Press.

Kalyvas, S. and Sánchez-Cuenca, I. (2005). Killing without dying: The absence of suicide missions. In: D. Gambetta, *Making Sense of Suicide Missions* (pp. 209–232). Oxford: Oxford University Press.

Kepel, G. (1993). *Muslim Extremism in Egypt: The Prophet and Pharaoh*. Berkeley: University of California Press.

Kfir, I. (2007). The Crisis in Pakistan: A dangerously weak state. *The Middle East Review of International Affairs*, Vol. 11, No. 3, Article 8/9, available at: http://meria.idc.ac.il/ journal/2007/issue3/jv11no3a8.html

Kimhi, S., & Even S. (2003). Who are the Palestinian suicide terrorists? *Strategic Assessment, 6*(2) (Tel Aviv: Tel Aviv University, Jaffee Center for Strategic Studies).

Kira, I. (2002). Suicide terror and collective trauma: A collective terror management paradigm. A paper presented at the annual convention of the American psychological Association, Chicago, Ill.

Klerman, G. (1987). Clinical epidemiology of suicide. *The Journal of Clinical Psychiatry*, *48*(12, suppl.), 33–38.

Koenigs, T. (2007). Suicide attacks in Afghanistan. United Nations Assistance Mission in Afghanistan report, September 1, Available at: http://www.unama-afg.org/docs/_UN-Docs/UNAMA%20-%20SUICIDE%20ATTACKS%20STUDY%20-%20SEPT%209th%202007.pdf. Accessed: February 19, 2008.

Kramer, M. (1990). The moral logic of Hizballah. In: W. Reich (Ed.), *Origins of Terrorism: Psychologies, Ideologies, Theologies, States of Mind* (pp. 131–160). Washington, D.C.: Woodrow Wilson Center Press.

Kramer, M. (1991). Sacrifice and Self-Martyrdom in Shi'ite Lebanon. *Terrorism and Political Violence*, *10*(3), 30–47.

Kramer, M. (2004). *Sheikh Obeid, Now Free, on Women Suicide Bombers*. Sandstorm Weblog. Available at: http://www.geocities.com/martinkramerorg/2004_01_30.htm. Accessed: October 24, 2005.

Krueger, A. (2007). *What Makes a Terrorist: Economics and the Roots of Terrorism*. Princeton: Princeton University Press.

Krueger, A., and Malecková, J. (2002). Education, Poverty, Political Violence and Terrorism: Is There A Causal Connection? Working Paper 9074, National Bureau of Economic Research. Available at: http://www.nber.org/papers/w9074. Accessed: October 23, 2004.

Krueger, A., and Malecková, J. (2003). Seeking the roots of terrorism. *The Chronicle of Higher Education* (June 6). Available at: http://chronicle.com/cgi2-bin/printable. cgi?article=http://chronicle.com/free/v49/i39/39b01001.htm. Accessed: June 9, 2006.

Kruglanski, A. (2002). Inside the terrorist mind. Paper presented at the annual meeting of the National Academy of Science, April 29, Washington, D.C. Available at: http://www.wam.umd.edu/~hannahk/ULTIMATE%2029%20APRIL%20TALK.doc. Accessed: October 27, 2005.

Kruglanski, A. and Fishman, S. (2006). The psychology of terrorism: Syndrome versus tool perspective. *Terrorism and Political Violence*, *18*(2), 193–215.

Lachkar, J. (2002). The Psychological make-up of a suicide bomber. *The Journal of Psychohistory*, *29*(4). Available at: www.psychohistory.com/htm/01_journal.html. Accessed: December 1, 2005.

Lawrence, B. (2005). *Messages to the World: The Statements of Osama Bin Laden*. London: Verso.

Leenaars, A. & Wenckstern, S. (2004). Altruistic suicide: Are they the same or different from other suicides? *Archives of Suicide Research*, 8, 131–136.

Lester, D. (1989). Experience of personal loss and later suicide. *Acta Psychiatrica Scandinavica*, *79*, 450–452.

Lester, D. (2000). Alcoholism, substance abuse, and suicide. In: R. Maris, A. Berman, and M. Silverman (eds.), *Comprehensive Textbook of Suicidology* (pp. 357–375). New York: The Guilford Press.

Lester, G. & Lester, D. (1971). *Suicide*. Englewood Cliffs, NJ: Prentice Hall.

Lester, D., Yang, B., and Lindsay, M. (2004). Suicide bombers: are psychological profiles possible? *Studies in Conflict and Terrorism, 27,* 283–295.

Levav, I. and Aisenberg, E. (1989). Suicide in Israel: cross national comparisons. *Acta Psychiatrica Scandinavia, 79*(5), 468–473.

Lewis, B. (1967). *The Assassins: A Radical Sect in Islam.* New York: Oxford University Press.

Litman, R. (1996). Sigmund Freud on suicide. In: J. Maltsberger & M. Goldblatt (eds.), *Essential Papers on Suicide* (pp. 200–220). NY: New York University Press.

Ludwig, A. (1992). Creative achievement and psychopathology: Comparison amongst professionals. *American Journal of Psychotherapy, 136,* 331–354.

Ludwig, A. (1995). *The Price of Greatness: Resolving the Creativity and Madness Controversy.* New York: Guilford.

Luft, Gal (2002). The Palestinian H-bomb. *Foreign Affairs, 81*(4), July/August. Accessed: August 22, 2006.

Maltsberger, J. (1993). Confusions of the body, the self, and others in suicidal states. In: A. Leenaars (Ed.), *Suicidology* (pp. 195–6). Northvale, NJ: Jason Aronson.

Maltsberger, J. (1999). The psychodynamic understanding of suicide. In: D. Jacobs (Ed.), *The Harvard Medical School Guide to Suicide Assessment and Prevention* (pp.72–82). San Francisco: Jossey-Bass.

Margalit, A. (2003). The suicide bombers. *New York Review of Books, 50,* January 16. Available at: http://www.nybooks.com/articles/15979. Accessed: December 15, 2003.

Maris, R., Berman, A., & Silverman, M. (2000). *Comprehensive Textbook of Suicidology.* New York: The Guilford Press.

Martindale, C. (1972). Father's absence, psychopathology, and poetic eminence. *Psychological Reports, 31,* 843–847.

Martindale, C. (1990). *The Clockwork Muse: The Predictability of Artistic Change.* New York: Basic Books.

McCauley, C. (2002). Understanding the 9/11 perpetrators: crazy, lost in hate, or martyred? In N. Matuszak (Ed.), *History Behind the Headlines: The Origins of Ethnic Conflicts Worldwide, Volume 5,* (pp. 274–286). New York: Gale Publishing Group.

McCauley, C. (2004). Psychological issues in understanding terrorism and the response to terrorism. In: C. Stout (Ed.), *The Psychology of Terrorism.* Westport, CT: Greenwood.

MEMRI (2002). A May 2002 Interview with the Hamas Commander of the Al-Qassam Brigades. The Middle East Media Research Institute (MEMRI) Special Dispatch Series No. 403, July 24, quoting Islam Online (http://www.islam-online.net/arabic/politics/2002/05/article25.shtml, May 29, 2002). Available at: http://memri.org/bin/articles.cgi?Page=subjects&Area=jihad&ID=SP40302#_edn1. Accessed: February 5, 2006.

Meninger, K. (1938). *Man against himself.* New York: Harcourt Brace Jovanovich.

Merari, A. (1990). The readiness to kill and die: Suicidal terrorism in the Middle East. In: W. Reich (Ed.), *Origins of Terrorism: Psychologies, Ideologies, Theologies, States of Mind.* (Vol. 9, pp. 192–207). Cambridge: Cambridge University Press.

Merari, A. (1994). Terrorism. In: *Encyclopedia of Human Behavior* (Vol. 4, pp. 399–409) San Diego: Academic Press.

Merari, A. (2000). Testimony before the Special Oversight Panel on Terrorism of the Committee of Armed Services, U.S. House of Representatives, July 13.

Merari, A. (2002). Suicidal terrorism. Lecture at the Institute of Social Research, University of Michigan, Ann Arbor, MI, February 11, 2002. Available at: http://www.umich. edu/~newsinfo/Releases/2002/Jan02/r012802a.html.

Merari, A. (2005). Suicidal Terrorism. In: R.I. Yufit & D. Lester (eds.), *Assessment, Treatment, and Prevention of Suicidal Behavior.* (pp. 431–453). Hoboken, NJ: Wiley.

Merari, A. (2005). Social, organizational, and psychological factors in suicide terrorism. In: T. Bjorgo (Ed.), *Root Causes of Terrorism.* (pp. 70–86). London: Routledge.

Merari, A. (2006). The psychology of suicide terrorism. In: B. Bongar, L. Brown, L. Beutler, J. Breckenridge, and P. Zimbardo (eds.), *Psychology of Terrorism.* Oxford: Oxford University Press.

Merari, A. and Braunstein, Y. (1984). Shi'ite Terrorism. Tel Aviv: Jaffee Center for Strategic Studies Special Report, Tel Aviv University.

Merari, A., Diamant, I., Bibi, A. Broshi, Y. & Zakin, G. (2010). Personality characteristics of suicide bombers and organizers of suicide attacks. *Terrorism and Political Violence, 22*(1) (in press).

Merari, A., Fighel, J., Ganor, B., Lavie, E., Tzoreff, Y. & Livne, A. (2010). Making Palestinian "martyrdom operations" / "suicide attacks": Interviews with would-be perpetrators and organizers. *Terrorism and Political Violence, 22*(1) (in press).

Miller, M. & Paulsen, R. (1999). Suicide assessment in the primary care setting. In: D. Jacobs, *The Harvard Medical School guide to suicide assessment and intervention* (pp. 520–539). San Francisco: Jossey-Bass.

Minois, G. (1999). *History of Suicide.* Baltimore: The Johns Hopkins University Press.

Mishal, S. and Sela, A. (2000). *The Palestinian Hamas: Vision, Violence, and Coexistence.* New York: Columbia University Press.

Moghadam, A. (2006). Suicide terrorism, occupation, and the globalization of martyrdom: A critique of Dying to Win. *Studies in Conflict and Terrorism, 29,* 707–729.

Moghadam, A. (2008). The Globalization of Martyrdom: Al Qaeda, Salafi Jihad, and the Diffusion of Suicide Attacks. Baltimore: The Johns Hopkins University Press.

Moscicki, E. (1999). Epidemiology of suicide. In: D. Jacobs, *The Harvard Medical School guide to suicide assessment and intervention* (pp. 40–51). San Francisco: Jossey-Bass.

Myatt, R. and Greenblatt, M. (1993). Adolescent suicidal behavior. In: A. Leenaars (Ed.), *Suicidology* (pp. 195–6). Northvale, NJ: Jason Aronson.

Nock, M., and Marzuk, P. (1999). Murder-suicide: phenomenology and clinical implications. In: D. Jacobs (Ed.), *The Harvard Medical School Guide to Suicide Assessment and Prevention* (pp. 188–209). San Francisco: Jossey-Bass.

Ohnuki-Tierney, E. (2002). *Kamikaze, Cherry Blossoms, and Nationalisms: The Militarization in Aesthetics in Japanese History.* Chicago: University of Chicago Press.

Oliver, A. and Steinberg, P. (2005). *The Road to Martyrs' Square: A Journey into the World of the Suicide Bomber.* New York: Oxford University Press.

O'Malley, Padraig (1990). *Biting at the Grave: The Irish Hunger Strikers and the Politics of Despair.* Boston: Beacon Press.

Orbach, I. (2004). Terror suicide: How is it possible? *Archives of Suicide Research, 8,* 115–130.

Pape, R. (2003). The strategic logic of suicide terrorism. *American Political Science Review, 97,* pp. 343–361.

Pape, R. (2005). *Dying to Win: The Strategic Logic of Suicide Terrorism*. New York: Random House.

Paz, R. (2001). The Islamic legitimacy of suicide terrorism. In: *Countering Suicide Terrorism* (pp. 86–96). Herzliya, Israel: The International Policy Institute for Counter-Terrorism at the Interdisciplinary Center.

Paz, R. (2005). *Arab Volunteers Killed in Iraq: An Analysis*. Hezliya, Israel: The Project for Research of Islamic Movements (PRISM), Occasional Papers 3, No.1 (March 2005). Available at: www.e-prism.org.

Paz, R. (2005). Zarqawi's Strategy in Iraq – Is there a New Al-Qaeda? Hezliya, Israel: The Project for Research of Islamic Movements (PRISM), Occasional Papers 3, No.5 (August 2005). Available at: www.e-prism.org.

Phillips, D. (1974). The influence of suggestion on suicide: Substantive and theoretical implications of the Werther effect. *American Sociological Review*, *39*, 340–354.

Piazza, J. (2008). A supply-side view of suicide terrorism: A cross national study. *The Journal of Politics*, *70*(1), 28–39.

Pinguet, M. (1993). *Voluntary Death in Japan*. Cambridge, UK: Polity Press.

Pleven, L. (2005). The innocence is over. *Newsday*, July 20. Available at: http://www.newsday.com/news/specials/ny-womoro204350336jul20,0,1086529.story?coll=ny-news-specialreports , accessed on Nov. 16, 2005.

Post, F. (1994). Creativity and psychopathology: A study of 291 world-famous men. *British Journal of Psychiatry*, *165*, 22–34.

Post, F. (1996). Verbal creativity, depression and alcoholism: An investigation of one hundred American and British writers. *British Journal of Psychiatry*, *168*, 545–555.

Post, J. (2003). When Hatred is Bred in the Bone: Social Psychology Dimensions of Terrorism (abstract). Paper presented in the International Expert Meeting on Root Causes of Terrorism, Oslo, Norway, 9–11 June. Available at: www.nupi.no/IPS/filestore/Root_Causes_Summaries.pdf Accessed: Dec. 14, 2005.

Post, J. (2007). *The Mind of the Terrorist*. New York: Palgrave Macmillan.

Post, J, Sprinzak, E., and Denny, L. (2003). The terrorists in their own words: Interviews with 35 incarcerated Middle Eastern terrorists. *Terrorism and Political Violence*, *15*(1), 171–184.

Pritchard, C. (1996) *Suicide — The Ultimate Rejection? A Psychological Study*. Buckingham: Open University Press.

Ramasubramanian, R. (2004). *Suicide Terrorism in Sri Lanka*. New Delhi: Institute of Peace and Conflict Studies, Research Paper No. 5, August 2004. Available at: www.ipcs.org/IRP05.pdf . Accessed on Nov. 28, 2005.

Rapoport, D. (1984). Fear and trembling: Terrorism in three religious traditions. *American Political Science Review*, *78*(3), 658–677.

Reuter, C. (2004). *My Life is a Weapon: A Modern History of Suicide Bombing*. Princeton: Princeton University Press.

Reuter, J. (2004). Chechnya's Suicide Bombers: Desperate, Devout, or Deceived? The American Committee for Peace in Chechnya, September 16. Available at: http://www.peacein-chechnya.org/reports/SuicideReport/SuicideReport.pdf. Accessed on Nov. 26 , 2005.

Richardson, L. (2006). *What Terrorists Want: Understanding the Enemy, Containing the Threat*. New York: Random House.

Ricolfi, L. (2005). Palestinians, 1981–2003. In: D. Gambetta, *Making Sense of Suicide Missions* (pp. 77–130). Oxford: Oxford University Press.

Rosenberger, J. (2003). Discerning the behavior of the suicide bomber: The Role of Vengeance. *Journal of Religion and Health*, *42*(1), 13–20.

Rosenthal, F. (1946). On suicide in Islam. *Journal of the American Oriental Society*, 66, 239–259.

Rubin, M. (2004). Ansar al-Sunna: Iraq's new terrorist threat. *Middle East Intelligence Bulletin*, *6*(5). Available at: http://www.meib.org/articles/0405_iraq1.htm, accessed February 18, 2008.

Sageman, M. (2003). The *Global Salafi Jihad. Statement of Marc Sageman to the National Commission on Terrorist Attacks Upon the United States*, July 9. Available at: http://www. globalsecurity.org/security/library/congress/9-11_commission/030709-sageman. htm. Accessed: May 29, 2005.

Sageman, M. (2004). *Understanding Terror Networks*. Philadelphia, PA: University of Pennsylvania Press.

Sageman, M. (2005). Understanding jihadi networks. *Strategic Insights*, *4*, (April 2005). Available at: http://www.ccc.nps.navy.mil/si/2005/Apr/sagemanApr05.asp. Accessed: October 27, 2005.

Saleh, B. (2003). Deprivation theory offers an answer. *Interdisciplines*, July 2. Available at: http://www.interdisciplines.org/terrorism/papers/1/5/printable/discussions/view/733. Accessed: November 13, 2005.

Saleh, B. (2004). Palestinian Suicide Attacks Revisited: A Critique of Current Wisdom. *Peace & Conflict Monitor*, available at: http://www.monitor.upeace.org/archive. cfm?id_article=237#_ftn2. Accessed: June 10, 2006.

Salib, E. (2003). Suicide terrorism: a case of *Folie à plusieurs? British Journal of Psychiatry*, *182*, 475–6.

Sarraj, E. (2002). Suicide bombers: Dignity, despair, and the need for hope. *Journal of Palestine Studies*, *29*(4), 71–76.

Schmid, A. (1983). *Political Terrorism: A Research Guide to Concepts, Theories, Data bases and Literature*. Amsterdam: North-Holland Publishing Company.

Schmid, A. & Jongman, A. (1988). *Political Terrorism: A New Guide to Actors, Authors, Concepts, Data Bases, Theories and Literature*. Amsterdam: North-Holland Publishing Company.

Schweitzer, Y. (2000). Suicide Terrorism: Development & Characteristics. The Institute for Counter-Terrorism (ICT), April 21. Available at: http://www.ict.org.il/. Accessed: May 31, 2002.

Schweitzer, Y. (2001a). Suicide terrorism: Developments and main characteristics. In: The International Policy Institute for Counter-Terrorism, *Countering Suicide Terrorism* (pp. 75–85). Herzliya, Israel: The Interdisciplinary Center.

Schweitzer, Y. (2001b). Suicide bombings: the ultimate weapon? Herzliya, Israel: The International Policy Institute for Counter-Terrorism (ICT), August 7. Available at: http://www.ict.org.il/. Accessed: June 6, 2006.

Segal, D. (1988). The Iran-Iraq War: A military analysis. *Foreign Affairs*, *66*(5), 946–963.

Shay, S. (2002). Ha'Islam Vepiguei Hahiabdut (Islam and suicide attacks). Tel Aviv: Department of History, Israel Defense Force General Headquarters [Hebrew].

Shiqaqi, K. (2001). The views of Palestinian society on suicide terrorism. In: *Countering Suicide Terrorism* (pp. 155–164). Herzliya, Israel: The Interdisciplinary Center, International Policy Institute for Counter-Terrorism.

Shikaki, K. The future of Palestine. *Foreign Affairs*, November/December 2004. Available at: http://www.foreignaffairs.org/20041101faessay83605/khalil-shikaki/the-future-of-palestine.html. Accessed: August 13, 2006.

Shneidman, E. (1977). The Psychological Autopsy. In: L. Gottschalk et al. (Eds.) *Guide to the Investigation & Reporting of Drug-Abuse Deaths*. Rockville: HEW.

Shneidman, E. (1985). *Definition of Suicide*. New York: Wiley.

Silke, A. (2003). The psychology of suicidal terrorism. In: A. Silke (Ed.), *Terrorists, Victims and Society: Psychological Perspectives on Terrorism and Its Consequences*, (pp. 93–108). Chichester: Wiley.

Silke, A. (2006). The role of suicide in politics, conflict, and terrorism. *Terrorism and Political Violence, 18*, 35–46.

Sprinzak, E. (2000). Rational fanatics. *Foreign Policy, 120*, 66–73.

Stack, S. (2000). Work and economy. In: R. Maris, A. Berman, and M. Silverman (eds.), *Comprehensive Textbook of Suicidology* (pp. 193–221). New York: The Guilford Press.

Stern, J. (2003). *Terror in the Name of God: Why Religious Militants Kill*. New York: Harper Collins.

Strenski, I. (2003). Sacrifice, gift, and the social logic of Muslim human bombers. *Terrorism and Political Violence, 15*, 1–34.

Swerdlow, A. (1993). *Women Strike for Peace: Traditional Motherhood and Radical Politics in the 1960s*. Chicago: University of Chicago Press.

Taarnby, M. (2003). Profiling Islamic Suicide Terrorists. A Research Report for the Danish Ministry of Justice. Available at: http://www.jm.dk/image.asp?page=image& objno=71157, accessed: June 14, 2006.

Taheri, A. (1987). *Holy Terror: Inside the World of Islamic Terrorism*. Bethesda, Maryland: Adler & Adler.

Tanney, B. (2000). Psychiatric diagnoses and suicidal acts. In: R. Maris, A. Berman, & M. Silverman (eds.), *Comprehensive Textbook of Suicidology* (pp. 311–341). New York: The Guilford Press.

Taylor, M. (1988). *The Terrorist*. London: Brassey's Defence Publishers.

Tobeña, A. (2004). Individual factors in suicide terrorism. *Science, 304*, 47.

Townsend, E. (2007). Suicide terrorists: Are they suicidal? *Suicide and Life-Threatening Behavior, 31*(1), 35–49.

United Nations (2002). *Report of the Secretary-General Prepared Pursuant to General Assembly Resolution ES 10/10 (Report on Jenin)*. Available at: http://www.un.org/peace/jenin/. Accessed: April 4, 2006.

Van Henten, J.W., & Avemarie, F. (2002). *Martyrdom and Noble Death*. London: Routledge.

Volkan, D.V. (2001). September 11 and societal regression. *Mind and Human Inter-action, 12*, 196–216. Available at: http://shr.aaas.org/transitionaljustice/traumaandtj/societal_regression_sept11.pdf . Accessed: December 16, 2005.

Weinberg, L., Pedahzur, A., & Cenetti-Nisim, D. (2003). The social and religious characteristics of suicide bombers and their victims with some additional comments about the Israeli public's reaction. *Terrorism and Political Violence, 15*(3), 139–153.

Weisman, A. & Kastenbaum, R. (1968). The psychological autopsy. *Community Mental Health Monograph*, No. 4. New York: Behavioral Publications.

Williams, B.G. (2007). The Taliban Fedayeen: The world's worst suicide bombers? *Terrorism Monitor*, 5(14). Available at: http://www.jamestown.org/terrorism/news/article.php?issue_id=4183 .

Wilson, J. & Herrnstein, R. (1985). *Crime and Human Nature*. New York: Simon and Schuster.

Witztum, E. & Lerner, V. (2009). *Genius and Madness*. Tel Aviv: Arie Nir [Hebrew].

World Health Organization (1993). *Guidelines for the Primary Prevention of Mental, Neurological and Psychosocial Disorders, 4. Suicide*. Geneva: Division of Mental Health, World Health Organization Publication WHO/MNH/MND/93.24.

World Health Organization (2001). The World Health Report 2001 (Chapter 2: The Burden of Mental and Behavioural Disorders). Available at: http://www.who.int/whr2001/2001/main/en/chapter2/002g.htm (as of July 11, 2003).

World Health Organization (2003). *Suicide Rates (per 100,000) by Country, Year and Gender*. Available at: http://www.who.int/mental_health/prevention/suicide/suiciderates/en/. Accessed: November 29, 2005.

Wright, R. (1985). *Sacred Rage: The Wrath of Militant Islam*. New York: Linden Press / Simon & Schuster.

Yom, S. & Saleh, B. (2004). Palestinian Suicide Bombers: A Statistical Analysis. Paper published at the Economists for Peace and Security website: http://www.ecaar.org/Newsletter/Nov04/saleh.htm, retrieved on November 18, 2005.

Zedalis, D. (2004). *Female Suicide Bombers*. Carlisle, PA: Strategic Studies Institute, U.S. Army War College. Available at: http://www.strategicstudiesinstitute.army.mil/pdffiles/PUB408.pdf. Accessed: November 12, 2005.

Zilboorg, G. (1996). Considerations on suicide, with particular reference to that of the young. In J.T. Maltsberger and M.J. Goldblatt, *Essential papers on suicide* (pp. 62–82). New York: New York University Press.

# APPENDIX 1

## Palestinian Population's Support for, or Opposition to, Armed Operations and Suicide Attacks

The table below summarizes the results of public opinion polls that measured Palestinian attitudes to armed struggle in general and suicide attacks in particular, during the period of September 1993 through January 2009. All the polls in the table were run by Palestinian polling institutions that used representative samples of the population in the West Bank and the Gaza Strip. One of these institutions has been the Center for Palestine Research and Studies (CPRS) based in Nablus, which was headed by Dr. Khalil Shikaki. CPRS conducted frequent polls on current political and social issues in the period of 1993–2000. Since July 2000 Shikaki continued his surveys at the Palestinian Center for Policy & Survey Research (PSR) in Bir Zeit. Both CPRS and PSR polls can be accessed on the web at http://www.pcpsr.org. Reliable public opinion surveys of the Palestinian population in the West Bank and the Gaza Strip have also been carried out since 1993 by the Jerusalem Media and Communication Center (JMCC). These polls can be accessed at http://www.jmcc.org. The table also includes a few relevant polls conducted by two other Palestinian centers: the Development Studies Programme (DSP) at Birzeit University, available at http://home.birzeit.edu/dsp/DSPNEW/polls/poll_2/index.html, and the Palestinian Center for Public Opinion (PCPO) at Beit Sahour, headed by Dr. Nabil Kukali, available at http://www.pcpo.ps/polls.htm.

The table contains polls that addressed the questions of support for armed struggle against Israel in general, and support for suicide attacks in particular. Questions and results concerning suicide attacks appear in **bold** letters. Because almost all armed attacks against Israeli civilians *inside Israel* (as differentiated from the Occupied Territories) consisted of suicide attacks, questions pertaining to support of armed attacks against civilians inside Israel were regarded as referring to suicide attacks. For the readers' benefit, however, the Comments column presents the questions as phrased by the pollsters. The Comments column occasionally mentions outstanding background events.

| Date | Pollster | Support | Oppose | Comments |
|------|----------|---------|--------|----------|
| 9/93 | CPRS | 42.6 | 46.5 | "Should the intifada be stopped." |
| 9/94 | CPRS | 32.7 | 55.7 | "Armed operations against Israeli targets in Gaza and Jericho." |
| 11/94 | CPRS | 32.7 | 55.7 | "Armed operations against Israeli targets in Gaza & Jericho." Poll was conducted in the wake of suicide attacks. Jordan peace treaty with Israel. |
| 2/95 | CPRS | 46.0 | 33.5 | "Armed attacks against Israeli targets." |
| 3/95 | CPRS | 32.5 | 43.5 | "Armed attacks against Israeli targets." Following Beit Lid double suicide attack and punitive closure. Pollster notes that some respondents feared answering the question. Support may be higher than poll shows. |
| 8/95 | CPRS | 18.3 | 73.9 | "Armed attacks against Israeli civilian targets." Following establishment of new settlements; two suicide attacks; closure; arrest of Hamas members by PA and Israel. |
| 8/95 | JMCC | **24.3** | **62.2** | **"Hamas and Islamic Jihad's suicide operations against Israeli targets"** |
| 8/95 | CPRS | 67.6 | 23.7 | "Armed attacks against Israeli army targets" |
| 8/95 | CPRS | 69.2 | 24.3 | "Armed attacks against Israeli settlers" |
| 3/96 | CPRS | **21.1** | **70.1** | **"Lately, armed attacks have taken place against Israelis in Jerusalem, Tel Aviv and Ashkelon. Do you support such attacks?" (Following suicide attacks and Israeli punitive measures).** |
| 3/96 | JMCC | **5.3** | **65.0** | **"Hamas suicidal bombings"** (14.7% "oppose but understand the reason"). 63% believe that the PA should prevent such attacks, but 50% of them maintain that the PA should do it by persuasion, not by force. 74.9% of the whole sample said that they were afraid of Israeli revenge, 19.8% said that they were not afraid. |
| 12/96 | CPRS | 39.1 | 48.7 | "Armed attacks against Israeli targets" |
| 3/97 | CPRS | 38.1 | 54.3 | "Armed attacks against Israeli targets" (in the wake of building Har Homa Jewish neighborhood in the outskirts of East Jerusalem). |

| Date | Pollster | Support | Oppose | Comments |
|------|----------|---------|--------|----------|
| 4/97 | CPRS | 40.3 | 47.9 | "Armed attack against the Israeli Cafe in Tel-Aviv last month" |
| 4/97 | JMCC | 39.8 | 47.7 | "Military operations against Israeli targets" |
| 4/97 | JMCC | **32.7** | **54.5** | **"Suicide bombing operations"** interesting comparison of "military operations" (39.8% support) and "suicide operations" (32.7% support) in the same poll. |
| 8/97 | JMCC | **28.2** | **56.0** | **"Suicide bombing against Israeli targets"** |
| 9/97 | CPRS | **35.5** | **55.5** | **"Several suicide attacks against Israelis took place in West Jerusalem during the past few weeks. Do you support or oppose these attacks?"** |
| 6/98 | CPRS | 49.7 | 44.8 | "Armed attack against Israeli targets" |
| 10/98 | CPRS | 50.8 | 43.5 | "Armed attacks against Israeli targets" |
| 11/98 | CPRS | 41.2 | 53.1 | "Armed attacks against Israeli targets" (Wye memorandum). |
| 1/99 | CPRS | 52.7 | 41.3 | Beginning of January: "Armed attacks against Israeli targets". (Israel suspended Wye agreement). |
| 1/99-A | CPRS | 40.8 | 52.8 | End of January: "Armed attacks against Israeli targets" (growing criticism in Israel of Netanyahu's government conduct concerning the peace process). |
| 3/99 | JMCC | 35.7 | 56.0 | "Resumption of military operations against Israeli targets" |
| 4/99 | CPRS | 44.6 | 49.4 | "Armed attacks against Israeli targets" |
| 6/99 | CPRS | 44.7 | 49.2 | "Armed attacks against Israeli targets" (Barak elected PM). |
| 7/99 | CPRS | 38.5 | 55.9 | "Armed attacks against Israeli targets" |
| 9/99 | CPRS | 35.7 | 57.3 | "Armed attacks against Israeli targets" |
| 10/99 | CPRS | 39.5 | 52.3 | "Armed attacks against Israeli targets" (After Sharm al-Sheikh agreement between Israel and the PA). |
| 12/99 | CPRS | 35.9 | 54.8 | "Armed attacks against Israeli targets" (after opening the Gaza-WB safe passage). |
| 1/00 | CPRS | 43.3 | 49.7 | "Armed attacks against Israeli targets" |
| 2/00 | CPRS | 39.4 | 52.6 | "Armed attacks against Israeli targets" |
| 3/00 | CPRS | 44.0 | 49.2 | "Armed attacks against Israeli targets" |
| 7/00 | PSR | 51.6 | 42.7 | "Armed attacks against Israeli targets" (following the Camp David Summit (Arafat, Barak, Clinton). |

*(Continued)*

| Date | Pollster | Support | Oppose | Comments |
|------|----------|---------|--------|----------|
| 11/00 | DSP | 52.3 | | The figure 52.3% is the sum of those supporting attacks against all Israelis (soldiers, settlers and civilians, 51.9%) and those supporting attacks against civilians (0.4%). The al-Aqsa intifada began on September 29, 2000. |
| 12/00 | JMCC | 73.0 | 15.5 | "Continuation of a military resistance Intifada"(18.5%) and "both a popular and military resistance Intifada" (54.5%) summed up. 15.5% were in favor of "popular resistance" only. |
| 12/00 | JMCC | 72.1 | 16.8 | "Resumption of military operations against Israeli targets" |
| 2/01 | DSP | **53.4** | **39.7** | **"Do you support or oppose suicide attacks against civilians inside Israeli cities (inside the Green Line)?"** |
| 4/01 | JMCC | **73.7** | **15.9** | **"Suicide bombing operations against Israeli civilians in Israel". "Support" combines "strongly support (54.4%) and "somewhat support" (19.3%). "Oppose" combines "strongly oppose" (5.8%) and "somewhat oppose" (10.1%).** |
| 6/01 | DSP | **74.8** | **18.6** | **"Do you support or oppose suicide attacks against civilians inside Israeli cities?"** |
| 6/01 | JMCC | **68.6** | **23.1** | **"What about the suicide bombing operations? Do you see them as a suitable response in the current political conditions or do you oppose them and see them harmful to national interests?"** |
| 7/01 | PSR | **58.1** | **39.0** | **58.1% support "armed attacks against Israeli civilians inside Israel" and 39.0% oppose them**; 91.7% support armed confrontations against the Israeli army in the West Bank and the Gaza Strip and 6.6% oppose them. |
| 9/01 | JMCC | 84.6 | 9.9 | "Do you support the resumption of the military operations against Israeli targets as a suitable response within the current political conditions, or do you reject it and find it harmful to Palestinian national interests?" |

| Date | Pollster | Support | Oppose | Comments |
|------|----------|---------|--------|----------|
| 12/01 | JMCC | **64.1** | **26.0** | **"What is your feeling towards suicide bombing operations against Israeli civilians, do you support it or oppose it?" "Strongly support" and "support" combined, "strongly oppose" and "oppose" combined.** |
| 12/01 | PSR | **58.2** | **39.8** | **"Armed attacks against Israeli civilians inside Israel."** Other questions: "Concerning armed attacks against Israeli soldiers in the West Bank and the Gaza Strip" – 92.3% strongly support or support, 6.5% oppose or strongly oppose. "Concerning armed attacks against Israeli Civilians settlers in the West Bank and the Gaza Strip" – 92.1% strongly support or support, 6.6% oppose or strongly oppose. |
| 3/02 | JMCC | **72.0** | **21.7** | **"What is your feeling towards suicide bombing operations against Israeli civilians, do you support it or oppose it?" "Strongly support" and "support" combined, "strongly oppose" and "oppose" combined.** |
| 3/02 | JMCC | 73.6 | 20.0 | "Do you support the resumption of the military operations against Israeli targets as a suitable response within the current political conditions, or do you reject it and find it harmful to Palestinian national interests?" |
| 5/02 | PSR | **52.0** | **46.9** | **"Armed attacks against Israeli civilians inside Israel."** Following "Defensive Shield" operation (April 2002). Also: 91.6% support and 6.9% oppose "armed attacks against Israeli soldiers in the West Bank and the Gaza Strip" and 89.3% support and 9.0% oppose "armed attacks against Israeli civilian settlers in the West Bank and the Gaza Strip." |
| 6/02 | JMCC | **68.1** | **26.0** | **"What is your feeling towards suicide bombing operations against Israeli civilians, do you support it or oppose it?" "Strongly support" and "support" combined, "strongly oppose" and "oppose" combined.** |
| 9/02 | JMCC | **64.3** | **27.7** | **"Suicide bombing operations against Israeli civilians" "somewhat" and "strongly support" combined.** |

*(Continued)*

| Date | Pollster | Support | Oppose | Comments |
|------|----------|---------|--------|----------|
| 11/02 | PSR | **53.2** | **43.2** | **"Armed attacks against Israeli civilians inside Israel."** Also: 91% support and 6.1% oppose "armed attacks against Israeli soldiers in the West Bank and the Gaza Strip," and 89.1% support and 7.8% oppose "armed attacks against Israeli settlers in the West Bank and the Gaza Strip." |
| 11/02 | DSP | **45.8** | **29.3** | "Do you believe that **attacks against Israeli civilians in Israeli cities** will lead to: Positive results for the Palestinian cause **(45.8%)**; Negative results for the Palestinian cause **(29.3%)**; Neither a negative nor a positive result for the Palestinian cause (18.6%). |
| 12/02 | JMCC | **62.7** | **29.8** | **"Suicide bombing operations against Israeli civilians" "somewhat" and "strongly support" combined.** |
| 4/03 | JMCC | **59.9** | **30.3** | **"Suicide bombing operations against Israeli civilians" "somewhat" and "strongly support" combined.** |
| 4/03 | PSR | **57.3** | **40.0** | **"Armed attacks against Israeli civilians inside Israel."** Also: 92.8% support and 5.0% oppose "armed attacks against Israeli soldiers in the West Bank and the Gaza Strip," and 91.2% support and 7.0% oppose "armed attacks against Israeli settlers in the West Bank and the Gaza Strip." |
| 9/03 | PCPO | **55** | **27** | **Continuation of suicide operations against Israel** |
| 10/03 | JMCC | **61.8** | **34.9** | **"Suicide bombing operations against Israeli civilians" "somewhat" and "strongly support" combined.** |
| 10/03 | PSR | **74.5** | **21.8** | **"With regard to the bombing operation in the Maxim Restaurant in Haifa, which led to the death of 20 Israelis, do you support or oppose this operation?" (74.5% support). However, in the same poll, only 54.4% supported and 43.2 opposed "armed attacks against Israeli civilians inside Israel"** (the standard question). *Specific attacks usually get greater support than the abstract question.* Also, 90.1% support and 8.0% oppose "armed attacks against Israeli soldiers in the West Bank and the Gaza Strip," 89.3% support and 8.7% oppose "armed attacks against Israeli settlers in the West Bank and the Gaza Strip." |

| Date | Pollster | Support | Oppose | Comments |
|------|----------|---------|--------|----------|
| 12/03 | PSR | | | 87% support for attacks on soldiers and settlers; 48% support for attacks against Israeli civilians. |
| 3/04 | PSR | 53.1 | 45.4 | **"Armed attacks against Israeli civilians inside Israel."** Also: 87.4% support and 11.0% oppose "armed attacks against Israeli soldiers in the West Bank and the Gaza Strip," and 85.8 % support and 12.5% oppose "armed attacks against Israeli settlers in the West Bank and the Gaza Strip." |
| 3/04 | PCPO | | | 87% support attacks against soldiers; 86% support attacks against settlers; 53% support attacks against civilians. |
| 4/04 | PCPO | 76.5 | 15.4 | **"Continuation of suicide operations"** |
| 6/04 | JMCC | 63.1 | 31.5 | **"What is your feeling towards suicide bombing operations against Israeli civilians, do you support it or oppose it?"** "Strongly support" and "support" combined, "strongly oppose" and "oppose" combined. |
| 6/04 | PSR | 58.6 | 37.1 | **"In recent weeks there is a sharp decrease in the level of violence exerted by both sides. In your opinion should Palestinians continue nevertheless the suicide bombings inside Israel if an opportunity arises?"** |
| 9/04 | PSR | 77.4 | 19.7 | **"With regard to the latest bombing attack in Beer Shiva in Israel early in this month which lead to the death of 16 Israelis, do you support or oppose this attack?"** Also: **53.8% support and 44.3% oppose "armed attacks against Israeli civilians inside Israel;"** 92.2% support and 6.3% oppose "armed attacks against *Israeli soldiers in the West Bank and the Gaza Strip*," and 90.1% support and 8.3% oppose "armed attacks against *Israeli settlers in the West Bank and the Gaza Strip*" (emphasis added). |

(*Continued*)

| Date | Pollster | Support | Oppose | Comments |
|------|----------|---------|--------|----------|
| 12/04 | PSR | **49.4** | **47.8** | **"Armed attacks against Israeli civilians inside Israel."** |
| | | | | 83.1% support or strongly support and 14.1% oppose or strongly oppose "armed attacks against *Israeli settlers in the West Bank and the Gaza Strip*" (emphasis added). Yasser Arafat died on November 11, 2004. |
| 12/04 | JMCC | 41.1 | 51.8 | "Do you support the resumption of the military operations against Israeli targets as a suitable response within the current political conditions, or do you reject it and find it harmful to Palestinian national interests?" |
| 3/05 | PSR | **29.1** | **67.1** | **"Two weeks ago a bombing attack took place in Tel Aviv leading to the death of four Israelis and the injury of 50 others in front of a night club. Do you support or oppose this attack?"** |
| 5/05 | JMCC | **49.7** | **48.0** | **"How do you feel towards suicide bombing operations against Israeli civilians? do you support them, or oppose them?"** |
| | | | | Also, a question on support for military operations in general: "Do you support the resumption of the military operations against Israeli targets as a suitable response within the current political conditions, or do you reject them and find them harmful to Palestinians national interests?" Interestingly, support is only 36.2% and opposition is 57.2%. |
| 6/05 | PSR | **46.3** | **50.8** | **"Armed attacks against Israeli civilians inside Israel"** |
| 9/05 | PSR | **37.8** | **59.8** | **"Armed attacks against Israeli civilians inside Israel"** (on the eve of the Israeli withdrawal from the Gaza Strip). |
| 12/05 | PSR | 36 | 60 | In the wake of Israel's withdrawal from Gaza: support for attacks from the Gaza Strip. |
| 12/05 | PSR | 33 | 61 | In the wake of Israel's withdrawal from the Gaza Strip: support for bombing attacks or the launching of rockets from the Gaza Strip. |
| *12/05* | *PSR* | *9* | *88* | *The questions related to the suicide bombing attacks in Amman in November. 77% see these attacks as criminal operations denounced by Islam while 10% see them as martyrdom operations supported by Islam.* |

| Date | Pollster | Support | Oppose | Comments |
|------|----------|---------|--------|----------|
| 3/06 | PSR | 52.4 | 45.2 | "Armed attacks against Israeli civilians inside Israel" |
| 6/06 | PSR | 69.4 | 26.6 | Concerning a suicide attack which took place on April 17, 2006: "A bombing attack took place in Tel Aviv last April leading to the death of 11 Israelis. Do you support or oppose this bombing attack?" |
| 6/06 | PSR | 56.1 | 42.0 | "Armed attacks against Israeli civilians inside Israel" |
| 9/06 | PSR | 57.4 | 40.9 | "Armed attacks against Israeli civilians inside Israel" |
| 3/08 | PSR | 77.4 | 18.5 | "What about the bombing attack in Dimona in Israel in early February of this year in which one Israeli woman was killed in addition to the two bombers, do you support or oppose this attack?" |
| 4/08 | JMCC | 50.7 | 46.5 | "Suicide bombing operations against Israeli civilians" |
| 6/08 | PSR | 54.8 | 41.7 | " Armed attacks against Israeli civilians inside Israel" |
| 1/09 | JMCC | 55.4 | 37.6 | "How do you feel about the suicide bombings operations against Israeli civilians? (following the Gaza war). |

# INDEX

Page numbers followed by "*f*" and "*t*" denotes figures and tables, respectively.